I0888663

AI-Driven Strategies for Sustainable Guest Experience in Intelligent Hospitality

Ahmed K. Elnagar
https://orcid.org/0000-0003-1787-8189
Taibah University, Saudi Arabia

Abdelkader Mohamed Sghaier Derbali
https://orcid.org/0000-0003-4098-3120
Taibah University, Saudi Arabia

Ahmad Mohammad Herzallah
https://orcid.org/0000-0002-9453-3777
Al-Quds University, Palestine

IGI Global
Scientific Publishing
Publishing Tomorrow's Research Today

Published in the United States of America by
IGI Global Scientific Publishing
701 East Chocolate Avenue
Hershey, PA, 17033, USA
Tel: 717-533-8845 | Fax: 717-533-7115
Website: https://www.igi-global.com E-mail: cust@igi-global.com

Library of Congress Cataloging-in-Publication Data

No LCCN (CIP Data Pending)
ISBN13: 9798337381978
EISBN13: 9798337381992

British Cataloguing in Publication Data
A Cataloguing in Publication record for this book is available from the British Library.

Table of Contents

Detailed Table of Contents

The geographical distribution of the population in Saudi Arabia plays a crucial role in climate risk management. The country is characterized by a high concentration of urban population, particularly in major cities such as Riyadh, Jeddah, and Dammam, while vast desert areas remain sparsely populated. This spatial configuration exacerbates the varying vulnerabilities to climate hazards: flash floods and heat islands in densely populated urban areas, water scarcity and desertification in rural and desert regions, and coastal threats related to flooding and sea-level rise. This study demonstrates that climate risk management must take into account this territorial heterogeneity to develop appropriate public policies. Recent initiatives, including those within the framework of Vision 2030 and innovative urban projects such as NEOM, illustrate the Kingdom's commitment to integrating sustainability and resilience into its spatial planning.

As environmental awareness grows worldwide, both consumers and businesses are becoming more conscious of sustainability. This study explores how green marketing strategies influence consumers' intentions to buy eco-friendly products. Companies today are adopting various green practices—such as eco-labeling, sustainable packaging, green advertising, and fair pricing—to appeal to environmentally aware customers. The research aims to understand how these strategies shape consumer trust, perception, and willingness to purchase green products. Using survey data and quantitative analysis, the study examines the strength of the relationship between different aspects of green marketing and consumers' buying intentions. The results reveal that honest, transparent, and credible green marketing practices can significantly improve consumer attitudes and encourage eco-friendly purchasing behavior. The paper also highlights ongoing challenges like greenwashing and the need for greater consumer awareness.

Algorithmic hospitality represents a transformative shift in the hospitality industry, where artificial intelligence (AI)–driven algorithms are increasingly embedded across the guest journey to deliver personalized, efficient, and predictive service experiences. From pre-arrival search and booking to on-site service encounters and post-stay engagement, AI-enabled systems analyze large volumes of guest data to anticipate preferences, automate decision-making, and tailor interactions in real time. Technologies such as machine learning, recommender systems, chatbots, facial recognition, and dynamic pricing engines are redefining how hotels and tourism organizations understand and respond to guest needs. The algorithmic personalization enhances convenience, operational efficiency, and customer satisfaction; it also raises critical concerns related to data privacy, transparency, bias, and the diminishing role of human agency in service encounters. This chapter explores the conceptual foundations of algorithmic hospitality and AI-driven personalization.

With the growing popularity of virtual and hybrid corporate events, artificial intelligence (AI) is becoming a critical component for improving event engagement and administration. AI technologies increase attendee engagement, simplify event management, and deliver real-time data insights, leading to more dynamic and personalised events. This chapter investigates how artificial intelligence has influenced the design and execution of virtual and hybrid events by automating activities, enhancing engagement, and personalising the attendance experience. It also looks into the economic and environmental benefits of using AI into event planning, notably in terms of reducing resource use and increasing output. This chapter adopts a conceptual approach to assess existing artificial intelligence applications in the event industry and to investigate the incorporation of Al technologies into virtual and hybrid event platforms. This study examines the impact of artificial intelligence on operational efficiency, event interactivity, and engagement through case studies and theoretical frameworks.

Preface

INTRODUCTION

The hospitality and tourism sector stands at a pivotal moment. Rapid advances in artificial intelligence are reshaping how destinations are managed, how services are delivered, and how guests experience travel. At the same time, the industry faces increasing pressure to operate responsibly, balancing innovation with environmental stewardship, social equity, and long-term economic viability. This edited reference book, *AI-Driven Strategies for Sustainable Guest Experience in Intelligent Hospitality*, is conceived at this important intersection of technology, sustainability, and guest-centric innovation.

As editors, our aim has been to bring together diverse scholarly perspectives and practical insights that collectively examine how AI can be strategically leveraged to enhance guest experiences while advancing sustainable tourism practices. The chapters in this volume explore a wide spectrum of applications, ranging from operational efficiencies—such as smart energy management systems, data-driven resource optimization, and predictive analytics to address overtourism—to customer-facing innovations including AI-powered personalization, service robotics, and generative AI for creating dynamic content, recommendations, and itineraries.

Beyond technological applications, this book deliberately engages with the broader implications of AI adoption in hospitality. Contributors critically address ethical and responsible AI implementation, workforce transformation and upskilling, biodiversity conservation, and the role of policy and governance in shaping intelligent tourism ecosystems. In doing so, the volume recognizes that technological progress must be accompanied by thoughtful human, environmental, and institutional considerations.

This reference work is intended for academics, researchers, policymakers, industry professionals, and advanced students seeking a comprehensive understanding of how AI-driven strategies can support intelligent, sustainable, and future-ready hospitality systems. We hope that the insights presented here will not only inform research and practice but also inspire collaborative efforts toward building tourism experiences that are innovative, inclusive, and environmentally responsible.

ORGANIZATION OF THE BOOK

Chapter 1, AI-Driven Sustainable Guest Experience in Intelligent Hospitality Ecosystems: Frameworks, Applications, and Future Pathways, establishes the conceptual foundation of the book by examining artificial intelligence as a core enabler of sustainable and intelligent hospitality ecosystems. This chapter synthesizes contemporary frameworks—including smart hospitality ecosystems, AI-enabled circular economy models, digital twins, and sustainable experience design—to demonstrate how advanced AI technologies such as predictive analytics, natural language processing, computer vision, and autonomous service robots enhance operational efficiency, reduce environmental impact, and deliver hyper-personalized guest experiences. By integrating applications ranging from AI-powered concierge systems and smart rooms to emotion-aware interaction tools, the chapter also foregrounds ethical AI practices, data privacy, and responsible automation as essential pillars of future-ready hospitality systems.

Chapter 2, The Importance of Green Finance on Climate Risk Management in the Case of Saudi Arabia, extends the sustainability discourse by exploring green finance as a critical mechanism for managing climate-related risks within a transforming national economy. Framed within Saudi Arabia's Vision 2030, this chapter examines the emergence of green bonds, green sukuk, ESG investing, and state-led initiatives such as the Saudi Green Initiative. While highlighting structural challenges—including ESG standardization gaps, greenwashing risks, and institutional constraints—the chapter underscores the strategic potential of green finance to attract foreign capital, support energy transition, develop new financial markets, and strengthen resilience against physical and transition climate risks.

Chapter 3, Reimagining Emotional Ergonomics through the Integration of Human Emotion and Artificial Intelligence for Sustainable Healthcare Wellbeing, broadens the application of AI beyond hospitality by examining how affective computing and emotional ergonomics can enhance sustainability in healthcare systems. The chapter demonstrates how AI-driven emotion recognition and analysis can support adaptive clinical interventions, improve patient satisfaction, reduce errors, and enhance workforce resilience. Through theoretical grounding, methodological discussion, and real-world case studies, the chapter also addresses ethical imperatives such as data privacy, algorithmic fairness, and trust, reinforcing the responsible deployment of emotion-sensitive AI technologies.

Chapter 4, Talent Transformation: Upskilling the Hospitality Workforce for an AI Era, focuses on the human dimension of intelligent hospitality. Drawing on theories of human–AI symbiosis, learning organizations, and competency-based education, this chapter explores how AI-driven transformation reshapes job roles, skill requirements, and workforce development strategies. Rather than framing AI as a substitute for human labor, the chapter positions technology as an enabler of creativity, empathy, and strategic thinking, emphasizing inclusive talent transformation, institutional responses, and supportive policy frameworks essential for sustaining service excellence in the AI era.

Chapter 5, The Nexus among Population Distribution and Climate Risk Management in the Case of Saudi Arabia, highlights the spatial and territorial dimensions of sustainability and climate resilience. By analyzing Saudi Arabia's uneven population distribution and associated vulnerabilities—ranging from urban heat islands and flash floods to water scarcity and coastal risks—the chapter demonstrates the importance of territorially sensitive climate risk management. Initiatives under Vision 2030 and innovative projects such as NEOM are presented as illustrative examples of integrating sustainability, resilience, and spatial planning into national development strategies.

Chapter 6, The Impact of Green Marketing Strategies on Consumer Purchase Intention of Green Products, examines the role of sustainability communication in shaping consumer behavior. Through quantitative analysis, this chapter investigates how green marketing practices—such as eco-labeling, sustainable packaging, green advertising, and transparent pricing—influence consumer trust, perceptions, and willingness to purchase eco-friendly products. The findings emphasize that credible and transparent green marketing can significantly enhance consumer attitudes, while also drawing attention to persistent challenges such as greenwashing and the need for greater consumer awareness.

Chapter 7, Algorithmic Hospitality: AI-Driven Personalization Across the Guest Journey, delves into the rise of algorithmic decision-making as a defining feature of contemporary hospitality. This chapter explores how machine learning, recommender systems, chatbots, facial recognition, and dynamic pricing engines personalize guest experiences across the entire journey—from pre-arrival to post-stay engagement. While highlighting gains in efficiency, convenience, and satisfaction, the chapter critically examines concerns related to data privacy, transparency, algorithmic bias, and the evolving balance between automation and human agency in service encounters.

Chapter 8, The Future of Corporate Events: The Role of Artificial Intelligence in Shaping Virtual and Hybrid Corporate Experiences, addresses the growing significance of AI in event management and experience design. Focusing on virtual and hybrid corporate events, this chapter demonstrates how AI enhances engagement, automates operations, and delivers real-time insights while generating economic and environmental benefits through reduced resource use. Through conceptual analysis and case-based insights, the chapter illustrates how AI-driven platforms are redefining interactivity, personalization, and operational efficiency in the events industry.

Chapter 9, Decoding AI Integrated Clinical Practice: A CNN-Based Intelligent Learning Approach for Medical Image Analytic Cases, explores the transformative impact of deep learning on medical imaging and clinical decision-making. Centered on convolutional neural networks, the chapter reviews advancements in segmentation, classification, and diagnosis across imaging modalities such as CT, MRI, ultrasound, and X-ray. By addressing technical challenges and emphasizing explainable AI, transfer learning, and ethical considerations, the chapter underscores the importance of fairness, transparency, and robustness in AI-enabled clinical practice.

Chapter 10, Technology and Customer Satisfaction in Hotels, investigates the relationship between technological adoption and guest satisfaction in modern hospitality operations. The chapter examines how digital innovations—including self-service kiosks, mobile applications, AI-powered concierge services, and smart room technologies—enhance service efficiency, personalization, and guest convenience. By analyzing guest perceptions, the chapter identifies ease of use, reliability, responsiveness, and personalization as key determinants of satisfaction, reinforcing the strategic role of technology in customer-centric hospitality models.

Chapter 11, Implementing AI in Heritage Tourism: Balancing Access and Preservation, addresses the challenge of preserving cultural heritage while expanding accessibility. This chapter explores AI-powered virtual tours that integrate 3D modeling, immersive media, and adaptive learning to provide personalized and interactive heritage experiences. By democratizing access and reducing physical pressure on fragile sites, the chapter positions AI as a powerful tool for sustainable heritage tourism, cultural education, and global engagement.

Chapter 12, Predictive Analytics for Overtourism Management and Destination Resilience, focuses on data-driven approaches to managing visitor flows in smart destinations. The chapter examines how predictive analytics models—drawing on historical data, real-time inputs, IoT sensors, and digital traces—can forecast congestion, optimize capacity, enhance safety, and support strategic decision-making. By addressing overtourism through anticipatory and adaptive management, the chapter contributes to building resilient and sustainable tourism destinations.

Chapter 13, An Intelligent Framework for Early Chronic Kidney Disease Prognosis, presents an advanced AI-driven approach to disease prediction using hybrid ensemble models and statistical feature selection. The proposed framework demonstrates high predictive accuracy and clinical relevance, enabling early risk detection and proactive intervention. By combining technical rigor with practical healthcare applications, the chapter highlights the potential of intelligent systems to improve patient outcomes while emphasizing robustness, validation, and ethical responsibility.

CONCLUSION

As this edited reference book demonstrates, artificial intelligence is no longer a peripheral innovation in hospitality and related service sectors; it is a foundational force shaping how experiences are designed, delivered, and sustained. Across the chapters, contributors collectively illustrate that AI-driven strategies—when thoughtfully integrated—have the capacity to enhance guest satisfaction, optimize operational efficiency, and support environmental and social sustainability. From intelligent hospitality ecosystems and algorithmic personalization to predictive analytics, green finance, workforce transformation, healthcare innovation, and heritage preservation, this volume reflects the breadth and depth of AI's transformative potential.

Importantly, the contributions in this book move beyond technological optimism to engage critically with the responsibilities that accompany intelligent systems. Ethical AI implementation, data privacy, workforce inclusion, transparency, and policy alignment emerge as recurring themes, underscoring that sustainable guest experiences cannot be achieved through technology alone. Rather, they require a balanced approach that integrates human values, institutional frameworks, and long-term ecological considerations into AI-enabled decision-making.

As editors, we view this book as both a scholarly reference and a practical guide for shaping intelligent, responsible, and future-ready hospitality and tourism ecosystems. The insights presented herein are intended to support academics advancing theory, practitioners implementing innovation, and policymakers designing enabling environments for sustainable growth. We hope this volume will stimulate ongoing dialogue, interdisciplinary collaboration, and evidence-based action, ultimately contributing to a hospitality industry that is not only smarter and more efficient, but also more inclusive, resilient, and aligned with the principles of sustainable development.

Ahmed K. Elnagar (Taibah University, Saudi Arabia)
Abdelkader Mohamed Sghaier Derbali (Taibah University, Saudi Arabia)
Ahmad Mohammad Herzallah (Al-Quds University, Palestine)

Chapter 1
AI-Driven Sustainable Guest Experience in Intelligent Hospitality Ecosystems:
Frameworks, Applications, and Future Pathways

Shivansu Sachan
https://orcid.org/0000-0002-9893-8018
Chhatrapati Shahu Ji Maharaj University, Kanpur, India

Ashi Singh
https://orcid.org/0009-0000-0139-8071
CSJM University, Kanpur, India

ABSTRACT

has emerged as a transformative force in the hospitality industry, especially in the creation of intelligent ecosystems that enhance sustainability and guest experience. This academic update examines recent advancements in AI applications within sustainable hospitality environments, emphasizing intelligent service delivery, operational efficiency, personalization, and eco-responsibility. The paper reviews contemporary frameworks such as smart hospitality ecosystems, AI-enabled circular economy models, digital twins, and sustainable experience design. It explores how AI technologies—such as predictive analytics, natural language processing, computer vision, and autonomous service robots—optimize resource consumption, reduce waste, and enhance energy management while delivering hyper-personalized guest services. Applications include AI-powered concierge systems, smart rooms,

DOI: 10.4018/979-8-3373-8197-8.ch001

dynamic pricing engines for green service offerings, and emotion-aware guest interaction tools. Additionally, the study highlights ethical AI practices, data privacy, responsible automation.

INTRODUCTION

The worldwide hospitality sector is going through a big change because of new technologies, a greater awareness of the environment, and changing visitor expectations. Artificial Intelligence (AI) has become a key part of this change, giving hospitality businesses new ways to improve guest experiences, make operations more efficient, and support sustainability across the industry. Travelers are asking for more personalized, seamless, and eco-friendly services. To meet these needs, hospitality providers are using smart technologies like AI-powered chatbots, smart rooms, robotic concierges, emotion detection systems, digital twins, and predictive analytics to offer unique value propositions. This change marks the move away from traditional hospitality models that focus on service to data-driven, smart, and sustainable ecosystems that follow the UN's Sustainable Development Goals (SDGs), especially SDG 7 (Affordable and Clean Energy), SDG 9 (Industry, Innovation, and Infrastructure), SDG 12 (Responsible Consumption and Production), and SDG 13 (Climate Action).

In the past, the hospitality business was known for its high-touch, labor-intensive services that concentrated on human relationships, cultural exchange, and experiencing value. But the post-pandemic age has forced hospitality businesses to change how they do business because of problems like limited resources, more consumers being conscious of sustainability, health and safety issues, and competition from around the world. AI technologies have become important instruments to deal with these problems by making it possible to personalize at scale, optimize resource use, automate repetitive operations, and get insights for making decisions based on data. AI is especially important for sustainability because hotels are one of the most resource-intensive types of commercial buildings, using a lot of energy, water, and materials. Smart thermostats, AI-based energy management systems, and predictive maintenance tools are examples of intelligent systems that can cut down on carbon emissions, waste, and the life of assets.

Also, the modern hospitality industry shows a change in what guests anticipate. Modern visitors want more than just comfort and luxury. They also want experiences that are meaningful, real, and good for the environment. More than 70% of travelers around the world now prefer eco-friendly places to stay, and more than 60% are prepared to pay more for services that are good for the environment (World Travel & Tourism Council, 2024). AI-driven personalization lets hotels meet these needs by employing data analytics to guess what people want, provide services that are right for them, and make interactions that are emotionally engaging. AI-powered smart rooms may automatically change the lighting, temperature, and entertainment systems based on how guests are acting. This makes them more convenient and eco-friendly at the same time.

Another important part of AI-enabled hospitality is making smart ecosystems where technology, people, and procedures all work together without any problems. These ecosystems combine IoT devices, big data platforms, cloud computing, AI algorithms, and human knowledge to produce value together. For example, AI-powered kiosks and service robots make front-office work easier, and backend systems employ predictive analytics to estimate demand, set dynamic prices, and optimize inventory. AI also helps hotel managers come up with ways to be more environmentally friendly by keeping track of their carbon footprints, trash, and green supplier chains. More and more hotels are using digital twins of their infrastructure, which are virtual copies that show how energy flows, how many people are staying, and how maintenance will be done. These are used for predictive sustainability planning.

However, using AI in the hospitality industry comes with moral, technological, and management problems. There are a lot of problems with integrating AI, including worries about data privacy, bias in algorithms, fears of losing jobs, high costs of implementation, and reluctance to change from both employees and guests. The digital divide between places that are technologically sophisticated and those that are not also raises problems about fairness and inclusion as we move toward smart hospitality ecosystems. So, we need a balanced strategy that focuses on responsible AI, working together with AI, improving skills, and making sure that policies are in place to make sure ethical deployment.

The goal of this chapter is to give a thorough look at AI-driven sustainable visitor experiences in smart hospitality ecosystems. It seeks to examine theoretical frameworks, technological applications, practical implementations, problems, and prospective trajectories. The chapter attempts to address fundamental research inquiries, including:

- How does AI help the hospitality industry provide guests with long-lasting experiences?
- What are the new paradigms and frameworks for AI-enabled smart hotel ecosystems?
- What are the best ways to do things and examples from the greatest hotels across the world?
- What problems and moral issues come up when AI is put into use?
- What future directions can lead the hotel sector towards regenerative and net-zero operations through the utilization of AI and other technologies?

A REVIEW OF THE LITERATURE AND THE THEORETICAL BACKGROUND

The incorporation of Artificial Intelligence (AI) into the hotel sector has generated significant scholarly interest, especially regarding guest experience, sustainability, and intelligent service ecosystems. Academics have progressively underscored that the hospitality industry is evolving from labor-intensive service models to technology-driven, data-centric, and ecologically sustainable systems (Buhalis & Amaranggana, 2015; Tussyadiah, 2020). This change is mostly based on theories like Service-Dominant Logic (SDL), Experience Economy Theory, Sustainable Development Theory, and Smart Tourism Ecosystem (STE) Theory. Vargo and Lusch (2004) came up with the idea of Service-Dominant Logic. This idea says that value is created through interactions between service providers and customers, not by the products themselves. In the hospitality industry, AI strengthens SDL by tailoring services to individual guests, anticipating their preferences, and increasing their participation in co-creating experiences through intelligent interfaces, smart rooms, and automated concierge systems (Lu et al., 2019). The Experience Economy Theory by Pine and Gilmore (1999) also says that firms need to provide memorable experiences to stand out. AI technologies like emotion detection, natural language processing, augmented reality (AR), and virtual reality (VR) improve the value of experiences by giving people services that are very individualized and can change based on how they feel (Tussyadiah, 2020; Gursoy et al., 2019).

The Brundtland Report (WCED, 1987) helped establish the Sustainable Development Theory, which stresses social fairness, environmental conservation, and economic viability. AI directly supports these concepts by making hotel operations more energy-efficient, using predictive maintenance to cut down on resource use, and using analytics to manage food and water to avoid waste (Jones et al., 2021). For instance, AI-based Energy Management Systems (EMS) have been proven to save energy use in hotels by up to 20% by controlling heating, ventilation, and air conditioning (HVAC) systems smartly (Sharma & Kumar, 2023). AI also helps the hospitality industry move toward a circular economy by employing blockchain integration and predictive analytics to make recycling, food redistribution, and green supply chains more efficient (Filimonau & De Coteau, 2020). The Smart Tourism Ecosystem (STE) framework is another important theory. It says that smart destinations are interconnected systems of stakeholders, such as tourists, service providers, governments, technology platforms, and data infrastructures, that are made possible by AI, the Internet of Things (IoT), big data, and cloud computing (Gretzel et al., 2015). Artificial intelligence is a big part of smart hospitality, smart governance, smart mobility, smart experiences, and using resources wisely (Xiang & Fesenmaier, 2017).

Recent literature has thoroughly chronicled AI uses within hotel operations. Ivanov and Webster (2019) placed various technologies into groups such predictive analytics, computer vision, natural language processing (NLP), robotics, and machine learning. AI chatbots, service robots, self-check-in kiosks, face recognition check-in systems, and smart voice assistants are all examples of front-end applications (Wirtz et al., 2018). Marriott's "ChatBotlr" and Alibaba's "FlyZoo Hotel" are two of the best examples of AI-powered hotel services (Li et al., 2021). Revenue management, dynamic pricing, demand forecasting, inventory optimization, and predictive maintenance are all part of back-end AI integration (Samara et al., 2020). Personalization based on AI improves customer satisfaction by looking at guest history, preferences, travel behavior, social media data, and real-time interactions to customize services like room temperature and meal suggestions (Tussyadiah, 2020). Emotion AI is another new technology that uses facial expressions, tones, and feelings to give emotionally intelligent service replies (Gursoy et al., 2019).

Researchers also spoke about how AI might help make hospitality more sustainable. Hotels use a lot of energy, water, and materials, but AI-powered solutions can help fix these problems (Jones et al., 2021). Winnow is an AI-powered technology for managing food waste that cuts food waste in hotel kitchens by 30–50% using image identification and analytics (Filimonau & De Coteau, 2020). AI sensors also help laundry, swimming, and irrigation systems use less water. AI also keeps an eye on carbon emissions, maintains environmental measures, and helps with certifications like LEED and ISO 14001 (Sharma & Kumar, 2023). Researchers like Sigala (2018) and Xiang and Fesenmaier (2017) say that the hospitality industry is changing into an intelligent ecosystem where digital technologies, people, and eco-friendly practices are all connected.

Even with more study being done, there are still some gaps. First, there are not many studies that put AI, sustainability, consumer experience, and intelligent ecosystems all together into one model. The majority of research examines these domains in isolation, exhibiting limited multidisciplinary integration (Gretzel et al., 2015; Sigala, 2018). Second, the literature is predominantly comprised of case studies from industrialized countries, including the United States, Japan, and Europe, whereas emerging regions such as India, Sri Lanka, Kenya, and Vietnam are inadequately represented (Sharma & Kumar, 2023). Third, the ethical ramifications of AI—encompassing data privacy, employment displacement, algorithmic bias, and human-AI collaboration—necessitate more profound academic investigation (Wirtz et al., 2018). Fourth, the long-term environmental consequences of AI in the hospitality sector, especially in regenerative and net-zero tourism frameworks, are little studied (Jones et al., 2021). This chapter seeks to address these deficiencies by offering a holistic view of AI-driven sustainable visitor experiences within intelligent hospitality ecosystems.

AI IN HOSPITALITY: IDEAS, GROWTH, AND TOOLS

AI, or artificial intelligence, has gone from being a theoretical idea in computer science to a game-changing technology that is changing several fields, including hospitality. AI is the term for computer systems that can do cognitive tasks that normally require human intellect, like learning, reasoning, perceiving, and solving problems (Russell & Norvig, 2016). AI is used in the hospitality business to automate everyday tasks, improve service, predict demand, make guests' experiences more personal, and make attempts to be more environmentally friendly (Ivanov & Webster, 2019). There are three stages in the development of AI in hospitality: AI 1.0 (Automation Era), AI 2.0 (Smart Interaction Era), and AI 3.0 (Cognitive and Sustainable Intelligence Era). In the early 2000s, when automation first started, hotels mostly used AI-driven systems for making reservations, managing revenue, managing customer relationships (CRM), and setting prices dynamically (Talluri & Van Ryzin, 2004). As technology progressed into the smart interaction era, AI facilitated real-time customer support via chatbots, robotics, and intelligent kiosks capable of processing natural language and responding contextually (Wirtz et al., 2018). In the current age of AI 3.0, the focus has moved to emotion-aware systems, digital twins, predictive analytics, and sustainability-oriented intelligence that connects guest experience with environmental responsibility and operational success (Tussyadiah, 2020).

Technologies including Machine Learning (ML), Deep Learning (DL), Natural Language Processing (NLP), Computer Vision, the Internet of Things (IoT), and Big Data analytics make it easier for hotels to use AI. Machine learning helps hotels predict how many customers they will have, determine the best prices, and look at big amounts of data to learn more about how customers act (Samara et al., 2020). Deep learning, which is a part of ML, is utilized in facial recognition, video surveillance, and image-based check-in systems like the ones at Alibaba's FlyZoo Hotel in China, where customers may get into their rooms using facial biometrics instead of keys (Li et al., 2021). AI chatbots and voice assistants like Marriott's ChatBotlr, Hilton's Connie (which is based on IBM Watson), and Amazon Alexa for Hospitality use natural language processing to let customers talk to them 24/7 in several languages (Pillai et al., 2021). Computer vision helps with security monitoring, attendance systems, service robot navigation, and recognizing emotions during service delivery (Gursoy et al., 2019). IoT is a vital part of smart rooms and linked hotel ecosystems. AI systems automatically control energy use, guest comfort, lighting, thermostats, and appliances based on how many people are in the room and what they like (Buhalis & Leung, 2018).

Service automation and robots are two of the most important ways that AI is being used in the hotel industry. Service robots like SoftBank's Pepper, Savioke's

Relay, and Yotel's YO2D2 can bring room service, move luggage, help at the front desk, and help guests in more than one language (Ivanov & Webster, 2019). Japan's Henn-na Hotel, which is known as the world's first robot-staffed hotel, has tried out robotic concierges, AI check-in counters, and robotic security systems (Smith, 2021). These new technologies save labor expenses and mistakes made by people, but they also make service faster and safer without touching anything, which is something that is especially important in the post-pandemic world. AI has also changed the way back-end operations work, such predictive maintenance, where systems keep an eye on energy units, air conditioning, elevators, and kitchen appliances and forecast problems before they happen. This cuts down on downtime and maintenance costs (Jones et al., 2021). AI algorithms look at past booking data, competition prices, market trends, and outside factors like the weather or local events to come up with dynamic pricing strategies for revenue and yield management (Talluri & Van Ryzin, 2004).

Due to growing demand on hospitality businesses to meet the United Nations Sustainable Development Goals (SDGs), AI solutions that are focused on sustainability have become more popular. AI-based Energy Management Systems (EMS) improve heating, ventilation, air conditioning (HVAC), and lighting based on real-time occupancy, cutting energy use by 15–30% (Sharma & Kumar, 2023). Winnow and other AI-enabled food waste management systems use computer vision to keep track of leftover food, create waste analytics, and help cooks change menus to cut down on waste (Filimonau & De Coteau, 2020). Smart AI meters keep track of how much water is used in laundry, pools, restrooms, and irrigation. They send alerts and use projections to help people use less water. Hotels are also using AI-based digital twins more and more. These are virtual copies of hotel infrastructure that show how energy is used, how many people are staying there, how resources are used, and how much carbon is released to help make decisions that are good for the environment (Gretzel et al., 2022). Integrating AI and blockchain into supply chains is making it easier to trace organic food, fair-trade goods, and eco-friendly materials used in hotel operations (Kshetri, 2021).

Even though AI is changing quickly in the hospitality industry, it is not easy to use. High installation costs, cybersecurity issues, algorithmic bias, employee resistance, and worries about job loss are all big problems (Wirtz et al., 2018). Moreover, ethical concerns with guest data privacy, surveillance, facial recognition, and permission necessitate the implementation of stringent policies and transparent AI governance frameworks (Morosan & DeFranco, 2016). Nevertheless, experts contend that AI ought not to supplant human service but rather to enhance it by increasing efficiency, so enabling personnel to concentrate on empathy-driven and creative service functions (Tung & Au, 2018). AI-driven hospitality is evolving into a synergistic human-AI collaboration model, wherein technology augments sustainability, experience customization, and astute decision-making, all while preserving human connection and cultural authenticity.

FRAMEWORK FOR AI-POWERED SUSTAINABLE GUEST EXPERIENCE IN SMART HOSPITALITY ECOSYSTEMS

The AI-driven sustainable guest experience in hospitality arises at the convergence of technical innovation, environmental stewardship, and human-centric service design. To understand how AI-enabled technologies, stakeholders, and sustainability principles come together to create intelligent hospitality ecosystems, you need to create a conceptual framework. The proposed framework in this chapter is based on four pillars that are all connected: (1) AI-Enabled Personalization and Guest Experience, (2) Sustainable Operations and Resource Optimization, (3) Intelligent Ecosystem Integration, and (4) Ethical, Human-Centric, and Governance Dimensions. These pillars are in line with the ideas of Service-Dominant Logic (Vargo & Lusch, 2004), Smart Tourism Ecosystems (Gretzel et al., 2015), and Triple Bottom Line sustainability (Elkington, 1997). They show how AI can create value in the economy, the environment, and society.

The first pillar, AI-enabled personalization and guest experience, shows how smart technologies improve service by making interactions along the guest journey hyper-personalized, emotionally adaptive, and seamless. AI gathers and analyzes data from booking sites, loyalty programs, social media, smart room sensors, and mobile apps to guess what people want and customize services like room temperature, meal suggestions, language settings, and entertainment choices (Tussyadiah, 2020). Chatbots that use Natural Language Processing (NLP), like Marriott's "ChatBotlr" and Hilton's "Connie," let people talk to one other in real time and get quick answers. They also learn from their conversations to make the service better (Wirtz et al., 2018). Emotion AI and sentiment analysis tools make personalization even better by using facial recognition, voice tone, and text feedback to figure out how guests are feeling, how stressed they are, and how happy they are (Gursoy et al., 2019). This is in line with Experience Economy Theory (Pine & Gilmore, 1999), which says that the most valuable things for customers are emotional engagement and memory generation.

The second pillar, sustainable operations and resource optimization, looks at how AI can help protect the environment and make operations more efficient. Hospitality uses a lot of resources, like energy, water, and materials. AI-powered solutions make it easier to manage energy smartly by adjusting HVAC systems, lighting, and appliances based on how many people are in the room and how they behave, which can save energy use by up to 30% (Sharma & Kumar, 2023). Machine learning algorithms estimate how much energy will be needed and improve the usage of renewable energy. AI-powered waste management solutions like Winnow employ computer vision to keep an eye on food waste and give useful tips on how to reduce loss (Filimonau & De Coteau, 2020). Predictive maintenance solutions use AI and IoT sensors to find problems in elevators, boilers, chillers, and plumbing systems before they break down. This cuts down on downtime, expenses, and waste of resources (Jones et al., 2021). This pillar follows the ideas of the circular economy, SCM 12: Responsible Consumption and Production, and regenerative hospitality, which focuses on repairing natural ecosystems instead of only reducing harm.

The third pillar, intelligent ecosystem integration, shows how AI links people, platforms, technologies, and places to create a smart hospitality network that works well. The Smart Tourism Ecosystem (STE) idea sees tourism and hospitality as systems that are linked to each other and where stakeholders share data to produce value for everyone (Gretzel et al., 2015). AI is the main intelligence in this ecosystem that connects different parts, like IoT-enabled smart rooms, digital twins, smart mobility systems, cloud-based property management systems, guest mobile apps, and green supply chains (Xiang & Fesenmaier, 2017). Digital twins—virtual reproductions of hotel infrastructure—simulate energy flows, visitor mobility, water usage, and carbon emissions to enhance predictive decision-making (Gretzel et al., 2022). Blockchain and AI work together to keep track of sustainable supply chains in a safe way. This makes sure that sourcing organic food, fair-trade tea, and locally-made amenities is open and fair (Kshetri, 2021). This pillar shows how AI, sustainability, and collaborative intelligence may work together with both internal and external stakeholders.

The fourth and last pillar, which includes ethical, human-centered, and governance aspects, makes sure that AI is used responsibly. AI has a lot of potential, but when it comes to hospitality, it needs to deal with ethical issues like privacy, surveillance, data ownership, bias, and job loss (Morosan & DeFranco, 2016; Wirtz et al., 2018). Hotels gather a lot of private information, like biometric facial scans and spending habits. This makes people worried about GDPR compliance, cybersecurity, and digital trust (Vu & Hoffman, 2021). Also, staff members, especially those who work in cleaning, reservations, and customer service, may be afraid about losing their jobs if AI is used. Researchers contend that AI should enhance rather than supplant human labor by assuming monotonous activities, so allowing staff to concentrate on empathy, creativity, and cultural storytelling—fundamental aspects of the human essence in hospitality (Tung & Au, 2018). This requires new ways of doing things that include AI ethics training, teaching employees how to use technology again, clear algorithms, ways for guests to give their consent, and rules for AI responsibility.

AI USES IN SMART HOSPITALITY ECOSYSTEMS

Using Artificial Intelligence (AI) in smart hospitality ecosystems has changed how services are delivered, how guests interact with them, how sustainable practices are used, and how efficient back-end operations are. These applications cover a lot of ground, such as smart rooms and the Internet of Things (IoT), AI-powered service automation, energy and waste management, predictive maintenance, improving the circular economy, and emotion-aware service delivery. AI is no longer only something that exists in the future; it is now a part of hotel operations in real time through gadgets, cloud systems, sensors, mobile apps, and service robots. This makes the hospitality industry more connected, responsive, and sustainable (Buhalis & Leung, 2018).

5.1 AI-Powered Personalization and Guest Experience

Personalization is a key part of luxury and happiness in the hospitality industry. AI has greatly improved this by making personalized guest profiles based on information from past stays, social media activity, loyalty programs, and real-time interactions (Tussyadiah, 2020). AI-powered recommendation engines look at what guests like and don't like to propose places to eat, spa treatments, hotel settings, and things to do nearby. The "Connected Room" technology at Hilton lets visitors use their phones or voice assistants like Amazon Alexa for Hospitality to manage the lights, drapes, air conditioning, and TV streaming options (Li et al., 2021). Using Natural Language Processing (NLP), Marriott's "ChatBotlr" is available 24/7 to help with room service requests, housekeeping, check-out, and travel advice. Emotion AI makes personalization even better. For example, NEC and Hilton worked together on AI that can read visitors' facial expressions and tone of voice to change how staff members talk to and treat guests in real time (Gursoy et al., 2019). This makes hospitality more proactive than reactive, moving from providing services to creating experiences together, which is in line with Service-Dominant Logic (Vargo & Lusch, 2004).

5.2 Smart rooms, IoT integration, and smart building management

The Internet of Things (IoT) and AI work together to make up the backbone of smart hospitality infrastructure. Smart rooms with IoT sensors keep track of how many people are in them, the temperature, the lighting, and the energy use to make the rooms more adaptable (Buhalis & Amaranggana, 2015). AI algorithms look at how guests are acting in real time to automatically change the temperature, lighting, window blinds, and entertainment systems. This makes guests more comfortable and saves energy. Crowne Plaza and Wynn Resorts have put Amazon Echo devices in their rooms so that guests may use voice commands such "Alexa, set room temperature to 22°C" or "Alexa, open curtains." This makes it easier for guests to communicate with technology (Pillai et al., 2021). AI-based Building Management Systems (BMS) find unusual patterns in how much electricity is used, improve heating and ventilation schedules, and stop energy waste. According to Sharma and Kumar (2023), AI-driven intelligent control systems at Accor Hotels cut energy expenses by 15–25% a year by automatically controlling air conditioning and power use. Digital twins are advanced tools that let you digitally mimic how a hotel works, including projecting how much energy it will need in the future, how many guests will come and go, and how sustainable it will be (Gretzel et al., 2022).

5.3 Robots that help with AI and contactless hospitality

Service automation using AI-enabled robots has become more popular, especially after COVID-19 made people want to avoid touch with others. Robots like Pepper (SoftBank Robotics), Relay by Savioke, Yotel's YO2D2, and Alibaba's FlyZoo Hotel's robotic butlers may help guests with their luggage, show them around, provide concierge services, and speak many languages (Ivanov & Webster, 2019). These robots do repetitive jobs for people, making sure that they are clean, fast, and accurate. Facial recognition and AI-enabled kiosks at the Henn-na Hotel in Japan let visitors check in without staff help, which makes the process faster and safer (Smith, 2021). Concierge robots with AI can also help you plan city tours, restaurants, and spa appointments, which cuts down on wait times. Service robots now work with cloud data systems to learn from how guests engage with them, keep their knowledge bases up to date, and adjust to changing service standards.

5.4 AI in Energy, Water, and Waste Management for Long-Term Use

AI plays a big role in reaching sustainability goals by making the best use of resources. Hotels usually use a lot of electricity, heat, water, and food. AI-powered Energy Management Systems (EMS) use predictive algorithms to control heating, ventilation, air conditioning (HVAC), and lighting based on occupancy trends, weather conditions, and guest behavior. This can save energy use by up to 30% (Sharma & Kumar, 2023). AI-controlled irrigation systems also look at soil moisture and weather data to use less water when gardening. Smart meters, on the other hand, keep track of how much water is used in kitchens, laundry rooms, and swimming pools. Winnow Vision is an example of a food waste management technology that uses computer vision and AI to scan trash food, take pictures, measure waste, and suggest changes to buffet planning and buying (Filimonau & De Coteau, 2020). Hotels like Accor and Hyatt use AI-based waste sorting systems to separate glass, metal, plastic, and organic waste. This helps promote circular economy principles.

5.5 Predictive Maintenance and Efficiency in Operations

Predictive maintenance is a strong AI tool that makes sure services are always available and cuts down on downtime. Sensors in elevators, dishwashers, HVAC systems, and boilers capture data in real time. AI models then use this data to figure out when something is likely to break down (Jones et al., 2021). For instance, Marriott International utilizes AI to keep an eye on boiler pressure and water leaks to avoid dangerous breakdowns. Predictive analytics can also help with planning staff schedules, allocating rooms, budgeting for energy, and buying things. AI-powered demand forecasting models are commonly utilized in revenue management systems to anticipate occupancy rates, establish dynamic pricing, and enhance promotional strategies (Samara et al., 2020). AI systems look at everything outside of the business, such local events, public holidays, the weather, and rival rates, to come up with the best pricing strategies that will keep the business going.

5.6 AI and Circular Economy Practices in the Hotel Industry

The circular economy concept puts a lot of stress on reusing, recycling, and buying things in a way that doesn't hurt the environment. AI helps with this change by making supply chains more efficient, keeping track of product lifecycles, and looking at waste trends. Blockchain and AI work together to make sure that hotels have eco-friendly materials, healthy food, and amenities that are made in a way that is fair to workers (Kshetri, 2021). Fairmont Hotels, for instance, utilize blockchain to track coffee and tea that comes from ethical sources. This makes sure that farmers get paid fairly and builds trust among eco-conscious customers. AI-powered procurement systems suggest vendors based on their carbon footprint, sustainability certification, and how well they save money. AI-powered linen reuse programs also urge guests to be more environmentally friendly by providing them targeted reminders through mobile applications or smart TVs. This cuts down on the amount of water and detergent used.

5.7 Managing Guest Sentiment and Emotion AI

One of the most cutting-edge types of AI in the hotel industry is Emotion Artificial Intelligence (Emotion AI). It employs facial recognition, voice analysis, and sentiment algorithms to figure out how guests are feeling right now (Gursoy et al., 2019). Emotion AI in hotels can change how they serve visitors based on their moods. For example, it can tell when a person is unhappy during check-in and send staff alerts to let them know what to do right away. AI uses sentiment analysis to look at guest evaluations on TripAdvisor, Booking.com, and social media to find patterns in satisfaction, complaints, and service gaps (Xiang et al., 2017). Voice-based Emotion AI technologies that work with call centers can pick up on changes in tone, tempo, or loudness that show irritation and recommend calm replies to human agents. This emotionally intelligent service fits with the idea of "High-Tech + High-Touch" service (Tung & Au, 2018).

GLOBAL BEST PRACTICES AND CASE STUDIES IN AI-DRIVEN SUSTAINABLE HOSPITALITY

Real-world examples from top hotel chains and smart tourism destinations show how AI-driven sustainable guest experiences may work in intelligent hospitality ecosystems. These case studies show how AI technologies are making operations more efficient, sustainable, personalized, and satisfying for guests. They offer empirical evidence for the implementation of conceptual models, demonstrating the synergy of innovation, environmental stewardship, and hospitality excellence.

6.1 Marriott International: Using AI to make things more personal and save energy

Marriott International is now a world leader in using AI to improve hotel operations and the guest experience. The chain introduced the "ChatBotlr" system through the Marriott mobile app. This lets visitors ask for towels, cleaning, hotel upgrades, and late check-outs through AI-powered chatbots (Li et al., 2021). Marriott also uses AI-based Customer Relationship Management (CRM) systems to look at guest preferences, loyalty program data, and behavior trends in order to offer very personalized services. Marriott worked with Samsung and Legrand to make smart rooms that use IoT sensors and AI to automatically control the lighting, air conditioning, and curtains depending on motion detection and temperature settings. This is a step toward sustainability. AI-driven Energy Management Systems have been said to cut energy use at some Marriott hotels by as much as 20% a year (Sharma & Kumar, 2023). The "Serve360" sustainability policy uses AI to keep track of carbon emissions, water use, and waste statistics. This is in line with the SDG goals.

6.2 Hilton Worldwide: New AI Concierge and Connected Room Features

Hilton has led the way in AI-enabled concierge services with "Connie," a robot made in partnership with IBM Watson and SoftBank Robotics. Connie helps guests with check-in, food suggestions, and information about things to do in the area by talking to them in natural language (Wirtz et al., 2018). Hilton also launched its "Connected Room" technology, which lets guests use their smartphones or voice assistants like Amazon Alexa for Hospitality to manage the lights, temperature, entertainment, and window shades. AI systems remember what guests like and dislike from previous stays, so they can set up rooms just the way they like them for future trips. LightStay, Hilton's program for sustainability, employs AI to keep track of energy, water, and waste at more than 5,000 hotels around the world. The chain has cut down on equipment failures and operating expenses by using AI to predict when maintenance is needed. This has resulted to a 30% boost in energy efficiency across all of its properties (Jones et al., 2021).

6.3 Alibaba's FlyZoo Hotel in China: A hotel that runs entirely on AI

The FlyZoo Hotel in Hangzhou, China, run by Alibaba, is one of the most advanced uses of AI in the hospitality industry. The FlyZoo Hotel is a futuristic example of hospitality that uses robots, AI, and contactless technology. Guests can check in using facial recognition without having to talk to the reception personnel. Biometric scanners in elevators only let people onto floors that have been approved (Li et al., 2021). Robots powered by AI bring food, laundry, and cleaning supplies to rooms. Through Alibaba's travel platform Fliggy, the AI system also suggests restaurants, spas, and shopping deals. Also, Alibaba Cloud keeps track of what customers like, so they may get personalized services when they come back. AI-driven electricity optimization, low-energy facial recognition systems, and robots that cut down on material waste and human mistake are all examples of sustainable practices.

6.4 Henn-na Hotel in Japan: The First Hotel in the World with Robot Staff

The Henn-na Hotel in Nagasaki, Japan, is known all over the world as the first hotel to have robots working there. The resort has multilingual robotic receptionists, mechanized luggage carriers, and robotic concierge services (Smith, 2021). Instead of room keys, facial recognition is used, and AI-based temperature sensors make the room's climate better. The Henn-na model shows both the good and bad sides of using AI in the hotel industry. There were problems with robots not working and guests not being happy in some circumstances. Even though there were problems with operations, the hotel was able to cut expenses for labor and energy by employing AI and IoT solutions for lighting, ventilation, and predictive maintenance (Ivanov & Webster, 2019).

6.5 Taj Hotels (India): AI for Heritage Hospitality and Sustainability

Taj Hotels, which is part of the Indian Hotels Company Limited (IHCL), has combined traditional hospitality with new technology and eco-friendliness. The chain has included AI-powered chatbots dubbed "Taj Assistant" for making reservations and talking to guests in the last few years (Sharma & Kumar, 2023). The Taj Palace in New Delhi and Taj Exotica in Goa are two of the Taj hotels that integrate AI-based HVAC systems and IoT-enabled smart meters to cut down on energy use and carbon emissions. The startup uses AI and picture recognition technologies to keep an eye on food waste in buffet restaurants. AI-driven sentiment analysis is also utilized to keep an eye on guest reviews on sites like TripAdvisor, Booking.com, and Google Reviews. This helps improve service quality while keeping cultural authenticity (Gupta & Srivastava, 2022).

6.6 Accor Hotels, France: AI and Circular Economy Practices

Accor has included AI to its "Planet 21" program for sustainability. The chain uses AI-powered predictive analytics to improve its linen and laundry services, which cuts down on the amount of water and detergent used (Filimonau & De Coteau, 2020). AI-powered robots help with cleaning at ibis and Novotel hotels, making it faster and cleaner. Accor also uses AI and blockchain technologies to keep an eye on its supply chains and make sure that coffee, tea, linens, and bath items are sourced in an ethical way. Some hotels have AI-powered equipment that autonomously sort glass, metal, food, and plastic trash. Using AI-based menu planning tools can help cut down on food waste, which can save up to 30% on food costs.

6.7 Smart Tourism Spots: Dubai and Singapore

Dubai and Singapore have become the world's best examples of smart tourist ecosystems, with a lot of AI used in transportation, hotels, and government. The "Smart Dubai" project in Dubai uses AI for smart hotel licensing, hospitality data dashboards, guest sentiment analysis, and real-time occupancy monitoring. The Burj Al Arab and Atlantis The Palm combine AI concierges, AI-driven boat services, and robotic housekeepers to give guests high-end, eco-friendly experiences (Al Nuaimi & Khan, 2022). The Singapore Tourism Board (STB) also employs AI-powered sentiment analysis to keep an eye on real-time input from tourists on digital platforms (Xiang & Fesenmaier, 2017). Hotels like Marina Bay Sands and Pan Pacific use AI to save energy, customize rooms, and make digital twins of guest foot traffic and utility needs.

PROBLEMS, MORAL ISSUES, AND LIMITS OF AI IN THE HOSPITALITY INDUSTRY

Artificial Intelligence has changed the hospitality business by making it more personalized, sustainable, and efficient. However, its use also comes with a number of problems and ethical issues that need to be thought about carefully. One of the main worries is data privacy and cybersecurity. Hotels collect a lot of guest data, such as personal information, face recognition records, browsing history, spending trends, and biometric information. This makes it easier for hackers to steal your identity, use your data without permission, and attack your computer (Morosan & DeFranco, 2016). For instance, Marriott International had a huge data breach in 2018 that affected 500 million guests. This showed how dangerous it is to have weak AI and data governance frameworks (Jones et al., 2021). When AI systems are put into use, they must follow data protection rules like the General Data Protection Regulation (GDPR) in Europe. These laws say that people must give their informed consent, that data usage policies must be clear, and that people have the right to have their data deleted (Vu & Hoffman, 2021).

Another big problem is the worry of losing jobs and having the workforce change. The growing usage of service robots, self-check-in kiosks, automated concierge systems, and AI-powered housekeeping technologies has made hospitality workers worry about losing their jobs and becoming less important. Research indicates that although AI eradicates monotonous, labor-intensive positions, it simultaneously generates new opportunities in digital service management, data analytics, AI maintenance, and the enhancement of guest interactions (Ivanov & Webster, 2019). But staff members typically oppose using AI because they don't have the digital abilities they need or because the training programs aren't good enough. Experts say that AI shouldn't take the place of human warmth, which is the heart of hospitality. Instead, it should work with human service to create a "high-tech, high-touch" service balance (Tung & Au, 2018).

AI systems can also be biased and unfair, especially when it comes to facial recognition, dynamic pricing, and targeted marketing. Biases in AI frequently arise from distorted or unrepresentative training data, leading to inequitable service delivery or erroneous visitor identification based on ethnicity, gender, or age (Gursoy et al., 2019). For example, facial recognition technologies are less accurate for women and people with darker skin tones. This could lead to unfair experiences for guests, being denied entry, or getting security alerts that aren't suitable (Morosan & DeFranco, 2016). Also, AI-powered revenue management solutions might use discriminatory pricing based on things like nationality or spending habits, which raises moral problems about fairness and openness (Samara et al., 2020).

The high cost of implementing AI is another problem, especially for small and medium-sized businesses (SMEs) in developing nations. This is bad for the environment and the economy. It costs a lot of money, trained workers, and long-term upkeep to set up smart energy systems, robots, digital twins, and complex property management systems (Sharma & Kumar, 2023). Hotels in less developed areas typically don't have the technology, stable internet connections, or qualified staff needed to promote AI adoption. This is making the global digital divide in hospitality innovation grow (Xiang & Fesenmaier, 2017). AI systems also depend a lot on cloud computing and data centers, which use a lot of electricity. This could make the environment worse unless they are supplied by renewable energy sources (Jones et al., 2021).

In the hospitality sector, which has always been based on emotional intelligence, empathy, human touch, and cultural connection, a big worry is that people are relying too much on AI and not enough on people. Too much automation can make service experiences less personal, which can make customers less happy, especially older guests, travelers who are sensitive to other cultures, or luxury tourists who appreciate human interaction (Wirtz et al., 2018). Cases from the Henn-na Hotel in Japan showed that robots failed when interacting with guests, had technical problems, and couldn't manage complicated customer questions. This shows that AI can't totally replace human staff in service situations that are emotionally complicated (Smith, 2021). Guests typically want realness, empathy, and cultural storytelling, which AI can't do well.

Lastly, there are holes in the ethical governance and regulation of AI use in the tourism and hospitality industries. Most countries don't have laws that make AI responsible, check for ethical issues, provide people rights to their data, or make decisions in a clear way (Vu & Hoffman, 2021). AI could be utilized for intrusive monitoring, worker exploitation, or biased service delivery if there aren't strict rules in place. So, politicians, hotel owners, and tech developers need to work together to create rules for Responsible AI that stress fairness, openness, human oversight, sustainability, and cultural sensitivity (Gretzel et al., 2022).

AI, THE METAVERSE, DIGITAL TWINS, AND REGENERATIVE HOSPITALITY ARE ALL POSSIBLE PATHS FOR THE FUTURE.

The future of AI-driven hospitality is at the crossroads of ethical governance, immersive technologies, predictive intelligence, and new ways to be environmentally friendly. As the hospitality industry continues to change into a smart ecosystem, new technologies like the metaverse, digital twins, blockchain, predictive AI, and regenerative hospitality models are expected to change the way guests experience and how businesses run in a sustainable way. These technologies make traditional AI applications better by making hospitality environments that are very interactive, predictive, and good for the environment. One of the most exciting things that could happen in the future is the rise of the metaverse in tourism and hospitality, which is a virtual space where physical and digital experiences come together. Travelers can use 3D virtual reality (VR) and augmented reality (AR) in the metaverse to see hotels, destinations, museums, and cultural heritage sites before they go there in person (Guttentag, 2020). Luxury hotel chains like Marriott, Atlantis Dubai, and Accor are already trying out blockchain-based metaverse platforms to offer virtual hotel tours, immersive booking experiences, digital concierge avatars, virtual conferences, and NFT-based loyalty programs (Mystakidis, 2022). This lets guests virtually customize the layout, decor, dining options, and event settings of their rooms before they arrive, which makes it easier for them to make decisions and be happy. The metaverse also helps the environment by cutting down on the carbon impact of long-distance travel for business meetings, virtual weddings, or MICE events (meetings, incentives, conferences, and exhibitions). This is in line with what people want after the pandemic, which is hybrid travel models that combine digital and physical experiences (Buhalis & Moldavska, 2022). The use of digital twins is another important future direction for AI-enabled hospitality. Digital twins are smart virtual copies of real hotels, resorts, or other places that show how things work, how much energy they use, how guests move around, how well equipment works, and how they affect the environment (Gretzel et al., 2022). These simulations allow hotel managers do "what-if" assessments to make smarter decisions. For example, they can use them to estimate occupancy patterns, optimize energy loads, test new architectural designs, or look at the carbon footprint of different operational scenarios. Digital twins are being used by resorts like Marina Bay Sands in Singapore and the infrastructure for Dubai's Expo 2020 to foresee maintenance needs, forecast energy use, and analyze crowd traffic. This makes them safer and more environmentally friendly (Al Nuaimi & Khan, 2022). Digital twins, which use AI, IoT, and real-time sensor data, help businesses run on net-zero energy, lower operational risks, and improve the guest experience by reducing service interruptions. The future of hospitality is moving from sustainability to regenerative hospitality, a model that not only minimizes environmental harm but also restores ecosystems and supports community well-being. AI helps make this change happen by making it possible to keep track of carbon footprints, monitor biodiversity, forecast when to save water, optimize renewable energy use, and manage supply chains in a circular economy (Elkington, 1997; Jones et al., 2021). AI-powered platforms can look at a hotel's energy mix and advise the best combinations of solar, wind, geothermal, and battery storage solutions to help the hotel reach its net-zero goals. Blockchain combined with AI also makes carbon credit trade, tea, coffee, linen, and spa product procurement more honest, and makes sure that local artists and farmers who work in eco-tourism get fair pay (Kshetri, 2021). Regenerative tourism goes beyond certifications like LEED or Green Key and focuses on improving the local ecology, cultural heritage, and indigenous knowledge. AI-driven data analytics and machine learning can help with resource planning and impact assessment in these areas. Another new area is AI-driven carbon benchmarking and predictive sustainability analytics. More and more, AI systems are being utilized to make real-time sustainability dashboards that keep track of things like energy use, water use, waste levels, greenhouse gas emissions, food waste, and how many guests are taking part in eco-friendly activities (Sharma & Kumar, 2023). Hotels can use predictive models to guess how the environment will change based on things like how many people are staying there, the weather, or special events. These insights are essential for decision-makers to comply with ESG (Environmental, Social, Governance) reporting standards and to conform with international climate regulations, including the Paris Agreement and the UN Sustainable Development Goals (SDGs) (Jones et al., 2021). Hilton, Marriott, Taj, and Accor are some of the hotels that are spearheading this change by adding AI-based sustainability dashboards to their corporate governance systems.

CONCLUSION

Artificial Intelligence is changing the future of hospitality by turning typical service interactions into intelligent, long-lasting, and experience-focused ecosystems. This chapter looked at how AI technologies including machine learning, natural language processing, robotics, emotion AI, digital twins, and predictive analytics are changing the way guests experience things while also making operations more efficient and protecting the environment. AI-driven personalization has allowed hotels to move away from traditional services and toward hyper-individualized ones that meet changing client needs for comfort, cultural authenticity, and convenience (Tussyadiah, 2020). Smart rooms, AI chatbots, service robots, and predictive maintenance systems have made operations more efficient, reduced human error, and improved safety. This is especially important in a post-pandemic world where contactless hospitality is now a necessity rather than a luxury (Wirtz et al., 2018). AI has also become a powerful force for sustainability, helping companies reduce waste, optimize energy use, keep an eye on carbon footprints, and manage resources responsibly (Sharma & Kumar, 2023).

This chapter also created a conceptual framework made up of four interrelated pillars: AI-enabled customization, sustainable operations, intelligent ecosystem integration, and ethical human-centered governance. These components together explain how intelligent hospitality ecosystems work as social and technological networks that bring together people, visitors, AI systems, and environmental goals. Case studies from Marriott, Hilton, Taj Hotels, Accor, FlyZoo, and Dubai's smart tourism initiatives show that the industry has successfully adopted these ideas, with clear benefits in guest satisfaction, lower operating costs, sustainability outcomes, and brand competitiveness (Li et al., 2021; Jones et al., 2021). But these implementations also show problems, like the high expenses of using AI, the digital divide between rich and poor countries, and the over-reliance on technology that could hurt emotional connection and human hospitality ideals (Ivanov & Webster, 2019).

Ethical considerations are paramount to the judicious advancement of AI in the hospitality sector. Concerns about data privacy, biometric surveillance, algorithmic bias, job loss, and loss of human warmth need strong governance frameworks and regulatory systems (Morosan & DeFranco, 2016; Vu & Hoffman, 2021). Responsible AI must be a top priority for the hospitality business. This means being open, fair, protecting data, getting guest agreement, and retraining employees. AI should add to, not replace, human workers. This will create a balanced "high-tech, high-touch" service model in which technology makes things more efficient and human workers provide empathy, cultural storytelling, and individualized, emotion-driven service (Tung & Au, 2018). To make sure that their businesses will continue and their employees will be able to adapt, hotels need to spend money on AI literacy programs, retraining their personnel, and working together with AI.

Future routes imply a transition from sustainability to regenerative hospitality, where AI not only minimizes environmental effect but actively contributes to ecological restoration, community well-being, and cultural preservation (Elkington, 1997). Digital twins, the metaverse, blockchain for eco-certification, and AI-driven carbon benchmarking are all technologies that will change the hospitality industry in the next phase (Gretzel et al., 2022; Mystakidis, 2022). These tools will help hotels test their operations before putting them into action, make virtual travel experiences more personal, make sure that tea, coffee, and wellness items are sourced ethically, and construct hotel infrastructures that are carbon-negative or net-zero. The metaverse will also make hybrid travel models that mix real and digital experiences. This will make virtual tours, digital conferences, and immersive cultural storytelling possible, which will help reduce the environmental impact of popular tourist spots (Guttentag, 2020).

REFERENCES

Buhalis, D., & Amaranggana, A. (2015). Smart tourism destinations. In Xiang, Z., & Tussyadiah, I. (Eds.), *Information and communication technologies in tourism* (pp. 553–564). Springer.

Buhalis, D., & Leung, R. (2018). Smart hospitality—Interconnectivity and interoperability towards an ecosystem. *International Journal of Hospitality Management, 71*, 41–50. DOI: 10.1016/j.ijhm.2017.11.011

Buhalis, D., & Leung, R. (2018). Smart hospitality — Interconnectivity and interoperability towards an ecosystem. *International Journal of Hospitality Management, 71*, 41–50. staffprofiles.bournemouth.ac.uk±2eprints.bournemouth.ac.uk±2DOI: 10.1016/j.ijhm.2017.11.011

Buhalis, D., & Moldavska, A. (2022). Metaverse and tourism: Hybrid experiences and smart ecosystems. *Journal of Tourism Futures, 9*(1), 105–120.

Elkington, J. (1997). *Cannibals with forks: The triple bottom line of 21st century business*. Capstone.

Filimonau, V., & De Coteau, D. (2020). Food waste management practices in hospitality operations: A critical review. *Tourism Management, 71*, 234–245. DOI: 10.1016/j.tourman.2018.10.009

Gretzel, U., Sigala, M., Xiang, Z., & Koo, C. (2015). Smart tourism: Foundations and developments. *Electronic Markets, 25*(3), 179–188. DOI: 10.1007/s12525-015-0196-8

Gretzel, U., Werthner, H., Koo, C., & Lamsfus, C. (2022). Conceptual foundations for understanding smart tourism ecosystems. *Computers in Human Behavior, 132*, 107–239.

Gupta, S., & Srivastava, R. (2022). AI-enhanced guest feedback analytics in heritage hotels: A case of Taj Group. *Journal of Heritage Hospitality, 14*(2), 88–102.

Gursoy, D., Chi, O. H., Lu, L., & Nunkoo, R. (2019). Consumers' acceptance of artificially intelligent (AI) device use in service delivery. *International Journal of Information Management, 49*, 157–169. DOI: 10.1016/j.ijinfomgt.2019.03.008

Guttentag, D. (2020). Virtual reality: Applications and implications for tourism. *Tourism Management, 71*, 315–327.

Ivanov, S., & Webster, C. (2019). *Robotics, artificial intelligence and the evolving nature of work in the tourism and hospitality industry*. Emerald Publishing.

Jones, P., Hillier, D., & Comfort, D. (2021). Sustainability in the global hotel industry. *International Journal of Contemporary Hospitality Management, 33*(1), 1–15.

Kshetri, N. (2021). Blockchain and sustainable supply chains in hospitality. *Tourism Management, 83*, 104–176.

Li, N., Zhang, T., & Wang, Y. (2021). AI in hotel operations: Case study of Alibaba's FlyZoo Hotel. *International Journal of Hospitality Management, 93*, 102–777.

Morosan, C., & DeFranco, A. (2016). It's about time: Revisiting hotel guests' intention to use biometric systems. *International Journal of Hospitality Management, 53*, 154–164. DOI: 10.1016/j.ijhm.2015.11.003

Mystakidis, S. (2022). Metaverse in hospitality and tourism: Opportunities and challenges. *Journal of Virtual Worlds Research, 15*(2), 1–21.

Pillai, S. G., Haldorai, K., Seo, W. S., & Kim, W. G. (2021). AI-powered smart hotels: Innovations and service delivery. *Journal of Hospitality and Tourism Technology, 12*(3), 449–464.

Pine, B. J., & Gilmore, J. H. (1999). *The experience economy: Work is theatre & every business a stage*. Harvard Business School Press.

Russell, S., & Norvig, P. (2016). *Artificial intelligence: A modern approach* (3rd ed.). Pearson.

Samara, D., Kattuman, P., & Khalil, S. (2020). AI-based revenue management in hotels. *Tourism Economics, 26*(6), 1132–1151.

Sharma, M., & Kumar, S. (2023). Artificial intelligence for sustainable hotel operations: Energy, water and waste optimization. *Sustainable Tourism Review, 11*(1), 50–67.

Sigala, M. (2018). Social media and customer engagement in the hospitality industry. *Service Industries Journal, 38*(11–12), 1–25.

Smith, A. (2021). Robot-run hotels: The Henn-na experience. *Journal of Hospitality Case Studies, 10*(2), 56–65.

Talluri, K., & Van Ryzin, G. (2004). *The theory and practice of revenue management*. Springer. DOI: 10.1007/b139000

Tung, V. W. S., & Au, N. (2018). Exploring customer experiences with robotics in hospitality: A service quality perspective. *Journal of Hospitality Marketing & Management, 27*(7), 855–876.

Tussyadiah, I. (2020). A review of AI applications in hospitality and tourism. *Journal of Travel Research, 59*(8), 1–18.

Vargo, S. L., & Lusch, R. F. (2004). Evolving to a new dominant logic for marketing. *Journal of Marketing, 68*(1), 1–17. DOI: 10.1509/jmkg.68.1.1.24036

Vu, H. Q., & Hoffman, M. (2021). Data privacy, GDPR, and AI in hospitality. *Journal of Hospitality and Tourism Technology, 12*(5), 733–750.

WCED (World Commission on Environment and Development). (1987). *Our common future (Brundtland Report)*. Oxford University Press.

Wirtz, J., Patterson, P., Kunz, W., Gruber, T., Lu, V., Paluch, S., & Martins, A. (2018). Brave new world: Service robots in the frontline. *Journal of Service Management, 29*(5), 907–931. DOI: 10.1108/JOSM-04-2018-0119

Wirtz, J., Patterson, P., Kunz, W., Gruber, T., Lu, V. N., Paluch, S., & Martins, A. (2018). Brave new world: Service robots in the frontline. *Journal of Service Management, 29*(5), 907–931. DOI: 10.1108/JOSM-04-2018-0119

Xiang, Z., Du, Q., Ma, Y., & Fan, W. (2017). A comparative analysis of major online review platforms: Implications for social media analytics. *Tourism Management, 58*, 51–65. DOI: 10.1016/j.tourman.2016.10.001

Xiang, Z., & Fesenmaier, D. R. (2017). Big data analytics, tourism design and smart tourism. *Journal of Destination Marketing & Management, 6*(2), 59–67.

Chapter 2
The Importance of Green Finance on Climate Risk Management in the Case of Saudi Arabia

Monia Ben Ltaifa
https://orcid.org/0000-0001-9202-2554
Applied College, King Faisal University, Saudi Arabia

ABSTRACT

This paper explores the role of green finance as a strategic lever for climate risk management in Saudi Arabia, a country undergoing a major economic transformation driven by Vision 2030. Despite its historical dependence on hydrocarbons, the Kingdom now aims to diversify its economy and strengthen its resilience to climate change. Through a review of current dynamics, this paper highlights the gradual development of a green financial ecosystem: green bond and green sukuk issuances, state initiatives such as the Saudi Green Initiative, and the rise of ESG investing. However, these dynamics remain hampered by major challenges: a lack of standardization of ESG criteria, the risk of greenwashing, weak local institutional capacities, and high upfront costs of sustainable projects. Despite these obstacles, green finance offers significant opportunities: attracting foreign capital, fostering the energy transition, developing new financial markets, and strengthening the management of climate-related physical and transition risks.

DOI: 10.4018/979-8-3373-8197-8.ch002

1. INTRODUCTION

Climate change is a major global challenge today, not only because of its environmental impacts melting ice, rising sea levels, and extreme weather events but also because of the risks it poses to economic systems, infrastructure, and financial stability (Guesmi et al., 2025; Madouri, 2025). In this context, the financial sector is increasingly emerging as a key player in mitigating greenhouse gas emissions and adapting to climate risks, through the financing of clean technologies, infrastructure resilience, physical risk management mechanisms, and transitions.

Among recent dynamics, the OECD and the GCF report that incentive regulatory frameworks including green taxonomy, climate reporting obligations, or standards for "green bonds" are spreading, but that current financing often remains insufficient to meet adaptation needs, particularly in regions subject to severe water constraints, extreme temperatures, or vulnerable ecosystems (Adeyemi et al., 2025; Al-Harbi, 2025; Madouri, 2025).

Saudi Arabia presents a profile distinguished by several characteristics related to climate, economy and national strategies (Bouzidi et al., 2024):

- Climate and physical risks: extreme heat, water stress, desertification, risks to agriculture, water resources, and biodiversity.
- Dependence on hydrocarbons: Oil and gas remain pillars of the national economy, both for government revenue, exports, and energy production. However, this dependence exposes the country to risks associated with the energy transition and global demand for cleaner energy.
- Vision 2030 and national strategies:
    - The commitment to achieve carbon neutrality by 2060 through the Circular Carbon Economy model.
    - The goal of reducing greenhouse gas emissions by 278 million tonnes per year by 2030 compared to the base year (2019).
    - The Saudi Green Initiative (SGI), launched in 2021, which combines several components: emission reduction, afforestation, land and marine protection (SGI, more than 77 initiatives for ~ $186 billion investment)
    - The Green Financing Framework, published by the Ministry of Finance in 2024 as part of the Financial Sector Development Program, aims to encourage public and private green investments and align financing with international standards such as the Green Bonds Principles.

These dynamics, however, leave several open questions regarding the real effectiveness of green finance as a lever for managing climate risks in Saudi Arabia. More specifically (Hussain et al., 2025):

- To what extent do the Kingdom's policies and institutional frameworks, strategies, regulations, incentives, generate dynamics favorable to green finance?
- What are the main obstacles, financial, technical, governance, capacity, transparency, that limit or slow down the implementation of these policies?
- What specific opportunities arise for Saudi Arabia, both to mitigate physical climate risks and to facilitate the energy transition, if green finance is effectively mobilized?

This paper proposes to explore these questions through a combination of recent literature review, analysis of Saudi frameworks and instruments, and illustrative case studies, in order to draw applicable political and strategic lessons.

2. THEORETICAL CONCEPTS AND LITERATURE REVIEW

2.1. Definition of green finance / sustainable finance / climate finance

Climate finance refers to all public and private financial flows that aim to support actions to mitigate greenhouse gas emissions or adapt to the effects of climate change (IMF, 2024). Green finance is a broader concept, including investments, loans, or capital allocated to activities that generate measurable environmental benefits, such as renewable energy, energy efficiency, ecosystem restoration, etc. (Angorani, 2024). Sustainable finance, on the other hand, encompasses not only environmental but also social and governance (ESG) dimensions, seeking to align financial decisions with long-term sustainable development principles.

Several recent studies highlight a lack of consensus on the precise definition of green finance, which creates challenges in monitoring, reporting, and comparison between jurisdictions (OECD, 2024).

2.2. Typologies of climate risks

The literature generally distinguishes three main categories of climate risks affecting economies, businesses and the financial sector:

- Physical risks: those linked to the direct effects of climate change, whether acute (extreme events such as floods, storms, heat waves) or chronic (rising average temperatures, persistent drought, rising sea levels). These risks can cause damage to infrastructure, disrupt value chains, and lead to significant economic losses. (Li and Wu, 2025).

- Transition risks: These risks arise from the institutional, political, regulatory, technological, and market changes required to transition to a low-carbon economy. For example, stricter carbon regulations, the abandonment of fossil fuel subsidies, the rise of clean technologies, or changes in consumer preferences. These risks may cause certain assets to become "stranded" or reduce their value, and impose significant costs on companies and financial portfolios with significant exposure to fossil fuels. (Li and Wu, 2025; Angorani, 2024).
- Reputational and legal risks: linked to the disclosure of misinformation, greenwashing, and increasing expectations of stakeholders (investors, regulators, civil society). Complaints or legal liabilities may arise if financial actors or companies do not respect their environmental commitments or if their practices are perceived as misleading. (Iqbal et al., 2025).

2.3. Review of relevant international experiences (GCC, MENA, oil-producing countries in transition)

Several studies offer useful lessons for comparing what Saudi Arabia is doing with similar trajectories:

- In the GCC, there is a strong momentum for the implementation of green financial instruments (green bonds, green sukuk, sustainable bonds) and sustainable finance policies. However, these countries face significant disparities in the volume of green issuance, the quality of ESG standards, reporting capacity, and local skills (Iqbal et al., 2025).
- A study titled Sustainable Finance is Transforming the GCC's Future shows that in the Gulf countries, sustainable investments and transition financing are already contributing to economic diversification, job creation, and are seen as essential to achieving carbon neutrality goals (KPMGFAB, 2025).
- MENA countries outside the GCC (e.g., Egypt, Morocco, Jordan) show that green finance projects can progress but are often limited by constraints: institutional capacity, high cost of capital, lack of standardization and strong environmental governance frameworks.
- In the case of oil-producing countries in transition, the literature indicates that success depends on the credibility of government commitments, the clarity and consistency of public policies, the active role of national financial institutions, and the attraction of international financing to offset the negative effects of the transition. (Angorani, 2024).

3. LEGAL, INSTITUTIONAL AND POLITICAL FRAMEWORK IN SAUDI ARABIA

Saudi Arabia, a key player in the global hydrocarbon market, has gradually integrated climate and sustainability issues into its institutional and economic reforms. As part of its economic diversification strategy, embodied in Vision 2030, the Kingdom has established a regulatory and institutional framework for green finance, consistent with its international commitments and its ambitions for transformation towards a more sustainable economy.

3.1. Strategic orientation and climate commitments

Vision 2030 is the cornerstone of Saudi Arabia's economic transformation. It aims to reduce dependence on oil, develop non-oil sectors, and promote sustainable growth, particularly through investments in renewable energy, energy efficiency, and green finance. In this spirit, the Kingdom announced in 2021 its goal of achieving carbon neutrality by 2060, through a so-called Circular Carbon Economy (CCE) approach, which is based on four pillars: reducing, reusing, recycling, and eliminating carbon emissions.

Furthermore, as part of its Nationally Determined Contribution (NDC) submitted under the Paris Agreement, Saudi Arabia has committed to reducing its greenhouse gas emissions by 278 million tons by 2030, while maintaining a balance between economic development and environmental protection.

3.2. Regulatory architecture and financial arrangements

One of the major developments in the legal framework is the publication of the Green Financing Framework in 2024 by the Saudi Ministry of Finance. This framework aims to direct sovereign debt issuance (green or sustainable bonds) towards projects with a positive environmental impact. It is based on international green bond principles, notably those defined by the International Capital Market Association (ICMA). It includes criteria for project selection, management of funds raised, impact reporting, and the independent evaluation of financial instruments issued.

Along the same lines, the Public Investment Fund (PIF), the Kingdom's sovereign wealth fund, has developed its own Green Finance Framework. This strategic document formalizes the PIF's sustainability commitments and provides a framework for the issuance of green financial securities (green bonds, green sukuk) to finance projects aligned with national environmental objectives. The PIF specifies eligible sectors (renewable energy, clean transportation, waste management, etc.), governance mechanisms, and monitoring and evaluation procedures.

Financial regulation has also adapted. In 2025, the Capital Market Authority (CMA) issued guidelines for the issuance of green, social, and sustainable debt instruments. These guidelines are part of a broader strategy to develop the Saudi capital market, with the aim of attracting international institutional investors while promoting the green transition.

3.3. Institutional actors and governance

Several institutions play a key role in operationalizing the green finance framework:

- The Ministry of Finance coordinates public policies on sustainable financing and leads the publication of regulatory frameworks for sovereign issues.
- The Public Investment Fund (PIF) acts as a catalyst for projects of national and international scope, in areas ranging from green infrastructure to clean energy.
- The Capital Market Authority (CMA) oversees financial markets and regulates sustainable investment instruments.
- The National Debt Management Center (NDMC) is responsible for the operational implementation of the green financing framework at the sovereign level, in conjunction with investors.

These institutions are working together to ensure consistency between national sustainability objectives, international investor expectations, and global financial standards. However, this architecture remains in a consolidation phase, and inter-institutional coordination challenges persist.

3.4. Limits and prospects for development

Despite these significant advances, several limitations remain. First, the lack of a unified national green taxonomy makes it difficult to standardize the identification of "green" projects, which can hamper private sector engagement. Second, the reporting and impact monitoring framework is still under construction, limiting the transparency and comparability of initiatives. Finally, the risk of greenwashing and the gap between strategic announcements and concrete implementation pose major challenges to the system's credibility.

In the medium term, institutional capacity building, training of local experts, regional cooperation within the framework of the Gulf Cooperation Council (GCC), as well as the adoption of binding ESG standards, could contribute to consolidating the Saudi legal and institutional framework.

Saudi Arabia's legal, institutional, and political framework for green finance is evolving. It reflects a strong desire to address climate challenges while diversifying the national economy. While recent initiatives demonstrate a genuine commitment, building a comprehensive, coherent, and credible ecosystem requires ongoing efforts in governance, transparency, and technical capacity. From this perspective, green finance can become a strategic lever, provided that legal frameworks are firmly anchored in a logic of efficiency, accountability, and alignment with international best practices.

4. CURRENT DYNAMICS OF THE GREEN FINANCE MARKET IN SAUDI ARABIA

Saudi Arabia, a major player in the global hydrocarbon market, has begun a transition to a more sustainable economy, notably through the development of green finance. This emerging sector is part of Vision 2030, which aims to diversify the national economy and reduce dependence on fossil fuels.

4.1. Green bond issues and sustainable financial instruments

Since 2022, the Public Investment Fund (PIF) has issued $8.5 billion in green bonds, becoming the first sovereign wealth fund to use this type of financial instrument. By mid-2024, $5.2 billion of these funds had been allocated to environmental projects, marking a significant increase from the previous year. Furthermore, in 2025, Saudi Arabia issued $6.25 billion in sustainable bonds, representing 66% of the regional market, consolidating its leading position in sustainable financing in the Middle East and North Africa.

4.2. Regulatory framework and sustainability standards

In 2024, the Ministry of Finance introduced the Green Financing Framework, aligned with the International Capital Market Association's (ICMA) Green Bond Principles. This framework aims to direct investments towards projects with environmental benefits, while ensuring transparency and accountability. In addition, in 2025, the Capital Market Authority (CMA) published guidelines for the issuance of green, social, sustainable, and sustainability-linked debt instruments, aimed at structuring and regulating the local sustainable capital market.

4.3. Sectoral initiatives and flagship projects

The Kingdom has launched several flagship projects in the field of green finance. The NEOM project, for example, involves the construction of a futuristic city powered by renewable energy, incorporating cutting-edge technologies to minimize its ecological footprint. Furthermore, initiatives such as smart waste management in Mecca, using artificial intelligence and the Internet of Things, illustrate the country's commitment to urban sustainability.

4.4. Challenges and prospects

Despite these advances, several challenges remain. The continued dependence on oil revenues exposes the Saudi economy to fluctuations in oil prices, thus impacting financial stability. Furthermore, the effective implementation of green projects requires substantial investments and effective coordination between various public and private stakeholders. However, ongoing institutional reforms and the country's commitment to global climate goals offer encouraging prospects for the development of green finance in Saudi Arabia.

5. IMPLEMENTATION CHALLENGES AND BARRIERS TO GREEN FINANCE IN SAUDI ARABIA

Despite the significant progress made in developing green finance in Saudi Arabia, several obstacles still hinder its full potential. These challenges are institutional, economic, and regulatory, as well as those related to financial culture and market maturity.

5.1. Low maturity of the green financial market

The green finance market in Saudi Arabia is still relatively young and immature. The issuance of green financial instruments, such as green bonds, is expanding but remains limited in volume compared to more advanced markets. This immaturity results in a still insufficient supply of suitable financial products and still moderate demand from local investors, who are often unfamiliar with these innovative instruments.

5.2. Lack of a clearly defined national taxonomy

The lack of a rigorous and harmonized national green taxonomy is a major obstacle. Without a clear and shared framework defining the eligibility criteria for green projects, the distinction between truly sustainable investments and those that fall under the umbrella of "greenwashing" remains blurred. This uncertainty undermines investor confidence and slows the mobilization of private capital.

5.3. Institutional limitations and technical capacities

Institutional capacity dedicated to the management, monitoring, and evaluation of green projects is still insufficient. Public and private organizations sometimes lack the technical expertise to conduct robust environmental impact assessments, ensure transparent reporting, and meet international sustainable finance requirements. Skills development, particularly in ESG (Environment, Social, and Governance) analysis, is necessary to ensure the credibility and performance of green financial instruments.

5.4. Persistent economic dependence on hydrocarbons

The Saudi economy remains heavily dependent on oil revenues, creating a structural contradiction. On the one hand, the state invests in green projects; on the other, taxes and public revenues still depend largely on the fossil fuel sector. This dual dynamic complicates the coherent orientation of public policies towards a low-carbon economy, while exposing financial markets to risks linked to oil price volatility.

5.5. Costs and complexity of compliance

Implementing international green finance standards entails high compliance costs, particularly with regard to external audits, project certification, and the publication of regular impact reports. These requirements can represent a barrier for small and medium-sized enterprises as well as some public actors, thus limiting access to green finance.

5.6. Inter-institutional coordination and fragmented regulatory framework

The regulatory framework, although recently strengthened, remains fragmented across several government entities and regulators. Coordination between ministries, financial authorities, and development agencies is not always optimal, which can slow down decision-making and the operational implementation of green finance projects.

Green finance in Saudi Arabia faces several significant challenges that limit its development. To overcome these obstacles, it is crucial to establish a clear national taxonomy, strengthen institutional and technical capacities, ensure better coordination between stakeholders, and support the economic transition with measures to reduce dependence on hydrocarbons. Only through an integrated and coherent approach can green finance fully play its role as a lever in managing climate risks and promoting sustainable development in Saudi Arabia.

6. OPPORTUNITIES OFFERED BY GREEN FINANCE IN SAUDI ARABIA

The emergence of green finance in Saudi Arabia opens up a range of major strategic opportunities, both economically and socially, and environmentally. These opportunities are part of the country's ambitions for energy transition and sustainable development, while also meeting the growing demands of international financial markets.

6.1. Economic diversification and reduction of dependence on hydrocarbons

Green finance is a key lever for supporting the diversification of the Saudi economy. By financing projects related to renewable energy, energy efficiency, sustainable natural resource management, and clean mobility, it helps reduce excessive dependence on oil revenues. This diversification promotes a more resilient economy in the face of external shocks and fluctuations in oil prices.

6.2. Capital mobilization and attractiveness for international investors

The development of a structured and regulated green financial market can attract significant international capital flows, particularly from institutional investors keen to integrate environmental, social, and governance (ESG) criteria into their portfolios. By aligning with international standards, Saudi Arabia can strengthen its competitiveness in global financial markets and improve access to long-term financing.

6.3. Technological innovation and development of green sectors

Green finance stimulates innovation by supporting the development of clean technologies and new sustainable economic models. Sectors such as solar energy, green hydrogen, smart waste management, and ecological construction benefit from a favorable financing framework. This dynamic can lead to the creation of skilled jobs and contribute to the development of local stakeholders' skills.

6.4. Improving governance and transparency

Adopting green finance principles encourages public and private stakeholders to strengthen transparency and accountability in the management of environmental projects. Mandatory reporting and impact assessments promote better governance and greater consideration of climate and social risks in financial decision-making.

6.5. Contribution to the achievement of climate commitments

Green finance helps mobilize the resources needed to achieve Saudi Arabia's greenhouse gas emission reduction targets set by its Nationally Determined Contribution (NDC) and its announced carbon neutrality by 2060. By financing mitigation and adaptation projects, it plays a central role in managing climate risks and the transition to a low-carbon economy.

6.6. Strengthening regional and international cooperation

The development of green finance promotes cooperation with regional and international financial institutions, as well as with other Gulf Cooperation Council (GCC) countries. These partnerships facilitate the exchange of best practices, technology transfer, and joint mobilization of financing for cross-border projects with high environmental impact.

In short, green finance offers Saudi Arabia considerable opportunities to support its economic transformation, strengthen its climate resilience, and improve its integration into global financial markets. To maximize these opportunities, it is essential to continue efforts to structure the market, improve the regulatory framework, and mobilize public and private actors in a collective and coherent approach. The success of this transition will also depend on the country's ability to reconcile environmental ambition and inclusive economic development.

7. IMPACTS OF GREEN FINANCE ON CLIMATE RISK MANAGEMENT IN SAUDI ARABIA

Green finance, as an investment lever geared toward environmentally friendly projects, plays a key role in climate risk management. In Saudi Arabia, where the effects of climate change are resulting in an intensification of extreme events such as drought, desertification, and sporadic flooding, the integration of green financial mechanisms helps mitigate these vulnerabilities while promoting structural adaptation.

7.1. Strengthening climate resilience through financing sustainable infrastructure

Green finance makes it possible to mobilize financial resources for the implementation of climate-resilient infrastructure projects. For example, the development of more efficient water supply networks, the construction of eco-responsible buildings, and the improvement of natural hazard management systems benefit from targeted funding. These initiatives reduce the vulnerability of territories and populations while ensuring better preparation for future impacts.

The NEOM project, a smart city currently being built on the Red Sea, is one of the most emblematic examples of the use of green finance. With a budget of over $500 billion, NEOM is designed to run entirely on renewable energy, including solar and wind power. Green finance has raised funds through green bonds and sustainable investments to finance this low-carbon infrastructure.

By financing large-scale, resilient, low-carbon infrastructure, this project illustrates how green finance can reduce vulnerability to climate risks while creating an innovative economic model. This type of investment reduces dependence on fossil fuels and prepares the country for future challenges related to climate change.

7.2. Support for the energy transition and reduction of greenhouse gas emissions

Investing in renewable energy (solar, wind, green hydrogen) through green finance helps reduce dependence on fossil fuels, the main source of greenhouse gas emissions in Saudi Arabia. This reduction in emissions directly contributes to limiting global warming, thereby reducing the risk of extreme weather events. Therefore, green finance plays a key role in preventing long-term climate risks at the national level (Ministry of Energy of Saudi Arabia, 2025).

Since 2022, Saudi Arabia has issued more than $8.5 billion in green bonds, a significant portion of which has been allocated to renewable energy, energy efficiency, and sustainable water management projects. This financing has notably supported the establishment of 300 MW solar power plants in the Sakaka region, inaugurated in 2019.

The ability to mobilize significant green financing demonstrates growing investor confidence in Saudi Arabia's energy transition. The precise allocation of funds to specific projects reflects targeted climate risk management, promoting sustainable solutions to environmental challenges.

7.3. Management of transition risks and adaptation of economic sectors

Climate risks are not limited to physical impacts, but also encompass transition risks related to regulatory, technological, and market changes. Green finance facilitates the adaptation of businesses and economic sectors by financing cleaner technologies and sustainable practices. This transition promotes better risk management related to decarbonization, thereby reducing the financial exposure of economic actors to market fluctuations and regulatory sanctions.

Saudi Arabia has committed to reducing its greenhouse gas emissions by 278 million tons of CO_2 equivalent by 2030, a significant reduction compared to a business-as-usual scenario. Green finance plays a central role in achieving this goal, particularly through the financing of low-emission technologies and energy efficiency initiatives in the industrial and urban sectors.

This quantified commitment underscores the strategic importance of green finance as an operational lever in the fight against climate change. It highlights the role of sustainable investments in decarbonizing the economy, an essential factor in limiting the physical impacts of climate risks.

7.4. Improving transparency and financial risk management

Integrating environmental, social, and governance (ESG) criteria into investment decisions increases transparency and the consideration of climate risks in financial portfolios. This approach leads to better identification, assessment, and management of climate risks by Saudi financial institutions, helping to stabilize the financial system and prevent shocks related to climate disasters or economic transitions.

In 2025, Saudi Arabia accounted for approximately 66% of the total volume of sustainable bond issuance in the MENA (Middle East and North Africa) region, totaling nearly $6.25 billion. This momentum illustrates a diversification of financial instruments dedicated to climate risk management.

The rapid growth of Saudi Arabia's green bond market signals the financial sector's growing maturity in addressing environmental issues. This diversification provides businesses and governments with a broader range of tools to finance the ecological transition, strengthening the country's overall capacity to effectively manage climate-related risks.

7.5. Encouragement of innovation and diversification of risk management tools

Green finance encourages the development of innovative financial instruments, such as green bonds, sustainable investment funds, and climate insurance. These tools diversify the means of hedging climate change risks, offering economic actors tailored solutions to absorb environmental shocks and strengthen their adaptive capacity.

Since the adoption of the Capital Market Authority's guidelines in 2025, more than 70% of large companies listed on the Tadawul (the Saudi stock exchange) have integrated ESG criteria into their annual reports. This movement contributes to better identification and management of climate and social risks.

The widespread adoption of ESG criteria promotes greater consideration of environmental risks in investment decisions. This development improves the financial resilience of economic actors in the face of climate hazards and strengthens the credibility of the Saudi market among international investors.

In summary, green finance positively impacts climate risk management in Saudi Arabia through several complementary mechanisms: financing resilient infrastructure, supporting the energy transition, managing transition risks, improving financial transparency, and promoting innovation. This integrated approach helps strengthen the country's capacity to anticipate, mitigate, and adapt to climate challenges, while ensuring a sustainable and resilient economic trajectory.

8. CONCLUSION AND RECOMMENDATIONS

Green finance is emerging as a key strategic lever for climate risk management in Saudi Arabia. By financing sustainable infrastructure, mobilizing green capital, and integrating environmental criteria into financial decisions, it helps strengthen the country's resilience in the face of growing environmental challenges. Moreover, recent momentum in the Saudi market, particularly through the issuance of green bonds and the development of specific regulatory frameworks, demonstrates a strong commitment to placing sustainable finance at the heart of the country's economic transformation.

However, several obstacles remain, including the low maturity of the green finance market, the lack of a clearly defined national taxonomy, and institutional and technical limitations. These challenges hamper the scale and effectiveness of ongoing initiatives and highlight the need for an integrated and coordinated approach.

Recommendations for this study are as follows:

- Establish a clear and harmonized national green taxonomy: In order to strengthen the credibility of green financial instruments and avoid greenwashing, it is imperative to develop a national classification of activities eligible for green financing, aligned with international standards while taking into account local economic and environmental specificities.
- Strengthening institutional and technical capacities: Developing skills in environmental assessment, ESG reporting, and climate risk management within public and private institutions is crucial. Training programs and the recruitment of specialized experts must be encouraged to effectively support market growth.
- Improving coordination between public and private actors: The establishment of a multi-sectoral governance mechanism promoting cooperation between ministries, regulators, financial institutions and businesses would make it possible to optimize the planning, implementation and monitoring of initiatives related to green finance.
- Encouraging financial innovation and diversification of instruments: Supporting the development of innovative financial tools, such as thematic investment funds, climate insurance or crowdfunding mechanisms, will help expand access to green financing, particularly for SMEs and local projects.
- Promoting investor awareness and education: Targeted information campaigns and educational initiatives are needed to increase institutional and retail investors' understanding and adherence to the principles of green finance, thereby strengthening market demand and liquidity.
- Integrate green finance into the national sustainable development strategy: Green finance must be fully integrated into national plans, such as Vision 2030 and the Saudi Green Initiative, to ensure coherence between environmental, economic and social objectives, and to guarantee a lasting impact.

In conclusion, green finance offers Saudi Arabia a unique opportunity to combine economic growth with environmental protection. The success of this ambition, however, will depend on the country's ability to structure its green financial market, strengthen its institutions, and mobilize all stakeholders in a concerted approach. Thus, green finance could become a central pillar of climate risk management and a driver of the transition to a more sustainable and resilient economy.

FUNDING

This work was supported by the Deanship of Scientific Research, Vice Presidency for Graduate Studies and Scientific Research, King Faisal University, Saudi Arabia [Grant No. KFU254189].

COMPETING INTERESTS

The author declares no competing financial or non-financial interests that are directly or indirectly related to the work submitted for publication.

ACKNOWLEDGEMENTS

This work was supported by the Deanship of Scientific Research, Vice Presidency for Graduate Studies and Scientific Research, King Faisal University, Saudi Arabia [Grant No. KFU254189].

REFERENCES

Adeyemi, F. A., Jempeji, A. A., Olaniran, A. O., Taliat, M. K., & Adeleke, A. T. (2025). Climate risks and financial stability: A global evidence. *Finance Research Open*, *1*(3), 100032. DOI: 10.1016/j.finr.2025.100032

Al-Harbi, A. (2025). Green financing for sustainable development in Saudi Arabia. *Journal of Environmental Management and Tourism*, *16*(2), 95–105. DOI: 10.14505/jemt.v16.2(78).01

Angorani, S. (2024). Green finance and sustainable development: A cross-sectional study of financial mechanisms driving environmental responsibility. *Indonesian Journal of Economics, Business, Accounting, and Management*, 2(4), 77–91. DOI: 10.63901/ijebam.v2i4.70

Bouzidi, F. M., Nefzi, A. A., & Al Yousif, M. (2024). Impact of international oil price shocks and inflation on bank efficiency and financial stability: Evidence from Saudi Arabian banking sector. *Journal of Risk and Financial Management*, *17*(12), 543. DOI: 10.3390/jrfm17120543

Guesmi, K., Makrychoriti, P., & Pyrgiotakis, E. G. (2025). Climate change exposure and green bonds issuance. *Journal of International Money and Finance*, *152*, 103281. DOI: 10.1016/j.jimonfin.2025.103281

Hussain, M. A., Alsayegh, M. F., & Boshnak, H. A. (2025). The role of ESG disclosure in enhancing profitability and market value: Insights from Saudi Arabia's corporate landscape. *The Economics and Finance Letters*, *12*(2), 158–182. DOI: 10.18488/29.v12i2.4171

IMF (International Monetary Fund). (2024). Global Financial Stability Report: Steadying the Course: Uncertainty, Artificial Intelligence, and Financial Stability. Washington. https://www.imf.org/-/media/files/publications/gfsr/2024/october/english/textrevised.pdf

Iqbal, J., Shahbaz, M., & Ozturk, I. (2025). The role of institutional quality in the nexus between green financing and sustainable development. Research in International Business and Finance, 73(Part A), 102531. https://doi.org/DOI: 10.1016/j.ribaf.2024.102531

KPMGFAB. (2025). The sustainable finance imperative: Driving multi-dimensional impact in the real economy, KPMG & First Abu Dhabi Bank Report, Publication No. 5336. https://assets.kpmg.com/content/dam/kpmg/ae/pdf-2025/the-sustainable-finance-imperative.pdf

Li, W., & Wu, D. (2025). Sustainability through business model innovation and climate finance in developing countries. *Humanities & Social Sciences Communications*, *12*(1), 66. DOI: 10.1057/s41599-024-04297-3

Madouri, H. (2025). Green finance and renewable energy investments: A comparative analysis of successes, challenges, and policy implications across regions. *Central European Review of Economics and Management*, *9*(2), 7–35. DOI: 10.29015/cerem.1022

Ministry of Energy of Saudi Arabia. (2025). Saudi Green Initiative: Progress report and future outlook. Government of Saudi Arabia. https://www.sgi.gov.sa/about-sgi/sgi-targets/reduce-carbon-emissions/?csrt=18277796921209943572

OECD (Organization for Economic Cooperation and Development). (2024). Leveraging De-Risking Instruments and International Co-ordination to Catalyse Investment in Clean Hydrogen (OCDE/World Bank), 2024. https://doi.org/DOI: 10.1787/9a377303-en

Vision 2030 Kingdom of Saudi Arabia. (2022). Vision 2030: Economic diversification and sustainability strategy. Government Publication. https://www.vision2030.gov.sa/media/rc0b5oy1/saudi_vision203.pdf

Chapter 3
Reimagining Emotional Ergonomics through the Integration of Human Emotion and Artificial Intelligence for Sustainable Healthcare Wellbeing

Krishnaveni Subramani
https://orcid.org/0009-0000-9785-4595
SR University, India

Geetha Manoharan
https://orcid.org/0000-0002-8644-8871
SR University, India

ABSTRACT

Combining emotional ergonomics and AI was a disruptive solution to improving the sustainability of healthcare by focusing on patient wellbeing and staff performance. Clinical decision-making, patient adherence, and professional performance are highly dependent on emotional states, which are usually not considered with the traditional healthcare system. AI-based affective computing can provide real-time identification and analysis of physiological, behavioral, and situational emotional cues to support adaptive interventions that can streamline the clinical processes and interactions between patients and staff. In this chapter, the theoretical background,

DOI: 10.4018/979-8-3373-8197-8.ch003

methodological principles, and practical use of AI-driven emotional ergonomics are reviewed, and pilot implementations and case studies are discussed, which show that patient satisfaction, reduction of errors, and resilience in the workplace have been improved. Ethical aspects such as privacy of data, fairness in algorithms, and trust are considered to promote responsible use of emotion-sensitive technologies.

INTRODUCTION

Healthcare systems are becoming more complicated environments with large patient flows, a wide range of medical conditions, and dynamic technology infrastructures (Cinar & Bilodeau, 2024). The quality, safety, and efficiency of care delivery are strongly determined in such settings by the emotional well-being of both patients and healthcare professionals (Dey, 2024). The accuracy of decision-making, the adherence to treatment, the engagement of a patient, or the staff performance are influenced by the emotional states, and stress, anxiety, or fatigue usually lead to negative outcomes (George, 2024). The main focus of traditional ergonomics has been on physical relationships and efficiency of the working process, but the emotional aspect was not studied thoroughly (Azour et al., 2024). Emotional ergonomics comes in to fill this gap by looking at the interaction between the emotional factors with task requirements, environmental conditions, and technological systems (Kolomaznik et al., 2024). The process of creating healthcare settings that support the emotional reaction of humans can alleviate stress, improve the performance of healthcare personnel, and build resilience in both staff and patients (Kaklauskas et al., 2022). By acknowledging emotion as a fundamental part of healthcare provision, one can have a ground to introduce technological solutions that can help improve emotional control and management in a clinical environment (Bibri & Jagatheesaperumal, 2023).

With the development of artificial intelligence (AI), new opportunities to implement operational emotional ergonomics in healthcare emerge (Kumar et al., 2023). The systems with affective computing can respond to emotional cues of a human in real time and identify them (Bekbolatova et al., 2024). Such systems are based on machine learning algorithms, natural language processing, and computer vision to process multi-mode data, such as physiological measurements, facial expressions, vocal intonations, and behavioral cues (Farahat et al., 2023). Transforming emotional data into actionable information, AI will make possible adaptive interventions to enhance interactions between patients and staff, optimize resource distributions, and enable personalized care (Stone et al., 2022). Not only do such technologies lead to a higher patient satisfaction level and better clinical outcomes but also facilitate workforce well-being by detecting and eliminating the sources of occupational stress

(Yu and Li, 2022). Incorporation of AI and emotional ergonomics was a transition fromreactive strategies towards a dynamic and proactive control of the emotional conditions in the healthcare systems (Priya et al., 2024).

The possible advantages of AI-based emotional ergonomics will also apply to the sustainability of operations and the organizations (Brown et al., 2024). Emotional stress among healthcare workers was one of the factors that lead to burnout, absenteeism, and turnover, causing a huge economic and operational burden on healthcare facilities (Mithas et al., 2022). Anxiety or frustration has also been found to result in poor adherence to treatment plans, extended recovery time, and lack of trust in medical services (Mahmud et al., 2022). The emotionally sensitive systems that are powered by AI offer round-the-clock monitoring, prompting stressor alerts and tailored interventions to overcome these obstacles (Bharadiya et al., 2023). Healthcare institutions can increase process efficiency, minimize human error, and promote positive patient experiences by developing emotionally responsive environments (Colorado–Aurora et al., 2024). Emotional ergonomics AI implementation was only one of the many goals of sustainable healthcare, where the human-centered design, technology, and organizational resilience will meet long-term wellbeing (Kamboj & A, 2024).

Implementations of AI-enhanced emotional ergonomics have important ethical, regulatory, and cultural considerations (Enholm et al., 2022). The sensitive emotional data must be processed according to strict guidelines to preserve the privacy, informed consent, and privacy (Ben Ahmed, 2024). A trustworthy and effective response by the system compromised by algorithmic bias and unfair responses of systems, which highlights the necessity of transparent and explainable models of AI (Jang and Landuyt, 2023). The presence of cultural and contextual variations in emotional manifestations also makes the implementation of AI more complicated in various medical settings (Saini and Montebello, 2024). Multi-stakeholder engagement, strict validation, and compliance with ethical standards to balance human values with technological development are some of the strategies used to address these issues (Jain and Alam, 2022). The incorporation of these protection measures was essential to assure the presence of AI interventions that will facilitate the provision of equitable, responsible, and ethical care (Van Velsen et al., 2022).

The intersection of emotional ergonomics and artificial intelligence was a vital boundary in improving the quality of health care, patient satisfaction, and employee well-being (Cinar and Bilodeau, 2024). Pilot tests and new uses reflect the ability of AI-driven emotional surveillance and adaptive interventions to make healthcare settings responsive and emotion-aware (Kolomaznik et al., 2024). The AI-based emotional ergonomics will improve the sustainability of healthcare systems by dynamically addressing the emotional requirements of patients and professionals by combining theoretical models, methodological rigor, and technological innovation

(Bibri and Jagatheesaperumal, 2023). The chapter has the purpose of examining these dimensions, providing evidence, practice, and future perspectives of instilling emotional intelligence into healthcare using the advanced AI technologies (Stone et al., 2022).

INTRODUCTION AND CONCEPTUAL FRAMEWORK

Defining Emotional Ergonomics in Healthcare Contexts

Emotional ergonomics was an advanced side of human factors engineering that goes beyond the traditional fact of physical comfort and task effectiveness. The emphasis placed on health care settings was not only on maximizing the physiological relationships but also the emotional condition of the patients and health care practitioners. Emotional ergonomics was the way that feelings, moods, and affective reactions affect cognitive functioning, interpersonal communication, and general execution of the tasks. The inclusion of these principles in healthcare systems aims at establishing the environment in which emotional well-being was not an incidental phenomenon but a part of the organizational design and patient care policy.

The healthcare industry was a high-pressure environment that was typified by a large workload, high-stress decisions, and high rates of emotional stressors. The effects of such stressors on clinical outcomes, staff satisfaction, and patient experiences are the areas of emotional ergonomics. It offers a set of guidelines to create interventions decreasing cognitive overload, coping with stress responses, and enhancing positive emotional states. The affective conditions of patients and professionals interrelate in the clinical area, with influences on empathy, concentration of attention, and mistakes. By understanding these interactions, it was possible to develop specific strategies, which can increase the level of engagement, communication, and resilience among the healthcare stakeholders.

Figure 1. Defining emotional ergonomics in healthcare contexts

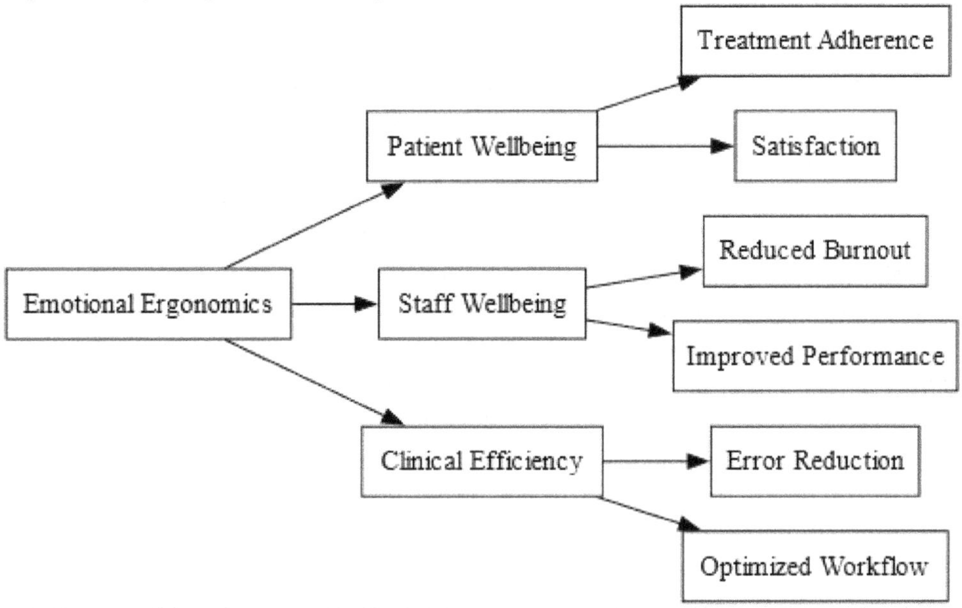

The implementation of emotional ergonomics in health care needs to be carefully evaluated in accordance with the measurement of emotional signs and their connection to the results of performance. The environmental conditions, the patterns of behavior, and physiological indicators are the primary parameters that help to learn about the emotional response to the complex healthcare processes. Emotional ergonomics was also concerned with the alignment of the organizational policies, workspace design, and technology implementation to the human affective requirements. With the recognition of the vital role of emotion in operational performance and patient care, healthcare systems will be able to create environments that allow staff and patients to enjoy sustainable well-being.

The Role of Human Emotion in Healthcare Performance and Wellbeing

Human feeling was an extremely critical factor when defining healthcare performance and well-being. The emotional conditions affect attention, decision-making, and cognitive processing, which are essential in the proper and timely performance of clinical duties. Stress or anxiety at a high level hamper memory, remembering, and problem-solving skills, leading to lower efficiency and a higher risk of mistakes in dealing with a patient. On the other hand, positive affective experiences increase focus, resilience, and interpersonal relationships and facilitate both personal performance and group cohesion in stressful healthcare settings. Emotional well-being was also associated with better communication with patients, and empathetic and emotionally attentive professionals show better patient satisfaction, adherence to treatment regimens, and trust in clinical relationships.

The influence of emotional conditions was not only on the individual performance but also on the entire organization. Critical patient situations, ethical dilemmas, and workload pressures are some of the emotionally demanding situations that healthcare professionals regularly face. The continuity of exposure to these stressors in the absence of sufficient emotional support leads to burnout, fatigue, and decreased job satisfaction, which undermine the sustainability of the healthcare delivery. The emotional states of patients combine dynamically with the well-being of the staff because an elevated level of anxiety, fear, or frustration contribute to making the provision of care more complicated and affecting the workflow efficiency and clinical outcome. Emotional awareness in the healthcare design and operation strategies was thus necessary in maximizing the human performance as well as system resilience.

The scientific knowledge and control of human emotion in healthcare used to inform health performance and well-being interventions. Strategic measurements of emotional workload, real-time measurements of stress indicators, and the establishment of emotionally supportive settings can offer avenues of alleviating the adverse emotional effects. Emotional ergonomics provides a model for the way the structure of the workplace, the assignment of duties, and the support of technologies should be aligned with the emotional reactions of human beings. The application of the knowledge based on the science of emotions to inform healthcare practice creates a premise of ongoing performance, better patient outcomes, and organizational well-being.

Historical Evolution: From Physical Ergonomics to Emotional Ergonomics

Ergonomics developed at the beginning of the 20th century and was a subject that was predominantly aimed at maximizing the physical interface between man and his work environment. Early initiatives were focused on enhancing the safety at the workplace and minimizing musculoskeletal stress and productivity of equipment, machines, and workstations. The first environment where these studies could be performed was in the industrial setting, where manual labor and repetitive tasks were performed and complicated machinery required systematic ways of reducing fatigue and injury. Integration of human factors into equipment design and organization of workflow was turned into a basic principle, which predetermined the further evolution of occupational health and efficiency. As time passed by, ergonomics developed to include cognitive factors, including mental load, attention, and decision-making in complex working environments, including aviation, manufacturing, and health care.

The shift of the physical and cognitive ergonomics to the emotional one was the natural move in the process of comprehending the human interaction with technology and workplace conditions. The difference between emotional ergonomics and physical comfort, as well as cognitive efficiency, was that the former also considers the importance of emotions in the process of performance, satisfaction, and well-being. Such emotional states as stress, anxiety, and frustration have quantifiable influence on the execution of tasks, error rates, and interpersonal relationships. Awareness of such effects has resulted in the establishment of measures that put into consideration human affective responses with an aim of developing systems and environments that not only prevent fatigue and error but also enhance resilience, engagement, and well-being in general. This trend can be traced back to a growing realization of the sophisticated interaction between physiological, thinking, and feeling aspects in human-centered design.

Figure 2. Historical evolution

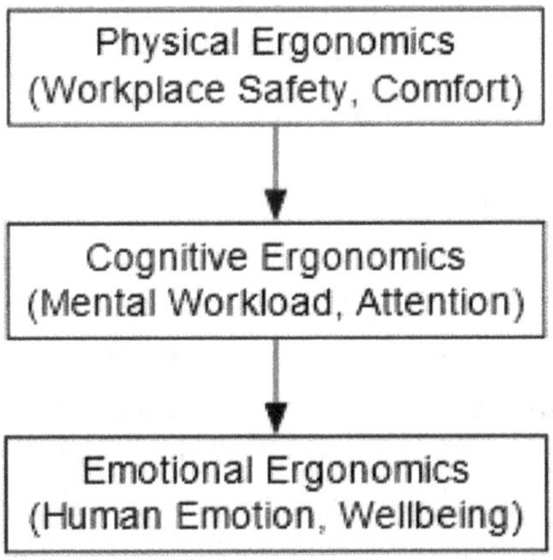

The healthcare setting was one of the most suitable areas in which emotional ergonomics can be applied because the environment was highly stressful in nature and human performance was necessary. Clinic decisions, interaction with the patients, and the organizational processes are all applied under the conditions that trigger severe emotions, which affect the effectiveness of staff members and patient outcomes. Emotional considerations in the design of the healthcare systems permit the development of adaptive supportive environments that react dynamically to the human needs.

Conceptual Models Linking Emotion, Cognition, and Work Efficiency

The emotional conditions significantly affect cognitive functioning and the effectiveness of work overall and high-stakes healthcare settings specifically. These are the effects of emotions on attention, memory, decision-making, and problem-solving, whose direct influence was the quality of patient care and the efficacy of healthcare teams. The cognitive load theory holds that the mental capabilities that can be used to perform a task are scarce and that the effects of emotional stress on the available capabilities leave the task performer with less efficiency and a high probability of error. An avenue to enhance cognitive performance was the incorporation of emotional understanding in the design of the work, which brings the tasks, the environment, and technological help in line with the natural emotional and cognitive rhythm of human beings. The conceptual models in this area are concerned with the processing of the two-way relationship between affective states and cognitive functioning, in which positive emotional processes have the potential to improve attention, strength, and cooperative problem solving in clinical practice.

Efficiency at work in healthcare goes hand in hand with the ability to control emotional reactions during the processing of complex information. Other models, like the affective/cognitive control framework, are based on the assumption that cognitive performance was regulated by the regulation of the attention to the task as well as the emotional states. Practically, clinicians capable of remaining emotionally stable even in stressful situations have been found to make better decisions when under pressure and have the ability to respond quickly and make correct clinical judgments. Application of these theoretical concepts in system design, workflow management, and technology deployment makes it possible to create environments that minimize cognitive overload and facilitate adaptive emotional regulation. Artificial intelligence, coupled with real-time tracking of emotional cues, has the potential to make these models operational by offering time-sensitive interventions that ensure optimal cognitive and emotional fit, which in the long term will allow sustainable performance in healthcare.

Theoretical Foundations For Ai-Enhanced Emotional Interventions

Emotional ergonomics was an extension of traditional ergonomics with an emphasis put on optimization of human emotional experiences in complex work environments. Emotions in a healthcare setting have a significant impact on cognitive ability, decision-making skills, and human relations. Anxious, stressed, or fearful patients are characterized by diminished treatment adherence and satisfaction, whereas health care providers working under long-term emotional pressure exhibit poor attention, higher rates of errors, and high burnout rates. Knowing how emotional states interplay with environmental and technological differences would create the basis of the design of systems that could facilitate the well-being of patients as well as support the efficiency of the professionals. The combination of these findings into the healthcare processes cannot be done without a systematic theoretical framework that explains human affective responses, environmental stimuli, and task requirements.

Figure 3. Theoretical foundations for AI-enhanced emotional interventions

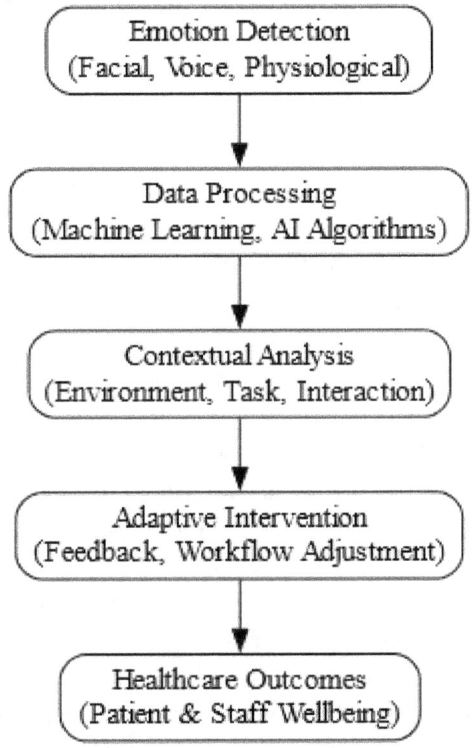

Artificial intelligence can support operationalization of emotional ergonomics through the translation of the dynamic human emotional data into operational informational insights. The detection and classification of emotions through multi-modal sources (physiological signals, facial expression, and vocal patterns) are possible using machine learning algorithms, natural language processing, and computer vision. The explanation of the theoretical foundation of AI-enhanced interventions was the integration of affective computing principles and human emotional processing models that enable the predictive and adaptive responses in the clinical working process. Emotional monitoring in real-time as a part of healthcare systems can enable dynamic adaptability to the environment, communication plans, and task distribution and help to ensure sustainable well-being of patients and staff members alike. These premises make AI not seem as an alternative to human judgment but as a more auxiliary system that can be used to add emotional dimension to the healthcare provision.

AI-enabled emotional intervention frameworks combine psychology, human factors engineering, and systems design concepts to form adaptive emotion-sensitive healthcare settings. Emotions are not only seen as quantifiable variables that interact with context and behavioral variables to determine the results, but AI algorithms also detect patterns and provide personalized interventions based on an individual's need. This practice will help in proactively dealing with stress, fatigue, and anxiety to stay resilient and to work efficiently.

HUMAN EMOTION AND HEALTHCARE WELLBEING

Emotional Determinants of Patient Satisfaction and Engagement

Emotional experiences in the course of healthcare have a powerful effect on patient satisfaction and engagement. Anxiety, fear, and uncertainty in the diagnosis and treatment process are emotions that decrease patient trust, compliance with medical guidance, and the overall attitude towards the quality of care. The positive emotional experiences like empathy, reassurance, and participation in decision-making lead to improved patient cooperation, retention, and reported satisfaction. Emotions are directly connected with the mental processes, which influence memory, attention, and judgment, influencing the way patients perceive medical information and engage with the health personnel. The knowledge of these determinants can be used to develop interventions that lead to positive emotional experiences and maximize the outcomes of patients.

Emotional involvement surpasses short-term response and includes long-term responses between healthcare settings, personnel, and systems. Noise, lighting, privacy, and accessibility are environmental factors that cause stress or comfort that will affect mood and responsiveness in the patients. Interpersonal relationships, such as the style of communication, empathy, and emotional support given by medical practitioners, influence perceptions of care and the willingness to be actively involved in the treatment regimen. Emotional engagement was an essential mediator of healthcare delivery processes and clinical outcomes, and a high level of engagement was associated with a higher adherence rate, fewer complications, and an increase in the level of satisfaction. Identification of the emotional and engagement interaction can support the creation of patient-centered approaches that cover the psychological and physiological aspects of care.

Emotional concerns built into healthcare design and operational planning lead to sustainable wellbeing because patient experiences are in line with organizational objectives. The empirical evaluation of emotional reactions enables the observation of the most stressful moments in the patient experience and makes informed direct actions. Emotional cues can be tracked and analyzed with the use of AI assistance in order to offer practical advice to boost satisfaction and engagement. Creating structures with these emotional determinants helps in resilience, trust, and effectiveness of healthcare delivery in the long run and the resultant creation of environments where both service needs and system efficiency are met simultaneously.

Psychological Stress and Burnout Among Healthcare Professionals

The healthcare professionals work in their industries that are characterized by high cognitive requirements, unpredictability of the workload, and constant exposure to critical or life-threatening circumstances. Chronic exposure to these stressors causes physiological and psychological stress, and this adversely impacts concentration, decision-making, and performance in general. The cognitive load was increased by emotional labor, which was the result of the necessity to control personal emotions and offer empathic care, which results in chronic exhaustion and emotional burnout. Empirical research indicates that long-term work stress was a contributing factor to high rates of burnout, low job satisfaction, and high turnover, which weakens the stability and quality of the workforce in terms of job performance.

Figure 4. Psychological stress and burnout among healthcare professionals

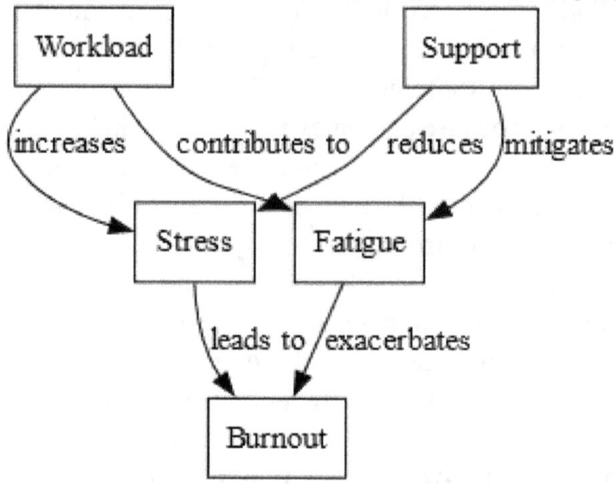

Burnout was a complex combination of emotions—exhaustion, depersonalization, and low personal achievement—that have a harmful effect on professional efficacy and personal well-being. Emotional exhaustion lowers the ability to interact with patients and colleagues, and depersonalization promotes indifference and lack of empathy. Reduction of personal perceived accomplishment undermines confidence in clinical competence, which forms a feedback loop that further increases the level of stress. The overall effect of these influences was not only a violation of personal health but also influences the organizational performance, such as an increase in error rates, decreased patient satisfaction, and operational efficiency. The knowledge of the stress and burnout mechanisms can help in developing interventions that can improve emotional resilience, maximize performance, and maintain the long-term wellbeing of healthcare professionals.

Cognitive Load, Decision-Making, and Emotional States in Clinical Settings

The cognitive load within a healthcare setting has a great impact on decision-making and the outcome of clinical practices. The multidisciplinary team coordination, speed in solving problems, and processing of complex information about patients are concomitant in high-intensity clinical environments. Emotions such as stress, anxiety, and fatigue have been found to compound with cognitive load to change the distribution of attention, the recall of memory, and accuracy in judgment. High levels of emotional arousal cause narrowing of focus or attentional tunneling, which makes one vulnerable to making mistakes in diagnosis, treatment planning, and procedure execution. Cognitive overload patterns alongside an increase in emotional strain are linked to poor patient safety, inefficient operations, and occupational stress among healthcare workers.

The interaction of human affective reactions and environment demands was evident in the decision-making in different emotional and cognitive situations. Emotion was a factor in the risk perception, prioritization of tasks, and understanding of clinical information, both in the short-term interventions and long-term care. It has been hinted that the environments that measure and react to the emotional state of healthcare providers can enhance cognitive performance and decrease the spread of errors. Affective awareness enables the implementation of the changes in allocation of tasks, information presentation, distribution of work, and promotion of adaptive decision-making by integrating affective awareness with clinical workflow management. These lessons enable a critical basis in the application of systems that would satisfy human emotional and cognitive abilities with organizational goals and long-term outcomes of patient care.

Socio-Emotional Factors Influencing Organizational Sustainability in Healthcare

Healthcare organizations are working under conditions marked by high emotional intensity, complicated social relationships, and high mental demands. The emotional relationship between personnel will impact the teamwork, interaction, and decision-making that will directly impact the quality and efficiency of care received by patients. Emotional fatigue, stress, and interpersonal conflict can interfere with workflow, decrease resilience, and undermine adherence to clinical protocols. Emotional responses of the patients, such as anxiety, fear, and frustration, further determine the outcomes of the organization, as influence the adherence to treatment, satisfaction, and utilization of healthcare services. The knowledge of these socio-emotional factors was important in insights into processes that lead to individual performance and overall organizational sustainability.

Employee health becomes one of the key factors of sustainable health care performance. The support structures, team building, and positive organizational culture have been observed to reduce burnout, job satisfaction, and retention of professionals in the healthcare field. Proper communication lines, emotional work acknowledgement, and stress reduction prospects would reinforce employees and increase their abilities in handling stressful and intense clinical situations. Emphasizing emotional needs, like support and sensitiveness in interaction with patients, and ensuring their environment was conducive to healing, patient-centered approaches strengthen organizational credibility and sustainability. Incorporation of socio-emotional factors into operational planning, resource allocation, and policy formulation can guarantee that healthcare organizations remain efficient and at the same time foster human-oriented care.

Figure 5. Socio-emotional factors influencing organizational sustainability in healthcare

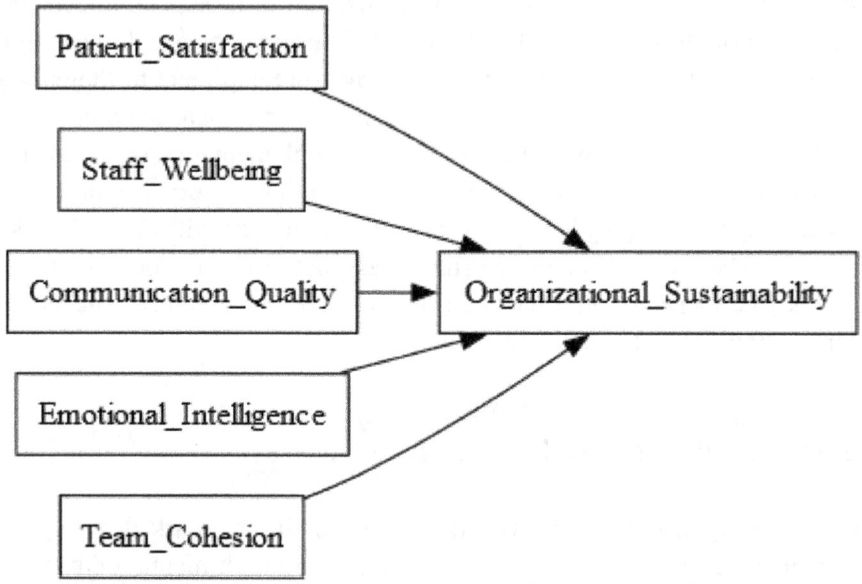

The interaction between organizational processes and emotional states creates a pattern of how to design an intervention towards sustainability. Surveys, behavioral observation, and digital monitoring of the emotional indicators give data to support strategic decision-making and ease of workflow. By integrating socio-emotional intelligence into the leadership behaviors, employee development, and technological interventions, one can be able to respond flexibly to the changing emotional needs. Healthcare systems that are systematic in the consideration of these factors exhibit better resilience, operational stability, and ability to continue improvement, which in turn uphold the twofold objective of delivering high-quality care to patients and the sustainability of the organization.

Patient-Staff Emotional Interactions: Impacts on Care Outcomes

Patient-healthcare provider emotional relations are of paramount importance in the determination of clinical outcomes and the quality of care in general. Patients undergoing supportive and empathetic treatments demonstrate increased trust, rate of compliance with treatment regimens, and satisfaction with care provision. When the healthcare personnel was emotionally attuned, it can reduce anxiety and perceived pain and increase cooperative behavior in patients when undergoing diagnostic and therapeutic processes. Conversely, patients tend to be less engaged and have a longer recovery time and receive a worse perception of healthcare services in the face of strained or emotionally distant interactions. Emotional climate in a clinical encounter was a predictor and determinant of physiological, psychological, and behavioral outcomes among patients.

The capacity of healthcare professionals to regulate their own emotional reactions as well as effectively react to the affective states of patients has a direct impact on the efficiency of care and safety. Emotional labor can be described as the control of one's own emotions to meet the professional demands, and this has been linked to both beneficial and adverse effects of employee performance. Emotional regulation helps patients by ensuring effective communication, making accurate decisions, and solving problems collectively. The emotional strain decrease attentional focus when excessive, make one prone to failure, and facilitate occupational burnout. The dynamics of these processes allow seeing how patient and staff well-being are interdependent and how critical it was to provide healthcare settings that facilitate emotional resiliency, mutual understanding, and responsiveness to the shifting affective conditions.

ARTIFICIAL INTELLIGENCE IN EMOTIONAL ERGONOMICS

Affective Computing and Emotion Recognition Technologies

Affective computing was a multidisciplinary intersection with computer science, psychology, and human factors engineering, with a goal of providing computers with the ability to recognize, understand, and react to human emotion. Emotion recognition systems can be based on the idea of using physiological, behavioral, and contextual information to deduce the affective state, which can be used as a starting point for emotion-aware and adaptive systems. The non-invasive approaches to measuring the level of emotional response in real time include facial expression analysis, voice modulation detection, and body gesture monitoring. These modalities can be integrated to make emotion recognition more accurate and reliable and allow healthcare systems to detect stress, anxiety, or discomfort in patients and staff with high time resolution.

Figure 6. Affective computing and emotion recognition technologies

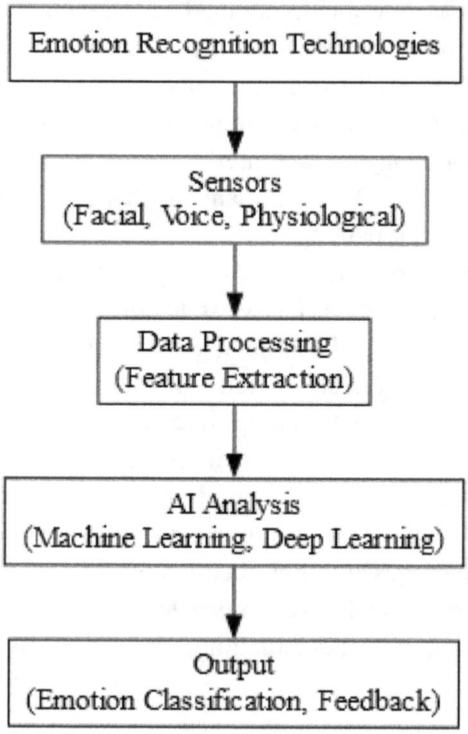

The use of physiological indicators such as heart rate variability, galvanic skin response, and electroencephalography can provide a complementary understanding of internal emotional conditions that cannot always be measured using behavioral indicators. Sensor fusion methods are able to integrate these physiologic signals with facial, vocal, and contextual information to produce a multi-dimensional emotional profile to enhance system responsiveness and prediction. These complex datasets are analyzed using machine learning algorithms to identify patterns and correlations so that can be continuously monitored and interventions taken in time within clinical settings. Affective computing has found its uses in healthcare through early detection of emotional distress, responsive patient engagement, and optimization of workloads for the medical staff, which promotes safety and well-being.

Emotion recognition technologies used in the healthcare industry should be cautiously implemented in terms of accuracy, scalability, and ethics. The adaptable system design can be based on data-driven insights, yet it requires alignment with the clinical goals, organizational culture, and patient-centered care principles to be integrated into the real-world workflows. Making these technologies constantly valid and refined improves the efficiency of these technologies and makes sure that AI systems do not substitute human judgment.

Machine Learning Approaches for Multi-Modal Emotion Detection

Machine learning offers a powerful model of recognizing and understanding the emotions of humans using the combination of multi-modal information sources. There are physiological indicators of emotional states, such as heart rate variability, electrodermal activity, and electroencephalography patterns, and behavioral ones, such as facial expression, speech prosody, and body posture. Multi-modal emotion detection uses the synergistic strengths of these streams of data to enhance accuracy, oversensitivity, and the individual variability of expression of emotions. Support vector machines, random forests, and neural networks are all examples of supervised learning algorithms that are used to classify emotional states using training datasets that have been labeled, then enabling systems to determine discrete emotional states like stress, anxiety, or engagement.

Deep learning systems, convolutional and recurrent neural networks, allow identifying multidimensional patterns in both time and space in multi-modal data. Time-varying behaviors in physiological responses along with space attributes in facial or gesture responses give way to dynamic modeling of emotional patterns as opposed to snapshot portraits. Early fusion, late fusion, and hybrid methods employ the use of feature fusion to combine information in heterogeneous modalities together in order to increase the predictive accuracy and ability to resist noise or missing data. Such methods make it easier to create real-time, adaptive systems that are able to track emotional states in real time in high-stakes healthcare settings.

The application of multi-modal machine learning models to the healthcare environment can help AI systems react on an emotional level to the state of patient and staff. Predictive emotion recognition facilitates interventions to decrease stress, enhance involvement, and maximize task distribution in the clinical processes. The systematic assessment of the model performance in the form of metrics (precision, recall, and F1 score) establishes the reliability and was used to guide further improvements.

Real-Time AI Monitoring of Patient and Staff Emotional States

Artificial intelligence-based emotional state and real-time monitoring are a new form of understanding and controlling practice and human affect in healthcare settings. Multi-modal sensors on AI systems record the physiological data of heart rate variability, galvanic skin response, and electroencephalography, as well as the behavioral data of facial expression, tone of voice, and posture. Machine learning algorithms are used to detect emotional states in real-time and objectively as these streams of data are being processed. Real-time monitoring can also be integrated, and therefore, stress, anxiety, fatigue, or distress can be identified instantly, and subsequently, timely interventions can be made to help improve patient health and staff performance. Ongoing evaluation of emotions will increase situational awareness in a clinical environment, enabling the prevention of interactions that affect the outcomes of care.

Figure 7. Real-time AI monitoring of patient and staff emotional states

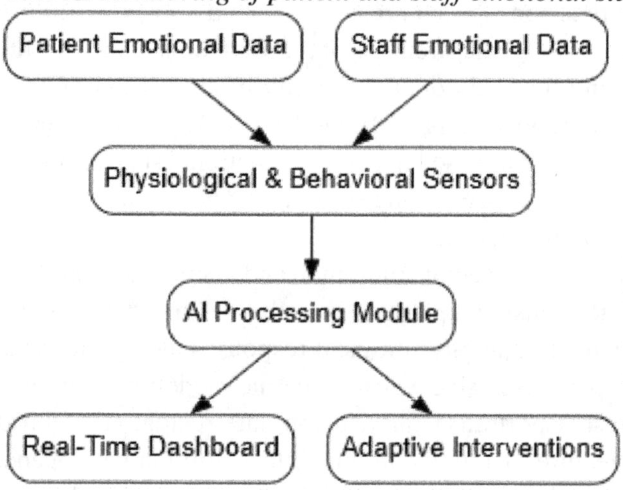

Emotional monitoring with the help of AI was not only applicable to the individual level of detection but also to the system-wide analysis of patterns within a healthcare system. Aggregated emotional information will give the information about the high stress levels, the distribution of workload, and other environmental factors contributing to emotional states. Healthcare systems can use predictive modeling on the basis of these patterns to predict high-risk scenarios, e.g., a time when patients are particularly anxious or staff was overworked, and act proactively, e.g., by dynamically staffing, redistributing tasks, or providing specific psychological assistance. The ability of AI to read complicated emotional cues in real time turns the traditional reactive models of care into the proactive models supporting resilience, operational efficiency, and overall patient care quality.

Real-time emotional monitoring needs to be integrated into the healthcare practices, but this should be aligned with ethical standards and data security measures and user acceptance issues. Effective and cultural interpretation of emotional cues will guarantee useful and fair interventions in patient and staff populations of various groups. The credibility of these technologies can be enhanced by systematic appraisal of AI performance both in terms of evaluation based on clinical outcome measures and staff feedback.

Predictive Models for Emotional Wellbeing in Healthcare Systems

Emotional wellbeing predictive models use artificial intelligence to interpret complex data: physiological data, behavioral data, and contextual data provided in healthcare settings. These models locate the trends in the emotional reaction of patients and the personnel, which allows them to implement anticipated interventions that improve the care quality and efficiency of operations. Predictive algorithms can alert of imminent states of stress, anxiety, fatigue, or other emotionally expressive conditions that adversely affect clinical outcomes by transforming raw data on emotional information into practical insights. Being able to predict emotional patterns can enable healthcare systems to take specific action, including workload rebalancing, environmental changes, or individualized patient contact strategies, to ensure the balance in the emotional state of stakeholders was the best possible.

Multi-modal data integration improves the reliability and accurateness of the predictive models since the emotional condition was displayed in a variety of physiological, behavioral, and contextual pathways. Machine learning methods, such as supervised and unsupervised methods, provide the ability to extract meaningful features in complex data and provide an analysis in real-time and adaptation. Resource allocation and workflow optimization are also enabled through predictive modeling to anticipate times of high emotional demand so as to manage the staff assignments, patient interaction, and clinical processes in advance. Integrating these models into healthcare information systems forms a feedback loop, where the emotional data will be used to guide operational decisions and interventions; this will support the long-term well-being of the patients and professionals.

Predictive emotional model implementation must be synchronized with the organizational goals, clinical guidelines, and ethical principles. Individual privacy, predictive transparency, and explainability of algorithm decisions are needed to adopt AI systems and have confidence in the health care industry. The predictive models are continuously validated and refined to ensure that responsive to the changing dynamics of emotions, cultural variations, and clinical complexities.

Human-AI Interaction and Trust in Emotion-Aware Technologies

The interaction between the human and the AI in the emotional-aware technology was one of the key considerations of whether AI-based emotional ergonomics in healthcare will be effective and adopted. The systems that detect, interpret, and react to the emotional state of a human being should have transparent mechanisms to ensure the confidence of the user. The confidence in these technologies was formed due to the consistency of performance, accuracy of emotional recognition, and lucidity of the AI-fueled feedback. The patients and medical personnel would be willing to use AI systems that show responsiveness to their emotional requirements and help in performing clinical and operational activities without compromising on human judgment. The sense of compassion, responsiveness, and situational awareness of AI interaction adds to the development of trust and continued usage.

Figure 8. Human-AI interaction and trust in emotion-aware technologies

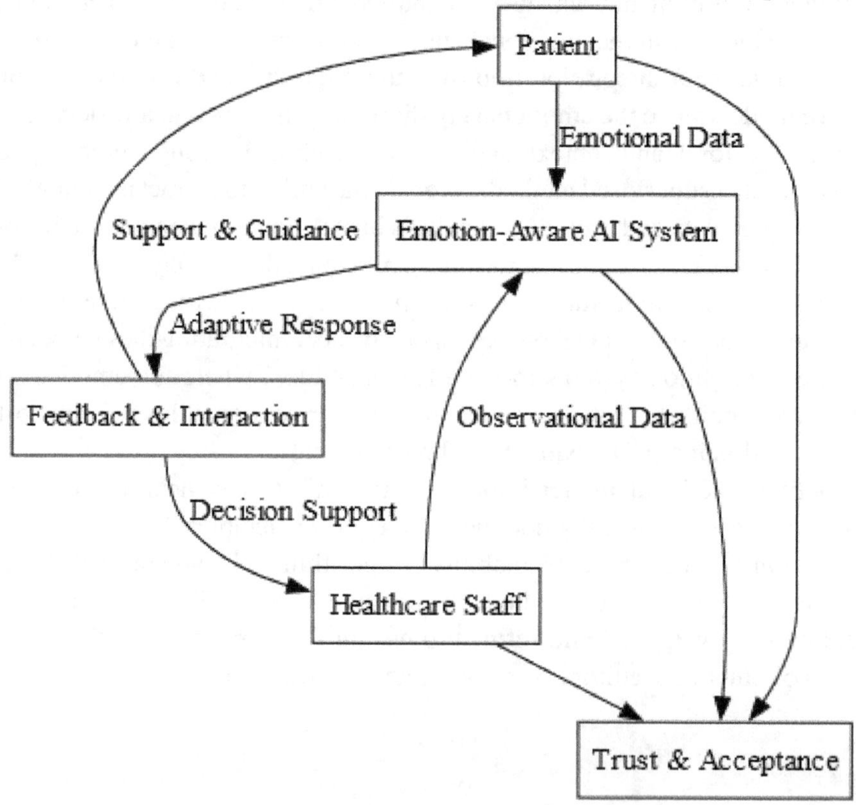

Emotion-aware AI principles focus on transparency and interpretability as well as being ethical and aligned with human values. Algorithms are designed in such a way that offer subjects of explanation that explain the reasoning behind recommendations or interventions so that the user can understand the relationship between their emotional conditions and reactions given by the system. Harmonious and sound emotional evaluations strengthen confidence, whereas wrong interpretations or unclear systems in decisions undermine trust and narrow the practical applicability of the system. Human-centered design methods allow making sure that AI operates in addition to existing clinical processes and improves the emotional aspect of healthcare interactions instead of causing another cognitive or emotional load to the staff and patients.

Emotion-aware AI can be successfully implemented with the help of a balance between technological skills and human trust in the reliability of the product and its objective justice. Ongoing monitoring of user experience, feedback systems, and emotional accuracy was useful to promote adaptive enhancement and keep pace with the changing healthcare requirements. The management of data privacy, consent, and ethical use of sensitive emotional data was an aspect of trust-building in which the organization was involved.

INTEGRATION OF EMOTION AND AI FOR SUSTAINABLE HEALTHCARE

Frameworks for AI-Driven Emotional Ergonomics in Hospitals

Systems of AI-based emotional ergonomics in hospitals offer systematic strategies on how emotional information can be incorporated in real-time into clinical practices and operational decision-making. These models integrate the concepts of affective computing, human factors engineering, and healthcare management into a set of adaptive systems that have the capacity to respond to the emotional conditions of the patient and staff. Multi-modal sensors gather emotional signals, such as physiological signals, facial expressions, language, and behavioral signals, which are then processed using machine learning algorithms to produce actionable information. Improved reception of these insights into the work of hospitals allows making dynamic changes in the work with patients and staff distribution, as well as in the environmental conditions, which adjusts the healthcare processes to human emotional needs.

These models are made up of core parts, which are emotion detection, contextual interpretation, and adaptive response mechanism. Emotion detection refers to the process of collecting real-time information on patients and medical staff and using it to detect stress, anxiety, or fatigue. These emotional conditions are contextualized to clinical, organizational, and environmental conditions, and the AI systems can suggest the interventions that facilitate well-being and efficiency. The analysis was then converted into actionable recommendations or system changes that are then implemented using adaptive response mechanisms, such as the scheduling of workflow, receiving decision support alerts, or changing environmental stimuli such as lighting or sound. The organized interaction of these elements was what makes sure that the functioning of a hospital was not only efficient but also contributes to the creation of emotionally supportive conditions.

The effectiveness of AI-based emotional ergonomics frameworks requires an assessment and ongoing improvement. The accuracy of emotion recognition, the effect of interventions on patient outcomes and the well-being of the staff, and the adoption of AI recommendations into regular clinical practice are performance measures. The framework considers ethical issues, such as the privacy of data, consent, and fairness in algorithm making in order to ensure trust and regulatory compliance.

Multi-Modal Data Fusion: Physiological, Behavioral, and Contextual Signals

Multi-modes are built upon the integration of physiological, behavioral, and contextual cues that are part of the foundation of multi-modes in emotion-sensitive healthcare. The objective measures of stress, arousal, and emotional states include physiological measures such as heart rate variability, electrodermal activity, and brainwave pattern. Facial expression, body language, hand gestures, and tone of voice are also some of the behavioral clues that provide complementary information about the affective reactions in the real-world interactions. The situational variables are further elaborated with contextual data such as environmental factors, task demands, and social dynamics that are needed to understand the effects of situational variables on emotional experience. The integration of these different sources will facilitate full-fledged modelling of the human emotion, and AI systems will be able to comprehend the intricate trends and produce valid and current information regarding the well-being of the patient and the staff.

Figure 9. Multi-modal data fusion

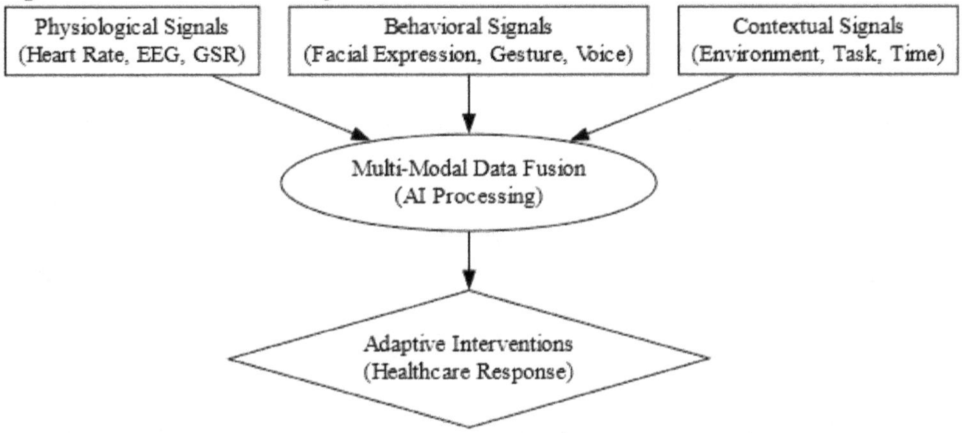

The latest machine learning methods support combining multi-modal data, which helps in identifying the slightest changes in emotions, which the uni-modality systems cannot achieve. Algorithms combine temporal, spatial, and relational data among data streams and generate strong predictions of emotional conditions under different circumstances. Context-aware models are able to fit in dynamic healthcare settings and adjust their response to individual baselines, clinical scenarios, and environmental cues. The resultant synthesis favors the adaptive interventions that bring the best levels of patient involvement, staff stress reduction, and overall operational effectiveness.

Multi-modal data fusion should also be implemented with special care on the quality of the data, calibration of sensors, and the ethical aspects of privacy and consent. Ongoing verification and reliability over time ensure that the AI systems are accurate and reliable by means of continuous monitoring and validation, whereas adaptive feedback loops enable the AI systems to narrow down predictive models as time goes on.

Adaptive Interventions: AI-Driven Feedback for Patients and Staff

Adaptive interventions based on AI alter the emotional ergonomics by offering instant feedback that can adjust to changing affective conditions of patients and medical workers. Machine learning algorithms are used to detect stress, anxiety, or fatigue using emotional signals, which are measured with the help of physical monitoring, face recognition, speech recognition, and behavioral observation. Personalized interventions to maximize the well-being of emotions then be activated by feedback mechanisms, including environmental modifications, guided relaxation sessions, or redistribution of tasks. These interventions increase patient engagement and adherence to treatment protocols and it lowers the chances of mistakes that can be triggered by emotional overload or cognitive exhaustion among healthcare personnel.

The adaptive feedback systems are designed with a focus on ongoing monitoring and context-dependent feedback that was geared towards clinical workflow. AI recognizes emotional fluctuation patterns, prioritizes the critical situations, and provides the interventions without interfering with the processes of care being implemented. The patient was guided in ways that help them feel comfortable, motivated, and emotionally strong, and the staff members have prompts to help them cope with workload, focus, and professional effectiveness. These systems are more responsive and human-centered in delivering health care, as offer the ability to change dynamically on the basis of real-time emotional evaluation, unlike other intervention models that operate based on rules and regulations.

Enhancing Workflow Efficiency and Reducing Occupational Stress

The working efficiency of a healthcare facility was directly associated with improving the mood of employees and the effectiveness of clinical machinery. AI that was sensitive to emotions promotes workload, cognitive exhaustion, and stress indicators in real-time in healthcare professionals. With a multi-modal approach to data, like the use of physiological signals or behavioral cues or task patterns, AI was able to detect bottlenecks and forecast when stress levels are high, as well as propose ways of modifying the allocation of tasks or the environmental conditions. This ongoing process of adaptation contributes to the minimization of the undue strain and equitable allocation of duties and allows personnel to stay focused on patient care and reduce the burden of emotions.

Figure 10. Enhancing workflow efficiency and reducing occupational stress

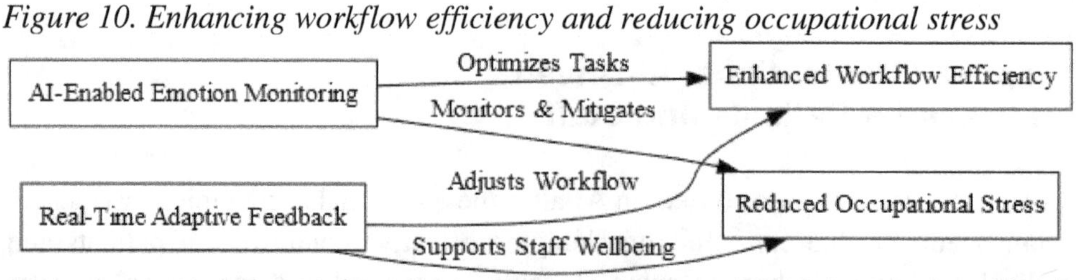

The impact of occupational stress on clinical performance, error rates, and long-term workforce sustainability has a direct relationship with healthcare professionals.

By incorporating AI-based emotional intelligence into the routine of work, it was possible to implement interventions that help to avoid a large amount of stress before it accumulates, as well as to help overcome it with the help of adaptive schedules, workload redistribution, or personal wellness reminders. The implementation of emotion-conscious technologies in workflow management helps to improve coordination of teams, create a supportive atmosphere, and build resilience to burnout. Such mechanisms form a positive feedback cycle, where emotional data has been used to make operational decisions, and better workflows have been used to maintain positive emotional conditions.

Sustainable health care processes are based on the focus on compatibility of technological innovation and human factors, on the complementary efficiency and well-being. Emotion-sensitive AI allows proactive decision-making and enables companies to forecast when demand or stress levels will be high and implement prevention measures in advance. The overall impact of streamlined operation and minimized job stress leads to increased quality patient care, enhanced staff satisfaction, and system sustainability in the long term.

Evaluating the Impact of AI-Integrated Emotional Ergonomics on Healthcare Sustainability

The analysis of AI-based emotional ergonomics in healthcare centers was the interaction of the technological intervention with human emotional control on the sustainability of the organization. Artificial intelligence systems that can observe and react to emotions affect both clinical productivity, patient satisfaction, and workforce wellness at the same time. Measures like decreased error rates, better treatment adherence, and decreased recovery time are beneficial to patients, while the decrease in the burnout rate, increase in job satisfaction, and optimal task allocation are indicators of benefits to healthcare professionals. These human and system-level considerations together create a holistic indicator of healthcare sustainability, on the one hand, focusing on the operational performance level and, on the other hand, the preservation of emotional well-being among the stakeholders.

Impact assessment frameworks utilize multi-dimensional data, such as physiological, behavioral, and operational data. Constant monitoring provides the opportunity to measure emotions, the responsivity of the systems, and the efficiency of the workflow and determine the causal links between AI interventions and healthcare outcomes. The comparative analysis of the traditional care model and the AI-enhanced emotional ergonomics shows that there was an increase in the efficiency of the processes, patient engagement, and resilience of healthcare staff. Longitudinal studies also indicate that the process of continuous incorporation of emotion-sensitive AI also leads to the decrease in the number of systemic stressors, the rise in adaptive organizational behavior, and the development of evidence-based decision-making processes in accordance with strategic healthcare goals.

Another aspect of the assessment was how the AI-based interventions can be aligned to the ethical and regulatory requirements so that the utilization of emotional data can improve care as well as not jeopardize privacy or equity. By combining human-centered design, algorithmic transparency, and organizational governance, healthcare institutions can strike a balance between technological development and human-oriented values.

APPLICATIONS IN HEALTHCARE SETTINGS

AI-Supported Emotional Monitoring for Patient-Centered Care

Emotional monitoring with artificial intelligence can offer real-time feedback about the affective condition of the patient and allow healthcare systems to provide patient care that was responsive to the emotional state. Anxiety, stress, and discomfort identified through continuous monitoring of the physiological signals, facial expressions, vocal patterns, and behavioral cues and affect the adherence rates and the progression of the recovery. These insights, when incorporated into care planning, aid in improving individualization of the interventions, such that clinical decisions are made in line with both the emotional and psychological state of the patient and in line with his or her medical needs. This strategy changes the reactive care model into proactive and responsive systems, predicting the emotionally critical situations and preventing their effect on the clinical outcomes.

Figure 11. AI-supported emotional monitoring for patient-centered care

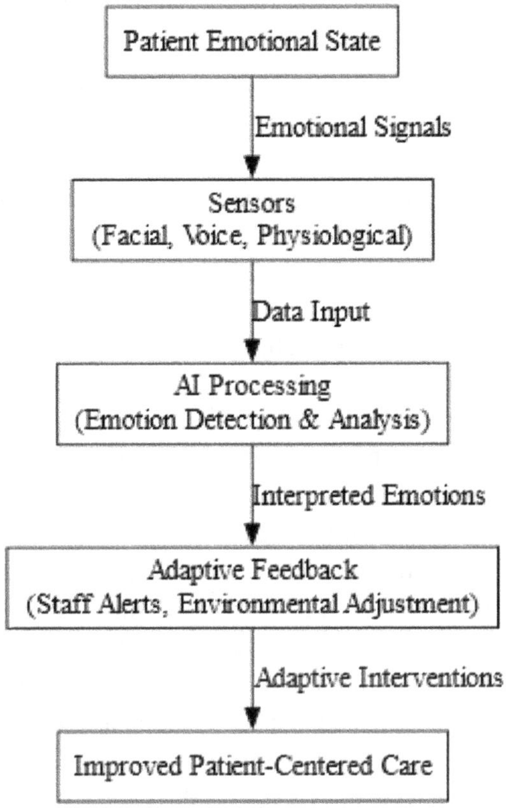

Application of the AI-based emotional monitoring can lead to communication between the patient and the health worker, allowing them to establish empathetic relationships and make necessary therapeutic changes on time. Offering objective and quantifiable information about the feelings of the patients, AI systems can help the staff prioritize the interventions, distribute attention efficiently, and achieve consistent quality of care with diverse patient groups. Multi-modal emotional data patterns can be used in predictive analytics to forecast early those patients who not adhere to treatment, experience emotional distress, or take a long time before recover. Connectivity to electronic health records and clinical decision-support systems makes sure that emotional data was used not only to initiate short-term care but also a long-term care plan.

Implementation of AI-based emotional monitoring must fit the clinical guidelines, ethics, and patient consent procedures. Openness in data processing, data security, and compliance with privacy laws will build patient confidence and allow the system to be constantly optimized. Employing emotion-sensitive AI in the long run leads to a higher patient satisfaction rate, better therapeutic interaction, and tangible viability of care.

Stress and Burnout Management for Healthcare Professionals

It was found that occupational stress and burnout of healthcare professionals represent one of the major factors influencing individual well-being and organizational performance. Chronic exposure to heavy workloads, emotional work, and high-stakes decision-making in the clinical setting are factors that lead to cognitive exhaustion, emotional fatigue, and diminished job satisfaction. These circumstances affect patient safety negatively, providing more chances of errors, and make the healthcare system less efficient overall. A combination of emotional ergonomics and AI technologies gives a chance to follow, anticipate, and reduce stress in real-time, which offers adaptive solutions to stress based on the individual needs and clinical settings.

AI-based systems process physiological indicators, behavioral aspects, and workflow records to detect the signs of stress and emotional exhaustion at an early stage. Predictive algorithms assist in proactive prevention, i.e., redistribution of work, adaptive scheduling, and well-being-focused measures, which form a responsive work environment in response to the dynamic emotional conditions of healthcare personnel. Feedback loops between the AI systems and the professionals enable awareness of the situation and make appropriate changes to the workloads, communication strategies, and support systems in time.

Smart Environments and Emotion-Adaptive Healthcare Workspaces

Smart healthcare spaces are designed to combine superior sensing and computational intelligence and adaptive feedback systems to form spaces that are dynamic to the emotional conditions of patients and personnel. Physiological indicators, behavioral patterns, and environmental variables, which are observed using sensors embedded in workspaces, give continuous streams of data to be analyzed in real time. The AI systems use these cues to modify lighting, sound, temperature, and spatial structure so that can promote emotional control, mental attention, and comfort. Emotion-adaptive design was known to improve patient experiences by making them feel less anxious and more relaxed and motivated to participate in treatment, whereas it also makes staff more focused, efficient, and resilient.

Figure 12. Smart environments and emotion-adaptive healthcare workspaces

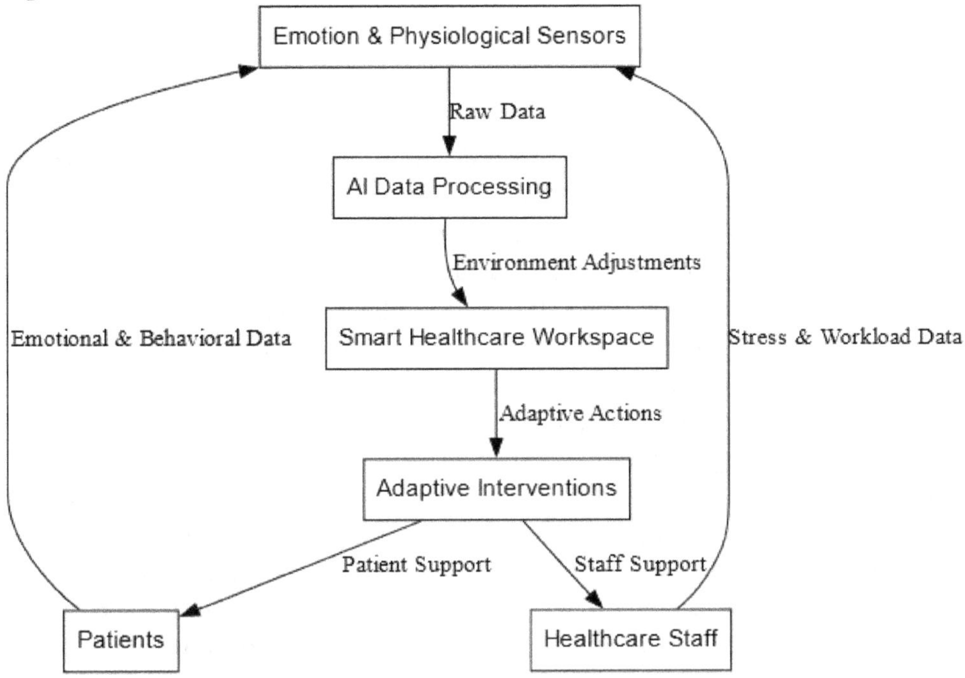

The use of smart workspaces was based on the multi-modal emotional detection mechanisms that combine facial expression recognition and speech sentiment analysis with physiological data collection with the context data (workflow requirements and patient urgency). AI algorithms process such a complicated set of data and produce actionable information to inform interventions to maximize both operational performance and feelings. This can be automated environmental changes in patient rooms to reduce stress or automated task distribution to the staff depending on perceived fatigue or emotional burden. These adaptive strategies can create a receptive healthcare ecosystem, which correlates human-oriented design theories with technology opportunities to facilitate sustainable healthcare delivery.

The assessment of smart, emotion-adaptive healthcare areas considers both the subjective and objective results. Patient-centered measures involve perceived comfort, patient satisfaction, and compliance with care procedures, whereas staff-centered measures measure stress reduction, efficiency in performing tasks, and job satisfaction. The ongoing evaluation will make sure that AI-based changes are consistent with clinical goals, ethics, and organizational sustainability targets.

Telemedicine and Remote Emotional Assessment Using AI

Telemedicine has revolutionized the provision of healthcare through remote access to medical services, a wider scope of clinical knowledge, and elimination of barriers to care. By incorporating artificial intelligence into the telemedicine platforms, one can judge the patient in real time by their emotions to improve the quality of virtual communication. Emotion-sensitive AI applications are able to analyze facial features, speech patterns, and physiological cues that were recorded by using webcams, microphones, and wearable devices and inform clinicians about the affective state of patients. Such abilities contribute to the early identification of emotional distress, anxiety, or cognitive overload with the opportunity to have timely interventions that enhance patient engagement and adherence to treatment plans.

Remote emotional assessment also supports the process of individualized care plans, including changing the communication style, therapeutic advice, and follow-up plans according to the specifics of the emotional patterns. Evidence-based information can help healthcare providers to focus more on interventions for patients that are under increased stress or emotionally susceptible, and care delivery can be responsive and patient-centered. Continuity of care was enhanced by the application of AI in telemedicine to ensure that it was aware of the emotional well-being of its patients in the long run despite the absence of physical consultations.

Emotional assessment based on AI was an adoption in telemedicine, which has helped in the efficiency of operations and sustainable healthcare outcomes. By pinpointing the obstacles to treatment compliance and eliminating emotional strain at a distance, healthcare systems will decrease unnecessary hospitalization, make better use of resources, and improve patient satisfaction. By creating safe and privacy-appropriate data collection and processing systems, it will be possible to use sensitive emotional information ethically without losing the confidence of the technologically mediated interactions in healthcare.

Case Studies and Pilot Implementations of AI-Enhanced Emotional Ergonomics

Pilot projects of AI-based emotional ergonomics in healthcare facilities prove the usefulness of involving emotion-related technology in clinical practice. The implementation of AI systems with affective computing capabilities within a variety of hospital settings has seen the use of AI systems to track patient stress, anxiety, and the level of engagement in the process of treatment and recovery. Information received through physiological sensors, facial expression analysis, and speech sentiment recognition has allowed the staff to change communication approaches and environmental settings and offer specific emotional assistance. Initial results show that there was an increase in adherence to treatment plans by patients, perceived discomfort reduction, and improved satisfaction with care experiences.

Healthcare staff also experience measurable benefits through the use of AI-driven emotional ergonomics. Systems that provide real-time insights into workload-induced stress and emotional fatigue support adaptive task allocation and proactive wellbeing interventions. Pilot programs reveal a decline in occupational stress markers, better team coordination, and a more supportive work environment, suggesting that the integration of AI technologies enhances staff resilience and efficiency. Operational metrics, including reduced error rates and improved workflow continuity, further reinforce the value of emotion-aware AI systems in fostering sustainable healthcare delivery.

CONCLUSION

A combination of emotional ergonomics and artificial intelligence was a paradigm shift in the direction of having sustainable healthcare wellbeing. The role of emotional dynamics in clinical care, patient collaboration, and employee performance cannot be overstated, and it was incredible that traditional healthcare systems usually neglect all these important aspects. Emotional ergonomics offers a framework towards human knowledge and maximization of the relationship between human feelings, the environment, and technology. This can be expanded by the use of AI-based affective computing that will allow real-time tracking, interpretation, and reaction to complicated emotional conditions. This kind of integration creates healthcare cultures that are sensitive, strong, and able to nurture the well-being of patients and professionals.

Practical experience of pilot implementation and case studies proves the measurable advantages of emotional ergonomics with AI addition. The advancement in patient satisfaction, compliance with treatment procedures, decrease in medical mistakes, and occupational resilience highlight the possibility of these systems radically changing how healthcare was provided. AI helps in the proactive management of emotional stressors, efficient workflow management, the improvement of communication, and the development of adaptive interventions that meet individual needs. Its operational effect was not merely beneficial to the individual level but also to the sustainability of the entire organization, through the reduction of burnout, absenteeism, and inefficient systems. All the results mentioned above reveal the importance of implementing emotion-sensitive technologies into the strategic context of contemporary health care systems.

The critical aspect of successful adoption of emotion-aware AI was still dependent on ethical considerations and contextual challenges. The privacy protection, informed consent, fairness of the algorithms, and cultural sensitivity must be strictly covered to be used responsibly. Clear, understandable, and human-focused design aspects are mandatory so as to ensure trust between patients and healthcare providers. Compliance with ethical, legal, and organizational standards will help make sure that technological innovations do not undermine but increase the quality and equity of care.

There was encouraging future research and practice direction upon the intersection of AI and emotional ergonomics. Further research on the multi-modal emotion detection, predictive analytics, and adaptive intervention models will develop the field and improve the approach to sustainable healthcare. The introduction of emotional intelligence into both technological and organizational design will allow healthcare systems to create a harmonious balance between human well-being, their operation, and resiliency in the long term, eventually turning the business of care provision into a more responsive, empathetic, and sustainable process.

REFERENCES

Azour, L., Goldin, J. G., & Kruskal, J. B. (2024). Radiologist and radiology practice wellbeing: A report of the 2023 ARRS wellness summit. *Academic Radiology*, *31*(1), 250–260. DOI: 10.1016/j.acra.2023.08.025 PMID: 37718125

Bekbolatova, M., Mayer, J., Ong, C. W., & Toma, M. (2024, January). Transformative potential of AI in healthcare: definitions, applications, and navigating the ethical landscape and public perspectives. In Healthcare (Vol. 12, No. 2, p. 125). MDPI. DOI: 10.3390/healthcare12020125

Ben Ahmed, M. (2024). Modern Trends in Green Interior Architecture Applications with Smart Systems. *International Journal of Multidisciplinary Studies in Art and Technology*, *7*(1), 1–21. DOI: 10.21608/ijmsat.2024.293946.1027

Bharadiya, J. P., Thomas, R. K., & Ahmed, F. (2023). Rise of artificial intelligence in business and industry. *Journal of Engineering Research and Reports*, *25*(3), 85–103. DOI: 10.9734/jerr/2023/v25i3893

Bibri, S. E., & Jagatheesaperumal, S. K. (2023). Harnessing the potential of the metaverse and artificial intelligence for the internet of city things: Cost-effective XReality and synergistic AIoT technologies. *Smart Cities*, *6*(5), 2397–2429. DOI: 10.3390/smartcities6050109

Brown, O., Davison, R. M., Decker, S., Ellis, D. A., Faulconbridge, J., Gore, J., Greenwood, M., Islam, G., Lubinski, C., MacKenzie, N. G., Meyer, R., Muzio, D., Quattrone, P., Ravishankar, M. N., Zilber, T., Ren, S., Sarala, R. M., & Hibbert, P. (2024). Theory-driven perspectives on generative artificial intelligence in business and management. *British Journal of Management*, *35*(1), 3–23. DOI: 10.1111/1467-8551.12788

Cinar, A. B., & Bilodeau, S. (2024). Incorporating AI into the inner circle of emotional intelligence for sustainability. *Sustainability (Basel)*, *16*(15), 6648. DOI: 10.3390/su16156648

. Colorado–Aurora, U. S., Hardman, L., Boston, U. S., Marai, G. E., Ynnerman, A., & Yuan, X. (2024). 4.5 The Role of Data Visualization in Instigating Behavior Change to Promote Healthy Lifestyles. Visualization of Biomedical Data–Shaping the Future and Building Bridges, 17.

. Dey, D. N. C. (2024). Harmonizing The Threads of Well-Being: Ai (Artificial Intelligence), Spirituality, Healthcare, And Management. Spirituality, Healthcare, And Management (April 24, 2024).

Enholm, I. M., Papagiannidis, E., Mikalef, P., & Krogstie, J. (2022). Artificial intelligence and business value: A literature review. *Information Systems Frontiers, 24*(5), 1709–1734. DOI: 10.1007/s10796-021-10186-w

. Farahat, M. A., Darwish, A., & Hassanien, A. E. (2023). The implication of metaverse in the traditional medical environment and healthcare sector: applications and challenges. The Future of Metaverse in the Virtual Era and Physical World, 105-133.

George, A. S. (2024). The evolution of economic models: From knowledge to intuition and optimization. *Partners Universal Multidisciplinary Research Journal, 1*(2), 1–25.

Jain, S., & Alam, M. A. (2022). Applications of Human-Computer Interaction in Health Psychology. *Journal of Digital Art and Humanities, 3*(1), 36–57. DOI: 10.33847/2712-8148.3.1_5

Jang, K., & Landuyt, N. G. (2023). Limited benefits of technological advances in human service organizations: Going beyond the hype using sociotechnical knowledge management system. *Journal of Social Service Research, 49*(4), 426–446. DOI: 10.1080/01488376.2023.2236131

Kaklauskas, A., Abraham, A., Ubarte, I., Kliukas, R., Luksaite, V., Binkyte-Veliene, A., Vetloviene, I., & Kaklauskiene, L. (2022). A review of AI cloud and edge sensors, methods, and applications for the recognition of emotional, affective and physiological states. *Sensors (Basel), 22*(20), 7824. DOI: 10.3390/s22207824 PMID: 36298176

Kamboj, J., & A, E. (2024). Mapping the green human resource management practices: A systematic scoping review and its implications for employees' well-being. *Human Systems Management, 43*(6), 1062–1081. DOI: 10.1177/01672533241305207

Kolomaznik, M., Petrik, V., Slama, M., & Jurik, V. (2024). The role of socio-emotional attributes in enhancing human-AI collaboration. *Frontiers in Psychology, 15*, 1369957. DOI: 10.3389/fpsyg.2024.1369957 PMID: 39474095

Kumar, P., Dwivedi, Y. K., & Anand, A. (2023). Responsible artificial intelligence (AI) for value formation and market performance in healthcare: The mediating role of patient's cognitive engagement. *Information Systems Frontiers, 25*(6), 2197–2220. DOI: 10.1007/s10796-021-10136-6 PMID: 33948105

Mahmud, S., Rahman, A., & Ashrafuzzaman, M. (2022). A systematic literature review on the role of digital health twins in preventive healthcare for personal and corporate wellbeing. *American Journal of Interdisciplinary Studies, 3*(04), 1–31. DOI: 10.63125/negjw373

Mithas, S., Chen, Z. L., Saldanha, T. J., & De Oliveira Silveira, A. (2022). How will artificial intelligence and Industry 4.0 emerging technologies transform operations management? *Production and Operations Management, 31*(12), 4475–4487. DOI: 10.1111/poms.13864

Priya, N., Satpathy, I., Patnaik, B. C. M., & Thaichon, P. (2024). Transforming workplace wellness in the next-generation hospitality industry by leveraging transformational digital technologies and tools. In *Technology and luxury hospitality* (pp. 295–313). Routledge. DOI: 10.4324/9781003488248-20

Saini, A. K., & Montebello, M. (2024). Exploring the Educational Frontier: A Deep Dive into VR and AI-Enhanced Learning Environments. In *Trust and Inclusion in AI-mediated Education: Where Human Learning Meets Learning Machines* (pp. 141–162). Springer Nature Switzerland. DOI: 10.1007/978-3-031-64487-0_7

Stone, P., Brooks, R., Brynjolfsson, E., Calo, R., Etzioni, O., Hager, G., . . . Teller, A. (2022). Artificial intelligence and life in 2030: the one hundred year study on artificial intelligence. arXiv preprint arXiv:2211.06318.

Van Velsen, L., Ludden, G., & Grünloh, C. (2022). The limitations of user-and human-centered design in an eHealth context and how to move beyond them. *Journal of Medical Internet Research, 24*(10), e37341. DOI: 10.2196/37341 PMID: 36197718

Yu, L., & Li, Y. (2022). Artificial intelligence decision-making transparency and employees' trust: The parallel multiple mediating effect of effectiveness and discomfort. *Behavioral Sciences (Basel, Switzerland), 12*(5), 127. DOI: 10.3390/bs12050127 PMID: 35621424

Chapter 4
Talent Transformation: Upskilling the Hospitality Workforce for an AI Era

Amrik Singh
https://orcid.org/0000-0003-3598-8787
Lovely Professional University, India

ABSTRACT

The hospitality sector is undergoing a disruption like never before due to the coming together of Artificial Intelligence (AI) technologies. Although automation and data analytics are beneficial to boost efficiency, personalization, and decision-making, they also transform workforce structures and competencies. The chapter is based on theories of human-AI symbiosis, learning organizations, and competency-based education, and it addresses the issue of the co-expansion of technology and human capital to maintain service excellence. Among the most important themes are the changing job description, skills gap, and workforce development pedagogy, institutional reactions, and policy frameworks to inclusive talent transformation. The chapter emphasizes that the future of hospitality does not consist of substituting the human workforce but rather in enhancing it- in which AI enables human creativity, empathy and strategic thinking.

INTRODUCTION

People have always characterized the hospitality industry. The ability to anticipate, empathize and surpass expectations is the characteristic feature of hospitality, whether it is the luxury resort or a quick-service restaurant, or even a boutique travel agency. However, the 21 st century has brought forth the influence of strong technology which is transforming not only the way services are offered in this human-centered

DOI: 10.4018/979-8-3373-8197-8.ch004

industry but also the kinds of competencies that are needed to offer the services. The fourth industrial revolution that has occurred as a result of merging Artificial Intelligence (AI), robotics, the Internet of Things (IoT), big data, and immersive technologies has made hospitality a digitally enhanced service ecosystem. There is a blurring of the formerly distinct boundaries between the operation of the human service and the machine. Nowadays, AI systems are functioning as digital co-workers and enhance the potentials of human workers and redesign organizational structures and processes (Hussain et al., 2023). Chatbots, multilingual booking and guest requests 24/7; facial recognition, quicker check-in; predictive analytics in the inventory, staffing and pricing decisions, robotic helpers in housekeeping, room service and food preparation. These innovations make operations more efficient, lower costs and make guests happier because they allow them to be personalized on a large scale. Nevertheless, they are also problematic as they unleash messiness by pushing out normal work processes and requiring a re-conceptualization of human positioning. Algorithms and machines have replaced the tasks that could be done in the past only with physical presence or manual work, and the new positions have appeared, which focus on analytical, creative, and interpersonal aspects. These new horizons have meant that in the new landscape, hospitality employees must be able to interpret information, operate automated systems, and bring in the emotional intelligence that AI never has, and therefore, the central issue that hospitality organizations will encounter is not whether AI will transform the nature of work, but how it will be possible to prepare and empower employees to embrace the new environment and thrive. This problem is not only technical but very human and it needs to be changed not only on the education, leadership, and organizational culture level.

1.1 Strategic Imperative of Talent Transformation.

The main principle of this change is the idea of talent transformation- the strategic process of the matching of workforce abilities with technological, cultural and business shifts. The process of transforming talent does not just consist of retraining staff; talent transformation is a complete re-evaluation of the process of attracting, developing, and retaining people in the age of smart automation (Arora et al., 2024). It entails the incorporation of AI literacy, emotional intelligence, as well as adaptability into the DNA of the hospitality profession. This need has been heightened under the post-pandemic era. The COVID-19 is what drove the digital adoption across the hospitality industry with contactless technology, mobile ordering, and automated service protocols becoming a norm. With the struggle of businesses to reconstruct operations with labor shortages and increased guest demands, AI-driven solutions became one of the primary resilience enablers. A large number of workers were not digitally fluent to use new systems and many managers were not able to manage a hybrid human-machine team. In this respect, both of the concepts of upskilling and reskilling have become pivotal to competitiveness and inclusion: the former technique of introducing new skills to the employees in order to improve their existing jobs, and the latter one of training their skills to fit fully new jobs. Effective talent changes need hospitality organizations as not only employees but also as learning systems, which promote curiosity, creativity, and human development continually. Learning, unlearning and relearning has turned out to be the specialty of the contemporary hospitality professional. Finally, the hospitality of the future will rely on symbiotic interaction between human resource and intelligent technology, in which AI will complement and not substitute the art of service that is unique to human beings (Metta & Kumar, 2026; Singh & Ansari, 2024; Ambardar et al., 2023). The competitive edge of the future hospitality organizations will not be because of the technology but the way in which they develop the human resources to work with the technology that will change the employees into adaptable and tech-savvy experience-creators.

2. HUMAN-AI SYMBIOSIS WITHIN THE HOSPITALITY

The idea of human-AI symbiosis, meaning a paradigm in which people and machines have to cooperate rather than to compete, is the theoretical foundation on which one can consider talent transformation in the era of AI. This model dispels the old belief of automation as an inevitable cause of job losses. Rather it imagines a world in which AI enhances the human potential and workers are able to engage in higher-order cognitive, creative, emotional work that introduces new value to the experiences of the guests.

2.1. Socio-Technical Systems Theory (Trist and Emery, 1951)

Socio-Technical Systems Theory suggests that both technological systems and social systems are dependent on each other and they have to be optimised together so as to attain sustainable performance. AI systems in the hospitality setting will never work well without the presence of human supervision, empathy, and situational awareness. As an illustration, an AI chatbot will be effective in answering guest questions, but it is not as emotionally sensitive as someone needs to be to deal with the upset or unhappy client (El Hajal & Yeoman, 2024; Singh & Sihmar, 2025; Singh, 2025; Supina & Singh, 2024). Symbiotic approach makes sure that the AI-driven processes are developed in such a way that they complement the human strengths instead of substituting them. It is a form of joint optimization, i.e. balancing technical efficiency and human satisfaction, which is the keystone of sustainable digital transformation in the hospitality industry.

2.2. Human Capital Theory (Becker, 1964)

The Human Capital Theory emphasizes the economic and social payoffs of investing in humans using education, training and skill building. In hospitality, employees constitute the greatest asset, and their imagination, innovativeness, and flexibility establish the service quality and innovation (Ercik & Kardaş, 2024; Singh, 2025; Supina & Singh, 2024). Upskilling and reskilling are not functions of HR, thus, they are strategic investments, which bring about productivity, profitability, and competitive differentiation. The rate of skills depreciation is high in the AI age when technology changes at a rather high rate. Companies that keep investing in their employees are agile and able to retain their human advantage in an increasingly automated world.

2.3 Learning Organization Theory (Senge, 1990)

The Learning Organization Theory developed by Peter Senge further evolves the idea that it is the ability of an organization to learn and to adapt as a whole that will result in long-term success. The cultures of inquiry, reflection, and common vision are promoted in learning organizations. This in the AI-based hospitality setting has been translated into the development of systems that encourage constant feedback, knowledge transfer, and cross-functional development. Even AI can become an enabler of learning- analytics can be used to determine the needs of individual learning, prescribe individual training modules, and evaluate the effect of skill acquisition programs. The hospitality organizations can also make sure that their employees are future ready by inculcating continuous learning into their daily activities.

2.4 The AI-Human Augmentation Model

With these theoretical grounds, the AI-human augmentation model comes into the limelight as a theoretical framework of comprehending the changing workforce. This model regards AI not as the substitute of human work but as the multiplier of the human potential. Machines are good at working on large volumes of data, repetition, and making anticipatory conclusions; humans are good at empathy, moral judgment, creativity, and interpretation of culture (Ersanlı et al., 2025; Supina & Singh, 2024; Singh & Singh, 2022; Singh & Hassan, 2024). The synergistic outcomes of the AI-human alliance are achieved through the distribution of tasks based on these strengths. To illustrate a case, AI systems can be used in a customer service operation of a hotel to analyze preferences of guests, purchase trends and their feedback to draw conclusions. With this information, human workers are able to make service interactions personalized, make empathetic choices, and establish authentic relationships. The outcome is an elevated data-driven, and deeply human experience of the guests.

2.5 Re-Imagining the Workforce of the Hospitality

The overlap between these theories transforms the hospitality workforce into a group of augmented human beings; people with the power of technology to provide high-quality service. These are professionals who integrate digital literacy and emotional intelligence to use data to predict needs and technology to boost personalization. The frontline worker turns into a digital artisan, able to process algorithmic insights with compassion; the manager turns into a data-driven leader, leading hybrid teams of people and machines, and the organization becomes an ever-changing living organism, constantly coping with technology. The success in this re-invented structure relies on balance.

Literature Review

Automation threatens to diminish the nature of the hospitality industry which is characterized by warmth and authenticity. On the other hand, inefficiency and lack of competitiveness are caused by technology resistance. The trick is to establish a symbiotic relationship, that is, one in which technology gives accuracy and scope and humans give meaning and feeling (Singh & Hassan, 2024; Singh, 2024). Finally, the human-AI symbiosis changes the traditional service paradigm into the enhanced humanity paradigm. Hospitality professional of the future will not be competing with machines, but use them as innovative collaborators in developing intelligent, ethical, and deep-human experience.

3. THE CHANGING WORK CHARACTERISTICS

Hospitality business has been one of the most labor intensive industries of the world economy traditionally. It has based its identity on the principles of face to face, manual service delivery and the art of building memorable experience using human warmth and attentiveness. It was either a concierge who helped a guest in booking a room or a chef creating a special meal, or a housekeeper who made sure that one feels comfortable and clean in the room, but the point of hospitality was on human labor and emotional intelligence. In the 21st century, however, this paradigm has changed radically. The wave of rapid digital transformation, which is driven by Artificial Intelligence (AI), automation, and data analytics, started to transform the very nature of work in the hospitality industry. The contemporary hospitality working environment is now in a phygital (physical + digital) ecosystem, which combines seamlessly the digital technologies with the conservative service spaces (Ersanlı et al., 2025; Singh & Kumar, 2021; Singh & Ansari, 2024; Ambardar et al., 2023). The notion of phygital hospitality is indicative of the industry that is working across digital and physical areas at the same time, i.e., the visitors can reserve a room with the help of an AI-controlled chatbot, scan their face to check in, and communicate with a digital version of a concierge with the help of an augmented reality (AR) interface, but they still anticipate a real, human-focused experience. Human service is not eroded by the combination of technology and human service but re-structured to require additional competencies, attitudes, and organizational frameworks. The technologies based on AI have already affected almost all aspects of the hospitality value chain. Predictive analytics are used to optimize prices, demand prediction, and inventory management, robotic systems are used to clean and provide room services, and digital platforms are used to make marketing more precise and provide guest interactions. Due to this, old-fashioned occupations are redefined, and new jobs completely appear in areas as data management, web experience design, and systems analysis. Also, the future workforce is not limited to operational proficiency anymore, it is required to incorporate technical skillfulness, analytical thinking and emotional acuity.

3.1. Operational Automation

The initial significant revolution is the automation of operations. Jobs that were previously repetitive or strenuous are being increasingly assigned to machines and artificial intelligence. Robots take care of the floors, housekeeping, autonomous delivery robots collect room service orders, and self-service kiosks process check-ins and check-outs. Not only these technologies enhance efficiency but also reduce the human factor error and improve hygiene, which became especially important during the COVID-19 pandemic. Nonetheless, this automation does not remove the human labor, but it changes its point of focus (Alhelal et al., 2025; Singh & Ansari, 2024; Ambardar et al., 2023). Automated systems require employees to have supervisory, maintenance, and problem-solving capabilities as a way of managing and troubleshooting. As an illustration, a front-desk associate should know how to manage self-check-in kiosks and make exceptions where this service cannot be done automatically. Equally, housekeeping personnel are also becoming robot handlers, keeping the cleaning robots in proper and safe operation. Digital dexterity, which is the capacity to operate across numerous digital platforms and react dynamically to technological challenges, is also required in this automation.

3.2. Data-Driven Decision-Making

The second significant change in the work of the hospitality field is the emergence of the data-based decision-making. The modern hospitality business works in the sea of information that is created through the interactions with guests, social media, booking systems, and IoT solutions. This data is processed by AI and machine learning algorithms to produce information about the preferences of guests, their spending patterns, and the level of their satisfaction. The insights allow developing more specific marketing plans, effective resource distribution, and better personalization of services. Therefore, the work of a hospitality professional is becoming more and more connected with the ability to handle data, visualize, and interpret it. Revenue managers will have to know how predictive modeling works with dynamic price setting; marketing specialists will need to convert data insights into personal offers; operations specialists will need to analyze the performance insights to optimize staffing and logistics (Wider et al., 2025; Singh & Supina, 2024; Singh & Kumar, 2024). This change is an indicator of the transition between the management by intuition and evidence-based decision-making. Although experience and intuition have been long-term assets in the hospitality industry, the contemporary setting requires the level of emotional intelligence and analytical rigor to be balanced. The skill of interpreting and taking action on the data information has become the hallmark of the 21 st century hospitality employee. In addition, AI-based analytics can also help front-line employees make better decisions, democratizing knowledge and promoting decentralized and nimble operations.

3.3. Hybrid Customer Engagement

The third innovation is the hybrid customer engagement where digital and human interactions are combined to create a guest journey. The current day travelers are demanding immediacy, personalization and convenience, which is achieved through technology. Chatbots, virtual assistants, and AR-based concierge systems enable guests to access any information or order any service any time, anywhere. A case in point is the AI-driven mobile application created by Marriott that allows the customer to control the room environment or order the service by voice. However, despite the fact that these technologies make life more convenient, they cannot replace the emotional connection that humans have (Seyitoğlu et al., 2023; Supina & Singh, 2024; Singh & Singh, 2022; Singh & Hassan, 2024). Being an effective hospitality professional in the era of AI, one thus has to master digital empathy, the capacity to project the warmth, authenticity and attentiveness using technology mediated interactions. The employees should be able to easily transition between the online environment and real-life visitation without losing the human face of the brand. This blended interaction also reinvents service training. The staff is no longer being taught on interpersonal skills but is being trained on the digital communication skills, virtual etiquette, and responsiveness in multiple channels.

3.4. The Rise of Hybrid Professionals

All these changes are the harbingers of a radical change in workforce composition, not so much of traditional service providers but of hybrid professionals, who possess some evidence of technical literacy and interpersonal excellentia at the same time. The new hospitality professional is not only information-driven but also emotionally intelligent, who will not hesitate to work with the AI system but still possess the empathy and cultural awareness that drive the guest satisfaction. There is greater fluidity between technology and hospitality service. These are some examples of how technological fluency is being wrapped up around creativity and service ethics. Continuous learning and adaptability are the competencies in the industry as it starts to shift to this hybrid model. The lifespan of skills- the duration of time of relevance of a skill- has radically decreased in the digital era (Santandreu Calonge et al., 2025; Singh, 2024; Singh & Supina, 2024). It is therefore the responsibility of employees to continuously acquire learnings in order to be able to stay applicable and productive. Organizations, on their part, have to develop a culture of learning that promotes experimentation, curiosity and innovation.

Discussion And Interpretation

The nature of work in the hospitality industry is shifting, which eventually points to a bigger fact: technology will probably change the operations, but cannot substitute the human ability to empathize, tell stories and connect. The most successful hospitality businesses will be those that embrace technology to enhance and not to reduce the emotional and the sense of experience that is characteristic of the industry. The hospitality industry can also prevail in a more automated and at the same time more human world by creating hybrid professionals who possess the ability to connect digital intelligence with human warmth.

4. THE WORKFORCE READINESS OF AI IN THE AGE OF SKILLS

Artificial Intelligence (AI) has also transformed the skills that a professional in the hospitality industry should possess. The industry previously focused on the manual dexterity and service etiquette, but currently requires a hybrid skill set that lies between technical literacy and interpersonal intelligence. However, the speed of the technological adoption has exceeded the development of the workforce potential. Deloitte (2023) estimates that half of the employees in the hospitality industry do not have the digital skills required to succeed in AI embedded jobs. This expanding divide is a major source of concern in terms of productivity, service quality, and innovation in the industry (Singh & Singh, 2022; Singh & Hassan, 2024). The shortcomings in hospitality skills can be loosely divided into three areas namely technical skills, soft skills and managerial skills. Both are essential building blocks of workforce preparedness in the AI age, and the solution to each of them involves a systemic change in education, training and human resource development.

4.1 Technical Skill Gaps

The observable void is the most in technical and digital skills. The environment that hospitality employees work in has become highly data-rich and analytics-driven in decision-making. Between AI-driven customer relationship management (CRM) systems and machine learning implementations in revenue optimization, the new workplace place demands employees to be able to interpret and use data insights in the most efficient way possible. Nevertheless, the majority of the vocational and educational hospitality programs are rooted in the conservative service competencies, namely, culinary arts, housekeeping, front office management, but do not involve much exposure to digital tools and AI applications (Das et al., 2025; Singh & Hassan, 2024; Singh, 2024; Singh & Supina, 2024). This leads to a high number of graduates joining the market without being digital ready to perform in the modern world. Lack of AI literacy, which is knowledge of how algorithms take information, identify patterns, and make judgments, presents a major obstacle in successful technology use. Now stockers need to understand the principles of machine learning, workflows with automation, and the systems based on data. To illustrate this, by learning how predictive analytics systems predict occupancy rates or how sentiment analysis can understand methods of interpreting guest feedback staff can work well together with artificial intelligence. In addition, AI is still infiltrating areas like marketing and human resources, meaning that hospitality workers need to become experts in the area of software management, cybersecurity knowledge, and data privacy regulations. The technical divide is not restricted to front-line functions, but it takes in managerial and strategic functions as well. Top managers and heads of departments need to be digitally fluent to make sound decisions based on technology investment and to be able to understand the insights provided by artificial intelligence. In the absence of these competences, organizations will find the implementation and underutilization of costly digital tools inefficient. Therefore, technical upskilling has to be institutionalized, incorporated into pre-employment training as well as into continuous professional training.

4.2 Soft Skill Gaps

Paradoxically, with several more routine chores becoming automated by technology, there is a greater need than ever to have certain uniquely human skills. Emotional and social intelligence also become key distinguishing factors in the AI-driven hospitality setting, where the guests are in contact with machines more and more. Competitive advantage of human labor force lies in the capacity to empathize, adapt and establish meaningful relationships. Emotional intelligence, flexibility, creativity and cultural empathy are some of the soft skills that are very crucial in preserving the human touch in hospitality. Emotional intelligence will help employees to perceive the needs of guests that cannot be predicted by the algorithms, and flexibility will help them to go through the digital systems and conditions of services that are quickly changing. Innovation, in its turn, is driven by creativity in designing a personalized guest experience that balances the use of technology with the authenticity. All the same, the hospitality workforce in most cases underestimates the complexity of these soft skills (Singh, 2025; Supina & Singh, 2024; Singh & Singh, 2022; Singh & Kumar, 2021). Training programs are often directed towards procedural service delivery as opposed to reflective or situational learning to develop the emotional aspect and critical thinking. Besides, because workers are increasingly interacting more virtually and in hybrid forms, as with digital concierge services or online guest relations, they too will be required to learn how to show warmth and attentiveness using mediated communications means. The AI era therefore turned soft skills into periphery traits to strategic competencies. Employers now realize that machines will be able to streamline operations but only humans will produce a sense of trust, emotional connection and brand loyalty. Developing the required capabilities would need pedagogical creativity, such as experiential learning, simulation-based training, and development of emotional intelligence incorporated in the hospitality curriculum.

4.3 Managerial Gaps

The third area of weakness has to do with managerial and leadership skills. With the implementation of AI systems in the organizational environment, managers are forced to manage hybrid teams, which include both human workers and digital agents. This novel leadership environment requires rearranging the conventional philosophies of management to be more digitally savvy and ethically based leadership. The hospitality managers of the modern era need to have the knowledge of data-driven decision-making, digital transformation policy, and AI ethics. They are not merely bosses of individuals anymore but directors of socio-technical systems. Knowing how AI can be used in human processes helps them to create jobs that are as efficient and engaging as possible. To take an example, any automation adopted by managers should not replace human advantages, it should complement them- morale should be preserved, and services should retain their authenticity. Change management is another managerial skill that is critical (Tan et al., 2025; Singh & Supina, 2024; Singh & Kumar, 2024; Singh & Kumar, 2021). The implementation of AI tends to cause anxiety to the employees as it is accompanied by the fear of being excluded or losing independence. Good leaders therefore need to communicate openly, establish trust and be able to create a learning environment where experimentation is encouraged and there is less resistance. Moreover, managers need to build a good foundation in digital ethics and governance. The leaders must provide the assurance of adherence to privacy policies and ethical data usage because AI applications work with sensitive data of guests. This is because the knowledge of algorithmic bias, transparency, and accountability can be instrumental in not only complying with regulations but also ensuring the ethical validity of the brand. These managerial gaps need systemic workforce planning and learning interventions that are agile. Organizations have to establish continuous development programs in professional development that involve training that entails leadership coaching, technical, and ethical training. A culture of innovation and mutual digital competence can also be promoted by cross-functional working of the HR, the IT, and operations departments.

4.4 Developing workforce Preparedness

The preparation of the workforce in the era of AI is not confined to the process of acquiring specific skills but to building the attitude of learning and the flexibility of the organization. Hospitality employees should become a group of lifelong learners, and digital learning environments should enable them to tailor developmental journeys with AI analytics. Institutions are also advised to work with industry partners to make the redesign of curricula around the AI-built-in competencies so that graduates are employment-ready in a digital-in-the-first world (Singh & Kumar, 2024; Singh & Kumar, 2021; Singh & Ansari, 2024; Ambardar et al., 2023). After all, the problem is not merely to address the gaps in the available skills but to redefine the concept of the work in the hospitality sector in the world of the human-machines cooperation. The workforce of tomorrow will be technologically fluent, emotionally and ethically aware- a new breed of professional, who will be able to maintain the human side to hospitality, as well as harness the potential of smart technologies.

5. ARTIFICIAL INTELLIGENCE AND DIGITAL ECOSYSTEM

Artificial Intelligence (AI) has become one of the revolutionary impacting forces throughout the hospitality value chain, which is fundamentally altering the working models and the redefinition of work. A service-focused business that used to be based on personal contact and physical performance has now turned into an augmented digital ecosystem. Smart technologies are transforming every aspect of hospitality business, including involvement with guests and the activities that support decision-making and experience personalization behind the scenes. As a result, the competencies demanded by hospitality workers have shifted to the level of basic service provision abilities to a set of technological skills and data literacy, as well as human responsiveness (Singh & Kumar, 2021; Singh & Ansari, 2024; Ambardar et al., 2023). The implementation of AI tools in the various functional sectors is an indication that talent needs are becoming more diverse. The human touch and machine intelligence in the hospitality industry have become a compromise where the human experience has to be mediated by the machine intelligence to be able to add and not to displace the emotional aspect of the interaction of the guest. The subsequent paragraphs identify the key fields in which AI is redefining the competencies of the workforce and transforming the talent strategy.

5.1. Front Office and Interaction with Guests

The front office has remained the most humanistic section of the hospitality sector in terms of receiving the guests, taking requests and checking-in and checking-out of the guests. Nowadays, AI systems are becoming popular to support those functions, which include chatbots, voice assistants, and facial recognition technologies. Chatbots manage the preliminary booking requests, offer multilingual support and solve frequent customer problems on the spot. Hotel rooms can have voice assistants, such as Amazon Alexa Hotel or IBM Watson Assistant, which allow guests to turn on and off the lights, regulate the temperature, or order housekeeping services without resorting to human assistance (Singh & Hassan, 2024; Singh, 2024; Singh & Supina, 2024). In the case of front office workers such technologies cause a two-fold task to control AI-based interfaces and preserve individualized service quality. Employees should be aware of protocols and cybersecurity measures of the system, as well as data privacy laws, particularly since facial recognition and biometrics systems deal with sensitive data. In addition, the employees must learn how to decipher the insights of guest data to find out the behavior patterns and customize service offerings. Therefore, the front desk agent is no longer a solely transactional operator; it is a digital relationship manager, that is, a person who can combine emotional intelligence with data-driven acumen. The modules in AI literacy, privacy ethics, and customer experience analytics now need to be incorporated in the training programs so that the staff can work together with intelligent systems without sacrificing the warmth and naturalness of human service.

5.2. Facility Management and Housekeeping

With housekeeping, AI-based automation has transformed housekeeping in terms of schedules, maintenance, and quality control. Repetitive and time-sensitive duties are now performed by intelligent systems with the help of robotic cleaning systems, IoT-based maintenance sensors, and AI-based scheduling systems. As an example, robots are able to clean up places of interest on their own and predictive maintenance computer software is able to know when equipment is in need of maintenance. Such technologies are very effective and require new skills in the employees. Housekeeping employees should learn technical troubleshooting, such as calibration of robots, fault building, and performance tracking with digital displays (Singh & Ansari, 2024; Ambardar et al., 2023). Supervisory officers, in their turn, have to make sense out of data provided by AI devices to distribute human resources effectively and ensure service quality. In addition, the introduction of AI into the facility management brings in the notion of data accountability. The workers should be aware of the way the performance measures are created and evaluated to make sure that this is transparent and fair. Consequently, the conventional housekeepers as manual service providers are becoming more of a technician-operators hybrid with both mechanical knowledge and digital flexibility.

5.3. Food and Beverage Operations

AI is changing the operations in food and beverage (F&B) departments in menu engineering, demand forecasting, and food wastage. Predictive analytics can make chefs and managers predict the consumption patterns according to seasonality, the guests profile, and previous data. The management systems of AI-powered kitchens will streamline the process of purchasing ingredients and automate the process of managing inventory, thereby lowering expenditures and improving sustainability. F&B managers and chefs will then need to acquire skills in the interpretation of data and in the operational analytics. It becomes a critical managerial role to understand the role of the algorithmic insights in the purchasing, pricing and makeup of the menu. As an illustration, customer sentiment information retrieved in online reviews can be used to redesign the menu or create recipes (Singh & Singh, 2022; Singh & Hassan, 2024; Singh, 2024). Besides, moral and creative aspects of culinary service are still very human. The next generation of gastronomic innovation will be characterized by employees who can synthesize algorithmic knowledge and culinary creativity i.e., interpreting data trends without undermining cultural authenticity or creativity. In this way, talent management in the F&B sector will have to be in a middle ground between online competency and old craftsmanship and sense of touch.

5.4. Financial Strategy and Revenue Management

Revenue management is perhaps no area that has been more radically changed by AI. The artificial intelligence of machine learning algorithms now make the dynamic pricing models adjust the price of rooms in real-time based on the dynamics of demand, competition pricing, and analytics of guest behavior. Another value of AI tools is accuracy in the forecasts, and this assists organizations in maximizing occupancy and revenue at the same time. Consequently, the task of the revenue manager has changed to the collection of data and manual reporting to the interpretation of AI-generated information in a strategic manner (Dhakal & Tjokro, 2024; Singh & Sihmar, 2025; Ambardar et al., 2023). The practitioners in this field should be able to comprehend the functioning of predictive models, their reliability, as well as make informed choices that conform to the organizational goals. More to the point, the integration of financial analytics and personalization of guests implies that revenue managers will be required to work hand-in-hand with the marketing and operations departments, which once again makes cross-functional digital competencies essential. It is no longer about data entry but critical thinking and analytical storytelling, that is, conveying insights gained with the help of AI in a form that drives strategic action.

Customer Relationship Management and Marketing

Hospitality marketing and customer relationship management (CRM) is another area where AI has transformed marketing. AI-based CRM systems will automatically divide customers by their preferences, booking history, and behavioral insights. Marketing specialists should thus have the ability to visualize data, automate processes and generate content. They have to be capable of designing, interpreting, and optimizing campaigns based on insights of AI and maintain brand authenticity as well as emotional appeal (Seraj et al., 2025; Singh & Kumar, 2024; Singh & Kumar, 2021). Additionally, with the further automation of content creation with the help of generative AI, marketing personnel will have to exercise moral judgment, imagination, and narrative skill to ensure that there is a human voice in online communication. The marketers working in the hospitality sector of the future will be able to combine algorithmic wisdom with narrative design to create messages that are informed by data and are emotionally evocative.

The emergence of Hybrid Talent Profiles

In all operations, the integration of AI is bringing together a merger of technology and interpersonal skills. The workforce of the future will have to reflect on hybrid talent profiles, i.e. the ability of professionals to be as fluent on reading data as on reading emotions, and troubleshoot machines and create memorable experiences of the guests in the meantime. These changing talent needs demand educational change, in-the-job reskilling, and leadership training that put more focus on the technical skill and human common sense. The digital craftsman, a mix of analytics and empathy, algorithms and authenticity will be the future hospitality employee (Gursoy, 2025; Supina & Singh, 2024; Singh & Singh, 2022). Finally, the effectiveness of AI in the hospitality industry will rest not only on the level of technological advancement but also on the ability of human talent to change, work in tandem, and develop with intelligent systems. It is the organizations that develop this hybrid labor force of balancing the interpretation of data with the human narration that will define the new frontier to excellence in the hospitality industry.

TALENT TRANSFORMATION AND UPSKILLING STRATEGIES

The process of talent transformation in the industry of hospitality should be intentional, participatory and never-ending. The shift to an environment with AI involvement in hospitality necessitates a critical consideration in developing a plan of action to align the organization of workforce with innovation, sustainability, and human welfare. The process involves the establishment of organizational ecosystems in which learning is inbuilt in the daily work, with the aid of technology and a collective vision of synergy between humans and machines. The strategies presented below provide a comprehensive roadmap to talent transformation- the roadmap that will introduce a continuous learning process, digital fluency, emotional intelligence, and ethical leadership into the culture of hospitality organizations.

6.1 Continuous Learning Ecosystems

The development of continuous learning ecosystems is the basis of talent transformation. These ecosystems turn organizations into a non-static trainers into a dynamic learning community where employees can learn, apply and update skills on a real time basis. Conventional, infrequent training classes are no more during the age of AI, where the development of technologies is continuous. Alternatively, hospitality organizations need to adopt the concept of lifelong learning that is facilitated by digital learning and adaptive technologies (Chin et al., 2024; Singh, 2024; Singh & Supina, 2024). Individualized and evidence-based learning is now possible through AI-powered Learning Management Systems (LMS). Such systems monitor the development of employees, detect skills deficiencies, and provide specific learning modules in accordance with personal performance and career expectations. As an illustration, international hospitality chains like Marriott International and Hilton Hotels have already adopted adaptive learning technology that bases content on the position, location, and skill level of the employee. This will make learning relevant and interesting and minimize skill obsolescence and improve retention. Microlearning modules- brief, narrow and easy to learn lessons are also crucial in keeping the engagement sustained. Workers can learn on the device, through office applications or just through their mobile phones, and professional development is incorporated into their daily workflows without obstruction. In the long run, this kind of digital ecosystem promotes a self-directed learning culture, whereby employees will own their own development, which is facilitated by AI analytics that can control the progress and anticipate future skill requirements.

6.2 Human-Machine Collaboration Skills

Now that AI is coming in as a coworker, employees are forced to evolve collaborative intelligence, or the skill to work with machines effectively. The training plans do not need to focus on the technical skills only but should develop an awareness of decision-making processes, restrictions and biases of AI. Practically, it would be to educate the employees to question and assess the results of algorithms so that human judgment would be at the heart of the decision-making. As an example, when an artificial intelligence system recommends that prices be changed or that guests have specific preferences, employees have to consider the suggestion in the context of a larger ethical and experience issue (Marlapudi & Lenka, 2024; Singh & Kumar, 2024; Singh & Kumar, 2021). The knowledge of the process of AI system learning, analysis, and even error enables employees to be a crucial mediator between technology and the authenticity of the service. Simulation-based training and workshops may expose personnel to a real-world situation of human-AI interaction, which may include controlling automated check-in kiosks at the front desk or processing predictive model to guest satisfaction. It is aimed at developing confidence and competence in the human-machine interaction, and transforming the possible fear of automation into the empowerment of the knowledge.

6.3 Data Competency and Digital literacy

Digital literacy is not an elective attribute anymore, it is a part of the fundamental skill sets of any hospitality worker. As the business becomes more and more data-oriented, all the people, regardless of their rank, should know how to use the digital ecosystem safely, comprehend analytics, and handle data effectively. A broad training program should thus comprise of cybersecurity awareness, data privacy compliance, and analytics interpretation. The employees should be capable of identifying the possible cyber threats, safeguarding guest information, and a sense of ethics in handling information. Knowing the details of how data is gathered and utilized would also increase openness and confidence of guests--two essential resources in the context of increased sensitivity regarding privacy (Singh & Supina, 2024; Singh & Kumar, 2024; Singh & Kumar, 2021). Moreover, companies must promote the use of certifications on digital hospitality management, e.g., in the case of "AI for Hospitality Professionals" or "Digital Guest Experience Design." Such certifications not only formalize learning but also make a person more employable and credible to the organization. Institutionalizing digital literacy allows hospitality organizations to implement a system, in which all employees, without exception, including entry-level employees or senior executives, are capable of making decisions based on data and innovate.

6.4 Personalization of services and Emotional Intelligence

The human touch can never be replaced despite the changing technology in service delivery. Interpersonal sensitivity and emotional intelligence (EI) are critical to maintaining the core hospitality behavior, which is the authentic concern of guests. The skills of emotional intelligence should be thus incorporated into upskilling strategies with digital training. Empathy, storytelling, and cross-cultural communication programs may make employees customize the experience of guests in a manner that cannot be achieved by technology alone. As an example, although AI systems can find out what a returning guest likes, human intuition is the contextualization of the information, it is recollection of the name of a person, awareness of his/her mood, or even cultural peculiarities in communication (Singh & Ansari, 2024; Ambardar et al., 2023). More to the point, since AI will be involved in more interactions with guests via chatbots or virtual assistants, employees should be trained to express empathy and warmth online, building what scholars refer to as digital empathy. This ability will make the use of technology in communication sensitive to the heart. Striking a balance between the technological accuracy and emotional sincerity, the hospitality organizations will be able to produce professionals who are digital savvy and emotionally sensitive, i.e., a blend that will make it possible to call out the excellence in the age of AI.

6.5 Leadership Development

Future leaders will be knowledgeable of AI tools, and will ensure these technologies are deployed in a responsible and equitable manner. Digital ethics, sustainable innovation, and human-centered transformation are the areas to focus on in the leadership development programs. The leaders need to be educated to understand the ethical consequences of using AI: including algorithmic bias, data insecurity and substituting human labor should they be trained to create organizational cultures that uphold transparency and trust. Besides, hybrid teams require leaders who can use adaptive communication and change management techniques to guide members through uncertainty and boost morale (Singh, 2024; Singh & Supina, 2024; Singh & Kumar, 2024). The engagement can be reinforced by promoting participatory leadership, in which employees can implement their ideas in technology utilization and service improvement. Digital leadership schools within institutions such as Accor and IHG have already provided technological training as well as sustainability and diversity training as an example of the global brand preparing leaders to work in AI-enabled futures. However, because the AI age requires more than technology and requires at the same time more humanity, leadership in the AI age must be not only technologically knowledgeable but also endowed with the ability to lead innovation without compromising the ethical and emotional well-being of the hospitality experience.

7. POLICY AND INSTITUTIONAL VIEWS OF WORKFORCE DEVELOPMENT

The Industry effort alone is not enough to transform the workforce in the hospitality industry in terms of artificial intelligence (AI) and automation. Governments, schools, and professional organizations have to work together in a strategic manner to create an enabling environment of mass and sustainable workforce up-skilling. Individual learning, organizational adjustment and sectoral innovation are constructed on the scaffolding of institutional and policy interventions. The ecosystem can also collectively equip the hospitality industry with Industry 4.0 and beyond by combining digital literacy with the creation of cross-sector partnerships and the future-oriented regulation.

7.1 Academic Integration

Educational institutions are the building blocks of development of talent in hospitality. Hospitality curricula should incorporate AI literacy, data analytics, and digital innovation into its major framework to be relevant. The age-old education on hospitality used to be focused on delivery of services and operational effectiveness but now, it is being technologically oriented. Training AI-related courses for operations, digital guest experience design, and ethical technology management must be added to the traditional training of operations front office management, food production and customer service. Industry-academia associations are needed to bridge the knowledge gap between theory and reality.

7.2 Public- Private Partnerships (PPP)

States are very important in facilitating workforce change in the form of public-private partnerships (PPP). India's Skill India Mission is an illustration of how a program at the national scale can fast-track workforce preparation to digital transformation. Such alliances can finance AI-powered skill development hubs, virtual educational platforms and micro-credential programs that address the requirements of the hospitality industry.

7.3 Policy Frameworks

The regulatory base of digital upskilling and workforce inclusion should be developed by national and regional policies. Governments ought to incorporate digital competency, AI ethics, and life-long learning policies in tourism and hospitality policies (Singh & Hassan, 2024; Singh, 2024). Organizational commitment to skill development can be facilitated by policy frameworks that promote investment into training by companies either by tax incentives or grant-based subsidies. Moreover, the ministries of tourism are supposed to encourage AI-preparedness standards of hospitality businesses, so that the development of the technology is not accompanied by insufficient training of the workforce.

7.4 Contributing Collaborative Industry and World Governance

The role of industry associations and international organizations in the transformation of the workforce is critical in making it fair and inclusive. Ethical and inclusive digital transitions have been highlighted by the World Travel and Tourism Council (WTTC), the International Labour Organization (ILO) and the United Nations World Tourism Organization (UNWTO). Those bodies are able to come up with global training standards, certification frameworks, and best practice toolkits, which can lead the hospitality organizations in incorporating technology without rendering human labor redundant. Joint efforts may be aimed at safeguarding the vulnerable workers such as those in low-skill or seasonal jobs as reskilling and redeployment programs (Singh & Supina, 2024; Singh & Kumar, 2024). Alliances throughout the industry can also be encouraging in terms of sharing common AI learning repositories, benchmarking, and open-access training modules to democratize knowledge across the industry. Connecting international policy orientation to the domestic application, these organizations will be able to contribute to the equitable distribution of benefits of AI use in hospitality and make the process socially accountable. The sustainable change in the hospitality workforce cannot take place without institutional and policy alignment.

8. INTERNATIONAL CASES AND BEST PRACTICES

The reshaping of the hospitality workforce based on AI and automation is a trend that takes place across the world, as major organizations implement new approaches to learning and talent development. These projects show that talent transformation needs to be effective and should be based on the incorporation of digital technologies, ongoing learning environments, and human-technological capabilities appropriateness. The case studies presented below globally demonstrate the finest examples in workforce development that makes an AI-ready hospitality workforce.

8.1 Digital Learning Academy of Hilton

The Hilton has been at the frontline in transforming digital talent by setting its Digital Learning Academy. This platform was created to provide the employees in various departments with the skills in AI-based revenue management, data analytics and guest personalization systems. The academy is based on adaptive learning approach and the employees can complete their specific learning paths depending on their position, level of skills and their level of learning preferences. The Hilton initiative is anchored on the philosophy of learning in the flow of work and allows the staff to encounter microlearning modules as well as real-time AI simulation and simulation as part of the daily operations. As an illustration, front-office teams will be educated on the predictive guest behavior analytics, which allows them to anticipate requirements, whereas revenue managers will connect with machine-learning dashboards that help predict the occupancy patterns.

8.2 AI-based Analytics of Talent at Accor

Accor Hotels has adopted an analytical attitude to workforce development of AI-based human resource analytics. Using the functions of machine learning algorithms to implement them on its HR systems allows Accor to detect high-potential candidates, evaluate performance trends and forecast leadership requirements in the future. This data-based strategy makes the training investment focused and leadership pipelines strong during the period of technological change. Predictive talent analytics can help Accor to synchronize the corporate strategy and human resource planning. As an example, the system determines the skills gaps that involve digital skills and provides specific developmental programs to each employee.

8.3 Marriott ChatGPT-Powered Concierge Training.

The Marriott International has borne the AI-driven conversational learning via the ChatGPT-powered concierge training program. This is a pilot program based on the application of generative AI simulations where front-desk associates are trained to act in real-life communication situations (Singh & Sihmar, 2025; Ambardar et al., 2023). Employees converse with an AI-based chatbot who will simulate guest requests, inquiries, and complaints, and gives immediate feedback on the tone, empathy, and ability to solve a problem. Marriot incorporates the idea of scenario-based learning and natural language processing to improve the interpersonal and adaptive capabilities of its employees-qualities that cannot be eliminated by automation in the process of guest relations.

8.4 Tourism SkillsFuture Singapore Initiative

On the national level, the Singapore Tourism Board (STB) has put in place the Tourism SkillsFuture Initiative which is an all-round framework that aims at empowering tourism and hospitality professionals with digital and sustainable transformation skills. The short courses and certifications in the field of AI application, robotics management, and digital marketing will be available to professionals, which guarantees their ongoing professional development. This is a good example of productive public-private partnership, in which government facilitation, knowledge of the academic community, and industry demands intersect. The visionary attitude of Singapore indicates that the policy alignment and institutional encouragement are essential to the workforce preparedness at the sector level (Singh & Kumar, 2024; Singh & Kumar, 2021). In all these instances, the same trend is observed; the success of talent transformation is achieved when the learning technologies, organizational culture, and human values are aligned. Hilton and Marriott highlight the focus on digital learning ecosystems including AI implementation in training; Accor proves the analytical capacity of AI in the labor force planning; and Singapore proves the ability of national strategies to transform more than individual businesses.

9. IMPLICATIONS, AND FUTURE PROJECTIONS

Artificial intelligence (AI) application in the field of hospitality development of the workforce opens unprecedented prospects of efficiency, customization, and crisis. However, its implementation also reveals some of the structural, ethical, and cultural issues that lie deep-rooted and influence the way organizations and employees adjust to this change. Technological preparedness is not the only factor that determines the success of AI-based upskilling, but the ability of institutions to address change in a human and inclusive way is also crucial. It is important to comprehend these issues and trace the future directions in order to make sure that AI can be used to improve, but not totally destroy, the human spirit of hospitality.

9.1 Access and Equity

Digital divide is one of the most challenging issues of the workforce transformation by AI. The big international hotel corporations like the Marriott, Accor, and Hilton have the resources and the structure required to implement the AI systems, adaptive learning systems, and analytics-driven talent management software. Nonetheless, SMEs that make up most of the global hospitality industry do not have the resources necessary to invest in such technologies. The outcome is an increase in the disparity between large corporations and smaller, locally owned establishments with regard to the capabilities and productivity of their workforce. The disparity is not only based on access to technology but also training. The hospitality industry in developing economies has a large number of workers in informal/semi-skilled jobs with a low level of exposure to digital tools.

9.2 Job Displacement Apprehension and Organizational Retaliation

The intrusion of AI into the work of conventional services has provoked the increasing anxiety related to job loss among the hospitality workers. Elimination of jobs due to automation in check-ins, housekeeping and customer service is a matter of concern due to its redundancy aspect particularly in jobs that are characterized by repetitive duties (Singh & Sihmar, 2025; Singh, 2025). This fear may be in the form of opposition to adoption of AI, low morale to AI, or even active resistance against technological endeavors. Change management strategies that organizational leaders should embrace should therefore be based on transparency, communication, and reassurance. The employees are to be involved in the process of transformation at its initial stage and informed about the ways in which AI will help them rather than dwindle their work.

9.3 Ethical Use of Data

The implementation of AI in hospitality is also based on data-based decision-making, which includes the preferences of the guests, data on employee performance, and forecasting. But this reliance creates some vital ethics and privacy issues. The fact that the employee and guest data are being collected and analyzed brings up the issue of consent, surveillance, and the ownership of data. Mishandling of sensitive information may result in loss of trust and reputational and legal consequences to organizations (Singh & Ansari, 2024; Ambardar et al., 2023). To prevent such problems, hospitality organizations need to introduce clear data governance schemes in accordance with the international regulations like the General Data Protection Regulation (GDPR). Data ethics should be taught to the employees, and they should be familiar with the capabilities and limitations of AI analytics. Ethical applications of AI should be based on explicit guidelines on how personal data is gathered, treated and used in training or human resource management.

9.4 Curriculum Lag and Educational Adaptation

The other important impediment is present in the system of hospitality education and training, most of which are still rooted on the old pedagogical model (Singh & Hassan, 2024). The industry is quickly changing with the aid of AI, robotics, and analytics, but the curricula do not always keep up with the changes, graduates end up unprepared to work in the modern field. Resolving this gap in the curriculum involves a strong partnership between the academic, industry and the government. At the same time, faculty training and the investment in the system of online teaching are required to make sure that teachers are able to provide the new-age skills.

FUTURE DIRECTIONS

In the future, human-AI symbiosis is the future of AI-based workforce development in the hospitality industry, where technology will not compete but support human creativity and empathy. Such inventions indicate a greater change in job-centered training to lifelong learning ecosystems-flowing adaptive systems that train employees to perpetual change. Agility, creativity and digital resilience will be the defining traits of the future workforce, rather than the fixed skill sets. Even in the context of the increased innovation in the hospitality industry, which is moving in the direction of an AI-enhanced future, the industry needs to base its innovations on the ethical and humanistic foundations. Artificial intelligence ought to complement but not to crowd out human employees. It is ultimately hoped to foster environments in which technology enhances the factors that have always made hospitality distinctly human responsive, empathy, warmth, and creativity and ensure that technological advancement is not made at the cost of humanity.

CONCLUSION

The acceptance of the hospitality industry into the realm of AI is forcing the definition of the skillfulness, competency, and employability to be redefined. Talent transformation is not a unanimous project but an ongoing transformation process, in which education, industry and policy have to converge. AI has remodeled the work structure acting to substitute the monotonous task but enhancing creativity, empathy, and strategy. The issue is to make sure that the workforce keeps up with technology, and it becomes digital-deft and human-sensible. Upskilling and reskilling are hence both moral and strategic needs. The future of hospitality relies on professionals who are capable of interpreting data in an insightful manner, employing technology in an ethical way, and engaging the guests in an authentic manner. The industry can become sustainable and human-focused by cultivating learning organizations and adopting collaborative intelligence and instilling AI literacy. Simply stated, AI era does not decrease the worth of the hospitality, it raises it. The human touch, smartened by smart technology, ceases to be a thing of the past, and a foundation of the excellence in the future.

REFERENCES

Alhelal, A. A., Alshiha, A. A., & Al-Romeedy, B. S. (2025). AI-Driven Sustainable Competitive Advantage in Tourism and Hospitality: Mediating Roles of Digital Culture and Skills. *Sustainability (Basel)*, *17*(19), 8903. DOI: 10.3390/su17198903

Ambardar, A., Singh, A., & Singh, V. (2023). Barriers in Implementing Ergonomic Practices in Hotels- A Study on five star hotels in NCR region. *International Journal of Hospitality and Tourism Systems*, *16*(2), 11–17.

Arora, M., Ahmad, V., Arora, T., & Kumar, R. (2024). Digital Transformation and Talent Management. In Green Metaverse for Greener Economies (pp. 50-70). CRC Press. DOI: 10.1201/9781032638188-4

Chin, Y. S., Mohamad, A. A., & Lo, M. C. (2024). Harnessing the power of artificial intelligence (AI): A paradigm shift in HRM practices for employee sustainable performance. *Global Knowledge, Memory and Communication*. Advance online publication. DOI: 10.1108/GKMC-06-2024-0355

Das, R. C., Basavaraj, S., Thankachan, J., & Thaliyan, D. (2025). The Impact of AI and Agile HR on Talent Acquisition and Onboarding in the Service Industry. In *AI and Innovation in HRM* (pp. 394–416). Routledge. DOI: 10.4324/9781003522157-24

Dhakal, S. P., & Tjokro, S. (2024). Local Tourism Businesses in the Digital Era: Implications for Bridging the Critical Skills Gap in Indonesia. In The Future of Work in the Asia Pacific (pp. 146-157). Routledge.

El Hajal, G., & Yeoman, I. (2024). AI and the future of talent management in tourism and hospitality. *Current Issues in Tourism*, ●●●, 1–18. DOI: 10.1080/13683500.2024.2439395

Ercik, C., & Kardaş, K. (2024). Reflections of digital technologies on human resources management in the tourism sector. *Worldwide Hospitality and Tourism Themes*, *16*(5), 646–663. DOI: 10.1108/WHATT-09-2024-0208

Ersanlı, C. Y., Çelik, F., Barjesteh, H., Duran, V., & Manoochehrzadeh, M. (2025). A review of global reskilling and upskilling initiatives in the age of AI. *AI and Ethics*, *5*(6), 1–10. DOI: 10.1007/s43681-025-00767-9

Gursoy, D. (2025). Artificial intelligence (AI) technology, its applications and the use of AI powered devices in hospitality service experience creation and delivery. *International Journal of Hospitality Management*, *129*, 104212. DOI: 10.1016/j.ijhm.2025.104212

Hussain, S., Singh, A. M., Mohanty, P., & Gavinolla, M. R. (2023). Next generation employability and career sustainability in the hospitality industry 5.0. *Worldwide Hospitality and Tourism Themes, 15*(3), 308–321. DOI: 10.1108/WHATT-01-2023-0011

Marlapudi, K., & Lenka, U. (2024). Unlocking the potential: Redefining talent and competency mapping for Industry 4.0. *Management Research Review, 47*(11), 1805–1832. DOI: 10.1108/MRR-07-2023-0496

Metta, S., & Kumar, S. V. S. (2026). AI-Driven HR Transformation in Service Industry: Opportunities, Challenges, Ethical Considerations and Strategic Implications. AI and Innovation in HRM, 191-205.

Santandreu Calonge, D., Kamalov, F., Medina Aguerrebere, P., Hassock, L., Smail, L., Yousef, D., ... & Abdulla, N. (2025). Upskilling and reskilling in the United Arab Emirates: Future-proofing careers with AI skills. Journal of Adult and Continuing Education, 14779714251315288.

Seraj, A. H. A., Hasanein, A. M., Al-Romeedy, B. S., & Elziny, M. N. (2025). Redefining the Digital Frontier: Digital Leadership, AI, and Innovation Driving Next-Generation Tourism and Hospitality. *Administrative Sciences, 15*(9), 369. DOI: 10.3390/admsci15090369

Seyitoğlu, F., Costa, C., Martins, M., & Malta, A. M. (2023). The future of tourism and hospitality labour: Challenges, requirements, trends, skills and the impact of technology. *Current Issues in Tourism*, •••, 1–15. DOI: 10.1080/13683500.2023.2286291

Singh, A. (2024). Quality of Work-Life Practices in the Indian Hospitality Sector: Future Challenges and Prospects. In Valeri, M., & Sousa, B. (Eds.), *Human Relations Management in Tourism* (pp. 208–224). IGI Global., DOI: 10.4018/979-8-3693-1322-0.ch010

Singh, A. (2025). Analysis of Perceptions on Employment of differently-abled People in the Indian Hotel Industry. *Pasos (El Sauzal), 23*(1), 167–183. DOI: 10.25145/j.pasos.2025.23.011

Singh, A., & Ansari, A. I. (2024). Role of Training and Development in Employee Motivation: Tourism and Hospitality Sector. In Mazurowski, T. (Ed.), *Enhancing Employee Motivation Through Training and Development* (pp. 248–261). IGI Global., DOI: 10.4018/979-8-3693-1674-0.ch011

Singh, A., & Hassan, S. C. (2024), "Identifying the Skill Gap in the Workplace and Their Challenges in Hospitality and Tourism Organisations", Thake, A.M., Sood, K., Özen, E. and Grima, S. (Ed.) Contemporary Challenges in Social Science Management: Skills Gaps and Shortages in the Labour Market (Contemporary Studies in Economic and Financial Analysis, Vol. 112B), Emerald Publishing Limited, Leeds, pp. 101-114. DOI: 10.1108/S1569-37592024000112B006

Singh, A., & Kumar, S. (2021). Identifying Innovations in Human Resources: Academia and Industry Perspectives. In Pathak, A., & Rana, S. (Eds.), *Transforming Human Resource Functions With Automation* (pp. 104–120). IGI Global. DOI: 10.4018/978-1-7998-4180-7.ch006

Singh, A., & Kumar, S. (2024). Effective Talent Management Practices Implemented in the Hospitality Sector. In Christiansen, B., Aziz, M., & O'Keeffe, E. (Eds.), *Global Practices on Effective Talent Acquisition and Retention* (pp. 126–144). IGI Global., DOI: 10.4018/979-8-3693-1938-3.ch008

Singh, A., & Sihmar, P. (2025). Higher Education Institution Sustainability: Role of Green Human Resource Management. In Adu-Gyamfi, M., Boateng, F., & Atiku, S. (Eds.), *Green HRM Awareness and Training in Higher Education Institutions* (pp. 1–14). IGI Global Scientific Publishing., DOI: 10.4018/979-8-3693-2956-6.ch001

Singh, A., & Singh, V. K. (2022). The impact of ergonomic practices on housekeeping employee retention and efficiency in hotels during COVID-19 in India. Turyzm/Tourism, 32(2), 29–50. DOI: 10.18778/0867-5856.32.2.02

Singh, A., & Supina, S. (2024). Talent Acquisition and Retention in Hospitality Industry: Current Skill Gaps and Challenges. In Christiansen, B., Aziz, M., & O'Keeffe, E. (Eds.), *Global Practices on Effective Talent Acquisition and Retention* (pp. 363–379). IGI Global., DOI: 10.4018/979-8-3693-1938-3.ch020

Supina, S., & Singh, A. (2024). Exploring the Presence and Adoption of Quality of Work-Life Dimensions in the Hotel Industry? *African Journal of Hospitality, Tourism and Leisure, 13*(2), 421–429. DOI: 10.46222/ajhtl.19770720.524

Tan, K. L., Yeap, P. F., Cheong, K. C. K., & Loganathan, S. R. (2025). Crafting an organizational strategy for the new era: A qualitative study of artificial intelligence transformation in a homegrown Singaporean hotel chain. *Business Process Management Journal, 31*(8), 104–123. DOI: 10.1108/BPMJ-11-2024-1086

Wider, W., Ho, C. P., Wu, C., Lee, H. P. T., & Tee, M. (2025). Adopting AI for HRM in the Malaysian hotel industry: A Delphi study. *Journal of Hospitality and Tourism Technology*, •••, 1–21. DOI: 10.1108/JHTT-03-2025-0202

Chapter 5

The Nexus Among Population Distribution and Climate Risk?

Management in the Case of Saudi Arabia

Walid Chouari
https://orcid.org/0000-0001-7038-8678
College of Arts, King Faisal University, Saudi Arabia

ABSTRACT

The geographical distribution of the population in Saudi Arabia plays a crucial role in climate risk management. The country is characterized by a high concentration of urban population, particularly in major cities such as Riyadh, Jeddah, and Dammam, while vast desert areas remain sparsely populated. This spatial configuration exacerbates the varying vulnerabilities to climate hazards: flash floods and heat islands in densely populated urban areas, water scarcity and desertification in rural and desert regions, and coastal threats related to flooding and sea-level rise. This study demonstrates that climate risk management must take into account this territorial heterogeneity to develop appropriate public policies. Recent initiatives, including those within the framework of Vision 2030 and innovative urban projects such as NEOM, illustrate the Kingdom's commitment to integrating sustainability and resilience into its spatial planning.

DOI: 10.4018/979-8-3373-8197-8.ch005

1. INTRODUCTION

Saudi Arabia lies at the intersection of extreme climate zones: both deserts, with low and erratic rainfall, and coastal, exposed to the effects of global climate change such as sea-level rise, coastal erosion, and flooding. The country experiences summers with temperatures frequently exceeding 50°C, increasing energy demands, causing health stress, and reducing the productivity of outdoor activities (Atlantic Council, 2023). Furthermore, its renewable water resources are limited and significantly dependent on desalination and fossil aquifers, making water stress a major current concern (Atlantic Council, 2023; G20 Climate Risk Atlas, 2024).

The issue of population distribution is of crucial importance for vulnerability to climate risks. In Saudi Arabia, the population is highly concentrated in large cities such as Riyadh, Jeddah, and Dammam, while vast desert regions remain sparsely populated or virtually uninhabited. This spatial distribution directly influences the ability to anticipate, prevent, and respond to climate hazards. For example, in dense urban areas, the combination of impermeable surfaces, insufficient drainage, and intense rainfall events favors flash floods, as observed in Jeddah (Water, 2024; "Flood Risk and Vulnerability…", 2023). Conversely, in rural or desert areas, the challenges relate more to water availability, desertification, geographic isolation, and limited infrastructure.

The problem of this work can be formulated as follows: How does the spatial distribution of the population in Saudi Arabia influence the management and adaptation to climate risks? The central hypothesis is that highly urbanized areas (such as Riyadh, Jeddah, Dammam) face specific challenges vulnerable infrastructure, urban flooding, heat islands, pressure on public services while sparsely populated areas present other types of vulnerabilities, including difficult access to essential resources (water, health), desertification, and a lower capacity to react quickly to extreme events.

2. THEORETICAL AND METHODOLOGICAL CONTEXT

2.1. Definitions

- Climate risk: Climate risk is any weather or climate phenomenon that is likely to cause human, economic, or environmental damage. This includes drought, extreme heat waves, flash floods, sandstorms, and coastal impacts related to rising sea levels.
- Geographic distribution of the population: This concept refers to the way in which individuals are spatially distributed across a territory, in particu-

lar the difference between urban concentration (high density in cities, large agglomerations) and rural dispersion (sparsely populated areas, isolated villages, desert areas). This distribution influences exposure, vulnerability and adaptive capacity to risks.

2.2. Theoretical framework

The work is based on two main approaches:

1. Geography of risks: This approach studies how hazards (physical, climatic) interact with the vulnerabilities of populations and infrastructures according to their spatial location, density, socio-economic organization, etc. It allows us to understand how topography, proximity or not of resources, urban planning, or even infrastructures influence the severity of climate impacts.
2. Climate resilience: This concept concerns the capacity of systems (urban, rural, ecological) to anticipate, absorb, recover from extreme events, and adapt to changing climatic conditions. It is linked to governance, territorial planning, sustainable infrastructure, as well as social participation.

These theoretical frameworks make it possible to articulate how spatial distribution (urban vs. rural, coastal areas, desert areas) modifies not only exposure to climate risks but also the management capacity (prevention, adaptation, response) of the State and communities.

2.3. Methodology

To investigate how the geographical distribution of the population in Saudi Arabia influences the management and adaptation to climate risks, the methodology will follow the following axes:

- **Documentary analysis**: Review and synthesis of recent and relevant sources, including:
    - IPCC reports for climate projections and patterns of increased climate hazards.
    - The G20 Climate Risk Atlas for the specific situation of Saudi Arabia.
    - Recent national statistics: The Saudi General Authority for Statistics' (2024) average population estimates indicate that the total population exceeds 35 million, with an annual growth rate of around 4.7%.
    - Urbanization/rurality data: for example, the percentage of rural (~15%) and urban (~85%) population in recent years.

- **Case studies**: Selection of representative areas according to their geographical and climatic characteristics:
    - o Jeddah and its flash floods: a coastal urban case subject to intense rainfall and poor drainage, highlighting urban vulnerability.
    - o Najd region (inland desert areas): low population density, challenges related to water stress, desertification, access to services.
    - o Gulf Coastal Areas: Threats from rising sea levels, coastal erosion, storms, and high concentrations of infrastructure and population.
- **Quantitative and qualitative analyses**:
    - o Quantitative: use of demographic data (urban vs. rural population, growth rates), historical climate data and projections (rainfall, temperature, frequency of extreme events).
    - o Qualitative: interviews or analysis of political documents (urban plans, climate adaptation plans), governance reports, project evaluations (drainage infrastructure, water policies, Vision 2030 projects).
- **Spatial comparison**: comparison between densely populated regions vs. sparsely populated areas to identify divergences in terms of exposure, vulnerability and response capacity.

2.3. Recent empirical data

Some key data to provide context:

- By 2024, the population of Saudi Arabia will exceed 35.3 million, according to estimates by the Saudi General Authority for Statistics.
- The percentage of rural population is about 15% of the total (i.e. ~5.2-5.3 million people), while about 85% live in urban areas.
- The G20 Climate Risk Atlas predicts a significant increase in the frequency of droughts and heatwaves if emissions trajectories remain high, increasing risks for vulnerable areas.

3. GEOGRAPHICAL DISTRIBUTION OF THE POPULATION IN SAUDI ARABIA

The spatial structure of the Saudi population is characterized by pronounced urbanization and a very high concentration in a few major agglomerations, contrasting with vast, sparsely populated interior spaces. These structural features result from recent historical trajectories industrialization, oil development, and infrastructure investment policies that have accelerated migration to cities and the formation of large metropolitan centers.

3.1. Urban concentration

The share of the population living in urban areas is currently very high: recent data indicate that urbanization reaches around 84–85% of the total population, placing Saudi Arabia well above the world average (≈ 62%) (The Global Economy, 2024; World Bank, 2024). This concentration is reflected in the dominance of a small number of cities: Riyadh, Jeddah, Makkah, Madinah, and the East Coast urban complex (Dammam/Khobar/Dhahran) account for a disproportionate share of the population and economic activity. Large cities are administrative, industrial, and commercial centers that attract population, investment, and services (Saudi General Authority for Statistics, 2024; World Population Review, 2025).

This rapid urbanization has produced high-density spatial configurations in rapidly expanding urban cores and peripheries, with direct consequences on exposure to climate risks: increased impervious surfaces, pressures on drainage systems, urban heat islands and a high concentration of critical infrastructure.

3.2. Low density in desert areas

In contrast, vast inland regions particularly the Najd Plateau and the immense Rubʿ al-Khali (Empty Quarter) desert complex have very low population densities. These spaces, sometimes virtually uninhabited over hundreds of thousands of square kilometers, are home to dispersed communities (oases, small towns, Bedouin populations) and limited infrastructure (Britannica; recent geographical studies). Low density poses specific challenges in terms of access to services, the cost of emergency response, and sustainable water resource management: protection or adaptation measures must be designed for large and sparsely populated territories, which changes operational priorities relative to urban areas.

3.3. Strategic coastline and concentration of infrastructure

The coasts of the Red Sea (west) and the Arabian Gulf (east) are home not only to major urban areas but also to most of the economic infrastructure ports, petrochemical complexes, industrial and tourist areas. Coastal cities such as Jeddah (Red Sea) and the East Coast complex (Dammam/Khobar/Dhahran) play a central role in the national economy; however, their coastal location makes them particularly vulnerable to climate risks associated with intense rainfall, coastal erosion, and, in the medium to long term, sea-level rise (Almheiri, 2024; reports and studies on coastal development). The concentration of activities on the coast partly explains the policy-making attention paid to coastal development projects (tourism, logistics) and the need to strengthen the resilience of maritime and urban infrastructure.

3.4. Summary and implications for risk management

The spatial distribution of the population in Saudi Arabia creates a dual challenge: on the one hand, dense urban areas require adaptation strategies focused on resilient urban planning, stormwater management, and heat island reduction; on the other, sparsely populated areas require solutions adapted to dispersion (warning networks covering large territories, intervention logistics, preservation of water resources). Finally, the concentration of critical infrastructure on the coasts makes the integration of coastal planning into national climate risk management policies a priority.

4. MAJOR CLIMATE RISKS IN SAUDI ARABIA

Saudi Arabia is subject to a range of climate risks closely linked to its geographical characteristics and arid climate. The main identified threats include drought and water stress, extreme heat waves, flash floods, and sandstorms. These increasingly frequent and intense phenomena are amplified by global climate change and the rapid growth of urban areas.

4.1. Drought and water stress

Drought is the most persistent climate risk in the Kingdom. The country receives an average of less than 100 mm of precipitation per year, with significant spatial and temporal disparities (World Bank, 2024). Renewable water resources are extremely limited, and more than 80% of the water used comes from desalination and non-renewable groundwater (Ministry of Environment, Water and Agriculture, 2023).

The consequences of water stress are particularly felt in rural and agricultural areas, particularly in the Najd and western regions of the country, where increasing water scarcity is compromising agricultural productivity and food security (Alotaibi et al., 2023). This situation is aggravated by rising temperatures and increased evaporation, making traditional agricultural practices increasingly difficult to maintain. Reliance on irrigation technologies and fossil resources increases the long-term vulnerability of the agricultural sector.

4.2. Extreme heat waves and urban heat islands

Extreme heat waves pose another major threat, particularly in major cities such as Riyadh, Jeddah, and Dammam. Temperatures frequently exceed 48°C during the summer, with peaks reaching 52°C in some inland areas (Saudi Meteorological Authority, 2024).

These extreme conditions exacerbate the phenomenon of urban heat islands, where the concentration of impermeable surfaces, the density of buildings and the low vegetation cover lead to local temperatures 3 to 7 °C higher than those of peripheral areas (Maghrabi, 2024). This phenomenon increases health risks (heat stroke, dehydration), energy consumption (air conditioning) and electricity-related emissions, creating a vicious circle between urbanization and global warming.

Recent urban policies tend to integrate the fight against heat islands through urban greening, the use of reflective materials and the design of more sustainable development plans, in line with the objectives of Vision 2030.

4.3. Flash floods

Despite its arid climate, Saudi Arabia regularly experiences intense rainfall events causing flash flooding, particularly in coastal urban areas. The cities of Jeddah, Makkah, and Madinah have been repeatedly hit by destructive floods, including in 2009, 2011, and 2020, causing significant human and material losses (Almazroui et al., 2022; Water, 2023).

These events result from a combination of rapid urbanization, an inadequate drainage network, and topography that favors rapid runoff. Recent climate models predict an increase in the intensity and frequency of extreme rainfall events in some parts of the country, emphasizing the need to invest in resilient water infrastructure and early warning systems.

4.4. Sandstorms and desertification

Sandstorms, which are frequent in the Arabian Peninsula, represent an environmental, health, and economic risk. They affect air quality, visibility, and transportation, while also impacting respiratory health (Alghamdi et al., 2023). These phenomena are linked to soil degradation, loss of vegetation cover, and increased desertification in several regions of the country, particularly in the north and center.

According to the G20 Climate Risk Atlas (2024), desertification is progressing due to the combined effects of global warming, overexploitation of groundwater, and agricultural pressure. Reforestation and soil restoration programs, such as the

Saudi Green Initiative, have been implemented to mitigate these effects and improve the ecological resilience of the territory.

4.5. Summary

Saudi Arabia faces a diversity of climate risks, the spatial distribution of which reflects the country's geographical contrasts. Coastal urban areas experience recurrent flooding and intense heatwaves, while inland areas face drought, desertification, and sandstorms. This diversity of hazards requires differentiated strategies across territories and reinforces the need for integrated planning based on sustainable resource management, urban resilience, and institutional coordination.

5. IMPACT OF GEOGRAPHICAL DISTRIBUTION ON RISK MANAGEMENT

The geographic distribution of Saudi Arabia's population profoundly influences climate risk management strategies and capacities. The contrasts between dense urban areas, dispersed rural areas, and coastal regions require differentiated approaches to infrastructure, land-use planning, and public policy. This spatial diversity creates asymmetries of vulnerability and resilience to climate hazards.

5.1. Dense urban areas: infrastructure and resilience

Major Saudi cities, including Riyadh, Jeddah, and Dammam, concentrate a major share of the population and economic infrastructure. This urban density increases risks in the event of extreme weather events, including floods and heat waves. The Jeddah floods of 2009, 2011, and 2020 revealed the limitations of drainage systems and insufficient urban planning in the face of intense rainfall (Almazroui et al., 2022; Water, 2023).

In these areas, risk management requires strengthening resilient infrastructure: modernizing stormwater drainage networks, improving urban planning, and integrating green spaces to mitigate heat islands (Maghrabi, 2024). Vision 2030 emphasizes urban sustainability through programs such as the Saudi Green Initiative and smart city projects aimed at optimizing energy and environmental management (Ministry of Municipal and Rural Affairs and Housing, 2024).

However, the concentration of population in a small number of urban centers makes the system more vulnerable to localized crises: an extreme climatic event can affect a large number of inhabitants and disrupt essential economic functions.

5.2. Dispersed rural areas: accessibility and structural vulnerability

Rural areas, characterized by their dispersion and low density, pose specific challenges in terms of accessibility and risk management. The remoteness of urban centers makes it difficult to quickly implement relief and emergency infrastructure in the event of sandstorms, drought, or flash floods (Alotaibi et al., 2023).

These territories are also more exposed to the effects of drought and desertification, due to their reliance on traditional agriculture and groundwater exploitation. The scarcity of water resources limits the adaptive capacity of rural communities, increasing their socio-economic vulnerability (Ministry of Environment, Water and Agriculture, 2023). Public policies now encourage the diversification of water sources and the adoption of more sustainable irrigation technologies, but their application remains uneven across regions.

5.3. Coastal zones: vulnerability and adaptation issues

The coastal areas of the Red Sea and the Arabian Gulf are home to strategic infrastructure (ports, refineries, industrial complexes, tourist areas) and a dense population. These areas are exposed to a combination of climate risks: urban flooding, coastal erosion, salinization of groundwater, and sea level rise (Almheiri, 2024).

Recent studies highlight that sea level rise could threaten some coastal infrastructure by 2050–2100 if global emissions do not decrease (G20 Climate Risk Atlas, 2024). In response, Saudi authorities are integrating coastal adaptation measures into their development plans, notably in the NEOM and The Line projects, which aim to create climate-resilient and technologically sustainable cities. These projects are experimenting with new approaches to linear urban planning, energy efficiency, and carbon neutrality (Ponzini, 2024).

5.4. Public policies and risk governance

Vision 2030 is the central strategic framework for integrating sustainability into national policies. It includes energy diversification, environmental protection, and the creation of smart urban areas that are resilient to climate change. Programs such as the Saudi Green Initiative and the National Environment Strategy reinforce this momentum by promoting reforestation, integrated water resource management, and carbon emission reduction (Ministry of Economy and Planning, 2023).

However, several researchers emphasize that the success of these policies depends on institutional coordination between the national and local levels, and the ability to integrate geographical specificities into planning (Alharbi & Alotaibi,

2024). The effectiveness of climate risk management thus relies on the differentiated implementation of strategies adapted to the density, location and environmental conditions of each region.

5.5. Summary

In short, the geographic distribution of Saudi Arabia's population decisively shapes priorities and methods for managing climate risks. Urban areas require infrastructure and planning solutions; rural areas require increased resource and community resilience support; and coastal areas require an integrated approach combining physical adaptation and urban innovation. The challenge for the Kingdom lies in building territorial governance capable of articulating these different scales of vulnerability.

6. DISCUSSION

Analysis of the geographic distribution of population and climate risks in Saudi Arabia highlights a series of structural tensions between rapid urban growth, environmental fragility, and institutional adaptation capacities. This discussion offers a critical reading of the results presented, comparing them with regional dynamics and the prospects for sustainable climate governance.

6.1. Urban concentration and systemic vulnerability

Urban concentration is both a driver of development and a source of vulnerability. Major Saudi cities—Riyadh, Jeddah, and Dammam—concentrate most of the country's economic, logistical, and administrative infrastructure. In the event of a major climate crisis (floods, extreme heat waves, sandstorms), these urban centers can become points of systemic fragility where disruptions quickly spread throughout economic and social networks (Almazroui et al., 2022).

Recent studies highlight that unplanned urbanization amplifies heat islands, increases energy demand for cooling, and increases the health vulnerability of populations (Maghrabi, 2024). This observation is consistent with the conclusions of international literature according to which urban densification, without integrated ecological management, tends to aggravate the impacts of climate change (Revi et al., 2024). The challenge is therefore to integrate sustainable urban planning as a central lever of resilience, through green infrastructure, natural ventilation corridors, and materials with high thermal reflectivity.

6.2. Sustainability challenges in desert and rural areas

The desert areas of Najd and Rubʿ al-Khali, although sparsely populated, present considerable sustainability challenges. Their isolation, combined with limited water availability and accelerated land degradation, makes any adaptation strategy difficult without advanced water management technologies (Alotaibi et al., 2023).

Chronic water stress is driving the Kingdom to invest in desalination, wastewater recycling, and agricultural modernization but these solutions remain energy-intensive and costly in the long term (Ministry of Environment, Water and Agriculture, 2023). The challenge is therefore to balance local development needs with ecological sustainability, particularly in regions where agriculture relies on non-renewable fossil aquifers. Pilot experiments conducted in certain oases, integrating precision irrigation practices, illustrate the beginnings of an adjustment towards territorial water resilience.

6.3. Regional comparison: lessons from the Gulf

Comparisons with other Gulf states, such as the United Arab Emirates and Qatar, reveal similar trends but differentiated approaches. All share a reliance on rapid urbanization and desalination, but the Emirates stand out for their more advanced integration of green urban planning and early warning systems (Almheiri, 2024; Reiche, 2023). Qatar, for its part, is investing in research on extreme heat management and climate-responsive building design.

These regional examples highlight the need for Saudi Arabia to accelerate the implementation of a multi-level adaptation strategy, combining technological innovation, territorial governance, and citizen participation. While massive investments in projects like NEOM or The Line embody a futuristic vision of resilience, their transferability to other regions of the country remains limited by geographic and socioeconomic disparities (Ponzini, 2024).

6.4. Perspectives: towards integrated climate governance

The results of this study suggest that climate resilience in Saudi Arabia will depend on the ability to integrate spatial planning, green infrastructure, and early warning systems. Developing spatial modeling and real-time climate data management tools could improve crisis prevention and response, particularly in high-density urban areas (G20 Climate Risk Atlas, 2024).

Furthermore, integrating nature into urban policies parks, green roofs, green buffer zones represent a promising avenue for reducing local temperatures, improving air quality, and increasing hydrological resilience. Finally, the transition to participatory climate governance, involving local authorities, businesses, and citizens, represents a necessary evolution for the objectives of Vision 2030 to translate into concrete territorial actions (Alharbi & Alotaibi, 2024).

6.5. Interim conclusion

Ultimately, the geographic distribution of Saudi Arabia's population shapes not only the country's climate vulnerability, but also its potential forms of adaptation. Challenges vary across contexts urban, rural, or coastal but addressing them requires a systemic approach that combines innovation, territorial equity, and ecological sustainability. From this perspective, Saudi Arabia has significant potential to become a regional laboratory for climate resilience, provided it fully integrates the spatial dimension into its environmental governance.

7. CONCLUSION AND RECOMMENDATIONS

7.1. Reminder of the problem and summary of the results

This study examined the influence of population distribution on climate risk management in Saudi Arabia. It showed that the spatial configuration of the population marked by high urban concentration, low rural density, and strategic coastal occupation directly conditions the country's vulnerability and adaptive capacity to climate hazards.

Dense urban areas, such as Riyadh, Jeddah, or Dammam, are particularly exposed to the risks of flooding and extreme heat waves, due to their increasing impermeability and energy dependence (Almazroui et al., 2022; Maghrabi, 2024). Conversely, rural and desert areas face structural challenges related to water scarcity, desertification, and remoteness from emergency services (Alotaibi et al., 2023). Finally, coastal regions, although vital to the national economy, are threatened in the medium and long term by rising sea levels and coastal erosion (Almheiri, 2024).

Thus, the geographical distribution of the population is not a simple demographic factor: it constitutes a strategic parameter of climate management, determining the priorities, the necessary infrastructures and the distribution of resources in public resilience policies.

7.2. Towards differentiated territorial planning

The results suggest the need for a territorialized approach to climate risk management, in which each type of space urban, rural, desert, or coastal benefits from policies adapted to its environmental and socio-economic specificities.

- In dense cities, it is a priority to strengthen urban resilience through the provision of efficient drainage infrastructure, sustainable transport networks and green spaces capable of reducing the effects of urban heat (Ministry of Municipal and Rural Affairs and Housing, 2024).
- In rural areas, policies should aim to improve water security and agricultural resilience, by supporting the modernization of irrigation systems, crop diversification and the promotion of water-efficient technologies (Ministry of Environment, Water and Agriculture, 2023).
- In desert regions, priority must be given to the protection of natural resources and the development of renewable energy projects, which can stimulate sustainable development while limiting environmental pressures.
- Finally, in coastal areas, it is essential to develop climate change adaptation plans integrating coastal management, protection of port infrastructure and long-term urban planning (G20 Climate Risk Atlas, 2024).

7.3. Strategic recommendations

In light of this analysis, several directions can be formulated:

- Developing sustainable and resilient cities: Integrating environmental sustainability into the heart of urban planning, promoting compact, climate-adapted city models with green infrastructure. Pilot projects such as NEOM or The Line can serve as laboratories for urban innovation, provided that their lessons are disseminated throughout the territory (Ponzini, 2024).
- Strengthening hydraulic and drainage infrastructure: Investing in the modernization of stormwater management systems, hydrological monitoring, and water recycling. Better interconnection between water and urban policies is necessary to anticipate drought and flood events.
- Implementing differentiated policies according to geographical areas: Develop regional risk management plans adapted to local contexts: urban resilience in metropolitan areas, agricultural sustainability in rural areas, and coastal protection in maritime areas. This spatial differentiation must be based on detailed climate data and territorial modeling tools.

- Strengthening early warning and local governance systems: Deploy integrated climate monitoring networks capable of rapidly detecting emerging risks. At the same time, strengthen the capacity of local authorities to respond effectively by promoting training, participatory planning, and inter-institutional coordination (Alharbi & Alotaibi, 2024).
- Integrating resilience into Vision 2030: Anchoring climate resilience objectives in the pillars of Vision 2030 sustainability, innovation, and economic diversification to ensure coherence between economic development and environmental adaptation (Ministry of Economy and Planning, 2023).

7.4. General conclusion

Ultimately, climate risk management in Saudi Arabia cannot be separated from the geographic distribution of its population. This spatial dimension determines the nature of vulnerabilities and guides political, economic, and technical adaptation choices. To successfully transition to integrated climate resilience, the Kingdom will need to articulate the dynamics of urban growth, environmental sustainability, and territorial governance, while drawing inspiration from regional and international best practices.

Saudi Arabia is thus at a pivotal moment: aligning its spatial and climate policies could not only reduce its internal vulnerability, but also make it a key regional player in sustainable climate governance.

ACKNOWLEDGEMENTS

We would to think the Deanship of Scientific Research, Vice Presidency for Graduate Studies and Scientific Research in the King Faisal University, and the anonymous reviewers and the editor in chief for their support to improve this the quality of this paper

FUNDING

This work was supported by the Deanship of Scientific Research, Vice Presidency for Graduate Studies and Scientific Research, King Faisal University, Saudi Arabia, [Grant No. KFU 254140].

COMPETING INTERESTS

The author declares no competing financial or non-financial interests that are directly or indirectly related to the work submitted for publication.

REFERENCES

Alghamdi, M., Alharbi, B., & Khoder, M. (2023). Dust storm frequency and air quality implications in central Saudi Arabia. *Atmospheric Environment*, *298*, 120056.

Alharbi, F., & Alotaibi, M. (2024). Integrating climate adaptation into local governance: A Saudi perspective. *Sustainability*, *16*(8), 5124.

Almazroui, M., Islam, M. N., & O'Brien, E. (2022). Extreme rainfall and flood risk in Saudi Arabia under climate change scenarios. *Climate Dynamics*, *59*(3), 987–1004.

Almheiri, A. (2024). Climate change hazards and the resilience of coastal cities in the GCC: A review. *Regional Environmental Studies Journal*, *12*(2), 45–63.

Alotaibi, M., Al-Sahli, M., & Hussein, K. (2023). Water scarcity and sustainable agriculture in arid Saudi regions. *Environmental Management*, *72*(4), 812–825.

Atlantic Council. (2023). *Climate Profile*.

Britannica, T. Editors of Encyclopaedia. (2024). Rubʿ al-Khali. In Encyclopaedia Britannica.

Exploring Climate-Induced Agricultural Risk in Saudi Arabia: Evidence from Farming Communities of Medina Region. (2024*Sustainability16*104245DOI: 10.3390/su16104245

Flood Risk and Vulnerability from a Changing Climate Perspective: An Overview Focusing on Flash Floods and Associated Hazards in Jeddah. (2023). Water, 15(20), 3641.

G20 Climate Risk Atlas. (2024). Saudi Arabia Climate Profile.

Maghrabi, A. (2024). Urban thermal vulnerability mapping for climate mitigation: A case study of Jeddah. *Journal of King Abdulaziz University: Environmental Design Sciences*, *15*(1), 93–111.

Ministry of Economy and Planning. (2023). National Environment Strategy 2023.

Ministry of Environment, Water and Agriculture. (2023). Annual. *Water Reports*, •••, 2023.

Ministry of Municipal and Rural Affairs and Housing. (2024). Urban Resilience and Smart Cities Framework 2024.

Ponzini, D. (2024). NEOM and the future of urban resilience in arid environments. *Cities (London, England)*, *144*, 104561.

Potential flood risk due to urbanization expansion in arid environments, Saudi Arabia. (2020). Natural Hazards, 104, 795–809.

Reiche, D. (2023). Energy transition and climate adaptation policies in the Gulf Cooperation Council (GCC) states. *Energy Policy*, *179*, 113483.

Revi, A., Satterthwaite, D., & Solecki, W. (2024). Urban resilience and climate governance: Global lessons for local adaptation. *Urban Climate*, *52*, 101864.

Saudi General Authority for Statistics. (2024). Population Estimates Publication 2024.

Saudi Meteorological Authority. (2024). Climate Data Summary 2024.

The Global Economy. (2024). Saudi Arabia — Percent urban population (1960–2024).

The World Bank. (2024). World Development Indicators. Rural population, total and urban population statistics for Saudi Arabia.

Water. (2023). Flood risk and vulnerability from a changing climate perspective: A focus on flash floods in Jeddah. Water, 15(20), 3641.

World Bank. (2024). World Development Indicators — Urban population (% of total).

World Bank. (2024). World Development Indicators: Precipitation and renewable water resources.

World Population Review. (2025). Saudi Arabia cities by population 2025.

Chapter 6

The Impact of Green Marketing Strategies on Consumer Purchase Intention of Green Product

Devi Mano
https://orcid.org/0009-0007-3707-8310
Vels Institute of Science, Technology, and Advanced Studies, India

D. Anitha Kumari
https://orcid.org/0009-0000-4863-8714
Vels Institute of Science, Technology, and Advanced Studies, India

N. Mari Anand
https://orcid.org/0000-0002-6443-249X
University of Technology and Applied Sciences, Salalah, Oman

ABSTRACT

As environmental awareness grows worldwide, both consumers and businesses are becoming more conscious of sustainability. This study explores how green marketing strategies influence consumers' intentions to buy eco-friendly products. Companies today are adopting various green practices—such as eco-labeling, sustainable packaging, green advertising, and fair pricing—to appeal to environmentally aware customers. The research aims to understand how these strategies shape consumer trust, perception, and willingness to purchase green products. Using survey data and quantitative analysis, the study examines the strength of the relationship be-

DOI: 10.4018/979-8-3373-8197-8.ch006

tween different aspects of green marketing and consumers' buying intentions. The results reveal that honest, transparent, and credible green marketing practices can significantly improve consumer attitudes and encourage eco-friendly purchasing behavior. The paper also highlights ongoing challenges like greenwashing and the need for greater consumer awareness.

INTRODUCTION

Growing concerns about climate change, pollution, and the depletion of natural resources have brought sustainability to the center of global attention. As people become more aware of environmental issues, both consumers and businesses are rethinking their choices. Companies are moving away from traditional marketing approaches and adopting green marketing, which focuses on creating, promoting, and delivering products that are environmentally friendly and socially responsible. The goal is not just to meet consumer needs but also to reduce the environmental impact of production and consumption. In recent years, growing environmental concerns and global sustainability movements have significantly influenced consumer behavior and business practices. As issues such as climate change, resource depletion, and pollution gain prominence, both consumers and organizations have become increasingly aware of the need for eco-friendly alternatives. This shift has given rise to green marketing, a strategic approach that emphasizes the promotion of environmentally sustainable products and practices. Green marketing not only focuses on highlighting the ecological benefits of products but also aims to build a positive corporate image and foster long-term consumer trust.

In today's marketplace, green consumerism is on the rise. Consumers are increasingly making purchase decisions based on ethical and environmental values. To meet these changing preferences, businesses across sectors—such as food, fashion, electronics, and automobiles—are embracing green marketing strategies like eco-labeling, recyclable packaging, green advertising, and sustainable pricing. These initiatives aim to build trust and project an image of environmental care, appealing to customers who value sustainability. However, the real effectiveness of these strategies depends on how well they shape consumer attitudes, trust, and ultimately, their intention to purchase green products.In today's competitive marketplace, consumers are increasingly evaluating products not only based on quality and price but also on the ethical and environmental practices of the companies behind them. This shift in consumer values has compelled businesses to integrate sustainability into their core marketing philosophies. As a result, green marketing is no longer viewed merely as a promotional tactic but as a holistic approach encompassing product innovation, supply chain management, and corporate responsibility. Companies that demonstrate genuine commitment to environmental protection often experience stronger brand loyalty, improved corporate image, and increased consumer trust. However, skepticism regarding "greenwashing"—false or exaggerated environmental claims—remains a significant challenge that can undermine consumer confidence. Thus, the credibility and authenticity of green marketing communications play a crucial role in determining their overall impact on consumer purchase intentions and behavior.

Even with the growing popularity of green marketing, several challenges remain. Many consumers express positive attitudes toward eco-friendly products but do not always follow through with actual purchases. This gap between what people say and what they do—often called the attitude-behavior gap—is influenced by factors such as price sensitivity, lack of product information, and skepticism caused by greenwashing (false or exaggerated environmental claims). Understanding how and why green marketing affects consumer decisions is therefore crucial for both marketers and policymakers.This study explores the impact of green marketing strategies on consumer purchase intention of green products, seeking to determine how various marketing efforts—such as environmental awareness campaigns, product labeling, and brand credibility—influence consumer attitudes and decision-making. By examining this relationship, the research aims to provide valuable insights into how organizations can effectively design and implement green marketing strategies that not only support environmental goals but also drive market success.Despite the increasing popularity of green products, there remains a gap between consumers' positive environmental attitudes and their actual purchasing behavior—a phenomenon often referred to as the "attitude-behavior gap." This gap raises important questions about the factors that drive or hinder green purchase intentions. Elements such as green advertising credibility, environmental labeling, perceived consumer effectiveness, and brand image play a significant role in shaping consumer decisions. Understanding these factors can help marketers design more effective strategies that convert environmental concern into actual purchase behavior.

Research shows that factors like environmental awareness and brand credibility play key roles in shaping green purchase intentions. For instance, green advertising helps educate consumers, eco-labels build trust, and sustainable packaging improves brand image. Studying these relationships can help companies develop marketing strategies that not only promote sustainability but also drive genuine consumer engagement and loyalty.The adoption of green marketing strategies has become a vital tool for organizations seeking to align with the values of environmentally conscious consumers. These strategies may include eco-labeling, sustainable packaging, green advertising, and corporate social responsibility initiatives. However, the effectiveness of such strategies ultimately depends on how they shape consumer purchase intentions—the likelihood that a consumer will choose a green product over conventional alternatives. Understanding the impact of green marketing on consumer purchase intentions is therefore essential for businesses striving to achieve both environmental sustainability and competitive advantage.

This paper explores the impact of green marketing strategies on consumer purchase intention toward green products by examining key elements such as eco-labeling, green packaging, pricing, and advertising. It also draws insights from consumer behavior, environmental psychology, and marketing theory to provide a more complete understanding of how green marketing works.

The findings of this research are expected to guide businesses in building stronger sustainability-oriented brands and help policymakers design programs that encourage eco-friendly consumption. As global markets move toward more circular and responsible economies, understanding how green marketing influences purchasing decisions has become not only a business advantage but also a vital step toward a more sustainable future.

BACKGROUND OF THE STUDY

In recent years, green marketing has become an essential part of India's move toward sustainable business practices. As consumers become more environmentally conscious, their buying habits increasingly reflect a preference for brands that show genuine concern for the planet. Businesses are responding by adopting eco-friendly approaches—such as recyclable packaging, environmental labeling, and digital green campaigns—that not only appeal to these conscious consumers but also strengthen their brand reputation (Kumar, 2024). This shift marks a broader trend toward sustainable consumerism, where companies strive to balance profitability with ecological responsibility.

Raturi and Bhatnagar (2023) explored how the components of the green marketing mix—product, price, place, and promotion—affect consumers' intention to buy green products in urban India. Their study revealed that eco-friendly packaging, reasonable pricing, and a positive brand image significantly encourage purchase intentions, especially among younger, environmentally aware consumers.

Similarly, Verma (2024) examined how environmental concern, perceived behavioral control, and social norms influence green product purchases in cities like Delhi and Bengaluru. They found that social influence and environmental awareness play a major role in shaping consumers' willingness to choose eco-friendly products.

Kumar (2024) investigated how eco-label credibility and green packaging affect consumer behavior in India's FMCG sector. Their findings showed that trustworthy third-party certifications and clear environmental labeling enhance consumer trust and perceived product quality, ultimately increasing the intention to purchase green products.

Priya and Mehta (2025) looked at the role of digital marketing and influencer campaigns in promoting green products in the retail sector. They found that social media-based sustainability messages and endorsements from influencers create stronger emotional connections with green brands, encouraging consumers to make eco-friendly purchases.

Kaur et al. (2025) analyzed how environmental concern mediates the relationship between green advertising and purchase intention in northern India. Their study concluded that authentic environmental messages and practical product usefulness significantly strengthen both purchase intention and brand preference.

Kumar (2025) used structural equation modeling (SEM) to identify the main predictors of green purchase intention. His results showed that green brand knowledge ($\beta = 0.55$), eco-friendly packaging ($\beta = 0.60$), and brand trust ($\beta = 0.70$) are major influencing factors. He emphasized the importance of transparency and consumer education in converting environmental awareness into actual purchasing behavior.

Nair (2024) examined how corporate social responsibility (CSR) and green innovation affect consumer behavior in southern India. They found that CSR activities and innovative eco-friendly products build consumer trust and long-term loyalty toward green brands.

Patel et al. (2024) explored post-purchase satisfaction and loyalty in the context of green products sold through e-commerce platforms. Their findings revealed that satisfaction with product performance and brand credibility strongly predict repeat purchases and positive word-of-mouth for green products.

RESEARCH OBJECTIVES

1. To examine how key green marketing strategies—such as eco-labeling, green advertising, sustainable packaging, and green pricing—influence consumers' intention to purchase environmentally friendly products.
2. To analyze how consumer trust and environmental awareness act as mediating factors in the relationship between green marketing practices and consumers' purchase intentions.
3. To identify the major challenges and barriers—such as greenwashing, price sensitivity, and doubts about product quality—that limit the effectiveness of green marketing in encouraging actual green purchases.
4. To propose a strategic framework that helps businesses design more authentic and effective green marketing initiatives, fostering consumer trust, promoting sustainable consumption, and strengthening brand competitiveness in the green marketplace.

RESEARCH QUESTIONS

1. How do different aspects of green marketing—like green brand knowledge, eco-friendly packaging, environmental awareness, and green labelling—influence consumers' willingness to buy environmentally friendly products?
2. How do factors such as brand trust and brand attitude help connect green marketing efforts with consumers' actual intention to purchase green products?
3. In what ways do demographic factors such as gender, age, and income shape how consumers respond to green marketing strategies and decide whether to buy green products?
4. Which mix of green marketing practices and brand-related factors most effectively encourages consumers to choose sustainable products?

METHODOLOGY

This study adopts a qualitative research methodology, utilizing case studies and literature review to analyze the impact of green marketing strategies on consumer purchase intention of green products. Data is collected from academic journals, industry reports, and documented marketing campaigns that focus on sustainable branding, eco-labeling, and green advertising across various sectors.

ENHANCING CONSUMER PURCHASE INTENTION OF GREEN PRODUCTS THROUGH GREEN MARKETING STRATEGIES

The growing focus on sustainability and the rise of eco-conscious consumerism have transformed how companies design, market, and sell their products. Under the expanding green economy, environmentally friendly products are gaining popularity—but influencing consumer purchase decisions remains a complex behavioral challenge. Green marketing strategies such as eco-labeling, green advertising, and sustainability messaging play a vital role in shaping these decisions. These approaches not only raise awareness but also build trust, helping brands engage consumers meaningfully and encourage environmentally responsible buying behavior.

The foundation of effective green marketing lies in understanding key psychological factors that shape consumer behavior—such as environmental concern, perceived product effectiveness, and brand credibility. When consumers are repeatedly exposed to genuine sustainability messages, they begin to associate green product features with their personal values and lifestyle choices. This emotional and cognitive alignment strengthens their motivation to choose eco-friendly options in a crowded marketplace filled with competing claims.

One of the biggest challenges in green marketing is overcoming greenwashing—the use of misleading or exaggerated environmental claims. Such practices damage trust and make consumers skeptical about green products. Kumar (2024) emphasizes that transparency, backed by credible third-party certifications and clear communication, is far more effective than vague sustainability slogans in converting purchase intention into real buying behavior. In a sense, just as cybersecurity systems detect hidden threats, authentic green marketing must anticipate and counter consumer skepticism to preserve credibility.

Digital green marketing has further transformed how businesses connect with different consumer groups. By leveraging data analytics and personalization, marketers can tailor sustainability messages to specific audience segments—whether they are eco-conscious millennials, price-sensitive shoppers, or socially responsible families. Rakhmatov (2025) found that targeted campaigns on social media and through influencer collaborations generate stronger engagement and higher purchase conversion rates, much like how advanced algorithms enhance performance in other data-driven fields.

Moreover, the implementation of green marketing strategies allows companies to gain continuous insights into consumer attitudes and behavior. Verma (2024) notes that green marketing analytics can monitor consumer sentiment, categorize behavioral patterns, and provide real-time feedback. This helps marketers refine their messaging and product positioning proactively, ensuring that their campaigns remain relevant and effective.

Automation tools have also become a key element in green marketing. These systems manage repetitive promotional tasks while enabling real-time interaction with consumers. Through automation, marketing teams can deliver eco-messages efficiently, identify skeptical audiences, and initiate loyalty programs without manual delays. Bharti et al. (2024) point out that this responsiveness helps prevent consumer disengagement and keeps brands competitive in the fast-evolving green marketplace.

Scalability is another major advantage of digital green marketing. As consumer expectations and product diversity grow, traditional marketing approaches often struggle to adapt. AI-powered systems can analyze vast amounts of consumer data, track shifting environmental priorities, and modify marketing strategies in real time (Thapaliya & Bokani, 2024). This agility helps brands stay aligned with the dynamic values of sustainability-oriented consumers.

Ultimately, green marketing strengthens brand equity by combining ethical branding with consumer education. Unlike traditional marketing, green campaigns must appeal to both the heart and the mind—addressing emotional connections while providing rational evidence of environmental benefits. The success of green marketing depends on authenticity, consistency, and meaningful consumer engagement. When done well, it fosters trust, loyalty, and advocacy; when done poorly, it risks consumer indifference or backlash (García, 2024).

EFFECTIVE INFLUENCE OF GREEN MARKETING STRATEGIES ON CONSUMER PURCHASE INTENTION OF GREEN PRODUCTS

The modern marketplace has evolved dramatically with the rising global focus on environmental sustainability and responsible consumption. Green marketing has reshaped traditional marketing practices by embedding eco-friendly values, sustainable production methods, and honest communication about environmental impact. Today, businesses are not just promoting product performance—they are also aligning their campaigns with consumers' ethical and environmental beliefs. As a result, green marketing has become a key driver of purchase intention across diverse industries, including food, fashion, cosmetics, and technology.

The power of green marketing lies in its ability to create awareness and build positive perceptions among consumers. Companies now rely on eco-labels, recyclable packaging, organic certifications, and sustainability claims to demonstrate their commitment to the environment. These visible actions foster consumer trust and enhance the perceived value of products, motivating eco-conscious buyers to choose green options over conventional ones (Dahiya et al., 2025). Similarly, transparent and authentic environmental advertising strengthens brand credibility, leading to greater customer loyalty and even a willingness to pay more for genuinely sustainable products.

A brand's green image plays a crucial role in influencing consumer decisions. People are more likely to support brands that consistently display ecological responsibility—from sourcing raw materials sustainably to managing waste responsibly. When companies effectively communicate their environmental efforts, they create an emotional connection with consumers who see the brand as a responsible caretaker of the planet (Fernandes et al., 2024). This emotional attachment not only strengthens loyalty but also encourages actual purchase behavior.

Environmental awareness and knowledge also play an important part in shaping green purchase intentions. Consumers who are more informed about sustainability are better equipped to recognize authentic environmental benefits and value them. However, the rise of greenwashing—where companies exaggerate or falsify their environmental claims—can quickly damage trust. To avoid this, brands must ensure transparency and support their claims with credible certifications and endorsements (Li, 2025).

Beyond awareness, perceived product quality remains a decisive factor. Consumers evaluate not only how eco-friendly a product is but also how well it performs and whether it's affordable. When green products offer equal or superior quality compared to traditional alternatives, consumers are more likely to buy them (Upadhyaya & Sijoria, 2024). This shows that sustainability alone is not enough—performance and value must go hand in hand with environmental responsibility.

Social and psychological factors further enhance the effectiveness of green marketing. Social influence, peer recommendations, and shared cultural values encourage environmentally friendly behaviors, especially among younger generations like Gen Z. This group is particularly responsive to digital marketing campaigns that highlight sustainability, social ethics, and responsible production (Dubey et al., 2024). By leveraging social media and influencer advocacy, brands can shape collective norms and inspire widespread eco-conscious consumption.

Government policies and corporate social responsibility (CSR) initiatives also play a critical role. Companies that integrate green supply chain practices, renewable energy, and proper waste management not only comply with regulations but also gain public respect and long-term loyalty (Kathuria & Nigam, 2024). These practices support national sustainability goals and reinforce a company's credibility in the eyes of the public.

The success of green marketing depends on a holistic approach that combines ethical practices, consistent environmental communication, and genuine brand integrity. When businesses align their marketing efforts with the values of environmentally conscious consumers, they don't just boost purchase intentions—they help create a culture of sustainability. In doing so, they contribute to both long-term brand success and the broader goal of preserving the planet for future generations.

MAJOR CHALLENGES IN ADOPTING GREEN MARKETING STRATEGIES AND HOW TO ADDRESS THEM

In India's growing green economy, businesses are increasingly recognizing the importance of integrating sustainability into their marketing strategies. As environmental awareness rises, many companies are adopting practices such as recyclable packaging, green labeling, and carbon-neutral advertising to attract environmentally conscious consumers. However, despite these efforts, several challenges continue to hinder the effective implementation of green marketing — including high operational costs, consumer skepticism, and a lack of clear regulatory direction (Kumar, 2024).

One of the key examples is ITC Limited, which has successfully linked sustainability with marketing communication through its "Paperkraft" notebooks and "Fiama" eco-friendly product lines. While these initiatives use recyclable materials and minimize plastic use, the company faces the challenge of maintaining affordability. Green products often cost more due to expensive sustainable inputs, which can limit consumer adoption (Raturi & Bhatnagar, 2023). To overcome this, ITC focuses on life-cycle marketing — emphasizing long-term environmental and health benefits rather than competing purely on price.

Similarly, Tata Consumer Products promotes its beverages through eco-labeling and responsible sourcing claims. However, the company initially faced skepticism from consumers who doubted the authenticity of its green claims. To strengthen trust, Tata adopted credible third-party certifications like Rainforest Alliance and Fairtrade, ensuring transparency and reinforcing consumer confidence (Kumar, 2025).

Hindustan Unilever Limited (HUL) provides another strong example through its "Clean Future" initiative, which promotes detergents and personal care products with lower carbon and water footprints. Yet, a major obstacle for HUL lies in communicating these technical sustainability benefits to consumers with different levels of literacy and environmental understanding. To bridge this gap, HUL launched educational and relatable green advertising campaigns that translate complex sustainability messages into simple, meaningful narratives (Verma, 2024).

Patanjali Ayurved, known for its natural and herbal products, struggles with the perception of greenwashing—where consumers question the authenticity of its eco-friendly claims. To address this, the company enhanced transparency across its supply chain by showcasing its sourcing and production processes through digital storytelling and QR-based traceability systems. This move helped consumers see the brand's genuine environmental commitment, strengthening trust and purchase intention (Desai & Mehta, 2025).

In the automotive industry, companies like Tata Motors and Mahindra Electric face a different challenge: low consumer awareness about the environmental advantages of electric vehicles (EVs). Many consumers still view EVs as expensive or impractical. To counter this, these brands focus their campaigns on educating consumers about long-term savings, zero-emission benefits, and India's sustainability goals. By blending emotional appeal with factual evidence, they successfully position EVs as both eco-friendly and technologically advanced (Nair, 2024).

The retail sector, represented by BigBasket and Reliance Fresh, has also adopted green marketing practices through sustainable packaging and locally sourced products. Their biggest challenge lies in maintaining consistent environmental standards across multiple regions. To solve this, these companies use AI-driven logistics optimization and supplier training programs to ensure that sustainability goals and product quality remain uniform nationwide (Patel et al., 2024).

A recurring challenge across industries is consumer behavioral inertia—where people express environmental concern but fail to act on it when making purchases. Overcoming this requires strategies that make green purchasing a social norm.

Techniques like behavioral reinforcement marketing, influencer advocacy, and public-private partnerships help bridge this gap. For instance, initiatives such as the Swachh Bharat Green Consumer Campaign integrate government awareness programs with corporate green messaging to encourage consistent eco-friendly choices (Kaur et al., 2025).

The success of green marketing in India depends on how effectively companies address challenges of trust, cost, education, and standardization. Businesses that prioritize transparency, credible certification, and consumer engagement are more likely to build loyalty and long-term brand strength. By aligning marketing strategies with consumer psychology and sustainable values, companies not only boost purchase intentions but also contribute meaningfully to India's journey toward a greener and more responsible economy.

KEY COMPONENTS IN A RESILIENT AND EFFECTIVE GREEN MARKETING FRAMEWORK FOR ENHANCING CONSUMER PURCHASE INTENTION OF GREEN PRODUCTS

A strong and resilient green marketing framework is essential for promoting sustainable consumption and building consumer trust in India's rapidly evolving marketplace. To be effective, such a framework must combine multiple strategic elements that influence consumer perceptions, encourage eco-friendly behavior, and ensure long-term competitiveness.

The first and most fundamental component is green brand knowledge, which shapes how consumers perceive a company's environmental responsibility. When consumers understand a brand's eco-friendly values, sustainable production methods, and environmental initiatives, they are more likely to form positive attitudes and intentions to purchase. Clear and consistent communication—through informative advertising, eco-labels, and transparency about sustainability practices—builds credibility and trust (Kumar, 2024).

The second vital element is eco-friendly product packaging, which serves as a visible expression of a company's commitment to the environment. Using biodegradable materials, reusable containers, or minimal plastic packaging appeals strongly to environmentally conscious consumers. Leading Indian brands like ITC and HUL have adopted such practices across product lines like *Aashirvaad Nature's Superfoods* and *Love Beauty and Planet*. These initiatives not only reduce environmental impact but also resonate with consumers' ethical and social values, motivating them to choose green products (Kumar, 2024).

Another essential pillar is green labeling, which bridges the information gap between companies and consumers. Recognized eco-labels and certifications—such as EcoMark, Energy Star, and Rainforest Alliance—indicate that a product meets specific environmental standards. These labels enhance authenticity, reduce consumer uncertainty, and help differentiate genuine green products from misleading claims. In the Indian market, where skepticism about sustainability is still common, credible labeling plays a crucial role in influencing consumer trust and purchase decisions (Kaur et al., 2025).

Environmental awareness and education form the next major component of the framework. Awareness initiatives—whether through digital media, sustainability workshops, or corporate social responsibility (CSR) programs—help cultivate eco-consciousness among consumers. For instance, Tata Motors and Godrej Consumer Products actively engage in community outreach and environmental education programs that encourage responsible consumption. Such efforts shape positive social norms and increase consumers' likelihood of purchasing eco-friendly products (Verma, 2024).

Equally important is green advertising and communication transparency. Honest, evidence-based communication about environmental benefits, certifications, and sustainable practices is key to building long-term credibility. Misleading or exaggerated claims—known as greenwashing—can severely damage consumer trust. Brands such as Patanjali and Dabur have addressed this by using authentic messaging that connects environmental sustainability with health, purity, and tradition, making their campaigns relatable and trustworthy (Desai & Mehta, 2025).

A well-designed pricing strategy is also critical. While green products often cost more to produce, pricing them competitively is essential in a price-sensitive market like India. Companies can adopt a value-based pricing approach, highlighting long-term savings, product durability, and health benefits instead of focusing only on upfront costs. In addition, government incentives—such as tax reductions or subsidies for eco-friendly goods—can make green products more affordable and appealing to consumers (Raturi & Bhatnagar, 2023).

In recent years, digital green marketing and social media engagement have become transformative tools for influencing consumer behavior. Social platforms allow brands to interact directly with young, environmentally aware audiences through creative campaigns, influencer partnerships, and community storytelling. By promoting sustainable lifestyles, companies like *FabIndia* and *Forest Essentials* build emotional connections with consumers that translate into higher purchase intentions (Patel et al., 2024).

Finally, corporate environmental responsibility (CER) and supply chain transparency strengthen overall brand credibility. Companies that integrate sustainability into every stage of their operations—from raw material sourcing to production, distribution, and recycling—demonstrate genuine ethical commitment. This not only enhances environmental outcomes but also boosts consumer loyalty and advocacy (Nair, 2024).

A robust green marketing framework combines several interrelated components: green brand knowledge, eco-friendly packaging, credible labeling, environmental education, transparent advertising, strategic pricing, digital engagement, and responsible corporate practices. Together, these elements create an ecosystem where green products are seen not just as alternatives, but as meaningful choices for a sustainable lifestyle. When effectively implemented, this framework helps businesses drive consumer purchase intention, strengthen brand equity, and contribute to India's broader journey toward sustainable economic growth.

CASE STUDY EXAMPLES

Case Study 1: Forest Essentials – Luxury Ayurveda and Environmental Stewardship (2025)

Forest Essentials combines luxury branding with sustainable product creation, using recyclable glass bottles, eco-refills, and organically grown ingredients. The brand positions itself as both environmentally ethical and culturally rooted, aligning Ayurveda with modern sustainability ethics. Its campaigns emphasize purity, tradition, and respect for nature—values that deeply resonate with Indian consumers.

According to research by Kumar (2025), Forest Essentials' strategy has increased consumer loyalty and repeat purchase intention by associating personal well-being with ecological balance. The case demonstrates that cultural relevance combined with environmental ethics can form a powerful driver of purchase intention in India's high-end market segment.

Case Study 2: Dabur India's Eco-Labeling and Herbal Green Strategy (2024)

Dabur's focus on eco-labeling, herbal authenticity, and sustainable sourcing represents another successful application of green marketing. In 2024, the company introduced new labeling standards for its Dabur Nature Care and Real Juices product lines, ensuring transparency in ingredient sourcing and recyclability information.

This move significantly boosted consumer trust and purchase intention among environmentally aware buyers (Patel et al., 2024). The case confirms that authentic labeling and verifiable product claims are key to influencing consumer choice, especially in markets where greenwashing remains a concern.

Case Study 3: Godrej Consumer Products – 'Good & Green' CSR Initiative (2023)

Godrej's 'Good & Green' initiative integrates green manufacturing, waste reduction, and sustainable packaging into its brand identity. The company communicates these efforts through its CSR reports, digital campaigns, and community awareness programs. By linking sustainability with social progress—such as skill development and green livelihood training—Godrej built a multidimensional brand perception.

A survey conducted by the Indian Journal of Sustainable Business (Verma, 2024) found that CSR-oriented green marketing enhances corporate image and consumer purchase intention, especially among educated, urban populations. This case illustrates how sustainability-driven CSR initiatives can transform corporate credibility into tangible consumer loyalty.

DISCUSSION

Green marketing has become a powerful approach for companies aiming to promote environmentally friendly products while influencing consumer purchasing behavior. By incorporating eco-friendly branding, sustainable packaging, and green labeling, organizations are successfully shifting consumer perception toward sustainability. Today's consumers are not just looking for low prices—they are seeking products that reflect their values and support environmental and ethical causes. In this changing landscape, green marketing serves as both a business growth strategy and a driver of environmental responsibility, helping brands build stronger equity and long-term trust.

Research across India shows that green brand knowledge, environmental awareness, and the credibility of eco-labels play a major role in shaping consumer purchase intention. Consumers are more likely to buy green products when they believe the brand's environmental claims are authentic and transparent (Mehta et al., 2025). This underlines how crucial trust and information reliability are in converting positive environmental attitudes into actual buying behavior.

Another significant factor is eco-friendly packaging and sustainable product design. These not only demonstrate a company's environmental commitment but also visually communicate quality and sincerity. Studies in the Indian FMCG sector reveal that innovative, sustainable packaging—like biodegradable or minimal plastic materials—creates emotional appeal and improves brand perception, especially among younger and urban buyers (Raturi & Bhatnagar, 2023).

The rise of digital media and influencer marketing has also transformed how green marketing messages reach consumers. Social media storytelling, eco-influencer collaborations, and transparency tools allow companies to connect sustainability narratives with individual lifestyles. These digital strategies build emotional engagement and help consumers feel more in control of their green choices (Desai & Mehta, 2025).

However, a major barrier that persists is consumer skepticism toward greenwashing—when brands exaggerate or falsify their environmental claims. This distrust can seriously undermine purchase intentions. To overcome it, companies must use third-party certifications, authentic eco-labels, and transparent sustainability reporting. Such actions improve credibility and reduce consumer uncertainty, especially in developing markets like India where awareness levels differ widely (Kaur et al., 2025).

Demographic factors also influence how consumers respond to green marketing. Educated, urban consumers with higher income levels are typically more receptive to environmental messages, whereas rural or price-sensitive buyers often prioritize practicality and cost over sustainability. Hence, brands need to develop tailored marketing strategies that combine ecological messaging with tangible economic benefits to broaden green product adoption (Nair, 2024).

Furthermore, the integration of corporate social responsibility (CSR) within green marketing adds another dimension of trust and engagement. When companies showcase sustainability through social initiatives—such as clean energy use, community reforestation, or waste management programs—consumers view them as genuinely responsible and socially conscious. This CSR alignment strengthens emotional loyalty and creates a meaningful bond between consumers and the brand (Singh & Verma, 2024).

For long-term success, green marketing must evolve into a holistic and adaptive framework that blends innovation, transparency, and consumer education. Incorporating feedback mechanisms, digital traceability, and sustainability audits can enhance accountability while building consistent consumer confidence. In India, growing government support, credible eco-certification systems, and increased public awareness are collectively accelerating the move toward a more circular and sustainable economy.

The effectiveness of green marketing strategies in India depends on authentic communication, consumer awareness, and brand trust working together. When these factors align, they not only drive stronger purchase intentions but also promote sustainable consumption patterns—supporting both business growth and environmental well-being in the evolving green economy.

MAIN FINDINGS

The study finds that green marketing strategies have a strong and positive impact on consumer purchase intentions toward environmentally friendly products across multiple industries in India. Consumers respond favorably to sustainable practices such as eco-labeling, recyclable packaging, and transparent communication of environmental benefits. Integrating green brand values into marketing activities enhances both brand image and consumer trust—two essential drivers of green purchasing behavior.

A key finding highlights the importance of green brand knowledge. Consumers who are aware of a brand's environmental performance and sustainable product features tend to show greater willingness to purchase green products. When companies share clear, verifiable, and honest environmental information through their advertising, packaging, and corporate communication, it builds consumer confidence and long-term brand loyalty.

The study also identifies eco-friendly packaging and credible labeling as among the most influential factors shaping consumer behavior. Buyers often associate biodegradable, recyclable, and minimalistic packaging with high product quality and brand responsibility. Labels with authentic eco-certifications or sustainability claims create trust and transparency, helping reduce uncertainty and encouraging consumers to pay a modest premium for environmentally safer options.

Furthermore, environmental awareness and personal values emerge as powerful motivators for green purchasing. Consumers who are more environmentally conscious view green products as a reflection of their ethical and social responsibility. Awareness-building efforts through environmental education, social media campaigns, and sustainability reporting have been shown to strengthen this consciousness, especially among urban and semi-urban audiences.

Digital marketing also plays a transformative role. The study finds that social media engagement, influencer partnerships, and online storytelling help brands connect emotionally with consumers and build sustained interest in green products. Interactive digital communication enhances credibility and strengthens behavioral intention, particularly among younger, tech-savvy consumers.

However, the findings also caution that greenwashing and lack of transparency remain major obstacles. When brands exaggerate or falsify their environmental claims, consumer skepticism rises, weakening trust and purchase intention. The research stresses the importance of honest communication supported by third-party certifications and verifiable data to build authenticity and credibility in the Indian market.

Socio-demographic factors such as age, education, and income further influence how consumers respond to green marketing. Younger, educated, and urban consumers are generally more receptive to sustainability messages, while rural and price-sensitive segments tend to focus on practicality and affordability. This suggests that brands must design segment-specific strategies that balance ecological benefits with economic value.

Another important insight is the positive effect of corporate social responsibility (CSR) integration within green marketing. When brands connect their green products to larger sustainability goals—like renewable energy use, community initiatives, or waste reduction—consumers view them as more ethical and socially responsible. This perception increases both trust and long-term loyalty.

Results from the structural equation modeling (SEM) analysis confirm that all the main dimensions—green brand knowledge, eco-friendly packaging, environmental awareness, and green labeling—have a significant positive impact on purchase intention. Among these, green brand knowledge and eco-friendly packaging show the strongest influence, indicating their central role in shaping consumer attitudes and behavior.

Overall, the study concludes that the success of green marketing in India depends on the synergy of authenticity, awareness, and perceived value. Companies that combine transparent communication, consumer education, and genuine sustainability practices are better positioned to build consumer trust, achieve environmental objectives, and strengthen competitiveness in the growing green economy.

SUGGESTIONS

1. Invest in authentic green marketing practices

Organizations should prioritize genuine and transparent green marketing efforts that truly align with their sustainability goals. Green initiatives must be supported by measurable environmental actions rather than symbolic or exaggerated claims. Establishing internal sustainability audits, obtaining third-party certifications, and maintaining open communication with consumers can reduce skepticism and build trust. These measures will encourage stronger purchase intentions and long-term loyalty toward green products.

2. Integrate sustainability across the entire value chain

For green marketing to be truly effective, sustainability must be embedded throughout the product life cycle—from raw material sourcing and production to packaging, logistics, and waste management. Companies should adopt eco-friendly designs, energy-efficient technologies, and recyclable packaging solutions. This holistic approach enhances corporate credibility and reflects a genuine, long-term commitment to the environment, motivating consumers to choose green products over conventional ones.

3. Strengthen consumer education and awareness programs

Raising public awareness is essential for promoting sustainable consumption. Businesses and policymakers should work together to organize awareness campaigns, workshops, and educational programs that highlight the benefits of eco-friendly products. When consumers understand how their purchasing decisions contribute to environmental preservation, they are more likely to make conscious, sustainable choices. Integrating environmental education at school and community levels can also nurture long-term eco-conscious behavior.

4. Adopt digital and social media–driven green strategies

Digital platforms play a crucial role in shaping modern consumer behavior. Companies should use social media, influencer marketing, and digital storytelling to communicate their sustainability efforts in a relatable and engaging manner. Visual campaigns that showcase real environmental actions—such as tree-planting drives, plastic-free operations, or renewable energy adoption—can build emotional connections and increase trust. Additionally, digital tools like QR codes that share product sustainability information can help consumers verify claims easily and boost confidence in green brands.

5. Standardize eco-labeling and certification systems

To eliminate confusion and ensure credibility, the government and industry associations should collaborate to establish a unified national eco-labeling framework. A standardized and scientifically validated labeling system will help consumers easily identify authentic green products and reduce the impact of misleading marketing claims. Clear, accessible, and trustworthy labeling enhances consumer confidence and encourages more informed purchasing decisions.

6. Build organizational capacity and employee expertise

Companies need to invest in training and capacity-building initiatives focused on sustainability and green marketing management. Educating employees about environmental practices and effective sustainability communication ensures that marketing messages are both accurate and authentic. Partnerships with universities and environmental organizations can bridge skill gaps, promote innovation, and foster a corporate culture rooted in genuine environmental responsibility.

7. Incorporate consumer feedback into green strategy development

Understanding consumer perceptions and expectations is vital for improving green marketing effectiveness. Businesses should implement feedback systems, such as surveys, focus groups, and AI-based sentiment analysis, to assess how consumers respond to green initiatives. Using these insights, companies can refine their messages, enhance transparency, and develop products that align more closely with consumer preferences and values.

8. Encourage cross-sector collaboration for sustainable transformation

The transition to a green economy requires collective action among government agencies, corporations, NGOs, and consumers. Collaborative initiatives such as sustainability fairs, green product expos, and public-private partnerships can create stronger market visibility and credibility for eco-friendly products. Moreover, policy interventions like tax incentives, subsidies, and grants for certified green products can make sustainable options more accessible and appealing to the broader population.

FUTURE IMPLICATIONS

1. AI and Data Analytics:

Future green marketing will rely on artificial intelligence and big data to understand evolving consumer behavior. Predictive analytics will help firms design targeted campaigns and personalize messages that match eco-conscious preferences. This data-driven approach will improve marketing accuracy and influence purchase intentions more effectively.

2. Circular Economy Integration:

Companies will move beyond traditional eco-friendly practices to adopt circular economy models focused on recycling, reuse, and waste reduction. Marketing will highlight sustainable production cycles and resource recovery. This shift will strengthen long-term consumer trust and brand loyalty toward sustainable businesses.

3. Digital Transparency and Technology:

The integration of blockchain, IoT, and QR-based tracking will allow consumers to verify the authenticity of green claims. By accessing product lifecycle and supply chain data digitally, customers can make informed decisions. Such transparency will minimize greenwashing and build credibility for genuine green brands.

4. Standardized Green Certification:

The future will bring uniform national eco-labels and certification systems that verify sustainability standards. These standardized labels will simplify consumer understanding of eco-friendly claims and enhance trust. As a result, more businesses will be motivated to follow verified sustainable practices.

5. Collaborative Green Ecosystems:

Partnerships among governments, corporations, and NGOs will become essential for spreading environmental awareness. Joint initiatives like green expos and educational drives will promote eco-friendly consumption. This collective effort will create a strong foundation for sustainable market transformation.

6. Personalized Sustainability Marketing:

AI-powered profiling will enable marketers to tailor green campaigns based on lifestyle, values, and psychographics. Personalized sustainability communication will make consumers feel emotionally connected to eco-friendly brands. This deeper engagement will lead to stronger purchase intentions and loyalty.

7. Sustainability Education in Marketing:

Future campaigns will focus on educating consumers about the environmental impact of their choices. Storytelling and cause-based marketing will help nurture responsible consumption habits. Such awareness-driven marketing will create a more environmentally conscious customer base.

8. Policy-Driven Green Consumerism:

Strong government policies—such as tax incentives for green products and mandatory eco-labeling—will shape the future of sustainable marketing. Regulatory support will encourage fair competition and authentic environmental claims. This policy framework will ensure the long-term growth of ethical green marketing practices.

CONCLUSION

Green marketing has become a powerful force in shaping how modern consumers think and act, especially as more people seek out environmentally responsible products. Traditional marketing alone no longer connects with today's audience, who value transparency, ethics, and sustainability. This study confirms that key elements such as eco-friendly packaging, green labeling, environmental awareness, and green brand knowledge have a strong positive impact on consumers' intentions to purchase green products. Together, these factors build trust, strengthen brand authenticity, and increase consumers' willingness to pay for sustainable options.

The findings highlight that when companies communicate their sustainability efforts honestly and clearly, consumers respond more favorably to green products. Beyond influencing individual choices, green marketing supports the broader goals of sustainable production and consumption across India. However, challenges like greenwashing, limited public awareness, and consumer skepticism remain obstacles to genuine progress.

To make green marketing truly effective, businesses must align their marketing strategies with long-term environmental goals. This means backing every sustainability claim with real action, transparent labeling, and verified certifications. Collaboration among industries, government, and consumers—supported by strong environmental policies and awareness programs—is essential to drive meaningful change.

Overall, green marketing will continue to play a crucial role in the future of sustainable business. As environmental awareness grows and digital communication evolves, success will depend on authenticity, data-driven insights, and social responsibility. Companies that embrace transparency and genuine sustainability will not only earn consumer loyalty but also contribute meaningfully to global environmental preservation and the growth of a greener economy.

REFERENCES

Bharti, K., Agarwal, R., & Satsangi, A. K. (2024). *Behavioral Intention of Consumers for Green Marketing in India: The Mediating Role of Consumer Environmental Attitude*. Jindal Journal of Business Research., DOI: 10.1177/22786821241256188

Dahiya, A., Bhatt, P., Kumar, A., & Kant, S. (2025). Factors influencing green product purchase intention: A structural equation modelling approach utilising PEST framework. *Indian Journal of Marketing*, *55*(8), 69–88. Advance online publication. DOI: 10.17010/ijom/2025/v55/i8/175210

Desai, A., & Mehta, P. (2025). The Interplay of Brand Strength, Profitability, And Equity Valuation: Evidence from The Indian Market. *International Journal of Management and Business Development*, *2*(05), 1–6.

Dubey, D., Gupta, D., Agarwal, N., Jain, N., & Thapliyal, B. L. (2024). Generation Z's Green Purchase Intentions: Impact of Consumer Attitude, Brand Positioning, and Knowledge. Library Progress International, 44(3).

Fernandes, S., Sathish, M., & Shrivastava, P. (2024). Effect of Consciousness in Sustainable Consumption Habits on Purchase Intention of Green Products: Comparison Study Between India and USA. *Indian Journal of Marketing*, *54*(10), 8–24. DOI: 10.17010/ijom/2024/v54/i10/174602

Garcia, M. D. J. (2024). *Essays on Consumer Preferences and Economic Resilience in Latin American Food Supply Chain* (Doctoral dissertation).

Kathuria, A., & Nigam, A. (2024). Analysis of the Impact of Green Marketing on Purchase Intention in the Automobile Sector: Roles of Environmental Knowledge and Green Psychological Benefits. *Journal of Electrical Systems*, *20*(11s).

Kaur, P., Kaur, R., Sharma, S., & Kaur, S. (2025). Hybrid meat for flexitarian consumers: Technological advancements, diversity in plant proteins and consumer preferences. *Critical Reviews in Food Science and Nutrition*, •••, 1–17. DOI: 10.1080/10408398.2025.2564890 PMID: 41017443

Kumar, R. (2024). Achieving Sustainability in India Through Modern Payment System: An Empirical Study. *American Journal of Economics and Business Innovation*, *3*(1), 92–99.

Kumar, V. (2025). Role of Financial Literacy in the Financial Management Practices of Salaried Women in India: An SEM-HLM Study. *IUP Journal of Applied Economics, 24*(1).

Li, D. (2025). Impact of green advertisement and environmental knowledge on intention of consumers to buy green products. *BMC Psychology*, *13*(1), 220. DOI: 10.1186/s40359-025-02538-x PMID: 40059236

Mehta, K., Kumar, S., & Rawal, Y. S. (2025). Metaverse Tourism, Future Trends, and Sustainable Tourism Development. In *Tourism Entrepreneurship and the Metaverse: Opportunities and Strategies for Growth in the Digital Sphere* (pp. 355–376). Springer Nature Switzerland.

Nair, Y. V. I. V. (2024). Econometric Analysis of How Corporate Social Responsibility has Enabled Social Entrepreneurship and Innovation in India.

Patel, D., Deshpande, M., & Jadhav, A. (2024, August). Unveiling Consistency and Disparities: Exploring the Dynamics Between Customer Reviews and Ratings. In *International Conference on ICT for Sustainable Development* (pp. 223-231). Singapore: Springer Nature Singapore.

Rakhmatov, S. (2025). THE CONCEPT OF "UNIVERSITY 3.0" AND THE IMPORTANCE OF INNOVATIVE UNIVERSITIES IN THE DEVELOPMENT OF THE EDUCATION SYSTEM. *International Journal of Artificial Intelligence*, *1*(3), 1049–1051.

Raturi, S., & Bhatnagar, S. (2023). Influence of the Green Marketing Mix on Customers' Purchase Intentions for Sustainable Eco-Friendly Fashion Products. *NIFT JOURNAL OF FASHION*, 52.

Thapaliya, S., & Bokani, A. (2024). Leveraging artificial intelligence for enhanced cybersecurity: Insights and innovations. *Sadgamaya*, *1*(1), 46–52.

Upadhyaya, A., & Sijoria, C. (2024). Customers' Purchase Intention of Green Cosmetics in India: Empirical Validations Using an Extended Theory of Planned Behaviour (TPB). *Indian Journal of Marketing*, *54*(8), 60. Advance online publication. DOI: 10.17010/ijom/2024/v54/i8/174187

Verma, J. P. (2024). Green Marketing Practices: An Investigation into Consumer Perceptions and Purchase Intentions. ShodhKosh. *Journal of Visual and Performing Arts*, *5*(6). Advance online publication. DOI: 10.29121/shodhkosh.v5.i6.2024.3774

Chapter 7
Algorithmic Hospitality: AI-Driven Personalization Across the Guest Journey

Amrik Singh
https://orcid.org/0000-0003-3598-8787
Lovely Professional University, India

ABSTRACT

Algorithmic hospitality represents a transformative shift in the hospitality industry, where artificial intelligence (AI)–driven algorithms are increasingly embedded across the guest journey to deliver personalized, efficient, and predictive service experiences. From pre-arrival search and booking to on-site service encounters and post-stay engagement, AI-enabled systems analyze large volumes of guest data to anticipate preferences, automate decision-making, and tailor interactions in real time. Technologies such as machine learning, recommender systems, chatbots, facial recognition, and dynamic pricing engines are redefining how hotels and tourism organizations understand and respond to guest needs. The algorithmic personalization enhances convenience, operational efficiency, and customer satisfaction; it also raises critical concerns related to data privacy, transparency, bias, and the diminishing role of human agency in service encounters. This chapter explores the conceptual foundations of algorithmic hospitality and AI-driven personalization.

INTRODUCTION

The hospitality business has never been out of personalized service philosophy, which consists of anticipating guest needs, and providing comfort, and unforgettable experiences. Personalization was traditionally greatly dependent on the human sense, experience, and human skills. Nonetheless, digitalization of hospitality, which is

DOI: 10.4018/979-8-3373-8197-8.ch007

triggered by artificial intelligence (AI), big data, the Internet of Things (IoT), and machine learning (ML) has introduced a new era called algorithmic hospitality. Within the framework of this paradigm, the data-driven algorithms are becoming an essential influence on how hospitality organizations perceive guests, design services, use resources, and are increasingly tailored. Algorithms and algorithms are used in algorithmic hospitality where AI-based algorithms analyze data about the guests and automate all these processes based on the guest journey, including inspiration and booking, on-site experience, and post-stay interactions. This is not only an upgrading of technology but the reconstruction of service logic, in which machines supplement or even substitute much of the human-based judgmental functions traditionally. The increasing demands of digitally native customers, especially Millennials and Gen Z have only intensified the applicability of algorithmic personalization. Visitors are now demanding excellent digital experiences, dynamic rates, real-time response services, curated advice, and custom experiences in various touchpoints. At the same time, hospitality organizations have pressures of increasing efficiency, maximizing revenue, boosting the productivity of staff, and staying competitive in an ever platform-based economy. The conceptual underpinnings of algorithmic hospitality, technologies that make it possible, its uses in various parts of the guest lifecycle, its strategic value, ethical issues, workforce issues, and directions of the field. In such a way, the chapter adds to the further insight of how algorithmic systems are transforming the delivery of hospitality services and the experience of guests.

Ideological Underpinning of Algorithmic Hospitality

Long-held service ideology, the traditional approach to personalization in hospitality has been based on a human-centered approach to service, in which the quality of the guest experience was strongly determined by the responsiveness, recall, emotional intelligence, and social skills of frontline employees (Al-Romeedy & Singh, 2025a) . We focused on the personalized service. face-to-face interactions enabled staff to remember the names of repeat guests, note their room preferences, dining habits, and tailored service experience with observational and first-hand knowledge. Guest histories used to be kept in a manual form in guest comment cards, rudimentary property management systems or simply through informal departmental communication. Loyalty programs were premised on general segmentation strategies according to frequency of stay or amount of spending, and provided standard incentives, as opposed to personalized interaction. Although full of emotional warmth and authenticity, this personalization model was also inherently of restricted scope, consistency, and predictability: it was based on the human memory, manual record-keeping, and data systems fragments. Hospitality personalization has fundamentally changed with the swift development of artificial intelligence, machine learning, and big data analytics as a human-oriented interpretive process becomes a data-oriented, algorithmic, and predictive system (Dwivedi et al., 2025). The concept of personalization in modern hospitality setting does not only pertain to what guests are saying directly to the service desk. Rather, it is being derived more and more out of massive bodies of implicit data of behaviors, produced by digital interactions. These are the online browsing behavior, the pattern of clicking, the history of past booking, the location data of mobile, the social media interaction, the record of digital payments and the sentiment of online reviews. Each online interaction now generates behavioral intelligence. Billions of such micro-data points are processed in real time by algorithms in order to build dynamic guest profiles that change with each interaction. Consequently, hospitality firms are no longer just aware of the guest, as it has been previously, they are to the extent becoming predictive of the guest in terms of anticipating the preferences, needs and consumption patterns even before they are expressed (Al-Romeedy & Singh, 2025b; Gupta & Pareek, 2024). It is used to predictively personalize so as to provide hyper-customized recommendations, dynamic pricing, customized marketing communication, and automated service adjustments at a scale and speed never before possible. As an example, recommendation engines may provide recommendations on the type of rooms, food, spa activities, or local experiences based on previous behavior and patterns of other users of similar tastes. Revenue management algorithms are dynamic in the sense that it adjusts prices based on the sensitivity of individual demand. The Smart room technologies adjust the lighting, temperature, and entertainment preferences according to the stored guest profiles. These trends mean that there is a radical change in personalization, moving from the intuition-driven to the algorithmic personalization; the authority to make decisions gradually shifts to a machine intelligence (Ansari et al., 2024).It is under this context that the notion of algorithmic hospitality may be introduced, which can be described as the tactical use of artificial intelligence and algorithmic systems to automatize the process of personalization, optimization of service processes, and constantly adapt the guest experience throughout the hospitality value chain. Most algorithmic hospitality is characterized by a number of features. First, it is based on the ongoing data gathering of various digital and physical touchpoints, which means that the profiles of guests can be updated in real time. Second, it is pushed by prediction based on machine learning allowing systems to find invisible patterns, predict behavior, and optimize service strategies. Third, it is automated decision-making, in which algorithms automatically perform missions like price changes, room assignment, recommendations, and service scheduling. Fourth, it makes it easy to realize personalization in real time so that the experiences of the guests can be changed dynamically as the conditions and preferences evolve (Berry & Singh, 2024). Lastly, it provides scalability of service customization and it is possible to customize experiences of thousands of guests at the same time without significant labor increases. As opposed to conventional personalization that was limited by the capacity of human memory, the quantity of work, and inconsistency, algorithmic hospitality is by definition scaleable, dynamic, predictive as well as automated. It works as a back-off server, and services are modified automatically instantly on demand changes, guest dynamics, and environmental information. The personalization is no longer an episodic or reactive process; however, it has been transformed into a continuous and anticipatory process and formed a part of the operations fabric of hospitality organizations.

Theoretical Frameworks

There are various theoretical frameworks, which justify the logic of algorithmic hospitality. Technology Acceptance Model (TAM) is used to explain how guests and employees are willing to work with AI-assisted systems in terms of perceived usefulness and ease of use. These perceptions largely determine whether mobile check-in, chatbots, and smart rooms are accepted or not. Service-Dominant Logic reimburse the value as collaboratively generated in the process of interaction between guests and service systems; in algorithmic hospitality, such collaboration is mediated more and more by digital platforms and intelligent technologies (Bilgihan et al., 2025; Srivastava et al., 2025; Suhag et al., 2024). Experience Economy Theory does highlight that memorable experiences are planned and not accidentally provided, a fact that is in close accordance with AI-enhanced organization of personalized guest experiences. The Big Data Analytics Capability Theory describes the analytical capability of hospitality firms that can create a competitive edge by utilizing data-processing capabilities to improve the quality of decisions, customer understanding, and operational performance. Lastly, the Socio-Technical Systems Theory emphasizes the fact that the hospitality organizations are not technical entities as such but rather complicated relations among human labor force, technological systems, organizational structures, and social forces. This view is especially critical in the concept of the hybridity of algorithmic hospitality, whereby human service labor and machine intelligence will co-exist and interact. Together, these structures shed light on how the shift toward data-driven and away-from-human personalization is not only a technological modernization of the game but also a reorganization of the structure and culture of hospitality service logic.

LITERATURE REVIEW

Algorithms have already taken over functions that were previously the preserve of the human mind, but the human aspect of the process empathy, moral compass, and emotional attachment cannot be substituted. The personalization of personalization in hospitality is not in the takeover of people by the machines, but in the strategic blending of algorithmic intelligence with the human service artistry.

Empowerment Technologies of Algorithmic Hospitality

The fundamental motivation of the emergence of algorithmic hospitality is a confluence of new, high-tech powers, which, when combined, can make personalization of the hospitality value chain smart, autonomous, and even scalable (Chaudhary et al., 2025; Rai & Singh, 2026; Prakash et al., 2024). These technologies are not isolated devices but make up a technological ecosystem which captures, processes, analyses, and acts upon huge volumes of guest and operational data in real time. The technological foundation of algorithmic hospitality is made up of artificial intelligence, big data analysis, the Internet of Things, natural language processing and computer vision that will revolutionize service delivery and managerial decisions.

Machine learning and Artificial Intelligence

Algorithms in hospitality are based on artificial intelligence (AI) and machine learning (ML). The purpose of machine learning algorithms is to find complicated trends in large data sets and to enhance predictive accuracy as time progresses without being reprogrammed. These algorithms in the hospitality setting examine past and current data then produce predictions regarding the preferences, purchase behaviors, price sensitivity, demand variations, and the general level of satisfaction. Supervised learning models have been extensively applied to demand forecasting, revenue maximization and churn modeling using labeled data, including past bookings and cancelation history (Chaudhary et al., 2025; Sharma et al., 2024a). Unsupervised learning, however, helps in the customer segmentation of hidden behavioral groups that are not classified into categories. Applications of deep learning methods, especially neural networks, can improve image recognition, speech processing, and highly recommended engines. With constant learning, the ML systems are able to optimize room allocation procedures, target promotional packages, preempt occupancy with high accuracy and recognize failure in service delivery before it leads to complaints. In fact, as an example, AI-based recommenders systems personalize travel recommendations based on previous interactions and behavioral patterns of similar users, whereas predictive systems predict service demand including housekeeping or food choices. Simply put, AI and ML allow hospitality companies to change their reactive service models to the proactive service systems based on being adaptive and predictive, which signifies a radical change in operations.

Big Data Analytics

The analytical infrastructure used in AI-driven operations of hospitality is based on big data analytics. The hospitality organizations produce vast amounts of structured, semi-structured and unstructured data, which is generated by property management systems (PMS), customer relationship management (CRM) systems, booking engines, loyalty programs, online travel agencies (OTAs), social media interactions, digital payment systems, IoT sensors and mobile applications. All these varied data streams have high velocity, volume, variety and variability implying that traditional data-processing tools are not adequate. Big data analytics combines high quality data mining, cloud computing and real time processing applications to transform raw digital traces to actionable managerial information. Descriptive analytics allow hotels to track real-time performance indicators, including the occupancy, average daily rate, and guest satisfaction. Predictive analytics helps to predict demand in the future, bookings patterns and lifetime value of guests. Prescriptive analytics goes an extra mile by giving the best choices in terms of pricing, staffing, inventory management, and marketing promotion (Singh & Kumar, 2025a; Islam & Singh, 2025). The analytics of big data enables strategic agility, more precise services, and improved competitive advantage through the transformation of scattered and complicated information into the actionable intelligence of the algorithmic hospitality.

Internet of Things (IoT)

Internet of Things (IoT) is very important in adding intelligence to the physical structures in a hospitality setting. IoT can be described as a type of network that is made up of connected physical objects, which have sensors, actuators, and wireless connectivity that constantly gather and transmit data. IoT makes personalizing the service environment in algorithms with digital guest data in real time into a physical interpretation of the service environment. The use of smart rooms with sensors helps to computerize the process of regulating light, room temperature, air quality, curtain movement, and entertainment system depending on the personal preferences or behavioral patterns of a particular guest. Smart wristbands and mobile applications are examples of wearable devices that monitor the movement of guests, how they utilize facilities, and their location choices in resorts and cruise ships. Interconnected sensors are also used to track energy use, water usage, and equipment operation, which allows predictive maintenance and sustainable use of resources (Cherenkov et al., 2024; Sharma et al., 2024a). Hospitality companies by combining IoT-generated data and AI analytics implement responsive service ecosystems that dynamically adapt to the needs of the guests and increase efficiency and sustainability in operations and the environment. Natural Language Processing

(NLP) refers to the branch of computer science focused on analyzing, synthesizing, and comprehending natural languages.

Natural Language Processing (NLP)

Natural Language Processing (NLP) is the field of computer science that deals with the syntheses, analysis, and understanding of natural languages. Natural language processing (NLP) allows machines to comprehend, interpret, and produce human language, hence allowing a smooth interaction between humans and computers in the hospitality sector. The technology behind chatbots, voice assistants, automated messaging platforms, and sentiment analysis software used in hotel websites, mobile apps, social media, and in-room devices is based on NLP. The conversational AI agents are able to respond to guest queries on room availability, price, amenities, and local attractions in real-time, and offer 24/7 service support to guests without the involvement of human resources (Wang, 2025; Suhag et al., 2024; Singh, 2025). In-Room voice assistants enable guests to operate the lighting, temperature system, television, and order requests with the help of voice commands, which increases convenience and ease of use. Sentiment analysis using NLP identifies the degree of emotions and satisfaction in the form of client reviews, feedback forms, and social media posts, providing an excellent opportunity to enhance the services and manage reputation. NLP creates a wide range of opportunities to enhance communication between the hospitality operations by facilitating natural, real-time, and customized communication, which, in turn, substantially diminishes service friction and broadens the scope of hospitality operations.

Computer Vision

The ability to make visual conclusions using AI-based image and video recognition allows algorithmic hospitality to use computer vision to understand the visual data. The facial recognition technologies have made it easier to check-in with contactless facilities, conduct biometric authentication and identify the guest by name. Gesture recognition facilitates the interaction between customers and the self-service kiosk and interactive displays without the use of touch. Video analytics is used to track the number of people in a crowd, the movement of guests, and the security situation in the open areas and lobbies, airports, and entertainment facilities (Wang, 2025; Sharma et al., 2024c). Operationally, computer vision improves surveillance, threat identification, loss prevention and facility management.

In the personalization perspective, it facilitates the automatic identification of repeat guests who will receive personalised greetings, room preferences and service notifications. Nonetheless, there are also significant ethical, legal, and privacy issues associated with the implementation of the computer vision, which demand efficient governance systems. Artificial intelligence, big data analytics, IoT, natural language processing, and computer vision are all components of an intelligent technological ecosystem that will drive algorithmic hospitality. Their coherent nature allows them to capture data, analyze data in real-time, predict and execute automated services. They will further personalize operations in the hospitality industry in the digital era and make them more efficient and strategic, as these technologies evolve and converge further.

AI Powered Guest-Journey Customization

The concept of AI personalization is now seen as a ubiquitous element across all stages of the hospitality guest experience and has turned the linear nature of the service into an ever-evolving data-driven experience ecosystem. The guest experience is generally known to have five interconnected phases, such as pre-trip inspiration, booking and planning, arrival and check-in, on-site experience, and post-stay engagement, and all five phases are now undergoing an algorithmic system through all these phases in order to become relevant, efficient, and emotionally robust. At the pre-trip phase, artificial intelligence has a significant influence on how prospective tourists explore destinations, compare alternatives, and create expectations (Vashishth et al., 2024; Singh & Kumar, 2025a). The digital marketing space that runs with AI is used to analyze the behavior of users on search engines, social media, and traveling websites to determine the intent patterns and psychographic profiles that will be used to hyper-target ads via programmatic marketing systems. To stay in the market, the Marriott International and the Hilton Worldwide use AI-based marketing engines to provide personalized advertisements, dynamic email campaigns, and retargeted travel offers, based on the browsing history and previous stays. At the same time, the recommendation systems employed by such websites as Booking.com, Expedia, and Airbnb are based on collaborative filtering algorithms and content-based algorithms to propose the hotels, destinations, and experiences based on personal likes and dislikes. An already booked traveler of an eco-resort or wellness retreat is guided algorithmically to find similar sustainable luxury resources and, as a result, minimizes search fatigue and gets guaranteed to book. The conversational AI also goes further to provide inspiration by providing the personalized and real-time engagement of chatbots and virtual assistants (Turčinović et al., 2025; Sharma et al., 2024b). Hotels like Accor or IHG on their websites and apps have AI-based chat interfaces to answer pre-booking requests about rates and amenities, as well as local attractions in real time, simulating human interaction based on natural language processing.

Hospitality Operations and AI

Simultaneously, online review and social media sentiment and review analysis software summarize hundreds of thousands of online ratings and social media posts, losing emotional aura and determiners of satisfaction to impact platform rankings and consumer trust. An example is TripAdvisor using machine learning to summarize the sentiment of guests and rank the properties dynamically, according to the changing feedback. All these mechanisms make the pre-trip phase more personalized and predictive, form the impressions of the guests even before they physically come in touch with the hotel. The booking and planning phase is the business center of the guest experience, so the directly-related outcomes of algorithmic personalization are revenue maximization and operational efficiency. Revenue management systems based on AI actively regulate the price of rooms in real-time, combining demand indicators, seasonal patterns, competitor rates, and business-specific sensitivity to prices (Thaichon et al.,2025; Singh & Kumar, 2025b; Sharma et al., 2024a; Islam & Singh, 2025). Large hotel chains like Hyatt or Marriott use AI-powered pricing engines to optimize the RevPAR, but also provide personal discounts to the target groups of guests. This change in stagnant pricing technique to algorithmic yield management is necessary as a way of guaranteeing profitability as well as the perceived fairness. Machine learning can also be used to create tailor-made travel packages by smartly bundling accommodations, dining, transportation and experience services. Indicatively, AI-programmed wellness or adventure packages are being offered more often by luxury resorts, using their profile of guests and past consumption habits. The predictive demand forecasting also enables the hotels in a high level of accuracy of their forecast into the volume of booking, length of stay and probability of cancellation with the result that they will be able to optimize their staffing, inventory and plan procurement. Simultaneously, the detection algorithms of fraud are used to track the behavior of transactions in real-time, to detect suspicious payment patterns, which increases the level of digital security and trust in guests. Expedia and MakeMyTrip are examples of OTAs that use AI-based risk scoring systems to avoid payment fraud and chargeback losses. By these algorithmic interventions, the stage of booking will be able to smoothly transform interest into bookings and match guest value with business performance. The check-in and arrival stage is a very serious one because it forms immediate feelings and reactions. Personalization has been redefined by algorithms to make this step a smooth, touchless and extremely effective one. Guests can now avoid the normal front desk processes and check-in directly through mobile check-in apps, facial recognition, and touchscreen key cards (Talukder et al., 2025; Srivastava et al., 2025; Suhag et al., 2024). The biometric method of identity verification and entry to the hotel rooms is implemented in hotels in Asia and the Middle East like the FlyZoo Hotel in China operated by Alibaba and some properties in the Accor Smart Hotel program, where no queues or paperwork are required to complete the identification procedure.

Smart Rooms and AI

Smart room allocation system employs AI to allocate rooms according to the preferences of the guests, their loyalty level, access requirements, and past complaints, which means that returning clients will be automatically put in the room that will match their expectations. The workforce optimization tools also predict the patterns of guest arrival and peak traffic at the same time to schedule the staff predictively and reduce waiting time and maximising responsiveness to services. The transition of digital interaction to physical service is virtually seamless since by the time the guest gets on the physical property, much of the experience has been organized by algorithmic systems. The on-site experience can be seen as the operational core of algorithmic hospitality, in which the living experience of the guest is continuously being defined by real-time personalisation (Srivastava et al., 2025; Suhag et al., 2024). The IoT sensor-powered smart rooms are now able to automatically control lighting, temperature, curtains, and audiovisual systems according to the preferences of the guests stored in advance or according to the specifics of their actions in real-time. Other global brands like the IoT Guestroom Lab by Marriott and Connected Room concept by Hilton demonstrate that the individualization of the environment turns into a luxury requirement. Voice recognition systems like Alexa in Hospitality and Google Assistant also enable guests to manage lights, order food, call housekeeping and get local recommendations by speaking naturally, greatly lowering the response time of services and employee numbers. Within the food and beverage sector, AI-based menu recommendation applications recommend foods and beverages according to dietary needs, past orders, allergies, and wellness information.

AI and Inventory Systems

Robotic chefs, automated ordering systems, and AI-controlled inventory systems have also been implemented in some of the most high-tech hospitality settings to achieve faster speed, consistency, and cost control. Predictive maintenance systems rely on sensor-based generated data, which predicts the failure of equipment in HVAC systems, elevators, and kitchen infrastructure, reducing the service downtimes and enhancing energy conservation. The computer vision analytics control the number of guests entering and leaving lobbies, pools and dining areas, controlling the crowd density and movement patterns, which was particularly important during the post-pandemic period to guarantee safety and social distancing. These applications show that algorithmic systems are working invisibly and continuously in the background to influence comfort, convenience, safety, and reliability of the service in real time (Suhag et al., 2024; Singh, 2025; Maheshwari et al., 2024). The guest journey does not end at the check-out, but instead under the post-stay engagement stage, hospitality organizations will be able to further customize their services using AI as they no longer rely on transactional service but instead a long-term relationship management approach. Chatbots and email workflows, as well as mobile notifications delivered automatically upon departure, are used to gather feedback in order to capture the response of guests at the highest emotional recall.

Feedback and Surveys

Such systems have very high response rates due to feedback response rates than the traditional paper surveys. Textual reviews and open-ended feedback are then analyzed using natural language processing tools to identify emotional tone, service gaps, and satisfaction drivers to implement quick managerial intervention. Customization based on AI has also redefined loyalty programs. Loyalty rewards are no longer a standardized system, but are instead customized concerning an individual expenditure history, frequency of visits, lifetime value projectors and market segmentation. Marriott Bonvoy and Hilton Honors brands use machine learning to personalize at redemption offers of rewards, bonus plans, and frequency of communication. Predictive retargeting algorithms go on to evaluate the likelihood of returning again and activate custom offers at the best times, like a birthday present or anniversary present, location-based cues (Singh, 2025; Dwivedi et al., 2025). By such means, algorithmic hospitality goes beyond the physical stay and becomes a loop of engagement that builds brand loyalty and lifetime value of a customer. All these changes together demonstrate that the personalization provided by AI has radically transformed the process of the hospitality guest experience as a digitally mediated, constantly adaptive, and relational experience system.

DISCUSSION AND INTERPRETATION

Algorithms inspired to post-stay loyalty provide unprecedented accuracy in the customization of the services, at the same time optimizes the work performance. Nevertheless, this change, too, creates significant ethical, privacy, and human-oriented issues, especially in terms of data safety, openness, and emotional sincerity in hospitality experience. The future of AI-driven personalization thus will be in the extent to which it is made in the balance between automation and empathy, efficiency and trust, and data intelligence and human dignity between hospitality organizations.

Strategic Advantages of Algorithmic Hotel

Algorithms hospitality has great strategic benefits to hospitality organizations since it changes the ways in which services are provided, designed and managed. By integrating artificial intelligence, big data analytics, and automation, hospitality companies can become more efficient, profitable, and satisfy customers and be more competitive. The strategic advantages of algorithmic hospitality are not a strictly technological increase; they restructure the organizations, models of the services and market performance in the long run (Singh & Kumar, 2025a; Gupta & Pareek, 2024). The first and possibly the most obvious advantage of algorithmic hospitality is that it can significantly enhance operational efficiency. Routine and repetitive jobs like reservations processing, check-in and check-out, billing, housekeeping scheduling, inventory tracking, and maintenance monitoring are very automated and consequently the employees are not overworked and overburdened with administrative duties. The AI based systems reduce human error, standardize service implementation and bring uniformity in the quality-of-service delivery at various properties and service interactions. Machine learning-based predictive maintenance minimizes machine failures and service interruptions, which reduces the costs of repair and downtime. Optimization algorithms of the workforce also improve efficiency in the fact that they predict demand trends and schedule employees in accordance with real service demand. Consequently, hospitality organizations are able to offer quicker, dependable, and inexpensive services as well as enable human personnel to occupy jobs of greater value, such as experiential and relational work.

Revenue and Algorithmic Systems

The other significant strategic advantage is optimization of revenue because the algorithmic systems are fundamental in the way they alter classical pricing and sales approaches. Dynamic pricing models, which are powered by AI, keep the prices of rooms dynamic due to the real-time demand, market conditions, competitor pricing, seasonality, and sensitivity of a specific price. This helps the hotels to enable them to maximize revenue per available rooms (RevPAR) without over and under pricing during peak and low-demand seasons respectively. Custom promotional triggers and recommendation systems boost the rate of conversion and the mean value of transactions (Singh & Kumar, 2025b; Gursoy, 2025). Collectively, these competencies can help hospitality companies to shift toward non-static revenue management to highly flexible, data-driven yield management systems. The algorithmic hospitality also delivers high results in guest satisfaction with the ability to achieve high levels of personalization at all the guest touchpoints. Room set-ups, service suggestions, individualized diet, proactive service recovery and hassle-free online communications benefit the comfort, convenience, and emotional connection of guests.

Data-Driven Decision-Making

Another of the strategic strengths is the transition to data-driven decision-making. Historically, a lot of managerial choices in the hospitality were based on intuition, experience, and history. With algorithmic hospitality, the reactive and subjective approach is substituted with predictive and evidence-based management. Advanced analytics will give real-time information regarding demand patterns, guest behavior, service performance, market trends, and financial risks (Sharma et al., 2024a; Hardcastle et al., 2025). The managers are able to model other strategies, assess the effects of price adjustments, predict staffing needs and identify the new service issue before they go out of control. This saves confusion, increases the accuracy of strategic planning, and increases agility to changing market conditions in organizations. Lastly, hospitality firms can enjoy a strong competitive edge through the use of AI.

Algorithmic Hospitality

Successful organizations in the implementation of algorithmic hospitality enjoy greater level of market responsiveness, since they can easily adapt to changes in customer preferences, competition and other external disturbances. Individualized digital experience enhances brand differentiation through the delivery of individualized, personalized guest experiences that cannot be easily imitated by the competitors. Leadership in innovation and data accumulation are also some of the benefits of early adopters of AI. Algorithms are becoming an important source of sustained competitive advantage (as opposed to a technological addition) in the ever more platform-based and experience-based hospitality markets. Overall, the multi-dimensional strategic advantages of algorithmic hospitality improve the efficiency, profitability, satisfaction of visitors, effectiveness in management, and competitive positioning (Hardcastle et al., 2025). The achievement of these advantages however is not solely tied to technological investment but also ethical governance, employee upskilling and strategicity between the digital innovation and the values of human-oriented service.

Human-AI Collaboration and Hotel Workforce

Algorithms hospitality is not only a change in technology, but it is a restructuring of hospitality employment, frontline work, and organizational culture to the core. With the advent of artificial intelligence in the service operations, human labor, and machine intelligence are no longer defined in the classic way. Algorithms in hospitality have workforce implication that go beyond the efficiency improvement to include matters of professional identity, employment quality and human dignity. Another most observable transformation is in the frontline roles. Many routine and repetitive, rule-based processes, including reservations management, billing, check-in operation, housekeeping scheduling and simple guest inquiries are being automated with self-service kiosks, mobile apps, chatbots, and robotic process automation (Sharma et al., 2024b; Maheshwari et al., 2024; Islam & Singh, 2025). Frontline work is turning into guest relationship management, where employees are focused on or building trust, personal rapport, and building long term loyalty, emotional labor, where empathy, warmness, and personalization of services can only be authentically provided by human employees, service recovery, where human discretion is required to address complaints and regain guest satisfaction, and experience design, where employees are involved in creating memorable and emotionally charged service experiences. Automation is therefore not taking away the human aspect but realigning it to a greater value, relationship, and experiential aspect of hospitality. Such a change in job content is also accompanied by the need to change skills heavily. The future hospitality workers should not only have the conventional service skills but also high-level digital skills. The level of digital literacy becomes an essential skill, and the employees will be able to use AI-based systems, robotic service tools, smart room controls, and data dashboards (Jogarao, 2024; Islam & Singh, 2025). The interpretation of data is becoming a crucial skill as frontline supervisors and managers need to have the ability to interpret predictive analytics, which will be connected with the behavior of guests, demand trends, and service quality. Human-AI collaboration competencies are also crucial and should involve the skills to collaborate with automated systems, rely on recommendations by the algorithms without critical thinking, and take proper action in case of system failure or when ethical issues are present. Moreover, increasing anxieties about data privacy, cybersecurity, and algorithmic bias necessitate that employees should build moral and privacy consciousness in the daily functioning practices. As a result, hospitality education, business training systems, and professional development models should develop at a high pace to equip workers with digitally enhanced service settings.

Job Displacement

One of the main arguments of algorithmic hospitality is the question of job displacement, or job augmentation. The advent of AI, robotics, and automation has spawned universal concerns of massive layoffs, especially of less skilled service workers. The main tasks that are the focus of automation include routine and standardized tasks which leave employees with the freedom to focus on the guest engagement, creativity in services and complex decision making. At the same time, new professional positions are being developed in hospitality companies, such as trainers of AI systems, data analysts, designers of digital experience, specialists in the maintenance of robots, and cybersecurity managers. These jobs represent an even more widespread occupation transformation to hybrid digital-service jobs. Instead of seeing the killing of work, the industry is undergoing the structural redesign of the employment where the work content, skills demanded and career ladders are being redesigned. On one hand, AI-based monitoring systems have the ability to follow the productivity of employees, their response time, location, service transactions, performance metrics to a precision that has never been achieved before. Although this kind of monitoring promotes efficiency, accountability, it also presents real issues of workplace surveillance, loss of employee independence, and the aggravation of labor (Al-Romeedy & Singh, 2025b; Ansari et al., 2024). Algorithms can be used to schedule staff in the most cost-effective way, yet they can decrease predictability of the schedules and work-life balance among employees. Constant online surveillance can also add to psychological stress, preperformance anxiety and the feeling of loss of professional discretion. As more workflows become defined by algorithms, the distribution of tasks, and performance appraisals, employees can feel that the power balance has shifted towards the impersonal machine system against the human management.

Socially Responsible

To make algorithmic hospitality both sustainable and socially responsible, it is necessary to have a balanced approach to the integration of humans and AI. Although efficiency, accuracy, and scalability are valid organizational objectives, they should not be attained at the cost of employee welfare, dignity, and professional development. Open algorithmic regulation, democratic technology design, equitable performance measures, solid data security, and active upskilling programs are paramount to preserve healthy human-AI relations in the workplace of the hospitality industry (Sharma et al., 2024c; Saxena et al., 2024; Rai & Singh, 2026). The companies that manage to strike the right balance between technological progress and human-oriented management are the ones more prone to attaining not only the best practices in their operations but also loyal, strong, and future-focused employees. To summarize, the concept of algorithmic hospitality is radically reinventing the essence of hospitality labor. It minimizes a reliance on routine manual labor and maximizes the strategic, emotional and creative aspects of front line service. It is the quality of cooperation between human intelligence and artificial intelligence that will determine the future of the hospitality job, though not in the form of replacement of the latter by the former.

LEGAL, PRIVACY, AND ETHICAL HAZARDS

The promotion of the use of algorithmic systems in the hotel sector not only has operational and strategic advantages but also a range of ethical, legal, and privacy problems that essentially define confidence, governance, and social responsibility in the sector. With the growing reliance of personalization on the massive gathering, processing, and analysis of guest data, hospitality organizations have a delicate balancing act to walk in the area of data protection, fairness, transparency, and cybersecurity. The inability to handle these issues may destroy the trust of the guests, put the companies at risk of lawsuits, and negatively impact the long-term validity of algorithmic hospitality. Data privacy and informed consent are the major concerns of the concept of algorithmic personalization (Ansari et al., 2024; Berry & Singh, 2024; Liu et al., 2024). Visitors do not necessarily know how much their information are being monitored, distributed on different platforms and being used to make predictions and targeted advertising. Even in cases of consent, it is usually enshrined in long and cumbersome privacy policies, which not many users comprehend. This brings a moral clash between the exploitation of data in the business name and a basic right of a person to privacy, autonomy, and data ownership. The hospitality organizations have to ensure that they have transparent consent processes, have minimization of data and that they are fully adhering to the changing standards of regulations.

Algorithmic Unfairness & Discrimination

The other problematic issue is the issue of algorithmic unfairness and discrimination. Training AI systems is done based on historical data that could mirror the current social, economic and cultural disparities. When these prejudiced data are latent into algorithms they may accidentally reenact or even enhance discriminatory acts. Biased algorithms can affect the price of rooms, the ability to earn loyalty points and receive special services, prioritization of risk analysis, and marketing exposure in a manner that reduces members of some demographic groups (Saxena et al., 2024; Rai & Singh, 2026; Prakash et al., 2024). Indicatively, a dynamic pricing system can have a systematic provision of a higher rate to a particular group of customers, and a recommendation engine can marginalize or ostracize others based on the perceived socioeconomic status

Transparency and Explainability

Bias is closely associated with the problem of transparency and explainability, commonly referred to as the black box problem of artificial intelligence. Most algorithmic decision-making systems use complicated machine learning models to which even their creators may not fully be able to read. This makes guests and employees often unaware of how the decisions regarding pricing, the focus on services, or performance appraisal are created. Such transparency undermines trust and restricts responsibility, especially when the algorithm decisions are of great financial or personal importance (Prakash et al., 2024; Mishra et al., 2025). Ethically and legally, people are becoming more and more demanding of their right to know, question and contest automated decisions, which have an impact on them. The task of hospitality organizations should consequently be to achieve explainable AI systems and open data habits that enable the user to understand the mechanism of algorithmic personalization.

Cybersecurity

Lastly, the increased reliance on interconnected AI is a risk to cybersecurity of hospitality organizations. Smart hotels, mobile applications, biometric, reservation systems based on the cloud, and the IoT-powered rooms create very interconnected digital environments that can be easily hacked, breached, impersonated, or ransomware attacked. A single security breach would jeopardize sensitive guest information in a tremendous scale causing financial loss, legal fines, brand loss and deficit of trust in the long term. With the higher sophistication of cyber threats, hospitalsity companies will have to spend a lot of money on encryption systems, intrusion detection systems, secure cloud infrastructures, and efficient incident-response models (Mooi Kwong et al., 2024; Maheshwari et al., 2024). To sum up, ethical, legal, and privacy issues are some of the most challenging limitations to sustainable development of algorithmic hospitality. Protection of data, justice, openness, and cybersecurity are not technical considerations but key aspects of trust and social responsibility. The proactive discussion of these issues is a key to the creation of resilient, legally compliant, and ethically based algorithmic hospitality ecosystems that would reconcile technological innovation with human rights and societal values.

CASE STUDIES OF ALGORITHMIC HOSPITALITY

Global hotel chains, as an example, have been on the front to embrace artificial intelligence in the area of demand prediction and personalization of loyalties. These organizations can predict the predicted data with high accuracy using advanced machine learning models that are combined with property management systems and customer relationship management platforms that analyze past booking patterns, seasonal demand variations, competitor rates, and macroeconomic factors (Berry &

Singh, 2024; Singh, 2025; Jogarao, 2024). At the same time, loyalty programs are becoming more and more algorithmic, which allows them to offer hyper-personalized products in terms of guest lifetime value, spending patterns, frequency of traveling, and history of interaction with the brand. Guests are given customized upgrades, targeted discounts, and experiences instead of general ones, which in turn enhances the emotional connection and repeat visits. Another vivid example of algorithmic hospitality is offered by luxury resorts, which use voice-controlled smart rooms and adjust their lighting and environmental automation according to their moods. The Internet of Things (IoT) infrastructure and AI-powered systems of control would enable these resorts to customize the room environment on the fly. Guest profiles record their preferences in terms of temperature, intensity of lighting, type of music, location of the curtain and even the type of content that they would prefer to watch in the TV. These preferences are automatically taken into consideration in the room upon a check-in establishing an immediate feeling of familiarity and comfort. Voice assistants also allow the amenities, rooms service, spa, and concierge to be controlled without hands, which makes service delivery less frictional and experience-related exclusivity exclusive (Gupta & Pareek, 2024). These systems are also being incorporated in most luxury environments together with wellness technologies (circadian lighting, personalized climate controls, etc.), which further supports the positioning of luxury hospitality as an experience based on immersion and the use of technology to enhance it.

When it comes to the other side of the scale, the concept of algorithmic hospitality has been used by budget hotels mainly to enhance efficiency, decrease operational expenses and facilitate the movement of guests. The most noticeable one is the introduction of contactless check-in experience using the facial recognition and mobile-based identity verification (Al-Romeedy & Singh, 2025a; Mishra et al., 2025; Mooi Kwong et al., 2024). The systems minimize the number of front-desk employees, do away with long lines, and allow fast guest registration. To price-sensitive passengers, speed, convenience, and affordability tend to be more important than desire to communicate with a human, so algorithmic solutions are especially appropriate to the low-price niche. Automated check-in desks, electronic room keys and AI-enhanced help desks are additional features to improve service accessibility without raising labor expenses. It shows how algorithmic hospitality can facilitate a business model based on high volume and low margin in addition to enhancing personalization, as well as cost optimization and scalability.

Some of the most sophisticated instances of algorithmic hospitality can be found via digital accommodation platforms like Airbnb and larger online travel agencies (OTAs) that operate some of the most sophisticated recommender systems and dynamic pricing engines. These sites constantly examine the search actions of the user, the browsing history and booking history, location, peer evaluations, and seasonal demand cues in order to tailor the search results and price-setting suggestions to hosts (Turčinović et al., 2025; Singh, 2025; Singh & Kumar, 2025a). Listings are served to the guests and hosts are given optimal pricing suggestions, availability suggestions, and listing suggestions by the algorithm. This personalization on both sides will maximize the efficiency of transactions and revenue on the platform as well as influence consumer choice on a global level. These case examples, in total, can prove that algorithmic hospitality is not experimental and does not remain in a luxury setup.

FUTURE OF ALGORITHMIC HOSPITALITY

The future of algorithmic hospitality will shift much further than the state of the present automation and recommendation systems into immensely immersive, emotionally intelligent, and sustainability-focused service ecosystems. The systems of the future will likely combine biometric information (facial expressions, voice tones, heart rate, and stress indicators) with non-biometric data (location, time of the day, purpose of travel, social setting (Srivastava et al., 2025; Suhag et al., 2024). This convergence will enable hotels to actively change room settings, service levels, and engagement strategies in real time, which will produce experiences that are not merely personalized but also emotive. To give an example, a business traveler who is tired of his or her work can be offered soothing lights and quicker services, whereas a leisure guest can be given lively experiences and activity recommendations, which is detected by the mood. Generative AI-driven virtual concierge services will provide extremely natural, contextually aware experiences, providing insight into destinations, assistance in entertainment planning, problem-solving, and interaction with emotions on a request basis. This will greatly improve the availability and consistency of the services and minimize reliance on the standardized scripts of service (O. Abdullah et al., 2025; Manoharan & Ashtikar, 2025; Islam & Singh, 2025). The collaboration of the metaverse and virtual hospitality will also increase the limits of the guest experience outside of the physical space. The use of AI powered virtual worlds will allow the travelers to view virtual copies of the hotel, rooms, destinations and even experiences before deciding whether to book them or not. Visitors can have virtual tours around the sites, undergo faux spa sessions, or preview meals using immersive extended reality technologies. Virtual conferences can be held in branded hotel metaverse, which can incorporate both physical and online hospitality (Al-Romeedy & Singh, 2025b; O. Abdullah et al., 2025). The innovations will transform marketing, pre-trip experience, and even remote service consumption, placing hospitality in a larger ecosystem of immersive online experiences. In this regard, the individualized avatars, virtual interrelationship, and simulated flow of services across the world will be organized by algorithmic systems.

One of the future trends that may be critical will be the emergence of sustainable algorithmic hospitality where AI will be implemented strategically to help in the environmental management and the proper management of resources. Smart energy management system will streamline the heating, cooling, lighting, and water consumption in accordance with the real-time occupancy and behavioral trends. The food waste will be reduced by analyzing demand and optimizing the inventory with predictive analytics and improving recycling and the practices of the recycling economy by utilizing AI-powered waste management systems. Lastly, more human-centered AI models that enable a compromise between the technological efficiency and ethical responsibility and the dignity of the workers will be emphasized. The next generation of hospitality algorithm applications will focus on transparency, explainability, inclusiveness, and fairness in both customer and employee-facing applications. Instead of substituting human employees, AI will become a co-worker that will enrich human creativity, emotional intelligence, and decision-making process (Sharma et al., 2024a; Liu et al., 2024). The responsible use of biometric information, surveillance technology, and automated monitoring of performance will be informed by the principles of ethical design. Emotionally intelligent hyper-personalization, generative service design, and immersive virtual experience, sustainability-focused intelligence, and ethically oriented human-centered AI will characterize the future of algorithmic hospitality.

IMPLICATIONS OF RESEARCH AND GAPS

The fast penetration of algorithmic hospitality has spawned an increasing number of scholarly studies in the fields of hospitality management, information systems, marketing, and tourism studies. Yet, current literature is skewed and focused heavily on technical efficiency and system performance as well as the intentions to adopt the systems. Models like the Technology Acceptance Model (TAM), Unified Theory of Acceptance and Use of Technology (UTAUT) and service automation frameworks have dominated much of the existing literature and discussed the perception of usefulness, ease of use, trust, and behavioral intention towards AI-based services (Ansari et al., 2024; Berry & Singh, 2024). Although these studies have brought important information on adoption trends, revenue growth and optimization of operations, they still give a biased picture on the socio-psychological, ethical, and cultural changes that are prompted by algorithmic hospitality on a wider platform. A number of research gaps thus are not adequately addressed. Additional empirical research is needed to comprehend the effects of constant algorithmic surveillance and prophesy on the perceptions of autonomy, authenticity, and privacy by the guests during successive stays and travel situations (Chaudhary et al., 2025; Singh, 2025; Jogarao, 2024). Another similar and hardly researched area is the emotional aspect of algorithmic service experiences.

Hospitality Psychology

The perceived empathy, emotional resonance, discomfort, formation of trust, and emotional dissonance issues have not been thoroughly theorized. Future studies need to consider the combination of affective computing, emotional intelligence theory, and hospitality psychology to investigate the way emotional value is built, mediated, or even reduced in situations where algorithms are used to provide services. The second research gap is the power relations that exist between the algorithms, the workers, and the guests. A significant part of the literature is a neutral view of AI that helps to increase efficiency and the quality of services. Nevertheless, critical approaches demonstrate that algorithmic systems can be used to exercise control, surveillance, and performance control (Singh & Kumar, 2025b; Rai & Singh, 2026; Prakash et al., 2024; Mishra et al., 2025;]Maheshwari et al., 2024). Algorithms affecting employees are becoming more commonly used to schedule and measure productivity, monitor behavior, and even issue discipline. Simultaneously, the guest-facing algorithms also affect the pricing, prioritization of the service, visibility, and access to benefits. Such power structures of the algorithmic types redefine the authority, the autonomy of the employees, and the agency provided to the customers in significant ways. However, there are few empirical studies on algorithmic management, intensification of digital work, psychological stress, resistance, and negotiation of algorithmic control in hospitality workplaces. There is an urgent need to conduct interdisciplinary research based on the field of labor studies, critical management studies, and digital sociology in order to shed a light on such changing power relations.

Cross-Cultural Variations

The question of cross-cultural variations in the adoption and understanding of AI-driven personalization also describes a significant line of research. The majority of empirical research on algorithmic hospitality is clustered in economies that are technologically advanced (United States, Western Europe, and East Asia). The relationship between AI technologies and the perceptions and reactions of the guests are highly dependent on the particular cultural values of privacy, uncertainty avoidance, power distance, and human interaction (Thaichon et al.,2025; Sharma et al., 2024b; Maheshwari et al., 2024; Islam & Singh, 2025). As an example, a collectivist society might value relational warmth and face-to-face communication, whereas highly individualistic societies might want autonomy and efficiency. Although data protection legislation like GDPR are often discussed in general terms, no industry-specific research on how algorithmic hospitality intersects with consumer protection legislation, biometric surveillance legislation, work laws, liability principles, and platform regulations has been done.

Accountability In Algorithms

Other problems like accountability in algorithms used in pricing, legal accountability in case of AI-based failures in service provision, and ownership of behavioral and biometric data in the hotel ecosystems are still legally unclear in most countries. Strict legal and policy-based studies are needed to come up with governance models that safeguard the rights of the consumer, the dignity of the worker and the accountability of the organization without oppressing the innovation (Manoharan & Ashtikar, 2025; Maheshwari et al., 2024). The existing research is also limited methodologically as it is heavily based on quantitative survey designs with frequently student samples or hypothetical situations. Although these methods are useful when it comes to testing the theory, they do not reflect the intricate, embodied lives of guests, employees, and managers who have to deal with algorithmic systems in actual operational environments. Qualitative, ethnographic, longitudinal, and mixed-method methods are urgently required that would examine the role of algorithms in daily hospitality practices. It is possible to acquire deeper insights on dynamic human-AI interaction using action research, case-based studies, digital trace analysis and experimental field designs. Furthermore, new studies should embrace indeed interdisciplinary studies that incorporate the hospitality management, information systems, psychological, sociological, ethical, legal, and sustainability science due to the complex implications of algorithmic hospitality (Rai & Singh, 2026; Prakash et al., 2024; Jogarao, 2024; Islam & Singh, 2025). The future of hospitality is not in getting rid of humans in favor of machines, but in putting the human and algorithmic intelligence into a strategic and ethical balance. An actual sustainable example of algorithmic hospitality has to be people-oriented, based on ethical AI design, transparency, explainability, empowerment of employees, and meaningful engagement with guests. Companies should not see AI as a goal by itself but as an enabler that will enhance human creativity, service recovery, and experiences design.

CONCLUSION

The design, delivery and experience of hospitality services in the computer age is drastically changing into a completely different animal; it is algorithmic hospitality. AI, big data analytics, the Internet of Things, natural language processing, and computer vision are now invisibly potent yet powerful infrastructures that influence all phases of the guest experience, including pre-trip inspiration, algorithmic recommendations, and dynamic pricing and smart room customization, predictive maintenance, and post-stay loyalty interaction. Algorithms on the hospitality can be used at a strategic level to enable organizations to optimize revenue management, increase precision in the operational level, and build highly personalized guest experiences on predictive intelligence. On an experiential front, customers are getting more and more exposed to hospitality services that learn dynamically in response to their preferences, preempt needs, and provide interactions that are frictionlessly and seamlessly across both physical and digital touchpoints. In that regard, hospitality has ceased to be a model of reactive service provision to being proactive and data-driven experience orchestration. However, accompanying all these transformative advantages, the increasing role of algorithms creates severe social, ethical, and organizational problems. Algorithms bias, black box decision-making, and cyber threats further deepen the suggestion of individualized hospitality, placing visitors and companies in novel exclusionary, distrustful, and systemic operationalism. More importantly, algorithms are most effective at data processing, pattern recognition, and making decisions at scale, but they still lack the ability to emulate similar levels of emotional intelligence, empathy, cultural sensitivity and moral judgment characteristic of the nature of genuine hospitality. Hospitality is not simply a transactional type service industry, but a highly human practice based on care, relational interaction and emotional attachment.

REFERENCES

O. Abdullah, A. S.S., M. S. Khan, B. B. A. Qizi, S. J. Q. Usmanova and J. J.V., (2025). AI-Driven Solutions in Hospitality: Transforming Guest Experience and Streamlining Hotel Operations, Tashkent, Uzbekistan, 2025, pp. 01-07, .DOI: 10.1109/InTech64186.2025.11198397

Al-Romeedy, B. S., & Singh, A. (2025a). From Search to Stay: Mapping the Digital Journey of the Modern Traveler. In Azman, N., Valeri, M., Albattat, A., & Singh, A. (Eds.), *Decoding Tourist Behavior in the Digital Era: Insights for Effective Marketing* (pp. 283–308). IGI Global Scientific Publishing., DOI: 10.4018/979-8-3693-3972-5.ch012

Al-Romeedy, B. S., & Singh, A. (2025b). Reimagining Customer Relations Through AI Innovation. In Darwish, D., & Kumar, S. (Eds.), *Utilizing AI and Machine Learning in Financial Analysis* (pp. 351–368). IGI Global Scientific Publishing., DOI: 10.4018/979-8-3693-8507-4.ch019

Ansari, A. I., Singh, A., Pattanaik, S., Patnaik, R., & Suryawanshi, U. (2024). Exploring the Role of AI-Powered Virtual Assistants in Optimizing Self-Service Experiences for Customers Within the Service Sector. In Nadda, V., Tyagi, P., Singh, A., & Singh, V. (Eds.), *Integrating AI-Driven Technologies Into Service Marketing* (pp. 225–238). IGI Global Scientific Publishing., DOI: 10.4018/979-8-3693-7122-0.ch013

Berry, K., & Singh, A. (2024). AI-Driven Service Marketing: Transforming Customer Experience and Operational Efficiency. In Nadda, V., Tyagi, P., Singh, A., & Singh, V. (Eds.), *AI Innovations in Service and Tourism Marketing* (pp. 35–56). IGI Global Scientific Publishing., DOI: 10.4018/979-8-3693-7909-7.ch003

Bilgihan, A., Ostinelli, M., Zhang, Y., & Lorenz, M. (2025). Artificial intelligence (AI) agents and the future of customer loyalty. *International Journal of Contemporary Hospitality Management*, *37*(9), 3240–3262. DOI: 10.1108/IJCHM-03-2025-0373

Chaudhary, M., Sahani, G., & Ghouse, S. M. (2025). Artificial Intelligence and Hyper-Personalisation in Travel Platforms. In Impact of Digital Transformation on Business Growth and Performance (pp. 121-144). IGI Global Scientific Publishing. DOI: 10.4018/979-8-3693-9783-1.ch005

Cherenkov, E., Benga, V., Lee, M., Nandwani, N., Raguin, K., Sueur, M. C., & Sun, G. (2024). From machine learning algorithms to superior customer experience: Business implications of machine learning-driven data analytics in the hospitality industry. *Journal of Smart Tourism*, *4*(2), 5–14. DOI: 10.52255/smarttourism.2024.4.2.2

Dwivedi, Y. K., Helal, M. Y. I., Elgendy, I. A., Albashrawi, M. A., Hughes, L., Shawosh, M., Dutot, V., & Jeon, I. (2025). Artificial intelligence agents and agentic systems in hospitality and tourism: Challenges, opportunities and research agenda. *International Journal of Contemporary Hospitality Management*. Advance online publication. DOI: 10.1108/IJCHM-02-2025-0287

Gupta, P., & Pareek, R. (2024). AI-Enabled Guest Experience: Disrupting Hospitality Through Next-Generation AI Technologies. In Technology and Luxury Hospitality (pp. 165-181). Routledge.

Gursoy, D. (2025). Artificial intelligence (AI) technology, its applications and the use of AI powered devices in hospitality service experience creation and delivery. *International Journal of Hospitality Management*, *129*, 104212. DOI: 10.1016/j.ijhm.2025.104212

Hardcastle, K., Vorster, L., & Brown, D. M. (2025). Understanding customer responses to AI-Driven personalized journeys: Impacts on the customer experience. *Journal of Advertising*, *54*(2), 176–195. DOI: 10.1080/00913367.2025.2460985

Islam, N., & Singh, A. (2025). Role of Digitalization into Hospitality Businesses: Innovations and Trends. In Rana, V., Bathla, G., Raina, A., & Chhabra, D. (Eds.), *Transforming the Service Sector With New Technology* (pp. 447–458). IGI Global Scientific Publishing., DOI: 10.4018/979-8-3693-7447-4.ch027

Jogarao, M. (2024). AI in the hospitality industry: Revolutionizing guest experience. In Technology and International Conference on Technology Enabled Economic Changes (InTech),luxury hospitality (pp. 199-210). Routledge.

Liu, S. Q., Vakeel, K. A., Smith, N. A., Alavipour, R. S., Wei, C., & Wirtz, J. (2024). AI concierge in the customer journey: What is it and how can it add value to the customer? *Journal of Service Management*, *35*(6), 136–158. DOI: 10.1108/JOSM-12-2023-0523

Maheshwari, N., Singh, V., Singh, A., & Ansari, A. I. (2024). Understanding Artificial Intelligence Adoption in Tourism Services and Marketing: Boon or Bane? In Nadda, V., Tyagi, P., Singh, A., & Singh, V. (Eds.), *AI Innovations in Service and Tourism Marketing* (pp. 359–374). IGI Global Scientific Publishing., DOI: 10.4018/979-8-3693-7909-7.ch018

Manoharan, G., & Ashtikar, S. P. (2025). AI Era in Hospitality: The New Frontier in Guest Satisfaction and Operations. In Digital Disruption in Hospitality, AI, and Emerging Technologies: A Roadmap to Personalized Experiences, Enhanced Operations, and Revenue Growth (pp. 59-77). Emerald Publishing Limited.

Mishra, S., Anifa, M., & Naidu, J. (2025). AI-Driven Personalization in Tourism Services: Enhancing Tourist Experiences and Business Performance. In Integrating Architecture and Design Into Sustainable Tourism Development (pp. 1-20). IGI Global Scientific Publishing.

Mooi Kwong, A. T., Omar, S. I., & Nur Aliah, M. (2024). The Ethical Implications of AI-Powered Personalization in Hospitality and Tourism. In Talukder, M., Kumar, S., & Tyagi, P. (Eds.), *Impact of AI and Tech-Driven Solutions in Hospitality and Tourism* (pp. 103–122). IGI Global Scientific Publishing., DOI: 10.4018/979-8-3693-6755-1.ch006

Prakash, J., Singh, V., Singh, A., & Kumari, U. (2024). Investigating the Synergistic Impact of AI and Marketing Within Virtual Tourism Platforms for Millennials: A Review. In Nadda, V., Tyagi, P., Singh, A., & Singh, V. (Eds.), *Integrating AI-Driven Technologies Into Service Marketing* (pp. 419–438). IGI Global Scientific Publishing., DOI: 10.4018/979-8-3693-7122-0.ch020

Rai, V., & Singh, A. (2026). The Digital Renaissance of Hospitality: Workforce Mastery in the Smart Revolution. In Talukder, M., & Chowdhury, H. (Eds.), *Smart Operations and Enhancing Guest Experience in the Hospitality Industry* (pp. 125–144). IGI Global Scientific Publishing., DOI: 10.4018/979-8-3373-2145-5.ch005

Saxena, S. K., Gupta, V., & Kumar, S. (2024). Enhancing guest loyalty in the hotel industry through artificial intelligence-drive personalization. In *New Technologies in Virtual and Hybrid Events* (pp. 335–350). IGI Global. DOI: 10.4018/979-8-3693-2272-7.ch017

Sharma, M., Singh, A., & Rohit, . (2024b). Embracing Technological Disruption: Exploring the Adoption of AI-Driven Solutions in Tourism and Hospitality. In M. Talukder, S. Kumar, & P. Tyagi (Eds.), Impact of AI and Tech-Driven Solutions in Hospitality and Tourism (pp. 123-138). IGI Global Scientific Publishing. DOI: 10.4018/979-8-3693-6755-1.ch007

Sharma, M., Singh, A., & Rana, S. (2024a). Empowering Hospitality Brands AI Strategies for Enhanced Customer Experiences in Emerging Markets. In Nadda, V., Tyagi, P., Singh, A., & Singh, V. (Eds.), *Integrating AI-Driven Technologies Into Service Marketing* (pp. 173–190). IGI Global Scientific Publishing., DOI: 10.4018/979-8-3693-7122-0.ch010

Sharma, R., Sachdeva, T., Singh, A., & Nadda, V. (2024c). A New Era of Engagement and Satisfaction: Transforming Customer Experience With AI-Driven Technologies. In Nadda, V., Tyagi, P., Singh, A., & Singh, V. (Eds.), *AI Innovations in Service and Tourism Marketing* (pp. 1–16). IGI Global Scientific Publishing., DOI: 10.4018/979-8-3693-7909-7.ch001

Singh, A. (2025). Convergence of Generative Artificial Intelligence (AI)-Based Applications in the Hospitality and Tourism Industry. In Gaur, L. (Ed.), *Generative Artificial Intelligence and Ethics: Standards, Guidelines, and Best Practices* (pp. 127–142). IGI Global Scientific Publishing., DOI: 10.4018/979-8-3693-3691-5.ch006

Singh, A., & Kumar, V. (2025a). Organizational Innovation and Adaptation in Hospitality and Tourism: Strategies for Resilience and Leadership. In C. Ramos, T. Costa, R. Madeira, & J. Ferreira do Rosário (Eds.), Open Innovation and Technology in Tourism and Hospitality (pp. 355-372). IGI Global Scientific Publishing. DOI: 10.4018/979-8-3693-8633-0.ch018

Singh, A., & Kumar, V. (2025b). User-Centered Hospitality: UI/UX as the New Frontier in Hotel and Restaurant Innovation. In C. Ramos, T. Costa, R. Madeira, & J. Ferreira do Rosário (Eds.), Open Innovation and Technology in Tourism and Hospitality (pp. 395-410). IGI Global Scientific Publishing. https://doi.org/DOI: 10.4018/979-8-3693-8633-0.ch020

Srivastava, A., Singh, B. M., Singh, A., & Singh, A. (2025). Customer Immersiveness and Customer Retention: A Metaverse-Driven Study for Brands. In Al Aqad, M., Sorayyaei Azar, A., Albattat, A., & Singh, A. (Eds.), *Navigating AI and the Metaverse in Scientific Research* (pp. 475–500). IGI Global Scientific Publishing., DOI: 10.4018/979-8-3373-0340-6.ch023

Suhag, N., Sarkar, D., & Singh, A. (2024). Exploring the Impact of AI-Driven Chatbots on Customer Service in the Hospitality Industry. In Nadda, V., Tyagi, P., Singh, A., & Singh, V. (Eds.), *Integrating AI-Driven Technologies Into Service Marketing* (pp. 211–224). IGI Global Scientific Publishing., DOI: 10.4018/979-8-3693-7122-0.ch012

Talukder, M. B., Kabir, F., & Jibon, F. A. (2025). AI-Driven personalized room management in the modern hotel industry. In *AI technologies for personalized and sustainable tourism* (pp. 59–82). IGI Global.

Thaichon, P., Dutta, P. K., Haghi, A. K., & Dutta, S. (Eds.). (2025). *Digital Disruption in Hospitality, AI, and Emerging Technologies: A Roadmap to Personalized Experiences, Enhanced Operations, and Revenue Growth.* Emerald Publishing Limited. DOI: 10.1108/9781836087960

Turčinović, M., Vujko, A., & Mirčetić, V. (2025). Algorithmic Management in Hospitality: Examining Hotel Employees' Attitudes and Work–Life Balance Under AI-Driven HR Systems. *Tourism and Hospitality*, *6*(4), 203. DOI: 10.3390/tourhosp6040203

Vashishth, T. K., Sharma, V., Sharma, K. K., Kumar, B., Kumar, A., & Panwar, R. (2024). Artificial intelligence (AI)–powered chatbots: Providing instant support and personalized recommendations to guests 24/7. In *Technology and Luxury Hospitality* (pp. 211–236). Routledge. DOI: 10.4324/9781003488248-15

Wang, P. Q. (2025). Personalizing guest experience with generative AI in the hotel industry: There's more to it than meets a Kiwi's eye. *Current Issues in Tourism*, *28*(4), 527–544. DOI: 10.1080/13683500.2023.2300030

Chapter 8
The Future of Corporate Events:
The Role of Artificial Intelligence in Shaping Virtual and Hybrid Corporate Experiences

Pratim Narayan Moitra
Amity Institute of Travel and Tourism, India

Aruditya Jasrotia
https://orcid.org/0000-0002-8274-5609
Amity University, Noida, India

Alka Maheshwari
https://orcid.org/0000-0002-5204-1686
Amity Institute of Travel and Tourism, India

ABSTRACT

With the growing popularity of virtual and hybrid corporate events, artificial intelligence (AI) is becoming a critical component for improving event engagement and administration. AI technologies increase attendee engagement, simplify event management, and deliver real-time data insights, leading to more dynamic and personalised events. This chapter investigates how artificial intelligence has influenced the design and execution of virtual and hybrid events by automating activities, enhancing engagement, and personalising the attendance experience. It also looks into the economic and environmental benefits of using AI into event planning, notably in terms of reducing resource use and increasing output. This chapter adopts a conceptual approach to assess existing artificial intelligence applications in the event industry and to investigate the incorporation of Al technologies into virtual

DOI: 10.4018/979-8-3373-8197-8.ch008

and hybrid event platforms. This study examines the impact of artificial intelligence on operational efficiency, event interactivity, and engagement through case studies and theoretical frameworks.

1. INTRODUCTION

Business events are structured gatherings that serve as key platforms for networking, knowledge exchange, professional development, and economic stimulation. According to the Global Destination Report 2022 (Martin & Fullard, 2022), such events significantly influence both local and national economies by generating direct and indirect revenue through travel, hospitality, and service industries. Business events include a wide range of formats such as conferences, trade exhibitions, conventions, workshops, and corporate seminars, each requiring meticulous logistical coordination, including venue selection, scheduling, participant management, and resource allocation (Getz & Page, 2016).

With the rapid advancement of technology, particularly in the fields of communication and automation, the landscape of business events has undergone a profound transformation. The traditional in-person model is now increasingly complemented—or even replaced—by virtual and hybrid formats that leverage digital tools to enhance accessibility, scalability, and interactivity (Marques & Pinho, 2021). Virtual platforms allow for real-time collaboration, remote attendance, and digital networking opportunities, thus breaking geographical barriers and reducing operational costs (Lee & Hwang, 2020). This shift has been particularly accelerated by the COVID-19 pandemic, which catalyzed the adoption of digital solutions and redefined event delivery models globally (Sigala, 2020).

Furthermore, the integration of artificial intelligence (AI) into event technology has enabled more efficient planning and personalized experiences. AI-powered tools are increasingly used for automating administrative tasks such as registration and scheduling, as well as for analyzing participant behavior and preferences to curate more engaging content (Gretzel et al., 2015). As a result, the business events industry is not only becoming more technologically advanced but also more data-driven and user-centric, aligning with broader trends in digital transformation and smart tourism.

Virtual and hybrid events leverage technology to enhance participant experiences, offering cost-effective solutions while maintaining high satisfaction levels through innovative platforms and personalized event management Kulshreshtha & Webster. (2024). Hybrid events seamlessly combine in-person and online experiences, allowing participants the freedom to select how they wish to engage. The initial push for this change came from technological advancements, but the global

COVID-19 pandemic quickly speed things up, rendering large in-person gatherings impractical or even impossible.

Today, virtual and hybrid formats have evolved beyond mere temporary fixes; they are now vital elements of the business event landscape. These formats provide businesses with a chance to connect with broader audiences, lower expenses, and support sustainability by minimising travel and resource use. Adapting to these event formats has become essential for businesses looking to remain competitive in a world that is becoming more digital by the day. This chapter investigates how artificial intelligence has influenced the design and execution of virtual and hybrid events by automating activities, enhancing engagement, and personalising the attendance experience. Despite the expanding adoption of AI across various sectors, its strategic application in virtual and hybrid business events remains underexplored in academic literature. Most existing studies focus on general event technology or digital transformation trends, leaving a research gap in understanding AI's specific contributions to engagement, operational efficiency, and user experience within this niche (Marques & Pinho, 2021; Gretzel et al., 2015). This study seeks to fill that gap by providing a conceptual and evidence-based examination of AI-driven practices in event management.

2. TYPES OF BUSINESS EVENTS

Business events can currently be categorized into three principal formats: traditional (in-person), virtual, and hybrid. Each of these formats possesses distinctive characteristics, advantages, and limitations, shaped by evolving technological capabilities and the dynamic expectations of participants. Traditional business events, such as physical conferences, trade shows, and seminars, are valued for their face-to-face networking opportunities, immersive environments, and greater emotional engagement (Getz & Page, 2016). However, they are often constrained by geographic boundaries, high logistical costs, and environmental concerns related to travel and resource consumption (Arcodia & Whitford, 2006).

Virtual events, on the other hand, leverage digital platforms to deliver content and foster interaction entirely online. These events offer increased accessibility, cost efficiency, and scalability, allowing global participation without the need for physical presence (Marques & Pinho, 2021). Nevertheless, they may suffer from reduced audience attention spans, limited networking dynamics, and dependence on stable internet infrastructure (Lee & Hwang, 2020).

Hybrid events combine elements of both physical and virtual formats, offering a flexible model that caters to in-person and remote attendees simultaneously. This format allows organizers to maximize reach while retaining the experiential benefits of face-to-face interaction. Hybrid events have gained popularity as a post-pandemic solution, supported by advanced technologies such as live-streaming, real-time chat, AI-driven engagement tools, and virtual networking spaces (Sigala, 2020; Pencarelli et al., 2020). Despite their versatility, hybrid events present challenges in content synchronization, technical coordination, and ensuring equitable engagement between onsite and online audiences.

As participant needs become more diverse and technologically influenced, the selection of event formats increasingly reflects strategic decisions aimed at optimizing engagement, inclusivity, and impact. Understanding the unique dynamics of each format is essential for effective event planning and audience satisfaction in the modern era.

3. OVERVIEW OF VIRTUAL EVENTS

Virtual media significantly enhances event tourism by increasing participant engagement and creating new opportunities, as explored through surveys and interviews in the study.(Asha, John., Pankaj, Kumar, Tyagi., Vipin, Nadda. (2024). Virtual events are totally digital, carried out via online platforms allowing attendees to participate from anywhere with internet connection. Among these are:

Webinars are online seminars whereby a speaker addresses a live virtual audience. Interaction is generally limited to polls, Q&A sessions, or chat functions, making them effective for lectures and product demos but less suitable for in-depth collaboration (Marques & Pinho, 2021; Lee & Hwang, 2020).

Online conferences, in contrast, are larger, multi-session gatherings that replicate the structure of traditional conferences. They include breakout rooms, panel discussions, networking lounges, and keynote presentations, enabling participants to engage with both synchronous and asynchronous content (Sigala, 2020). These conferences aim to foster more dynamic interaction among attendees, often supported by AI tools for matchmaking and personalized session suggestions (Gretzel et al., 2015).

Virtual booths and exhibits simulate traditional trade fair environments, allowing users to explore products and services, interact with company representatives through live chat or video, and download marketing materials or brochures digitally (Pencarelli et al., 2020). These digital interfaces are increasingly designed to be immersive and interactive, enhancing user experience and data collection for exhibitors.

For organisers as well as attendees, virtual events have benefits like less expenses, more accessibility, and convenience. Engagement may be difficult, though, and staying focused over long stretches calls for inventive information delivery.

Synopsis of Mixed Events

Combining physical and digital components, hybrid **events** offer a dual-experience format that blends the advantages of both in-person and virtual participation. Attendees can choose to join either on-site or remotely, depending on their preference, location, or accessibility needs, thereby increasing inclusivity and reach (Marques & Pinho, 2021). Typically, hybrid events feature live keynotes, panel discussions, and breakout sessions hosted at a physical venue, which are simultaneously broadcast to online audiences through digital platforms. Virtual attendees can view these sessions in real time and often engage in interactive features such as live Q&A, polls, and chat forums, enabling active participation despite physical distance (Sigala, 2020).

The incorporation of technologies such as AI-powered chatbots, virtual networking lounges, and real-time translation tools further enhances the experience for remote participants, helping them navigate the event and connect with other attendees or exhibitors (Gretzel et al., 2015). From a strategic standpoint, hybrid events also enable data-driven decision-making by collecting analytics on attendee behavior, session popularity, and engagement levels across both physical and digital touchpoints (Pencarelli et al., 2020).

Moreover, hybrid formats are seen as a sustainable alternative to fully physical events, helping reduce carbon emissions and resource use while still delivering immersive experiences and networking opportunities (Jones, 2014). As a result, hybrid events are increasingly recognized as the future of the meetings and events industry, offering flexibility, resilience, and scalability in a rapidly evolving global landscape (Davidson et al., 2018).

Exhibitors of hybrid trade shows present items on-site and provide virtual booths for remote attendees—who may engage via chat or video conference. Physical participants participate in face-to--face networking; virtual attendees employ systems that enable video networking and virtual conferences.

Hybrid events give flexibility and appeal to those who prefer in-person engagement while also accommodating participants who are unable to attend physically. This inclusive format expands audience reach and supports accessibility for diverse groups, including international attendees, individuals with mobility limitations, or those constrained by budget or time (Marques & Pinho, 2021). Although this model demands more sophisticated technological integration, including high-quality audiovisual systems, reliable streaming platforms, and real-time interaction tools, it offers the potential for a more engaging and participatory experience for all attendees (Sigala, 2020). The dual-channel approach also promotes greater equity in knowledge sharing and networking opportunities, contributing to the democratization of professional events (Pencarelli et al., 2020).

Examining Virtual, Traditional, and Hybrid Events

Faced with restricted location, expense, and logistics, traditional events—which centre on in-person interactions—offer extensive networking possibilities but are typically constrained. For venue booking, transport, and lodging, they call for large resources.

Virtual events eliminate entrance obstacles like travel expenditures, hence provide scalability and cost-efficiencies. They could, however, lack the personal touch and lively intensity of in-person gatherings.

- Mixed Events: Give flexibility to close the difference between conventional and digital forms. They expand access to a worldwide audience while keeping the personal experience. To properly balance both forms, they do, however, necessitate sophisticated technical infrastructure and thorough planning.

Every kind of event has different benefits and drawbacks; the format chosen will rely on the objectives, audience, and resources at disposal of the planners.

4. TECHNOLOGICAL INFRASTRUCTURE FOR VIRTUAL & HYBRID EVENTS

The fundamental technology infrastructure determines much how successful virtual and hybrid events are. To guarantee flawless execution, significant involvement, and a seamless experience for both in-person and virtual participants, organisers must make use of several tools and platforms. The efficiency and influence of these events may be much improved with the proper mix of technology. Event technology includes software applications, mobile tools, and wearable devices that create immersive experiences (Kulshreshtha & Webster, 2024).

Fundamental Technologies

Several basic technologies are necessary for the implementation of virtual and hybrid events:

Hosting virtual gatherings depends critically on thorough platforms as Zoom, Microsoft Teams, or specialised solutions like Hopin and Whova. Live streaming, breakout rooms, audience polls, and Q&A sessions—among other tools—allow a dynamic virtual experience on these platforms.

Streaming Services: A basic element of hybrid events is live streaming. Organisers may broadcast events to a large online audience with services such YouTube

Live, Vimeo, and Twitch. Maintaining audience interest depends on these services guaranteeing low-latency, high-quality streaming.

Interactive tools are necessary in order to close the engagement difference between virtual and actual attendees. Real-time chat tools like Slido, virtual networking tools like Brella, and polling tools like Slido help people communicate and become involved. Additionally employed to keep guests interested during the event are gamification components such treasure hunts and tests.

Working together, these technologies provide an immersive event experience that guarantees everyone, wherever, feels involved and included.

How artificial intelligence (AI) may improve events experiences?

Virtual and hybrid events are now planned and experienced in ways that artificial intelligence has transformed. Several important uses for artificial intelligence consist in:

AI systems can examine attendance preferences and behaviour to provide pertinent session, speaker, or networking recommendations. By concentrating on material and relationships most important to them, this customising helps participants maximise their event experience.

Real-time translation and transcription capabilities enabled by AI-powered systems have significantly enhanced the accessibility and inclusivity of events for global audiences. These technologies help overcome language barriers and enable participants from different linguistic backgrounds to engage with content simultaneously (Gretzel et al., 2015). Platforms like Google Meet, Zoom, and Microsoft Teams already incorporate features such as automated captioning and multilingual support, allowing for live subtitles and translated audio in real time (Marques & Pinho, 2021). Such AI-driven tools not only broaden audience reach but also align with the principles of universal design and digital equity in event management (Sigala, 2020).

AI-driven chatbots and virtual assistants may help attendees by addressing questions, delivering event updates, and generating session recommendations. This automation simplifies correspondence and facilitates participants' more effective navigating of the event. Predictive analytics for engagement let organisers make data-driven, real-time changes include providing more resources or boosting interaction for high-interest subjects, based on AI's ability to forecast which sessions or areas of the event participants most likely would find appealing. Incorporating artificial intelligence can help event planners improve personalisation, accessibility, and involvement, therefore producing a more powerful event experience.

Problems and Solutions for Managing Technology for Major Events

Technology offers difficulties, especially for big events with thousands of attendees, even while it allows the virtual and hybrid events to be executed:

Maintaining consistent and high-quality streaming for a sizable virtual audience presents one of the most often occurring difficulties with bandwidth and connectivity. Reliable streaming services should be partners for organisers to make sure backup plans are in place to manage bandwidth surges or disruptions. Big virtual events run the danger of security issues including data leaks, hacking, or illegal access. Strong encryption techniques, safe login methods, and internet safety tips must all be followed by organisers. Technical Difficulties: Troubleshooting becomes crucial given users' vast spectrum of devices, internet speeds, and technical expertise. Providing real-time tech assistance, thorough user manuals, and committed workers to fix problems can help to minimise disturbance during the event.

Maintaining a sizable and diverse audience's engagement—particularly in a virtual environment—can be a significant challenge due to shorter attention spans, screen fatigue, and the lack of physical presence (Lee & Hwang, 2020). To sustain interest and encourage participation, event organizers increasingly incorporate strategies such as gamification, scheduled breaks, and interactive technologies including polls, live chats, and Q&A sessions (Marques & Pinho, 2021; Xu et al., 2017). These elements not only enhance cognitive engagement but also foster a sense of community among participants, thereby replicating some of the social dynamics of in-person events (Gretzel et al., 2015). By integrating such features, virtual and hybrid events can become more immersive, personalized, and effective in achieving their communication and networking goals. Dealing with these issues calls for careful planning, appropriate technology alliances, and proactive troubleshooting to guarantee a flawless and interesting event experience for all attendees.

5. BENEFITS OF VIRTUAL & HYBRID EVENTS

Virtual and hybrid events have various advantages that appeal to businesses, planners, and attendees alike, rising as attractive alternatives for traditional in-person meetings. Regarding cost-effectiveness, global reach, and flexibility, these systems provide most significant benefits.

Scalability and Affordability

One of its key advantages is the cost-effectiveness of virtual and hybrid events compared to traditional in-person ones. Especially virtual gatherings save several expenses connected to real-world meetings such venue rentals, food, housing, and transportation. Smaller businesses or anyone without the resources for big in-person events might find this drop in overhead costs to allow hosts of events with a much smaller budget.

Virtual events are essentially infinitely scalable, allowing organizers to accommodate thousands of participants without the constraints of venue capacity, travel logistics, or on-site resources (Marques & Pinho, 2021). This makes them particularly attractive for global audiences and cost-sensitive organizations. Similarly, hybrid events offer the advantage of scalability, as the virtual component can be expanded to reach a broader demographic without necessitating additional physical infrastructure (Sigala, 2020). The ability to scale seamlessly enables event planners to extend their reach beyond physical and geographic boundaries, increasing accessibility, inclusivity, and potential return on investment (Gretzel et al., 2015; Davidson et al., 2018). This flexibility supports strategic goals such as brand visibility, knowledge dissemination, and international collaboration, which are increasingly vital in the digitized events landscape.

Audience Variability and Global Reach

Virtual and hybrid events let businesses reach a global audience free from travel time or geographic limitations. Anyone from anywhere across the world may join substantially increasing the impact and reach of the event thanks to internet access. Because of this global accessibility, more diversified participation in terms of geography, culture, and industry representation arises from which the event experience is improved.

Virtual and hybrid events reduce the need for travel and might not have the means or capacity to personally participate, hence they attract a more broad spectrum of individuals. This diversity especially for under-represented groups may lead to more diverse opinions in arguments, more rich networking possibilities, and greater inclusivity.

User Convenience and Flexibility

The freedom virtual and hybrid events give attendees in terms of participation adds even another big advantage.

Virtual attendees might connect from anywhere, therefore reducing travel time and allowing them to participate from the comfort of their own offices or homes. Depending on their preferences or circumstance, hybrid events also provide participants the option to choose either physically or virtually.

Many virtual and hybrid events include on-demand access to recorded sessions, therefore allowing participants to interact with event content whenever it would be most convenient. Those who have trouble scheduling or those who live in different time zones really appreciate this flexibility. It also encourages increased participation since participants may go over missed sessions or ones they felt particularly significant.

Simplicity of these formats enhances the complete attending experience and promotes more participation and enjoyment. All things considered, virtual and hybrid events provide globally accessible scalable, reasonably cost options. These forms provide participants unmatched independence, so fit for the networked, fast-paced business world of today.

6. CHALLENGES OF VIRTUAL & HYBRID EVENTS

Even if they offer certain benefits, virtual and hybrid events have their own set of problems. Organisers have to address these issues if they want to ensure that every guest will find great and successful events. Among the primary challenges are low involvement, technological ones, and growing concern over "Zoom fatigue".

Interaction Restrictions and Involvement Limitations

Virtual and hybrid gatherings often find it challenging to replicate the natural interactions seen in-person conferences bring. Absence of tangible indicators, casual conversations, and face-to- face networking might change the flow of attendance in its natural condition.

Conventional gatherings have guests starting impromptu food-related discussions at booths, during breaks. Conversely, virtual platforms rely on controlled environments—such as chat rooms or virtual conferences—which might feel forced or less intimate.

Including far-off participants might prove challenging when distractions at home or the workplace force one to forget about the event. Even if they increase engagement, surveys, Q&A sessions, chat technologies, and other tools might not be able to genuinely capture the energy of in-person, live interactions.

Including interactive elements that encourage active participation—such gamification, breakout areas, or live polling—organisers can solve these issues. Still, developing intimate relationships virtually is challenging.

Technical Issues and Notes of Correction

Virtual and hybrid events rely on technology, hence technological issues might strike without notice and cause disturbance of the flawless operation of the event.

Presenting an unexpected loss of internet connectivity, platform faults, or audio/video issues might throw off presentations and annoy attendees as well as organisers. Technology management can be further complicated by juggling the needs of in-person and online participants during hybrid events.

Digital savvy participants: Participants might feel at ease utilising the device at several degrees of intensity. Some may leave meetings or decrease their participation if they struggle with virtual platforms or technological problems on their own.

To help to lower these risks, event planners should carefully test platforms, offer thorough instructions, and offer real-time technical support. Including backup plans with pre-recorded materials or other streaming options helps to minimise major disruptions.

Attendant attention spans: combating "zoom fatigue"

"Zoom fatigue," the phrase used to characterise the tiredness from prolonged virtual interactions, originates from participants in virtual events sometimes having to remain sitting and concentrated on a screen for lengthy durations.

Virtual participants are more prone to become sidetracked without the immersive environment of live events. When multitasking brought on by homes or businesses, presenting demands for less attention and commitment.

Spending hours in front of a screen from virtual interactions can physically and mentally tired one. Burnout brought on a lack of nonverbal cues and the need to stay focused on a fixed computer interface rapidly lowers general interest and enjoyment.

Organisers might divide the event in half, offer breaks, and change the presenting strategy by using interactive elements as virtual networking or Q&A sessions. Providing demand-driven event recordings can also help to be flexible and help to lower the need for actually attending live events. Basically, even if virtual and hybrid events have many benefits, they also present different difficulties that need for careful preparation and original concepts. Organisers may guarantee long-lasting effect and enhance the whole event experience by limiting engagement issues, controlling technology problems, and fighting virtual tiredness.

7. EVENT DESIGN AND USER EXPERIENCE

Designing virtual and hybrid events calls for great attention to user experience as well as the content. Organisers of events must balance offering an equally immersive experience for virtual guests with involving in-person visitors. Good event planning guarantees seamless interaction and maximises participation regardless of the participants' preferred mode of involvement.

Best Practices in Virtual and Hybrid Event Experience Design

A few recommended practices help to provide a flawless event experience for online and in-person viewers:

Create a unified experience whereby virtual and in-person audiences feel equally appreciated. Match event materials so that everyone, in whatever format, gets the same degree of involvement and attention. Live-streamed events could, for example, have real-time polls or Q&A available to both groups.

Plan for seamless transitions between real and virtual components; they should seem natural and fluid. Make sure presentations, activities, and event sessions fit one another naturally. For instance, pre-recorded materials could help to keep uniformity and prevent interruptions.

Plan events in sections or modules that let people come at various times and yet engage fully. In virtual events, where attendees could be in different time zones, this framework is quite helpful. This method also enables more flexible involvement, hence lowering participant weariness.

These techniques guarantee that both groups of viewers have the best, linked experience the event offers all around.

Tailoring Content Delivery for Online and In-person Audiences

A good hybrid event tailors material delivery to fit both in-person and online participants as their approaches of interaction differ.

Virtual participants gain from both live, synchronous (synchronous) and on-demand, asynchronous choices. While on-demand materials gives flexibility for individuals who cannot make it at the designated time, live sessions encourage real-time involvement. This guarantees highest involvement from an audience with different backgrounds.

Customise visual presentations—such as slide decks and videos—such that they are readily viewable from a distance. Virtual participants depend much on high-quality voice and images as low quality could cause disengagement.

Content Adaptation: Virtual attendees could want shorter, targeted sessions while in-person audiences flourish on physical connections. Change style and length of material to fit the tastes and attention spans of every target group. For example, although in-person audiences might value lengthier, more thorough sessions, virtual presentations may be more digestible when split into smaller, interactive portions. Customising material distribution to fit the particular requirements of every audience guarantees that both groups stay interested and happy with the event.

Tools for Audience Participation, Networking, and Gamification

Improving user experience depends on interactive components, especially for virtual and mixed models where keeping attention may prove difficult. Gamification, networking, and participation technologies taken together will increase involvement.

Including game-like components like leaderboards, tests, or reward systems helps gamification—that is, active participation—by means like Giving points or incentives for particular behaviours, such as showing up for particular sessions or participating in conversations, helps the event to be more lively and fun.

Virtual and hybrid events can profit from dedicated networking systems like Brella or Hopin, which let attendees plan one-on-one meetings or group conversations. Matchmaking tools based on artificial intelligence can also enable participants to meet others with same interests or objectives.

Live polls, Q&A sessions, and real-time feedback systems—e.g., Slido or Mentimeter—help close the engagement gap between physical and online guests. These instruments inspire every person to express their opinions, probe questions, and get active in the event.

Gamification and interactive technologies let planners design a more interesting, participative event that keeps guests engaged and targeted.

To sum up, the success of virtual and hybrid events depends much on careful planning of user experience and event design. Using interactive tools and customising material for both in-person and online audiences can help organisers provide a well-rounded experience maximising participation across all media.

8. ENVIRONMENTAL AND SUSTAINABILITY BENEFITS

Apart from changing the way businesses engage with their consumers, growing adoption of virtual and hybrid events has resulted in significant environmental benefits. These models are gradually recognised for their ability to reduce the carbon footprint connected with traditional in-person events and help the incorporation of sustainable practices into the sector of events.

Lower the carbon footprint of Virtual Events.

One major environmental advantage of virtual gatherings is their far reduced carbon emissions than traditional, in-person conferences. Virtual models allow many of the logistical needs supporting a significant carbon footprint to be waived, including:

Reduced Air Travel: Many times, in-person business meetings include attendees flying from various countries or regions, therefore increasing the CO2 emissions. Virtual event planning greatly reduces the overall environmental effect of the event by removing the need for travel.

Virtual events serve to reduce the demand for large physical venues running on energy for heating, cooling, lighting, and maintenance. The less energy is required to plan the event as guests from their own homes or companies use digital platforms.

Events held entirely online replace the demand for printed materials, food, and other physical resources traditionally used in-person. Reduced waste and resource consumption help to enable even more sustainable event design.

The trend towards virtual events clearly offers a way to lower emissions and other environmental impacts generally generated by traditional meetings.

9. THE FUTURE OF VIRTUAL & HYBRID EVENTS

Virtual and hybrid models are projected to be quite important in determining the direction of the events business as it develops. Changing attendee tastes and technological developments will improve the experiences provided by various forms even more, hence increasing their immersive and adaptability.

Integration of augmented reality (AR) with virtual reality (VR).

Offering audiences more immersive and engaging experiences, the combination of Virtual Reality (VR) and Augmented Reality (AR) is set to transform the virtual and hybrid event scene.

VR can create totally immersive surroundings that let virtual participants feel as though they are a part of the actual event. Trade events, product presentations, and networking lounges where attendees may explore 3D surroundings, communicate with others, and interact with materials as if they were personally can especially benefit from this as well.

Augmented reality (AR) improves the physical surroundings by layering digital components onto actual locations. AR may provide hybrid events extra levels of engagement for both in-person and virtual participants, such virtual information booths or interactive product displays available via tablets or smartphones.

The increasing usage of VR and AR at events will blur the barriers between real and digital involvement, therefore enhancing the whole experience for attendees all across the world.

Forecasts about Post-Pandemic Event Plans

The COVID-19 pandemic has significantly increased the prevalence of virtual events, highlighting the importance of managing them effectively alongside live and hybrid events (Tim, Brown., Claire, Drakeley. (2023). The following trends should help to guide post-pandemic event plans going ahead:

Large-scale events will probably adopt the hybrid model as the standard as it provides flexibility for both in-person and online involvement. Inclusivity and accessibility will be given top priority by organisers so that people who can't make it in person may still participate meaningfully via virtual possibilities.

For in-person hybrid event components, health and safety measures—such as improved cleanliness, contactless check-ins, and separated seating—will remain vital. Safety will be first priority for attendees, hence event planners should create a safe and healthy surroundings.

Future events will concentrate on hyper-personalizing experiences by means of data-driven techniques to fit every attendee. This might offer tailored networking possibilities, personalised session recommendations, and information delivery styles depending on particular tastes.

10. CONCLUSION

The move to virtual and hybrid business events marks a new era with many benefits and clear challenges for the global events sector. Even if they have advantages, virtual and hybrid events have some restrictions. Participation and involvement in virtual worlds might be more challenging to maintain; technological problems still exist and should be considered especially during important events. Furthermore combating "Zoom fatigue" and keeping participants' interest calls for inventive event design and unique participation instruments.

Virtual and hybrid events will be vital in the global economy as the planet adjusts to a more networked and digital future. Driving innovation in the Meetings, Incentives, Conferences, and Exhibits (MICE) sector, they provide companies a readily available, adaptable platform to interact with consumers, partners, and stakeholders all around. Future corporate events will be planned and experienced differently depending on the sustainability emphasis and continuous development of event technology. Combining the benefits of in-person engagement with the inclusiveness and environmental advantages of virtual involvement allows companies to use hybrid models. These advancements enable virtual and hybrid events to be a natural feature of the changing corporate environment, therefore promoting worldwide cooperation and progress.

REFERENCES

Arcodia, C., & Whitford, M. (2006). Festival attendance and the development of social capital. *Journal of Convention & Event Tourism, 8*(2), 1–18. DOI: 10.1300/J452v08n02_01

Asha, John., Pankaj, Kumar, Tyagi., Vipin, Nadda. (2024). 1. Examining the Impact of Virtual Media on Event Tourism Investigating New Possibilities. Advances in hospitality, tourism and the services industry (AHTSI) book series, DOI: 10.4018/979-8-3693-6755-1.ch011

Brown, T., & Drakeley, C. (2023). 1 From pixels to possibilities: Innovations within virtual and hybrid events. Virtual Events Management, 1.

Davidson, R., McPherson, G., & Ramos, A. (2018). *Events management: Principles and practice* (4th ed.). Routledge.

Getz, D., & Page, S. J. (2016). *Event studies: Theory, research and policy for planned events* (3rd ed.). Routledge. DOI: 10.4324/9781315708027

Gretzel, U., Sigala, M., Xiang, Z., & Koo, C. (2015). Smart tourism: Foundations and developments. *Electronic Markets, 25*(3), 179–188. DOI: 10.1007/s12525-015-0196-8

Jones, M. (2014). *Sustainable event management: A practical guide*. Routledge. DOI: 10.4324/9780203768723

Kulshreshtha, S. K., & Webster, C. (2024). Emerging Technologies in Virtual and Hybrid Events: Major Issues and Major Drivers. New Technologies in Virtual and Hybrid Events, 1-18.

Lee, S., & Hwang, J. (2020). The impact of virtual events on visitor experience and satisfaction. *Journal of Convention & Event Tourism, 21*(2), 103–121. DOI: 10.1080/15470148.2020.1752246

Marques, R. C., & Pinho, C. (2021). Virtual and hybrid events in the post-COVID-19 era: A strategic framework. *International Journal of Event and Festival Management, 12*(3), 345–360.

Martin, C., & Fullard, D. (2022). Global Destination Report 2022. *International Congress and Convention Association (ICCA).*

Pencarelli, T., Splendiani, S., & Fraboni, C. (2020). Smart tourism experiences: Value co-creation at cultural heritage sites. *Sustainability, 12*(2), 1–20. DOI: 10.3390/su12020669

Sigala, M. (2020). Tourism and COVID-19: Impacts and implications for advancing and resetting industry and research. *Journal of Business Research, 117*, 312–321. DOI: 10.1016/j.jbusres.2020.06.015 PMID: 32546875

Xu, B., Buhalis, D., & Weber, J. (2017). Serious games and the gamification of tourism. *Tourism Management, 60*, 244–256. DOI: 10.1016/j.tourman.2016.11.020

Chapter 9
Decoding AI Integrated Clinical Practice:
A CNN-Based Intelligent Learning Approach for Medical Image Analytic Cases

Rudra Kalyan Nayak
https://orcid.org/0000-0003-4447-8391
VIT Bhopal University, India

Nilamadhab Mishra
https://orcid.org/0000-0002-1330-4869
VIT Bhopal University, India

Ashwini Kumar Pradhan
https://orcid.org/0009-0005-7217-4936
Galgotias University, India

Ramamani Tripathy
Chitkara University, India

ABSTRACT

Medical imaging, which provides a non-invasive window into the complex mechanisms of the human body, has completely transformed the healthcare sector. The integration of deep learning techniques into medical image analysis is the primary focus of this work, which describes advances in segmentation, classification, and disease diagnosis tasks. After outlining traditional approaches and their shortcomings, this investigation examines convolutional neural networks (CNNs)—the underlying architecture for most deep learning applications in this discipline. The

DOI: 10.4018/979-8-3373-8197-8.ch009

paper discusses applications across various imaging modalities, including CT, MRI, ultrasound, and X-ray, highlighting real-world achievements, challenges, and the path to clinical adoption. Emphasis is placed on the importance of advanced approaches, such as transfer learning, data augmentation, and explainable AI, in addressing challenges. This exploration also highlights the ethical and regulatory aspects, emphasizing the importance of fairness, transparency, and robustness in clinical applications.

1 INTRODUCTION

The human body, a marvel of biological intricacy, continues to inspire extensive research in health and science. Unraveling the complex structures and functions is vital for understanding diseases, developing effective treatments, and improving healthcare outcomes. Central to this attempt is medical imaging, a technology that has altered modern medicine by enabling doctors to observe and evaluate the inside anatomy in extraordinary detail (McCollough et al., 2015; Bushberg et al., 2012). Imaging modalities, such as X-rays, computed tomography (CT), magnetic resonance imaging (MRI), and ultrasound, provide comprehensive insights into organs, tissues, and bones, thereby enhancing diagnostic accuracy and therapeutic decision-making (Boas & Fleischmann, 2012). These technologies have become vital tools in illness identification, treatment monitoring, and surgery planning, consequently playing a pivotal role in improving patient outcomes (Brady, 2017). In recent years, the integration of medical imaging with artificial intelligence (AI), particularly deep learning, has emerged as a ground-breaking advance.

Deep learning, a subset of AI, excels at learning complex patterns in large datasets, making it uniquely suited for the analysis of high-dimensional medical images (LeCun et al., 2015; Schmidhuber, 2015). Among various architectures, convolutional neural networks (CNNs) have demonstrated remarkable capabilities in detecting subtle abnormalities, segmenting organs, and identifying disease-specific markers with high precision (Litjens et al., 2017; Shen et al., 2017). For example, CNN-based models have been successfully applied to detect lung nodules in CT scans, classify breast lesions in mammograms, and predict cardiovascular risks using imaging biomarkers (Lakhani & Sundaram, 2017; Coudray et al., 2018; Poplin et al., 2018).

However, traditional medical imaging workflows rely heavily on human expertise, particularly from radiologists and clinicians. This manual analysis, while effective, is labour-intensive, time-consuming, and susceptible to human error, especially when interpreting large volumes of data or subtle imaging features (Doi, 2007; Brady et al., 2012). The increasing volume of medical imaging studies—driven by advancements such as 3D imaging and routine screening protocols—has further strained healthcare systems, creating a demand for automated solutions to enhance efficiency and accuracy (Litjens et al., 2017).

Deep learning offers a promising solution to these challenges. By automating repetitive tasks such as lesion detection, organ segmentation, and anomaly classification, AI-powered systems can significantly reduce the workload of radiologists while ensuring consistency in interpretation (Rajpurkar et al., 2017; Hosny et al., 2018). These technologies also hold the potential to enhance diagnostic precision, particularly in detecting early-stage diseases or rare conditions that might be overlooked by human observers (Ribli et al., 2018; Esteva et al., 2017). Moreover, deep learning can facilitate real-time decision-making in clinical settings, enabling immediate insights that improve patient outcomes (Zeiler & Fergus, 2014; Gulshan et al., 2016).

The integration of deep learning into personalized medicine further underscores its transformative potential. By combining imaging data with other patient-specific records, such as genetic profiles and clinical histories, AI systems can support tailored treatment strategies, especially in fields like oncology and cardiology (Hosny et al., 2018; Poplin et al., 2018). For instance, CNN-based models have been employed to predict tumour progression and optimize radiation therapy plans, enabling more effective and patient-centric care (Coudray et al., 2018).

Despite these advancements, significant challenges remain. The development of reliable deep learning models requires large, annotated datasets, which are often limited due to privacy concerns and the resource-intensive nature of expert labelling (Kaissis et al., 2020). Moreover, the "black box" nature of deep learning models raises issues regarding interpretability, as clinicians need to trust and understand AI-driven decisions, particularly when they impact life-critical outcomes (Rudin, 2019; Samek et al., 2017). Ensuring the generalizability of models across diverse populations and medical settings is another critical challenge, as biases in training data can lead to disparities in model performance (Nagendran et al., 2020).

Ethical and regulatory considerations further complicate the adoption of AI in medical imaging. Algorithmic bias, data privacy concerns, and the need for rigorous validation are key barriers that must be addressed to ensure fair and equitable healthcare delivery (Ghassemi et al., 2021; Amann et al., 2020). Regulatory bodies such as the FDA and EMA have begun establishing frameworks for approving AI-based medical devices, but ensuring compliance with evolving standards remains a complex task (Topol, 2019; Benjamens et al., 2020).

This paper aims to provide a comprehensive overview of the current state of deep learning in medical imaging, exploring its successes, challenges, and future prospects. By examining the intersection of technological innovation and clinical application, this review highlights the potential of deep learning to transform medical imaging into a more accurate, efficient, and personalized domain. Collaborative efforts among AI researchers, healthcare professionals, and policymakers will be crucial for overcoming existing barriers and realizing the full potential of this technology to enhance patient care and outcomes.

1.1 Medical Image Analysis: Traditional Approaches and Limitations

Medical image analysis, a cornerstone of modern healthcare, has traditionally relied on conventional computer vision techniques and manual interpretation by radiologists and clinicians. This process involves analyzing images to extract clinically meaningful information, playing a crucial role in the diagnosis and treatment of various medical conditions (Doi, 2007; Brady, 2017). The main tasks in medical image analysis include segmentation, classification, and registration.

Segmentation involves identifying specific regions or structures within an image, such as organs, tumors, or lesions. This is critical for understanding the spatial relationships and sizes of anatomical features, which can aid in disease diagnosis and treatment planning (Pham et al., 2000). Classification tasks aim to categorize medical images or specific regions based on pathological findings. For instance, classifying tissues as cancerous or non-cancerous is a common use case (Murphy et al., 2007). Registration aligns multiple images—either from different imaging modalities, such as CT and MRI, or from different time points—to allow for comparative analysis and monitoring of disease progression (Maintz & Viergever, 1998).

Traditional methods for these tasks often employed rule-based algorithms and machine learning techniques that relied on explicit feature engineering. For example, edge detection and thresholding techniques were widely used for segmentation tasks, while algorithms like Support Vector Machines (SVMs) and Random Forests were applied to classification problems (Belgiu & Drăguţ, 2016). While these methods provided valuable insights, they had several critical limitations.

1. **Feature Engineering Dependency**: Traditional approaches relied heavily on hand-crafted features, such as shape, texture, and intensity. The performance of these methods was often dataset-specific, making them prone to variability and limiting their generalizability to new or unseen datasets (Lowe, 2004; Shen et al., 2017).
2. **Inability to Handle Complex Patterns**: Medical images often contain high variability due to noise, artifacts, or subtle abnormalities, such as faint lesions or overlapping anatomical structures. Traditional methods have struggled to capture such complexities, resulting in suboptimal performance in challenging scenarios (Litjens et al., 2017).

3. **Scalability Issues**: The volume of medical imaging data has grown exponentially due to the increasing use of advanced imaging modalities and routine screenings. Traditional algorithms lacked the computational efficiency to process such large-scale datasets, further limiting their applicability in real-world clinical workflows (Brady, 2017).

1.2 Deep Learning: Theoretical Foundations

Deep learning, a transformative branch of artificial intelligence (AI), has revolutionized medical image analysis by overcoming many of the limitations of traditional methods. Its success stems from its ability to automatically learn hierarchical representations of data, eliminating the need for manual feature engineering (LeCun et al., 2015; Goodfellow, 2016).

At the heart of deep learning in medical imaging is the Convolutional Neural Network (CNN). CNNs are designed to mimic the human visual system, making them particularly effective for analyzing visual data. These networks consist of several key components:

- **Convolutional Layers**: These layers extract spatial features from images using filters, capturing patterns such as edges, textures, and more complex structures.
- **Pooling Layers**: These layers reduce the dimensionality of the feature maps while retaining essential information, making the model computationally efficient.
- **Fully Connected Layers**: These layers aggregate the extracted features for tasks such as classification or regression, enabling the network to make predictions based on the learned representations.

The hierarchical nature of CNNs allows them to excel in tasks such as segmentation, classification, and registration, which are critical in medical image analysis (Shen et al., 2017; Litjens et al., 2017).

1.3 Applications in Medical Imaging

Deep learning has demonstrated remarkable success across various imaging modalities, including X-rays, CT scans, MRI, and ultrasound. Each modality presents unique challenges and opportunities for AI-based solutions:

1. **X-rays**:

- *Disease Detection*: CNNs have been employed to detect pneumonia, tuberculosis, and lung cancer. For example, Rajpurkar et al. (2017) developed a deep learning model, CheXNet, which outperformed radiologists in identifying pneumonia on chest X-rays.

2. **Computed Tomography (CT)**:
   - *Tumor Segmentation*: Deep learning models have achieved high precision in segmenting liver, lung, and brain tumors, aiding oncologists in treatment planning (Menze et al., 2015).
   - *Cardiac Imaging*: CNNs are used to analyze cardiac structures, enabling better management of heart diseases such as coronary artery disease and cardiomyopathies (Zreik et al., 2018).
3. **Magnetic Resonance Imaging (MRI)**:
   - *Brain Imaging*: Automated segmentation of brain tumors and white matter abnormalities has facilitated the diagnosis of conditions like multiple sclerosis, Alzheimer's disease, and glioblastomas (Pereira et al., 2016; Shen et al., 2017).
   - *Functional Analysis*: Deep learning models have been applied to classify neurological disorders based on MRI features, providing insights into brain function and connectivity (Eshaghi et al., 2019).
4. **Ultrasound**:
   - *Obstetrics and Gynecology*: CNNs assist in fetal health monitoring, placental assessments, and anomaly detection during pregnancy (Baumgartner et al., 2017).
   - *Cardiac Imaging*: Echocardiograms analyzed using deep learning provide valuable insights into cardiac function and valve abnormalities, improving diagnostic accuracy (Madani et al., 2018).

1.4 Challenges in Clinical Integration

Despite its transformative potential, deep learning faces significant challenges in clinical adoption:

- **Data Availability**: Large annotated datasets are essential for training deep learning models. However, such datasets are often limited due to privacy concerns, the resource-intensive nature of expert labeling, and proprietary restrictions (Kaissis et al., 2020).
- **Explainability**: Deep learning models are often criticized as "black boxes." This lack of interpretability makes it challenging for clinicians to trust and adopt AI-driven decisions in critical scenarios (Rudin, 2019).

- **Regulatory and Ethical Hurdles**: AI systems must comply with stringent regulatory standards to ensure safety and efficacy. Ethical concerns, such as algorithmic bias and data security, further complicate the clinical deployment of these technologies (Amann et al., 2020; Topol, 2019).
- **Generalizability**: Models trained on specific datasets may fail to perform well on diverse populations or imaging equipment, necessitating robust validation across multiple clinical settings (Nagendran et al., 2020).

1.5 Future Directions

The future of medical image analysis with deep learning is brimming with possibilities:

1. **Multimodal Imaging**: Integrating data from multiple modalities, such as MRI and PET, can provide comprehensive insights into complex diseases like cancer and neurodegenerative disorders (Xu et al., 2022).
2. **Explainable AI**: Developing interpretable models will enhance clinician trust and facilitate regulatory approval (Samek et al., 2017).
3. **Generative Models**: Techniques such as Generative Adversarial Networks (GANs) can augment limited datasets by generating realistic synthetic images (Frid-Adar et al., 2018).
4. **Personalized Medicine**: Combining imaging data with genomic and clinical information can enable tailored treatment strategies, especially in oncology and cardiology (Hosny et al., 2018).
5. **Edge Computing**: Deploying deep learning models on portable devices can bring diagnostic capabilities to remote and underserved areas, addressing global healthcare disparities (Xu et al., 2020).

By addressing these challenges through collaborative efforts among researchers, clinicians, and policymakers, deep learning can redefine the standards of medical image analysis, ultimately improving patient outcomes.

2. LITERATURE SURVEY

Medical imaging serves as a cornerstone of modern medicine, providing non-invasive insights into the human body that are crucial for diagnosis, treatment planning, and disease monitoring. The emergence of deep learning has revolutionized this field, offering state-of-the-art methodologies for automating image analysis tasks, including classification, segmentation, and registration. This section provides a detailed review of the literature, focusing on significant developments, traditional methodologies, the impact of deep learning, applications across modalities, challenges, and future prospects.

1. Traditional Approaches in Medical Image Analysis

Traditional medical image analysis was predominantly based on manual interpretation and handcrafted algorithms. These conventional approaches relied on human-defined features such as intensity, texture, and edges to interpret medical images. Techniques such as thresholding, region growing, and clustering form the backbone of image segmentation.

Pham et al. (2000) explored these methods, detailing their application to segmentation tasks in brain MRI and CT scans. While such techniques were computationally efficient, they struggled with variability in image quality, noise, and artifacts, limiting their robustness. Similarly, statistical models such as Gaussian Mixture Models (GMMs) and K-means clustering were often employed for image segmentation, but they required extensive parameter tuning.

Machine learning techniques have introduced a level of automation, with algorithms such as Support Vector Machines (SVMs) and Random Forests demonstrating success in classification tasks (Murphy et al., 2007). These models relied on feature extraction pipelines tailored to specific datasets, but lacked scalability. Moreover, their dependence on domain-specific expertise for feature engineering often led to suboptimal performance when applied to diverse or unseen datasets.

Limitations of traditional methods included:

1. **Feature Engineering Dependency**: Required significant domain expertise to manually design and extract features.
2. **Limited Generalization**: Struggled with variations in imaging modalities, patient demographics, and acquisition protocols.
3. **Scalability**: Could not handle the increasing volume and complexity of medical imaging data.

2. Emergence of Deep Learning in Medical Image Analysis

The advent of deep learning marked a paradigm shift in medical image analysis, eliminating the need for handcrafted features by enabling the automatic learning of features directly from raw data. Deep learning models, particularly Convolutional Neural Networks (CNNs), have demonstrated remarkable performance across various imaging tasks.

2.1 Segmentation

Segmentation, the process of delineating anatomical structures or lesions, has been significantly advanced by CNN-based architectures. Ronneberger et al. (2015) introduced the U-Net, a fully convolutional network tailored for biomedical image segmentation. Its encoder-decoder design, with skip connections, allowed for precise localization and feature propagation, achieving exceptional results in tasks such as tumor segmentation and organ delineation.

For instance, Zhang et al. (2020) applied U-Net variants to brain MRI for glioblastoma segmentation, achieving high Dice scores and outperforming traditional algorithms. Advanced architectures, such as Attention U-Net (Oktay, 2018), incorporated attention mechanisms to focus on relevant regions, further enhancing performance.

2.2 Classification

Deep learning models have also achieved breakthroughs in disease classification. Esteva et al. (2017) developed a CNN for skin cancer detection, achieving dermatologist-level accuracy in identifying melanoma and other conditions. Similarly, Rajpurkar et al. (2017) proposed CheXNet, a deep learning model for detecting pneumonia in chest X-rays, which demonstrated superior diagnostic performance compared to radiologists.

2.3 Registration

Medical image registration aligns images from different modalities or time points, enabling comparative analysis. Balakrishnan & Rajendran (2020) introduced VoxelMorph, a deep learning-based framework for deformable image registration. The model, trained in an unsupervised manner, achieved state-of-the-art results in aligning MRI and CT images with significantly reduced computation time compared to traditional iterative methods.

3. Applications Across Imaging Modalities

Deep learning has been applied across various imaging modalities, each presenting unique challenges and benefits:

3.1 X-ray Imaging

As one of the most widely used imaging modalities, X-rays have benefited significantly from advancements in deep learning. CheXpert, developed by Irvin et al. (2019), provided a large annotated dataset for chest X-ray analysis, facilitating multi-label classification of thoracic diseases. CNNs have also been used for early detection of lung cancer, tuberculosis, and bone fractures, with models demonstrating robustness across diverse datasets.

3.2 Computed Tomography (CT)

CT imaging plays a crucial role in the management of oncology and cardiovascular diseases. Setio et al. (2016) demonstrated the effectiveness of 3D CNNs for lung nodule detection in CT scans, achieving high sensitivity and specificity. Christ et al. (2017) utilized cascaded CNNs for liver tumor segmentation, enabling precise tumor localization and volume estimation.

3.3 Magnetic Resonance Imaging (MRI)

MRI, known for its superior soft tissue contrast, has been extensively studied using deep learning. Kamnitsas et al. (2017) developed a multi-scale 3D CNN for brain lesion segmentation in multi-modal MRI. Their model combined spatial and contextual information, achieving superior performance in detecting lesions caused by multiple sclerosis and stroke.

3.4 Ultrasound

Deep learning has enhanced the utility of ultrasound imaging, which is often affected by noise and operator variability. Baumgartner et al. (2017) applied CNNs for automated fetal head circumference measurement, improving reproducibility and reducing inter-operator variability. Similarly, Zhang et al. (2019) utilized deep learning for breast cancer diagnosis, achieving comparable performance to that of expert radiologists.

4. Other Applications of Deep Learning for Medical Imaging

Despite its successes, the integration of deep learning into clinical workflows faces several challenges:

4.1 Data Scarcity and Annotation

Medical datasets are often limited due to privacy concerns and the high cost of expert annotation. Kaissis et al. (2020) explored federated learning as a potential solution, allowing collaborative model training without data sharing. Additionally, synthetic data generation using GANs (Frid-Adar et al., 2018) has shown promise in augmenting training datasets.

4.2 Explainability

The lack of interpretability in deep learning models hinders their clinical adoption. Rudin (2019) emphasized the need for interpretable models, advocating for techniques such as saliency maps, attention mechanisms, and layer-wise relevance propagation.

4.3 Generalization

Deep learning models often exhibit poor generalization when applied to datasets from different institutions or imaging protocols. Domain adaptation techniques, such as adversarial training (Ghafoorian et al., 2017), aim to address this issue by improving model robustness across diverse datasets.

4.4 Ethical and Regulatory Concerns

Ensuring fairness, transparency, and compliance with regulatory standards is critical for deploying AI in healthcare. Amann et al. (2020) highlighted the importance of addressing biases in training data and ensuring the ethical use of AI in clinical practice.

5. Innovative directions

5.1 Multimodal Fusion

Combining data from multiple modalities, such as MRI and PET, can provide comprehensive insights into complex diseases. Huang et al. (2020) demonstrated the benefits of multimodal fusion in improving diagnostic accuracy for Alzheimer's disease.

5.2 Explainable Models

Developing interpretable AI models remains a priority for building trust among clinicians and gaining regulatory approval (Samek et al., 2017).

5.3 Edge Computing

Deploying AI models on portable devices can enable real-time diagnostics in remote and underserved regions (Xu et al., 2020).

5.4 Personalized Medicine

Integrating imaging data with genomic and clinical information can enable the development of tailored treatment plans, paving the way for precision medicine (Hosny et al., 2018).

Key Achievements and Impact

Deep learning models have revolutionized medical imaging by enabling efficient processing of large-scale datasets, identifying subtle patterns in images that may elude human experts. CNN-based models, for instance, have achieved exceptional performance in segmenting lung regions, detecting chest abnormalities, and diagnosing eye diseases with explainable and reproducible methods (Ronneberger et al., 2015; Baltruschat et al., 2019). These innovations have significant implications for clinical workflows, reducing radiologists' workloads and ensuring early and accurate disease detection.

Additionally, AI-powered systems trained on these datasets have demonstrated robust performance in handling real-world challenges such as image noise, artifacts, and variability in imaging modalities. For example, the Chest X-Ray dataset has been utilized to train multi-label classification models capable of simultaneously detecting multiple thoracic diseases (Wang et al., 2017). In eye disease classification, deep learning systems like EyePACS have enabled rapid screening for diabetic retinopathy, especially in low-resource settings (Abràmoff et al., 2016).

3. DATASET DESCRIPTION

Datasets play a pivotal role in training and evaluating deep learning models for medical image analysis. The quality, diversity, and size of the dataset are crucial for achieving reliable, accurate, and generalizable results. This section provides a detailed description of three important datasets widely used in medical imaging research: Chest X-Ray Images 2 (Zhang et al., 2023), NIH Clinical Centre Dataset (Willemink et al., 2020), and Eye Disease Classification Dataset (Babaqi et al., 2023). Each dataset offers unique insights into specific medical conditions and presents opportunities for advancing the capabilities of convolutional neural networks (CNNs) in medical image analysis.

Significance of the Datasets

The NIH Clinical Center's Chest X-Ray dataset has played a pivotal role in advancing chest disease classification by providing over 100,000 labeled X-ray images, enabling models like CheXNet to achieve radiologist-level performance (Rajpurkar et al., 2017). This has drastically improved diagnostic efficiency for conditions such as pneumonia, tuberculosis, and lung nodules (Irvin et al., 2019). Similarly, the eye disease classification datasets have supported the development of automated tools for diabetic retinopathy and glaucoma detection, which are critical for preventing vision loss (Gulshan et al., 2016; Ting et al., 2017).

These datasets have also allowed for the application of transfer learning, wherein pre-trained models such as ResNet and DenseNet are fine-tuned for specific tasks, further improving diagnostic accuracy and reducing the need for massive annotated datasets (Huang et al., 2017). Moreover, their public availability has democratized access to medical imaging research, fostering collaboration across academia, healthcare institutions, and industry.

1. Chest X-Ray Images 2

The Chest X-Ray Images 2 dataset is a curated collection of chest radiographs used primarily for research in lung disease detection, particularly pneumonia. This dataset was originally introduced to evaluate the performance of CNNs in detecting pneumonia and distinguishing between bacterial and viral infections.

Dataset Characteristics

1. **Volume and Distribution**:

The dataset consists of approximately 6,000 chest X-ray images, which are categorized into three main classes: Normal (healthy lungs), Bacterial pneumonia and Viral pneumonia.

2. **Image Format and Resolution**:

The images are stored in standard formats (JPEG or PNG) with varying resolutions, but most are high-quality grayscale images optimized for radiological interpretation.

3. **Annotations**:

The dataset includes image labels verified by radiologists. Each image is annotated with a diagnosis, which serves as the ground truth for supervised learning.

Usage of the dataset

This dataset is widely used for:

- Pneumonia detection: Training CNNs to differentiate between healthy and diseased lungs.
- Classification: Distinguishing bacterial pneumonia from viral pneumonia, a critical task for clinical decision-making.
- Explainability studies: Investigating how CNNs focus on specific regions of the lung (e.g., areas of opacity) during diagnosis.

While valuable, the dataset has limitations, including:

- Imbalance in class distribution, with fewer examples of rare conditions like viral pneumonia.
- Lack of metadata, such as patient demographics, which could provide additional insights into disease patterns.

2. NIH Clinical Centre Dataset

The NIH Clinical Centre Dataset, also known as the ChestX-ray14 dataset, is one of the largest publicly available datasets of chest radiographs. Released by the National Institutes of Health (NIH), this dataset has become a benchmark for deep learning applications in chest X-ray analysis.

Dataset Characteristics

1. **Volume and Diversity**:

The dataset contains over 112,000 frontal-view chest X-rays from more than 30,000 patients. It covers 14 common thoracic diseases, including: Atelectasis, Cardiomegaly, Effusion, Infiltration, Mass, Pneumonia, Pneumothorax, and Nodule.

2. **Labels and Annotations**:

Each image is annotated with one or more labels indicating the presence or absence of specific thoracic conditions. The labels were generated using natural language processing (NLP) techniques on radiology reports.

3. **Image Format**:

The dataset includes grayscale images of varying resolutions, ensuring compatibility with CNN architectures.

Usage of the dataset

The NIH dataset has enabled advancements in:

- Multi-label classification: Training CNNs to identify multiple diseases in a single radiograph.
- Localization: Developing models to pinpoint abnormalities using techniques like Grad-CAM and saliency maps.
- Transfer learning: Pretraining CNNs on this dataset for application to smaller, disease-specific datasets.

While valuable, the dataset has limitations, including addressable points such as: large scale and diversity enable robust model training and evaluation, availability of metadata, such as patient age and gender, for advanced research. The limitations of dataset include: labels derived from NLP may contain errors, necessitating manual validation for critical tasks and the dataset lacks lateral-view X-rays, limiting its applicability in certain clinical scenarios.

3. Eye Disease Classification Dataset

The Eye Disease Classification Dataset is designed for the detection and classification of various ophthalmic conditions. It primarily focuses on retinal images obtained using fundus photography, a non-invasive imaging technique widely used in the diagnosis of eye diseases.

Dataset Characteristics

1. **Volume and Conditions Covered**:

The dataset comprises thousands of retinal fundus images, annotated for conditions such as: Diabetic retinopathy (mild, moderate, severe, proliferative), Age-related macular degeneration (AMD) and Glaucoma

2. **Image Format and Quality**:

The images are high-resolution color fundus photographs, often provided in standard formats like TIFF or JPEG. The high quality of these images facilitates detailed analysis of retinal structures.

3. **Annotations**:

The dataset includes expert-verified labels, often accompanied by severity grades for specific conditions. Some versions also include pixel-level annotations for segmentation tasks.

Comparative Insights

These datasets collectively represent a diverse range of imaging modalities and clinical conditions, each contributing to advancements in deep learning applications for medical image analysis.

- **Chest X-Ray Images 2** and **NIH Clinical Center Dataset** focus on thoracic imaging, addressing challenges in lung disease detection and multi-label classification.
- The **Eye Disease Classification Dataset** targets ophthalmology, emphasizing high-resolution analysis of retinal features.

By leveraging these datasets, researchers have developed CNN architectures that achieve high accuracy and generalization across tasks, demonstrating the transformative potential of deep learning in healthcare. However, challenges such as data imbalance, label quality, and generalizability persist, underscoring the need for continued innovation and collaboration in dataset curation and model development.

4. TECHNICAL METHODOLOGY

4.1 Case study-1

It is centered on creating a Convolutional Neural Network (CNN) model to automate the detection of diseases in chest X-ray images. This study aims to develop a reliable model that can accurately recognize a wide range of diseases. The development and evaluation of the model will involve methods such as data exploration, preprocessing, designing the CNN architecture, and analyzing performance metrics. The aim is to enhance medical image analysis, thereby potentially improving diagnostic accuracy and efficiency in healthcare environments.

4.1.1 Dataset Collection:

This model works on two datasets: 1. Chest X-Ray Images, 2.NIH Clinical Center.

The Chest X-Ray Images Dataset comprises 5,856 images, divided into two categories: Normal and Pneumonia. This dataset is frequently used for training and evaluating machine learning models designed to detect pneumonia. It is thoroughly annotated and features a balanced distribution of images between the two classes, making it ideal for binary classification tasks.

The NIH Clinical Center dataset is one of the largest publicly accessible collections of chest X-ray images, featuring over 100,000 anonymized images sourced from more than 30,000 patients. It includes 14 different disease labels, such as Atelectasis, Cardiomegaly, Effusion, Infiltration, Mass, Nodule, Pneumonia,

Pneumothorax, Consolidation, Edema, Emphysema, Fibrosis, Pleural Thickening, and Hernia. This dataset is widely used for multi-label classification tasks and has played a crucial role in advancing research in automated disease detection and diagnosis. The following table (Table 1) provides an overview of the dataset.

Table 1. Dataset description

Dataset	Number of Images	Classes/Labels
Chest X-Ray	5,856	Normal, Pneumonia
NIH Clinical Center	100,000+	14 different labels(Atelectasis, Cardiomegaly etc.)

Figure 1. Input images and preprocessed images

Figure 2. Subplots creation and Loop through train, val, and test sets

Figure 1 and Figure 2 represent the various forms of input images.

4.1.2 Data Preprocessing

Dataset Download

4.1.2.1 Leverage the Kaggle API or other platforms to obtain medical image datasets (such as X-rays or MRIs).
4.1.2.2 Extract and organize the data into training, validation, and test sets.

Data Exploration

4.1.2.3 Visualize sample images to grasp their structure and associated labels.
4.1.2.4 Examine the class distribution to determine if the data is balanced or imbalanced.

Preprocessing

4.1.2.5 Resize images to a uniform dimension (for instance, 150x150 pixels).
4.1.2.6 Normalize pixel values to a range of [0, 1] to facilitate faster and more stable training.

Data Augmentation

4.1.2.7 Implement transformations like flipping, rotation, and scaling to enhance dataset diversity.

Figure 3. Class distribution in the dataset

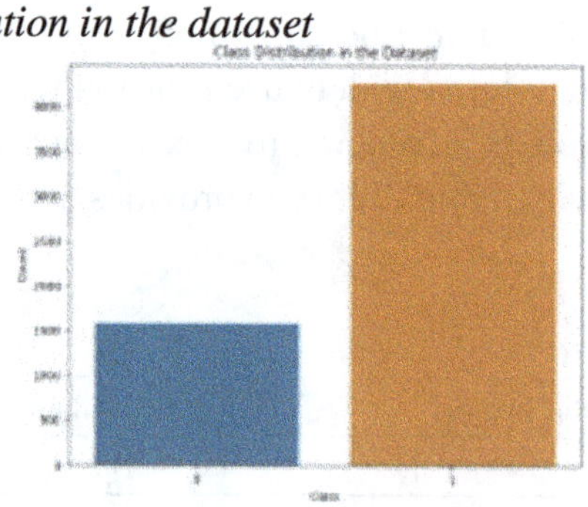

Figure 3 represents the class distribution in the described dataset.

4.1.3 Model Design

Custom CNN

4.1.3.1 We reate a Sequential model with the following layers.
4.1.3.2 Convolutional layers (Conv2D) to identify features within the images.
4.1.3.3 Pooling layers (MaxPooling2D) to decrease spatial dimensions while preserving essential features.

Dense layers for the classification process.

4.1.3.4 Incorporate activation functions (ReLU, Sigmoid) and Dropout for regularization purposes.
4.1.3.5 Pre-trained Models (Optional):
4.1.3.6 Load models like VGG16 or ResNet with pre-trained weights.
4.1.3.7 Adjust the output layer for either binary or multi-class classification tasks.

Algorithms Chosen

Convolutional Neural Networks (CNNs)

4.1.3.8 **Algorithm:** A specialized deep neural network that processes data structured in grids, such as images. This model uses convolutional filters to identify features like edges, textures, and patterns in medical imaging.
4.1.3.9 **Purpose:** To analyze medical images (such as X-rays and MRIs) for patterns that may indicate diseases or abnormalities. It also extracts spatial hierarchies of features to enhance image comprehension.

VGG16 (Pre-trained Model)

4.1.3.10 **Algorithm:** This is a deep convolutional neural network (CNN) architecture consisting of 16 layers, including 13 convolutional layers and 3 fully connected layers. It is often utilized with pre-trained weights for transfer learning.
4.1.3.11 **Purpose:** Utilize a model that has been trained on a vast dataset (ImageNet) to efficiently adapt to medical image datasets. Enhance accuracy by employing a well-established architecture instead of starting the training process from scratch.

ResNet (Residual Neural Network)

4.1.3.12 **Algorithm:** A convolutional neural network (CNN) that incorporates residual connections to address the vanishing gradient issue, facilitating effective training of very deep networks.

4.1.3.13 **Purpose:** Allow deeper models to effectively analyze intricate medical images. Enhance performance by preserving features from earlier layers via shortcut connections.

4.1.4 Model Compilation:

4.1.4.1 Select a loss function:

4.1.4.2 Use Binary Cross-Entropy for binary classification tasks.

4.1.4.3 Opt for Categorical Cross-Entropy for multi-class scenarios.

4.1.4.4 Choose an optimizer (such as Adam or SGD) to minimize the loss function.

4.1.4.5 Establish evaluation metrics like accuracy or AUC.

Figures 4, 5, and 6 illustrate the optimal parameters and scores obtained using the aforementioned models.

Figure 4. Optimal parameters and score using CNN

	params
0	{'units': 16, 'dropout_rate': 0.25}
1	{'units': 32, 'dropout_rate': 0.25}
2	{'units': 64, 'dropout_rate': 0.25}
3	{'units': 16, 'dropout_rate': 0.5}
4	{'units': 32, 'dropout_rate': 0.5}
5	{'units': 64, 'dropout_rate': 0.5}

Best parameters

```
random_search_results_cnn.best_params_
```

```
{'units': 64, 'dropout_rate': 0.25}
```

Best score

```
round(random_search_results_cnn.best_score_*100)
```

```
78
```

Figure 5. Optimal parameters and score using VGG16

	params
0	{'units': 16, 'dropout_rate': 0.25}
1	{'units': 64, 'dropout_rate': 0.25}
2	{'units': 128, 'dropout_rate': 0.25}
3	{'units': 16, 'dropout_rate': 0.5}
4	{'units': 64, 'dropout_rate': 0.5}
5	{'units': 128, 'dropout_rate': 0.5}

Best parameters

```
random_search_results_vgg16.best_params_
```

```
{'units': 16, 'dropout_rate': 0.25}
```

Best score

```
round(random_search_results_vgg16.best_score_*100)
```

```
78
```

Figure 6. Optimal parameters and score using ResNet

	params
0	{'units': 16, 'dropout_rate': 0.25}
1	{'units': 64, 'dropout_rate': 0.25}
2	{'units': 128, 'dropout_rate': 0.25}
3	{'units': 16, 'dropout_rate': 0.5}
4	{'units': 64, 'dropout_rate': 0.5}
5	{'units': 128, 'dropout_rate': 0.5}

Best parameters

```
resnet_random_search_results.best_params_
```

```
{'units': 16, 'dropout_rate': 0.25}
```

Best score

```
round(resnet_random_search_results.best_score_*100)
```

```
78
```

4.1.5 Model Training

Utilize a data generator or prepared datasets to feed data into the model in batches.

Specify

4.1.5.1 The number of epochs for training.
4.1.5.2 Batch size (for example, 32 images per batch).
4.1.5.3 Validation split for real-time performance assessment during training.

Employ callbacks

4.1.5.4 Implement early stopping to cease training when validation performance plateaus.

4.1.5.5 Use model checkpointing to save the best-performing model.

4.1.5.6

Figure 7. Predicted labels, model accuracy, model loss using CNN

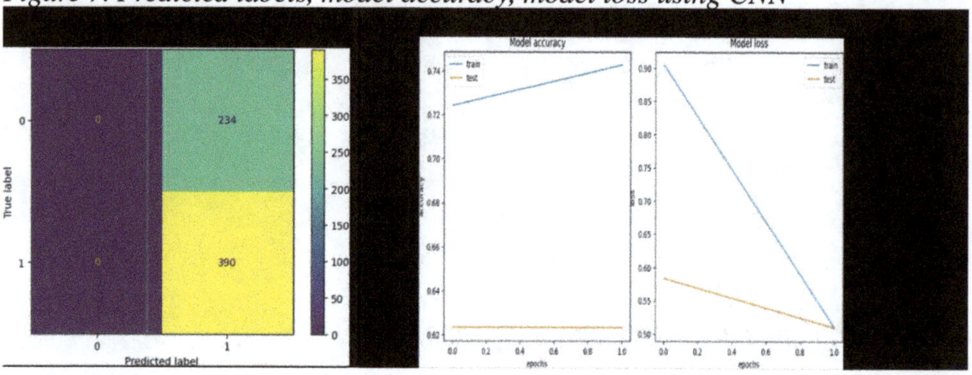

Figure 8. Predicted labels, model accuracy, model loss using VGG16

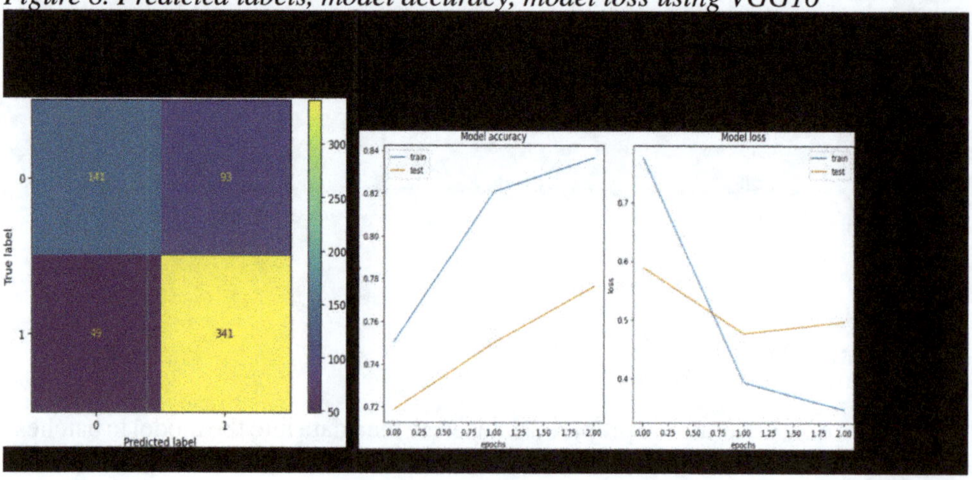

Figure 9. Predicted labels, model accuracy, and model loss using ResNet

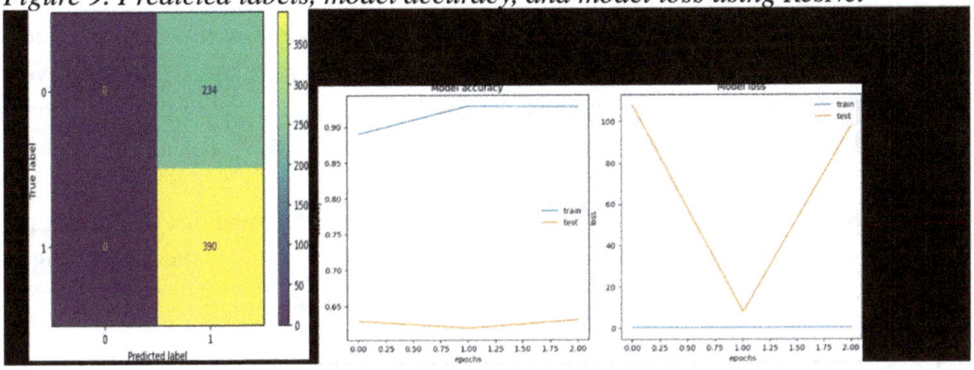

Figures 7, 8, and 9 display the predicted labels, model accuracy, and model loss for the CNN, VGG16, and ResNet models, respectively.

4.1.6 Result Analysis

Table 2 shows the comparison of the performances of various models.

Table 2. Comparison of model performance

Model	Support	Test Accuracy (%)	Train Accuracy (%)	Macro Avg F1-Score	Weighted Avg F1-Score	Optimal Parameters
CNN	234	62.5	74	0.38	0.48	Units 64, Dropout Rate 0.25
VGG16	234	77.24	84	0.75	0.77	Units 16, Dropout Rate 0.25
ResNet	234	62.5	93	0.38	0.48	Units 16, Dropout Rate 0.25

4.1.6.1 CNN (Custom Model):

- **Performance:** CNN recorded an accuracy of 62.5% during testing. The precision, recall, and F1-score were all zero, highlighting its poor prediction performance for class 0.
- **Training Accuracy:** The model shows slight overfitting, with a training accuracy of 74% that exceeds its testing performance.
- **Challenges:** The limited performance indicates that the model had difficulty generalizing, likely due to its simpler architecture or insufficient data preprocessing.

4.1.6.2 VGG16 (Pre-Trained Model):

4.2 **Performance:** VGG16 surpassed the other models with a test accuracy of 77.24%. It achieved the highest F1-score of 0.67 for class 0 and displayed balanced macro and weighted F1-scores, reflecting consistent performance.
4.3 **Training Accuracy:** With a training accuracy of 84%, the model is well-optimized and avoids significant overfitting.
4.4 **Key Factors for Success:** The use of pre-trained weights and a strong architecture enabled VGG16 to effectively learn complex patterns, making it ideal for binary classification.

4.1.6.3 ResNet (Residual Neural Network):

4.2 **Performance:** ResNet achieved a test accuracy of 62.5%, similar to CNN, but struggled to predict class 0 effectively.
4.3 **Training Accuracy:** Although it reached a high training accuracy of 93%, the model's testing performance reveals significant overfitting.
4.4 **Challenges:** ResNet's inability to generalize may be due to its deep architecture, which requires more training data or improved regularization.

VGG16 stood out among the three models, showcasing its superior ability to generalize across the test set, which makes it the most suitable option for deployment.

Challenges faced by CNN and ResNet:

Both CNN and ResNet likely encountered difficulties due to insufficient labeled data and challenges in managing class imbalance.

Improving data augmentation and regularization techniques could enhance the performance of these models.

The significance of Pre-Trained Models: VGG16's success highlights the importance of transfer learning in medical imaging, particularly for smaller datasets.

Consider investigating ensemble methods that integrate VGG16 and ResNet to enhance prediction stability. Additionally, implement advanced data augmentation techniques and explore the use of Generative Adversarial Networks (GANs) to boost dataset diversity.

4.2 Casestudy-2

Considering NIH Clinical Center dataset, we can proceed as earlier dataset as below.

4.2.1 Data Preprocessing

Data preprocessing involves converting raw data into a format that is easy to understand and use. This process involves tasks such as cleaning, normalizing, resizing, and augmenting the data. In the context of deep learning, effective preprocessing helps achieve better convergence and generalization.

Steps-

1. Load the raw data, including images and their corresponding masks, from files or a dataset.
2. Resizing: Make sure all images and masks are resized to the same dimensions, such as 256×256, to ensure consistency.
3. Normalization: Adjust pixel values to fall within the range [0, 1] or [-1, 1] to enhance learning speed and overall performance.
4. Mask Preparation: Transform masks into binary values (0s and 1s) for segmentation tasks.

4.2.2 **Evaluation:**

1. **Accuracy:** Accuracy is defined as the ratio of correctly classified samples (both true positives and true negatives) to the total number of samples. This is calculated using the accuracy_score function from the sklearn library.
2. **Precision:** Precision refers to the ratio of true positives to all predicted positives. It is computed using the precision_score function from sklearn, with zero_division=1 to prevent errors when the denominator is zero.

4.3 Casestudy-3

Eye disease classification is a research area that focuses on developing algorithms and models to accurately classify different types of eye diseases based on medical imaging data. It plays a critical role in assisting ophthalmologists and healthcare professionals in effectively diagnosing and treating eye diseases. The primary objective of eye disease classification is to leverage machine learning and computer vision techniques to analyze medical images and detect the four diseases: cataract, diabetic retinopathy, glaucoma, normal. For a human to find out about a disease in the eye can be difficult and inaccurate.

4.3.1 Data Preprocessing

Creating a DataFrame that links image paths to labels for an eye disease classification dataset. The dataset was built using torch.utils.data. Dataset for efficient loading of data. For data augmentation, only Random Horizontal and Vertical flip was used. Adding augmentations in colors, brightness etc made training difficult. 85% of the dataset was used for training while the remaining for validation/testing. Batch Size of 128 was chosen.

4.3.2 Model Architecture

We used the Resnet18 pretrained model for this task. ResNet-18 is composed of multiple residual blocks, which are designed to address the problem of vanishing gradients in deep neural networks. These blocks introduce skip connections, allowing information to bypass several layers and flow directly to deeper layers. This helps in mitigating the degradation problem and enables the network to learn more effectively, even with very deep architectures. We replaced the final layer with two new dense layers. 70% of the resnet18 was freezed while the remaining was kept trainable. The resnet18 block was trained with a lr of 5x10 -5 while the dense layers with lr = 8 x 10-4.

4.3.3 Model Training

The training step method calculates the loss (CrossEntropyLoss) and accuracy for each batch during training. It then performs backpropagation and updates the weights using the AdamW optimizer with separate learning rates for the ResNet18 layers and the custom block.

Once the model is trained, its performance is evaluated on the test dataset using the following metrics:

4.3.4 Model Evaluation

The model can be evaluated on the basis of

4.3.4.1 **Accuracy***:*

The percentage of correctly classified images out of the total test images.

4.3.4.2 The overall accuracy of the model is 0.92, indicating the percentage of correctly predicted instances across all classes.

4.3.4.3 **Precision***:*

The ratio of true positive predictions to the total positive predictions indicates the model's ability to avoid false positives.

4.3.4.4 **Recall (Sensitivity)***:*

The ratio of true positive predictions to the total actual positives reflects the model's ability to identify Pneumonia cases.

4.3.4.5 **F1-Score***:*

The harmonic mean of precision and recall provides a balanced measure of the model's performance.

4.3.4.6 **Confusion Matrix***:*

A matrix that summarizes the classification results, showing the number of true positives, true negatives, false positives, and false negatives.

The "glaucoma" class has a precision of 0.90, a recall of 0.83, and an F1-score of 0.86. This suggests that the model performs well in correctly identifying glaucoma cases, but there may be some false negatives. The "normal" class has a precision of 0.85, a recall of 0.90, and an F1-score of 0.88. The model performs well in both precision and recall for normal cases. The "diabetic retinopathy" class has a high precision, recall, and F1-score of 0.99. This indicates the model's excellent performance in correctly identifying cases of diabetic retinopathy. The "cataract" class also has high precision, recall, and

F1-score of 0.95 and above, indicating accurate identification of cataract cases.

5. CONCLUSION

The use of deep learning for medical image analysis, underpinned by comprehensive datasets such as the Chest X-Ray Images (NIH Clinical Centre) and eye disease classification datasets, has redefined healthcare diagnostics. These technologies not only address the limitations of traditional methods but also enable rapid, accurate, and scalable solutions for a wide range of medical challenges. The synergistic efforts of AI researchers, clinicians, and policymakers will be crucial in overcoming existing barriers and translating these advancements into widespread clinical adoption.

With continued advancements in dataset accessibility, model explainability, and ethical AI practices, deep learning is poised to revolutionize global healthcare systems. By aligning technological innovation with clinical needs, these efforts will improve patient outcomes, reduce healthcare disparities, and usher in a new era of precision medicine.

Despite the success in the medical domain, challenges remain in scaling deep learning models for diverse clinical applications. The dependence on large annotated datasets poses limitations due to privacy concerns, labelling costs, and variability in imaging protocols. To address these challenges, techniques like data augmentation, synthetic data generation using Generative Adversarial Networks (GANs), and federated learning are being explored (Frid-Adar et al., 2018; Li et al., 2020).

Another critical hurdle is the interpretability of deep learning models. Efforts to develop explainable AI (XAI) techniques, such as saliency maps and attention mechanisms, aim to enhance clinicians' trust in these systems while complying with regulatory standards (Rudin, 2019; Samek et al., 2017). Additionally, ensuring model generalizability across different populations and imaging equipment remains an essential area of focus, necessitating robust validation frameworks and domain adaptation strategies (Ghafoorian et al., 2017).

The future holds immense promise for leveraging these datasets to drive innovations in personalized medicine, multimodal imaging, and mobile health applications. By integrating imaging data with genomic and clinical information, AI systems can offer comprehensive diagnostic insights tailored to individual patients (Hosny et al., 2018). Edge computing and lightweight AI models also present opportunities to expand access to diagnostic tools in underserved regions (Xu et al., 2020).

REFERENCES

Abràmoff, M. D., Lou, Y., Erginay, A., Clarida, W., Amelon, R., Folk, J. C., & Niemeijer, M. (2016). Improved automated detection of diabetic retinopathy on a publicly available dataset through integration of deep learning. *Investigative Ophthalmology & Visual Science*, *57*(13), 5200–5206. DOI: 10.1167/iovs.16-19964 PMID: 27701631

Amann, J., Blasimme, A., Vayena, E., Frey, D., & Madai, V. I. (2020). Explainability for artificial intelligence in healthcare: A multidisciplinary perspective. *BMC Medical Informatics and Decision Making*, *20*(1), 310. DOI: 10.1186/s12911-020-01332-6 PMID: 33256715

Balakrishnan, N., & Rajendran, A. (2020). Computing WHERE-WHAT classification through FLIKM and deep learning algorithms. In *Advances in Electrical and Computer Technologies: Select Proceedings of ICAECT 2019* (pp. 593-608). Singapore: Springer Singapore. DOI: 10.1007/978-981-15-5558-9_52

Baumgartner, C. F., Koch, L. M., Pollefeys, M., & Konukoglu, E. (2017, September). An exploration of 2D and 3D deep learning techniques for cardiac MR image segmentation. In *International workshop on statistical atlases and computational models of the heart* (pp. 111-119). Cham: Springer International Publishing.

Belgiu, M., & Drăguţ, L. (2016). Random forest in remote sensing: A review of applications and future directions. *ISPRS Journal of Photogrammetry and Remote Sensing*, *114*, 24–31. DOI: 10.1016/j.isprsjprs.2016.01.011

Benjamens, S., Rijkse, E., te Velde-Keyzer, C. A., Berger, S. P., Moers, C., de Borst, M. H., Yakar, D., Slart, R. H. J. A., Dor, F. J. M. F., Minnee, R. C., & Pol, R. A. (2020). Aorto-iliac artery calcification prior to kidney transplantation. *Journal of Clinical Medicine*, *9*(9), 2893. DOI: 10.3390/jcm9092893 PMID: 32906789

Boas, F. E., & Fleischmann, D. (2012). CT artifacts: Causes and reduction techniques. *Imaging in Medicine*, *4*(2), 229–240. DOI: 10.2217/iim.12.13

Brady, A. P. (2017). Error and discrepancy in radiology: Inevitable or avoidable? *Insights Into Imaging*, *8*(1), 171–182. DOI: 10.1007/s13244-016-0534-1 PMID: 27928712

Bushberg, J. T., Seibert, J., Leidholdt, E., & Boone, J. (2012). Magnetic resonance basics, magnetic fields, nuclear magnetic characteristics, tissue contrast, image acquisition. *The Essential Physics of Medical Imaging*, 402-448.

Christ, P. F., Ettlinger, F., Grün, F., Elshaera, M. E. A., Lipkova, J., Schlecht, S., . . . Menze, B. (2017). Automatic liver and tumor segmentation of CT and MRI volumes using cascaded fully convolutional neural networks. *arXiv preprint arXiv:1702.05970.*

Coudray, N., Ocampo, P. S., Sakellaropoulos, T., Narula, N., Snuderl, M., Fenyö, D., Moreira, A. L., Razavian, N., & Tsirigos, A. (2018). Classification and mutation prediction from non–small cell lung cancer histopathology images using deep learning. *Nature Medicine*, *24*(10), 1559–1567. DOI: 10.1038/s41591-018-0177-5 PMID: 30224757

Doi, K. (2007). Computer-aided diagnosis in medical imaging: Historical review, current status and future potential. *Computerized Medical Imaging and Graphics*, *31*(4-5), 198–211. DOI: 10.1016/j.compmedimag.2007.02.002 PMID: 17349778

Esteva, A., Kuprel, B., Novoa, R. A., Ko, J., Swetter, S. M., Blau, H. M., & Thrun, S. (2017). Dermatologist-level classification of skin cancer with deep neural networks. *nature, 542*(7639), 115-118.

Frid-Adar, M., Diamant, I., Klang, E., Amitai, M., Goldberger, J., & Greenspan, H. (2018). GAN-based synthetic medical image augmentation for increased CNN performance in liver lesion classification. *Neurocomputing*, *321*, 321–331. DOI: 10.1016/j.neucom.2018.09.013

Ghassemi, M., Oakden-Rayner, L., & Beam, A. L. (2021). The false hope of current approaches to explainable artificial intelligence in health care. *The Lancet. Digital Health*, *3*(11), e745–e750. DOI: 10.1016/S2589-7500(21)00208-9 PMID: 34711379

Goodfellow, I. (2016). Deep learning.

Gulshan, V., Peng, L., Coram, M., Stumpe, M. C., Wu, D., Narayanaswamy, A., ... & Webster, D. R. (2016). Development and validation of a deep learning algorithm for detection of diabetic retinopathy in retinal fundus photographs. *jama, 316*(22), 2402-2410.

Hosny, A., Parmar, C., Quackenbush, J., Schwartz, L. H., & Aerts, H. J. (2018). Artificial intelligence in radiology. *Nature Reviews. Cancer*, *18*(8), 500–510. DOI: 10.1038/s41568-018-0016-5 PMID: 29777175

Irvin, J., Rajpurkar, P., Ko, M., Yu, Y., Ciurea-Ilcus, S., Chute, C., Marklund, H., Haghgoo, B., Ball, R., Shpanskaya, K., Seekins, J., Mong, D. A., Halabi, S. S., Sandberg, J. K., Jones, R., Larson, D. B., Langlotz, C. P., Patel, B. N., Lungren, M. P., & Ng, A. Y. (2019, July). Chexpert: A large chest radiograph dataset with uncertainty labels and expert comparison. *Proceedings of the AAAI Conference on Artificial Intelligence*, *33*(01), 590–597. DOI: 10.1609/aaai.v33i01.3301590

Kaissis, G. A., Makowski, M. R., Rückert, D., & Braren, R. F. (2020). Secure, privacy-preserving and federated machine learning in medical imaging. *Nature Machine Intelligence, 2*(6), 305–311. DOI: 10.1038/s42256-020-0186-1

Kaissis, G. A., Ziegelmayer, S., Lohöfer, F. K., Harder, F. N., Jungmann, F., Sasse, D., Muckenhuber, A., Yen, H.-Y., Steiger, K., Siveke, J., Friess, H., Schmid, R., Weichert, W., Makowski, M. R., & Braren, R. F. (2020). Image-based molecular phenotyping of pancreatic ductal adenocarcinoma. *Journal of Clinical Medicine, 9*(3), 724. DOI: 10.3390/jcm9030724 PMID: 32155990

Kamnitsas, K., Baumgartner, C., Ledig, C., Newcombe, V., Simpson, J., Kane, A., & Glocker, B. (2017, May). Unsupervised domain adaptation in brain lesion segmentation with adversarial networks. In *International conference on information processing in medical imaging* (pp. 597-609). Cham: Springer International Publishing. DOI: 10.1007/978-3-319-59050-9_47

LeCun, Y., Bengio, Y., & Hinton, G. (2015). Deep learning. *nature, 521*(7553), 436-444.

Litjens, G., Kooi, T., Bejnordi, B. E., Setio, A. A. A., Ciompi, F., Ghafoorian, M., van der Laak, J. A. W. M., van Ginneken, B., & Sánchez, C. I. (2017). A survey on deep learning in medical image analysis. *Medical Image Analysis, 42*, 60–88. DOI: 10.1016/j.media.2017.07.005 PMID: 28778026

Lowe, N. K. (2004). Context and process of informed consent for pharmacologic strategies in labor pain care. *Journal of Midwifery & Women's Health, 49*(3), 250–259. DOI: 10.1016/j.jmwh.2004.02.011 PMID: 15134679

Madani, A., Arnaout, R., Mofrad, M., & Arnaout, R. (2018). Fast and accurate view classification of echocardiograms using deep learning. *NPJ Digital Medicine, 1*(1), 6. DOI: 10.1038/s41746-017-0013-1 PMID: 30828647

Maintz, J. A., Meijering, E. H., & Viergever, M. A. (1998, June). General multimodal elastic registration based on mutual information. In *Medical Imaging 1998: Image Processing* (Vol. 3338, pp. 144-154). SPIE.

McCollough, C. H., Bushberg, J. T., Fletcher, J. G., & Eckel, L. J. (2015, October). Answers to common questions about the use and safety of CT scans. [). Elsevier.]. *Mayo Clinic Proceedings, 90*(10), 1380–1392. DOI: 10.1016/j.mayocp.2015.07.011 PMID: 26434964

Menze, M., & Geiger, A. (2015). Object scene flow for autonomous vehicles. In *Proceedings of the IEEE conference on computer vision and pattern recognition* (pp. 3061-3070).

Nagendran, M., Chen, Y., Lovejoy, C. A., Gordon, A. C., Komorowski, M., Harvey, H., ... & Maruthappu, M. (2020). Artificial intelligence versus clinicians: systematic review of design, reporting standards, and claims of deep learning studies. *bmj, 368.*

Oktay, A. B. (2018). Human identification with dental panoramic radiographic images. *IET Biometrics*, *7*(4), 349–355. DOI: 10.1049/iet-bmt.2017.0078

Pham, D. L., Xu, C., & Prince, J. L. (2000). Current methods in medical image segmentation. *Annual Review of Biomedical Engineering*, *2*(1), 315–337. DOI: 10.1146/annurev.bioeng.2.1.315 PMID: 11701515

Poplin, R., Varadarajan, A. V., Blumer, K., Liu, Y., McConnell, M. V., Corrado, G. S., Peng, L., & Webster, D. R. (2018). Prediction of cardiovascular risk factors from retinal fundus photographs via deep learning. *Nature Biomedical Engineering*, *2*(3), 158–164. DOI: 10.1038/s41551-018-0195-0 PMID: 31015713

Rajpurkar, P., Irvin, J., Zhu, K., Yang, B., Mehta, H., Duan, T., . . . Ng, A. Y. (2017). Chexnet: Radiologist-level pneumonia detection on chest x-rays with deep learning. *arXiv preprint arXiv:1711.05225.*

Ronneberger, O., Fischer, P., & Brox, T. (2015, October). U-net: Convolutional networks for biomedical image segmentation. In *International Conference on Medical image computing and computer-assisted intervention* (pp. 234-241). Cham: Springer international publishing. DOI: 10.1007/978-3-319-24574-4_28

Rudin, C. (2019). Stop explaining black box machine learning models for high stakes decisions and use interpretable models instead. *Nature Machine Intelligence*, *1*(5), 206–215. DOI: 10.1038/s42256-019-0048-x PMID: 35603010

Samek, W., Wiegand, T., & Müller, K. R. (2017). Explainable artificial intelligence: Understanding, visualizing and interpreting deep learning models. *arXiv preprint arXiv:1708.08296.*

Shen, D., Wu, G., & Suk, H. I. (2017). Deep learning in medical image analysis. *Annual Review of Biomedical Engineering*, *19*(1), 221–248. DOI: 10.1146/annurev-bioeng-071516-044442 PMID: 28301734

Ting, D. S. W., Cheung, C. Y. L., Lim, G., Tan, G. S. W., Quang, N. D., Gan, A., Hamzah, H., Garcia-Franco, R., San Yeo, I. Y., Lee, S. Y., Wong, E. Y. M., Sabanayagam, C., Baskaran, M., Ibrahim, F., Tan, N. C., Finkelstein, E. A., Lamoureux, E. L., Wong, I. Y., Bressler, N. M., & Wong, T. Y. (2017). Development and validation of a deep learning system for diabetic retinopathy and related eye diseases using retinal images from multiethnic populations with diabetes. *Journal of the American Medical Association*, *318*(22), 2211–2223. DOI: 10.1001/jama.2017.18152 PMID: 29234807

Topol, E. J. (2019). High-performance medicine: The convergence of human and artificial intelligence. *Nature Medicine*, *25*(1), 44–56. DOI: 10.1038/s41591-018-0300-7 PMID: 30617339

Wang, X., Peng, Y., Lu, L., Lu, Z., Bagheri, M., & Summers, R. M. (2017). Chestx-ray8: Hospital-scale chest x-ray database and benchmarks on weakly-supervised classification and localization of common thorax diseases. In *Proceedings of the IEEE conference on computer vision and pattern recognition* (pp. 2097-2106). DOI: 10.1109/CVPR.2017.369

Zreik, M., Lessmann, N., van Hamersvelt, R. W., Wolterink, J. M., Voskuil, M., Viergever, M. A., Leiner, T., & Išgum, I. (2018). Deep learning analysis of the myocardium in coronary CT angiography for identification of patients with functionally significant coronary artery stenosis. *Medical Image Analysis*, *44*, 72–85. DOI: 10.1016/j.media.2017.11.008 PMID: 29197253

Chapter 10
Dissertation on Technology and Customer Satisfaction in Hotels

Akhilesh Pandey
https://orcid.org/0000-0002-9172-9328
Galgotias University, India

Himanshu Sharma
Galgotias University, India

ABSTRACT

In the contemporary hospitality landscape, technology has emerged as a pivotal driver in enhancing customer satisfaction. This study explores the relationship between technological adoption and guest satisfaction in hotel operations, with a focus on digital innovations that streamline service delivery, personalize guest experiences, and improve operational efficiency. From self-check-in kiosks and mobile applications to AI-driven concierge services and smart room features, technology is transforming traditional service models. The research highlights how seamless connectivity, automation, and data analytics contribute to customer-centric strategies that elevate guest satisfaction. Furthermore, the study examines guest perceptions of technology-enabled services and identifies key factors such as ease of use, reliability, personalization, and responsiveness as crucial determinants of satisfaction. Findings suggest that while technological integration significantly enhances guest convenience and service quality.

DOI: 10.4018/979-8-3373-8197-8.ch010

INTRODUCTION

The hospitality industry has undergone a profound transformation in recent years, driven largely by rapid advancements in technology. In the hotel sector, the integration of innovative technological solutions has redefined the way services are delivered and experienced. With the increasing expectations of digitally-savvy guests, hotels are now compelled to adopt modern tools and platforms that enhance operational efficiency, personalize guest experiences, and ultimately, boost customer satisfaction. Technology plays a vital role in shaping customer perceptions at every stage of their journey—from booking and check-in to in-room services and post-stay engagement. Digital tools such as mobile apps, online booking engines, AI-powered chatbots, contactless check-in/check-out systems, and smart room controls have created new standards of convenience and personalization. These innovations not only streamline operations but also provide guests with greater autonomy, faster service, and tailored experiences, all of which contribute significantly to their overall satisfaction. Customer satisfaction in the hotel industry is closely tied to service quality, responsiveness, and emotional engagement. Technology has enabled hotels to collect and analyze guest data, understand preferences, and offer customized solutions in real-time. This data-driven approach helps hotels not only meet but anticipate guest needs, thereby exceeding expectations and fostering loyalty. At the same time, the challenge lies in maintaining a balance between digital convenience and the human touch that defines traditional hospitality This study explores the intricate relationship between technology and customer satisfaction in hotels. It aims to identify the technological interventions that most influence guest experiences, assess customer perceptions of tech-enabled services, and provide insights into how hotels can strategically leverage technology to enhance satisfaction and gain a competitive edge in a highly dynamic market. The hospitality industry, especially the hotel sector, has long been defined by its focus on service excellence, customer engagement, and memorable guest experiences. Traditionally reliant on face-to-face interactions and manual operations, the hotel industry is now witnessing a paradigm shift driven by technological advancement. This shift is not merely a reaction to customer demands but a strategic transformation intended to meet the expectations of a digitally oriented clientele, enhance operational efficiency, and maintain competitiveness in a rapidly evolving market. Over the past two decades, the role of technology in hospitality has expanded from back-end operations to front-line services and customer engagement. While earlier integrations focused on Property Management Systems (PMS) and basic online reservations, modern technology has enabled a much broader array of functionalities—from artificial intelligence (AI) and Internet of Things (IoT) to mobile technologies and data analytics. This transition is driven by several factors including increased internet penetration, mobile device usage, and the digital expectations of Generation Z and Millennials, who now represent a significant portion of the hotel customer base.

1. Objectives of the Study

1. To identify key technological tools and systems currently used in hotel operations.
2. To examine customer perceptions and satisfaction levels associated with technology-enabled services in hotels.
3. To evaluate the effectiveness of technological interventions (e.g., mobile apps, smart rooms, AI chatbots, contactless check-ins) in enhancing the guest experience.
4. To assess the relationship between technology usage and customer loyalty in the hospitality sector.

2. Significance of the Study

- **Industry Relevance**: As digital transformation accelerates across industries; the hospitality sector must keep pace to meet guest expectations. This research provides insights into how technology can be leveraged to create more satisfying and memorable guest experiences.
- **Operational Insight**: The study will help hotel managers understand which technologies are most valued by customers and how these technologies influence satisfaction, loyalty, and repeat business.
- **Academic Contribution**: The research contributes to the existing body of hospitality and service management literature by examining the technological determinants of customer satisfaction.
- **Policy and Investment Guidance**: For stakeholders, including investors and policymakers, the study offers data-backed insights that can inform decision-making regarding technological investments in the hotel sector.

3. Need for the Study

- **Changing Guest Expectations**: Today's customers demand fast, seamless, and personalized experiences, which are increasingly enabled by technology. Understanding these evolving needs is critical for hotels to remain competitive.
- **Post-Pandemic Trends**: The COVID-19 pandemic has heightened demand for contactless services and digital interactions. Studying their impact on customer satisfaction is essential for future preparedness.

- **Competitive Differentiation**: In an industry where services can appear homogenous, technology offers a means to differentiate brand experiences. There is a need to identify which technologies offer the most value to guests.
- **Gap in Localized Research**: While global studies have been conducted, region-specific or country-specific research (e.g., in India or emerging markets) remains limited. This study addresses that gap by focusing on customer experiences in local hotel settings.

4. Background of the Study

In recent years, technology has played an increasingly critical role in redefining customer experience in the hospitality industry. From the early days of computerized booking systems to today's AI-powered service bots and smart room features, technological innovations have become essential tools for enhancing service delivery. Modern guests expect more than just comfort—they seek efficiency, personalization, and control over their experiences, all of which technology facilitates. The rise of digital natives, the influence of online reviews, and the integration of mobile technologies have transformed the dynamics of customer interaction. At the same time, hotels face pressure to optimize operations, reduce costs, and improve service quality. Technology bridges these needs by offering automation, real-time data, and customer analytics. However, the success of these innovations largely depends on how well they are implemented and how positively guests perceive them. As competition intensifies and digital transformation continues, understanding the correlation between technology adoption and customer satisfaction becomes not only relevant but imperative. This study investigates that correlation, aiming to provide a comprehensive understanding of how technology is shaping guest satisfaction and loyalty in the hotel industry

LIMITATIONS OF THE STUDY

Despite offering meaningful insights into the influence of technology on customer satisfaction in the hotel industry, the present study is subject to several limitations that should be carefully considered when interpreting the findings and drawing conclusions.

First, the study is based on a relatively limited sample size, consisting mainly of respondents from 3-star to 5-star hotels located in metropolitan cities. While urban hotels are generally early adopters of advanced technologies, this geographic and segmental concentration limits the generalizability of the findings to other hospitality contexts. Budget hotels, rural tourism destinations, small independent properties, and unorganized accommodation sectors may operate under different technological constraints and guest expectations, which are not adequately represented in this study (Kandampully et al., 2018).

Second, the study relies primarily on self-reported data collected through structured questionnaires and interviews. Such methods are vulnerable to response bias, recall inaccuracies, and social desirability effects, where respondents may provide answers they perceive as favorable rather than entirely accurate. Although standardized instruments were used to enhance reliability and consistency, perceptual bias cannot be completely eliminated, potentially affecting the objectivity of the results (Podsakoff et al., 2003).

Third, the research places greater emphasis on customer perceptions, satisfaction levels, and behavioral intentions, while offering limited analysis of managerial, financial, and operational performance indicators. As a result, the direct impact of technological adoption on measurable organizational outcomes—such as cost reduction, productivity improvement, revenue growth, or return on investment—remains underexplored, despite being highly relevant for strategic decision-making in hospitality organizations (Piccoli et al., 2017).

Fourth, the adoption of a cross-sectional research design represents another limitation of the study. Data were collected at a single point in time, restricting the ability to examine changes in guest attitudes and satisfaction over longer periods. Given the dynamic nature of digital innovation and evolving customer expectations, longitudinal designs would be more effective in capturing shifts in technology acceptance and sustained satisfaction patterns (Ali et al., 2020).

Fifth, the study focuses predominantly on widely adopted technologies, such as mobile applications, contactless check-in and check-out systems, AI chatbots, and smart room features. While these technologies are currently prevalent, emerging innovations—including service robots, blockchain-enabled transactions, biometric authentication systems, and metaverse-based hospitality experiences—were not examined in depth due to time and scope constraints (Ivanov & Webster, 2017).

Sixth, although basic demographic variables such as age and gender were considered, other significant moderating factors—such as digital literacy, cultural background, technology readiness, and prior technological experience—were not analyzed comprehensively. Existing research indicates that these variables significantly influence technology acceptance, satisfaction, and continued usage intentions in service environments (Venkatesh et al., 2012).

Finally, data collection was conducted during a post-pandemic transitional phase, a period characterized by heightened guest sensitivity toward hygiene, safety, and contactless services. Consequently, respondent preferences may reflect temporary behavioral adaptations rather than stable, long-term attitudes toward technology use in hospitality settings (Buhalis & Sinarta, 2019).

SCOPE FOR FUTURE RESEARCH

In light of the above limitations, several directions for future research are recommended to enhance understanding of technology-driven customer satisfaction in the hotel industry.

Future studies may expand the sample scope to include budget hotels, boutique properties, heritage hotels, eco-resorts, and rural tourism establishments, thereby improving generalizability and enabling meaningful comparisons across different hospitality segments (Sthapit & Björk, 2020).

Researchers are encouraged to employ longitudinal research designs to examine how guest perceptions and satisfaction evolve as technologies mature and service familiarity increases. Such approaches would offer deeper insights into the sustainability of technology-led service enhancements and customer loyalty (Mittal & Kamakura, 2001).

Further research could integrate financial and operational performance indicators, such as occupancy rate, average daily rate (ADR), revenue per available room (RevPAR), and return on technology investment, to establish a clearer linkage between technological innovation, customer satisfaction, and business performance (Noone & McGuire, 2013).

Additionally, future studies may focus on emerging and disruptive technologies, exploring guest trust, privacy concerns, ethical considerations, and acceptance levels associated with advanced digital systems (Berezina et al., 2020). Cross-cultural and international comparative studies would further enrich understanding of how cultural values and technological readiness shape guest experiences globally (Hofstede et al., 2010).

In conclusion, while the present study makes a meaningful contribution to hospitality research, continued investigation is essential to develop resilient, customer-centric, and technology-enabled hospitality models suited to future industry demands.

LITERATURE REVIEW

The literature review explores the evolution of information technology in hospitality and its contribution to customer satisfaction. It emphasizes that technologies such as PMS and CRS improve internal operations, while online booking systems and digital marketing strategies enhance guest experiences. The authors argue that IT capabilities are directly correlated with perceived service quality (Law, R., Leung, R., & Buhalis, D.,2014).

Previous research investigates customer satisfaction in relation to hotel mobile applications. The study found that usability, visual appeal, and personalization features in apps strongly influence customer perceptions, especially among millennial travelers who value self-service options and digital convenience (Bilgihan, A.,2016)

My paper discusses the benefits and risks of Self-Service Technologies (SSTs). While SSTs reduce waiting times and increase operational efficiency, the study notes that poor design or technical failures can frustrate customers, thereby reducing satisfaction. Training and intuitive interfaces are critical success factors (Collier, J. E., & Sherrell, D. L.,2010).

The authors propose a framework for technology-enabled customer experiences in hotels. Their study finds that co-creation through digital platforms enhances guest satisfaction, particularly when the technology aligns with the customer's journey and needs (Neuhofer, B., Buhalis, D., & Ladkin, A.,2015).

The literature review work analyzes early adoption of hotel technologies such as kiosks and integrated communication systems. Although outdated, it remains relevant in showing how initial tech interventions paved the way for guest autonomy and faster service delivery (Kasavana, M. L., & Cahill, J. J.,2003).

Research paper investigates guests' intention to use mobile key technologies. It reveals that privacy concerns and technical reliability are key drivers of customer satisfaction and trust. Guests are more satisfied when technologies function smoothly and ensure data protection (Morosan, C., & DeFranco, A.,2016).

The authors examine how information systems and digital engagement affect loyalty and satisfaction. Their research shows that real-time digital communication—such as in-app messaging with hotel staff—creates emotional engagement, enhancing satisfaction (Piccoli, G., Lui, T. W., & Grün, B.,2017).

Previous studies have shown how CRM technologies influence customer loyalty and satisfaction in hotel settings. Their study concludes that when used effectively, CRM systems allow personalized services that meet individual preferences, resulting in higher guest satisfaction (Kim, W. G., & Lee, H. Y.,2013).

This has also been explored in prior studies the role of RFID and smart technologies in hotel rooms. The authors find that such innovations improve security, comfort, and personalization. However, satisfaction depends on how well guests are educated about these features (Kucukusta, D., Heung, V. C. S., & Hui, S.,2014).

The research focuses on digital touch points during the hotel booking and post-stay phases. The study finds that technological engagement throughout the customer journey positively affects satisfaction, especially when information is clear, accessible, and responsive (Tussyadiah, I. P., & Inversini, A. (2015).

The authors present a model linking technology, service quality, and customer satisfaction in hotels. Their results suggest that the presence of reliable Wi-Fi, smart TVs, and mobile concierge services boosts customer perceptions of modernity and responsiveness (Kandampully, J., Zhang, T., & Bilgihan, A. (2015).

This study introduces the concept of "Smart Hospitality," emphasizing the integration of IoT, big data, and AI. The authors found that technology alone does not drive satisfaction; it must be meaningfully integrated with human service elements (Buhalis, D., & Sinarta, Y.,2019).

Author studied the guest reactions to robotic technology in hotel services. While some customers found robots to be novel and efficient, others missed the emotional connection of human interaction. Satisfaction is therefore segmented based on traveler preferences (Berezina, K., Ciftci, O., & Cobanoglu, C.,2020).

This research explores the influence of in-room technologies (e.g., entertainment systems, smart lighting) on guest satisfaction. The study finds that high-tech rooms significantly enhance the perception of luxury and innovation, especially in 4-star and 5-star hotels (Ham, S., Kim, W. G., & Jeong, S.,2005).

The authors analyze the future of robotics and automation in hospitality. They suggest that although automation can increase efficiency, guest satisfaction may be compromised if the human touch is removed entirely. A balance is key (Ivanov, S., & Webster, C.,2017).

This paper focuses on how revenue management systems and dynamic pricing models impact guest satisfaction. It finds that transparent and fair use of pricing technology can enhance trust and loyalty, while inconsistent pricing may frustrate customers (Noone, B. M., & McGuire, Ks. A.,2013).

This research paper evaluates customer feedback on OTA platforms (e.g., Booking.com, Expedia) and finds that ease of booking, real-time availability, and digital communication with hotels through these platforms improve satisfaction and trust (Leung, R., & Law, R.,2013).

The research examines digital customer experiences in hotels through mobile and social media engagement. Results show that digital word-of-mouth and instant digital feedback channels (e.g., in-app surveys) enhance satisfaction and brand image (Ukpabi, D. C., & Karjaluoto, H.,2018).

The literature review shows that how service robots impact perceived service quality. The results show mixed reactions: business travelers were more satisfied due to speed and efficiency, while leisure travelers preferred human service for personalization (Ivanov, S., & Webster, C.,2018).

This The literature review shows that proposes a comprehensive model integrating technology, perceived value, and satisfaction. The authors found that perceived technological innovativeness directly impacts guest satisfaction, mediated by ease of use and service value (Ali, F., Rasoolimanesh, S. M., & Cobanoglu, C.,2020).

RESEARCH METHODOLOGY

The research methodology outlines the processes and tools used to collect, analyze, and interpret data regarding the impact of technology on customer satisfaction in the hotel industry. This study uses both primary and secondary data to provide a robust and holistic understanding of the subject.

1. Research Design

This study adopts a descriptive and analytical research design. It is descriptive because it aims to describe current trends and perceptions related to technology usage in hotels, and analytical because it investigates the relationship between technology and customer satisfaction using empirical data.

2. Sources of Data

A. Primary Data

Primary data is collected directly from hotel guests and staff through the following methods:

- **Questionnaires:** A structured questionnaire with both closed-ended (Likert scale) and open-ended questions is administered to hotel guests.
- **Interviews:** Semi-structured interviews are conducted with hotel managers and IT personnel to understand the back-end implementation of technologies.
- **Sample Size:** A sample of 150–200 guests from 3-star to 5-star hotels in a metropolitan city (e.g., Delhi, Mumbai, Bengaluru) is selected.
- **Sampling Technique: Purposive sampling** is used to target guests who have recently experienced technologically enhanced services (e.g., mobile check-in, AI-based concierge, room automation).

B. Secondary Data

Secondary data is sourced from:

- **Academic Journals** (e.g., International Journal of Hospitality Management, Tourism Management)
- **Industry Reports** (e.g., PwC, Deloitte, McKinsey hospitality insights)
- **Hotel Association Publications**

- **Online Databases:** Google Scholar, Science Direct, JSTOR, and hotel websites for technological trends and customer reviews.

3. Tools for Data Collection

- **Survey Questionnaire:** Designed using Google Forms or physical copies, including demographics, experience with hotel technology, satisfaction levels, and suggestions.
- **Interview Schedule:** A list of guiding questions to explore hotel management's view

4. Data Analysis Techniques

A. Quantitative Analysis (for Survey Data)

- **Descriptive Statistics:** Mean, median, mode, standard deviation to summarize satisfaction levels.

B. Qualitative Analysis (for Interviews & Open Responses)

- **Thematic Analysis:** To identify key patterns, attitudes, and themes in management responses.
- **Content Analysis:** Categorizing responses into areas like usability, responsiveness, personalization, and reliability.

5. Validity and Reliability

- **Pilot Testing:** Conducted with 10 respondents to refine the questionnaire for clarity and relevance.
- **Reliability Check:** Cronbach's Alpha is used to assess the internal consistency of survey items.
- **Triangulation:** Using both qualitative and quantitative methods helps validate the findings and improves credibility.

6. Ethical Considerations

- **Informed Consent:** Participants are informed about the purpose of the research and their right to withdraw.
- **Confidentiality:** Responses are anonymized and used solely for academic purposes.

- **Data Protection:** Data is stored securely and only accessible to the research team.

THEORETICAL PERSPECTIVE

The hospitality industry has undergone a significant transformation over the past few decades, primarily driven by technological advancements. These innovations have redefined service delivery, operational efficiency, and customer engagement, making technology an integral component of the modern hotel experience.

Technological Innovations in the Hotel Industry

Online Booking Systems

The advent of online booking platforms has revolutionized the reservation process. Guests can now compare prices, read reviews, and book rooms in real-time, enhancing transparency and convenience. Dynamic pricing algorithms adjust room rates based on demand, optimizing revenue for hotels.

Mobile Applications

Mobile apps have become essential tools for enhancing guest experiences. They allow for seamless check-ins/check-outs, room service orders, and real-time communication with hotel staff. Loyalty programs integrated into these apps encourage repeat bookings and foster brand loyalty.

Self-Service Kiosks

Self-service kiosks expedite the check-in/check-out process, reducing wait times and freeing up staff to focus on personalized guest services. These kiosks often support multiple languages, catering to a diverse clientele.

Smart Room Technologies

Smart rooms equipped with IoT devices allow guests to control lighting, temperature, and entertainment systems via voice commands or mobile apps. Such personalization enhances comfort and satisfaction. A study highlighted that smart room technology significantly enhances guest satisfaction and operational efficiency in the hospitality industry .carijournals.org

Artificial Intelligence and Chatbots

AI-powered chatbots provide instant responses to guest inquiries, handle bookings, and offer personalized recommendations. They operate 24/7, ensuring consistent service delivery. Research indicates that AI-powered response generators are transforming guest communication by delivering instant, personalized responses to inquiries, playing a crucial role in enhancing guest satisfaction .mara-solutions.com

Customer Relationship Management (CRM) Systems

CRM systems collect and analyze guest data to tailor services and marketing efforts. By understanding guest preferences, hotels can offer personalized experiences, increasing satisfaction and loyalty.

High-Speed Wi-Fi and Connectivity

Reliable internet connectivity is now a basic expectation. High-speed Wi-Fi supports guests' personal and professional needs, contributing to overall satisfaction.

Virtual and Augmented Reality

VR and AR technologies offer virtual tours of hotel facilities, aiding in decision-making for potential guests. They also enhance on-site experiences by providing interactive information about amenities and local attractions.

Impact of Technology on Customer Satisfaction

Enhanced Convenience

Technological tools streamline various processes, from booking to check-out, reducing friction and saving time for guests.

Personalization of Services

Data analytics enable hotels to customize services based on individual guest preferences, leading to more memorable stays.

Improved Responsiveness

AI and chatbots ensure prompt responses to guest inquiries, enhancing the perception of attentiveness and care.

Empowerment through Control

Smart technologies give guests control over their environment, allowing them to tailor their stay to their comfort.

Perceived Value and Modernity

The integration of advanced technologies enhances the hotel's image as modern and forward-thinking, positively influencing guest perceptions.

Challenges in Implementing Technology

High Initial Investment

The cost of acquiring and maintaining advanced technologies can be substantial, posing a barrier for smaller establishments.

Integration with Legacy Systems

New technologies may not seamlessly integrate with existing systems, leading to operational disruptions.

Staff Adaptation

Employees may resist adopting new technologies due to unfamiliarity or fear of redundancy, necessitating comprehensive training programs.

Cybersecurity Concerns

The increased reliance on digital systems heightens the risk of data breaches, requiring robust security measures.

Guest Adaptability

Not all guests are comfortable with advanced technologies, especially older demographics, necessitating alternative service options.

Strategies for Effective Technology Integration

User-Centric Design

Technologies should be intuitive and user-friendly to ensure widespread adoption among guests and staff.

Comprehensive Staff Training

Regular training sessions can equip staff with the necessary skills to utilize new technologies effectively and assist guests.

Hybrid Service Models

Combining technological solutions with human interaction caters to diverse guest preferences, ensuring inclusivity.

Robust Cybersecurity Protocols

Implementing advanced security measures protects guest data and builds trust.

Continuous Feedback Mechanisms

Regularly collecting and analyzing guest feedback helps in refining technological offerings and addressing issues promptly.

Future Trends and Research Directions

Integration of Artificial Intelligence

AI will play a more significant role in predictive analytics, helping hotels anticipate guest needs and preferences.

Sustainable Technologies

Eco-friendly technologies will gain prominence, aligning with the growing emphasis on sustainability in hospitality.

Block chain for Secure Transactions

Block chain technology could revolutionize payment systems, offering secure and transparent transactions.

Enhanced Virtual Experiences

Advancements in VR and AR will provide more immersive experiences, both in marketing and on-site engagement.

Personalized Marketing Strategies

Leveraging data analytics for targeted marketing campaigns will become increasingly prevalent, enhancing guest acquisition and retention.

The integration of technology in the hotel industry has significantly enhanced customer satisfaction by offering convenience, personalization, and control. While challenges exist in implementation, strategic approaches focusing on user-centric design, staff training, and robust security can mitigate these issues. As technology continues to evolve, staying abreast of emerging trends and aligning them with guest expectations will be crucial for sustained success in the hospitality sector. Technology has fundamentally transformed the hotel industry over recent decades. It has revolutionized how hotels operate, interact with guests, and deliver services. From booking systems to smart rooms and artificial intelligence, technology is now embedded in nearly every aspect of hotel management and guest experience. This essay explores technology in hotels in detail—defining key concepts, describing various technological applications, analyzing their impacts on service quality and operational efficiency, discussing challenges hotels face, and identifying future trends shaping the industry.

OVERVIEW OF TECHNOLOGY IN HOTELS

Definition of Technology in Hospitality

Technology in hotels refers to the use of electronic, digital, and automated tools and systems designed to enhance operational efficiency, improve guest services, facilitate communication, and support business management. It includes hardware (computers, kiosks, IoT devices), software (property management systems, mobile apps), and digital infrastructure (networks, databases).

Historical Evolution

The hotel industry initially relied on manual processes and face-to-face service. Over time, technology began with computerized reservation systems in the 1970s, evolving through property management systems in the 1990s, internet booking in the 2000s, and now to AI, IoT, and smart automation in the 2020s.

TYPES OF TECHNOLOGY IN HOTELS

Reservation and Booking Systems

Online booking platforms enable guests to browse availability, prices, and services 24/7. Integrated systems allow real-time updates of room inventory and rates. Channel managers synchronize bookings across multiple platforms like Expedia, Booking.com, and hotel websites, preventing overbooking.

Property Management Systems (PMS)

PMS software automates front desk operations, housekeeping management, billing, and reporting. It acts as the operational backbone, integrating data from reservations, payments, room status, and guest profiles.

Mobile Applications and Digital Check-in

Mobile apps allow guests to book rooms, check-in remotely, access digital room keys, order services, and communicate with staff. This reduces queue times and increases convenience.

Self-Service Kiosks

Kiosks enable guests to check-in/check-out without staff assistance. They reduce wait times, improve accuracy, and support contactless service, increasingly vital in a post-pandemic world.

Smart Room Technologies and IoT

Rooms equipped with IoT sensors and devices let guests control lighting, HVAC, entertainment, and curtains via mobile apps or voice commands. These technologies optimize energy consumption and enhance personalized comfort.

Artificial Intelligence (AI) and Chatbots

AI-driven chatbots provide 24/7 guest support, answer FAQs, make bookings, and offer personalized recommendations. AI also supports dynamic pricing, demand forecasting, and personalized marketing.

Customer Relationship Management (CRM) Systems

CRMs compile guest data from bookings, preferences, and feedback to tailor services, offer loyalty rewards, and run targeted marketing campaigns.

High-Speed Internet and Connectivity

Fast and reliable Wi-Fi is a fundamental guest expectation. Hotels invest in strong network infrastructure to support business travelers, streaming services, and IoT devices.

Virtual Reality (VR) and Augmented Reality (AR)

VR offers immersive virtual tours of hotel properties to entice bookings. AR can enrich on-site experiences by overlaying digital information about the hotel or nearby attractions.

Payment Technologies

Contactless payments, mobile wallets, and block chain-based systems provide fast, secure transactions and reduce cash handling risks.

APPLICATIONS AND BENEFITS OF TECHNOLOGY IN HOTELS

Enhanced Guest Experience

- **Convenience:** Technology enables 24/7 access to booking, check-in/out, and service requests.
- **Personalization:** Data analytics allow tailoring services like room preferences, dining, and local recommendations.
- **Faster Service:** Automation reduces wait times and streamlines interactions.
- **Increased Engagement:** Apps and chatbots maintain continuous guest communication.

Operational Efficiency

- **Resource Management:** PMS and IoT optimize housekeeping schedules, energy use, and inventory.
- **Revenue Management:** AI models forecast demand and adjust pricing dynamically.
- **Data-Driven Decisions:** Analytics inform marketing and service improvements.

Staff Productivity

Technology automates repetitive tasks, freeing staff to focus on personalized guest interactions and complex problem-solving.

Safety and Hygiene

Contactless technologies and digital communication minimize physical contact, important in health-conscious environments.

DETAILED CASE STUDIES

Marriott International: Mobile Check-in and Mobile Key

Marriott's mobile app lets guest's check-in remotely and unlock their rooms via smartphones. This technology improves guest autonomy and reduces front desk congestion.

Hilton's Connected Room

Hilton's smart rooms allow guests to control room features through an app or voice assistant, offering a personalized and futuristic experience.

The Wynn Las Vegas: AI-Powered Chatbots

Wynn uses AI chatbots to handle inquiries instantly, improving customer satisfaction and operational efficiency.

CHALLENGES AND LIMITATIONS

High Initial Investment and Maintenance Costs

Implementing cutting-edge technology requires substantial capital expenditure, ongoing maintenance, and periodic upgrades.

Integration Complexity

New technologies must integrate seamlessly with legacy systems to avoid disruptions.

Data Privacy and Security

Guest data must be protected against cyber threats; compliance with GDPR and other regulations is essential.

Staff Training and Adaptation

Effective adoption depends on staff's digital literacy and willingness to embrace change.

Digital Divide Among Guests

Not all guests are tech-savvy or comfortable with automated services, requiring alternative options.

FUTURE TRENDS IN HOTEL TECHNOLOGY

Increased AI and Machine Learning

AI will further personalize guest experiences, automate operations, and provide predictive insights.

Robotics in Service Delivery

Robots for room service, cleaning, and concierge roles will become more common.

Sustainability Through Technology

Smart energy management and green building tech will align with sustainability goals.

Block chain for Secure, Transparent Transactions

Block chain could revolutionize payments, identity verification, and loyalty programs.

Enhanced Virtual and Augmented Reality Experiences

More immersive marketing and on-property guest experiences will emerge. Technology is a cornerstone of modern hotel operations and guest satisfaction. Its evolving role encompasses convenience, personalization, efficiency, and safety. While adoption poses challenges in investment, integration, and training, strategic implementation unlocks significant competitive advantages. Future developments promise even deeper integration of AI, IoT, robotics, and immersive experiences, shaping the hospitality industry of tomorrow.

Customer Satisfaction in Hotels

Customer satisfaction is critical in the hospitality industry. In hotels, guest satisfaction not only affects the immediate experience but also drives loyalty, influences reputation, and directly impacts profitability. When guests' expectations are met or exceeded, they tend to become repeat customers and advocates. This essay elaborates on the concept, factors, measurement, impact, challenges, and future trends of customer satisfaction in the hotel sector.

UNDERSTANDING CUSTOMER SATISFACTION IN HOTELS

Definition and Concept

Customer satisfaction in hotels refers to a guest's holistic evaluation of their experience during a stay. This evaluation depends on the comparison between their expectations before arrival and their actual experiences. Satisfaction encompasses tangible elements like room comfort, decor, cleanliness, and facilities, as well as intangible elements such as the warmth and professionalism of staff, and the emotional satisfaction derived from feeling valued and cared for. For example, a guest may expect a clean, quiet room and friendly service; if these expectations are met or exceeded, satisfaction is high. If unmet, dissatisfaction arises. Understanding this perception gap is key for hoteliers aiming to improve service delivery.

Importance in Hospitality

Customer satisfaction drives business success in hospitality. Satisfied guests tend to return, helping build a loyal customer base. They also promote the hotel through word-of-mouth, social media posts, and positive reviews, which attract new customers at a relatively low acquisition cost. In contrast, dissatisfied guests can harm reputation and deter others. Thus, satisfaction is not just a customer metric but a strategic business asset, essential for revenue growth, brand building, and competitive positioning in a crowded market.

KEY FACTORS INFLUENCING CUSTOMER SATISFACTION

Service Quality

Service quality is often the most significant determinant of guest satisfaction. The SERVQUAL model breaks this down into five dimensions:

- **Tangibles:** Physical facilities, equipment, and appearance of personnel. For example, a modern, clean lobby or well-maintained gym.
- **Reliability:** The ability to perform promised service dependably and accurately, such as timely room service or consistent Wi-Fi connectivity.
- **Responsiveness:** Willingness to help guests promptly, like quick check-in/check-out and immediate issue resolution.
- **Assurance:** Knowledge and courtesy of staff, instilling confidence and trust.

- **Empathy:** Caring, individualized attention to guests, such as remembering preferences or accommodating special requests.

Hotels must excel in all five areas to meet diverse guest expectations and deliver exceptional experiences.

Room Quality and Cleanliness

The guest room is the core product of any hotel. Room quality includes comfort factors such as mattress and bedding quality, lighting, noise control, temperature regulation, and available amenities like a minibar or coffee maker. Cleanliness is non-negotiable; a spotless room ensures guest health and comfort. Issues such as stains, odors, or faulty equipment severely damage satisfaction levels and can prompt negative reviews or requests for compensation.

Staff Behavior and Professionalism

Frontline employees often shape the overall perception of the hotel. Courteous, empathetic, and knowledgeable staff create a welcoming atmosphere that fosters positive emotional connections. Professionalism includes politeness, promptness, cultural sensitivity, and problem-solving skills. Staff who can anticipate guest needs and personalize service enhance satisfaction by making guests feel valued rather than just another customer.

Food and Beverage Quality

Food and beverage (F&B) offerings form an essential part of the hotel experience. Guests expect high-quality food, diverse menu options catering to dietary preferences, and attentive service. Whether it's a hotel restaurant, room service, or bar, taste, presentation, hygiene, and ambiance significantly affect guest satisfaction. Special culinary experiences or local flavors can also add value.

Price and Value for Money

Price perception is relative to the quality and service received. Guests evaluate whether the overall experience justifies the cost. Competitive pricing combined with superior service and amenities fosters a perception of good value, which boosts satisfaction. Overpricing or hidden charges without matching service quality creates dissatisfaction.

Hotel Location and Accessibility

Location plays a strategic role. Proximity to business districts, tourist attractions, airports, or transport hubs is convenient and enhances the guest experience. Easy accessibility by public or private transport also reduces travel stress. Conversely, remote or difficult-to-reach locations may reduce satisfaction unless compensated by exceptional offerings.

Technology and Convenience

Modern travelers expect hotels to integrate technology to enhance convenience. Fast, reliable Wi-Fi, mobile check-in/out, digital room keys, smart room controls (lighting, temperature), and online concierge services are increasingly important. Such innovations reduce friction and elevate guest comfort, improving satisfaction.

Ambiance and Atmosphere

The hotel's atmosphere—including interior design, lighting, music, cleanliness of common areas, and the overall vibe—affects guests emotionally. An aesthetically pleasing and calming environment enhances relaxation and enjoyment. Cultural or thematic decor can also create memorable experiences.

Safety and Security

Guests prioritize feeling safe in the hotel environment. Visible security measures like surveillance cameras, secure locks, safes in rooms, well-lit premises, and trained security staff build trust. Safety also extends to hygiene and health protocols, particularly relevant post-pandemic.

MEASURING CUSTOMER SATISFACTION IN HOTELS

Surveys and Questionnaires

Surveys remain a direct and structured method to gauge satisfaction. Hotels use questionnaires with Likert scales (e.g., 1-5 ratings) covering various aspects like cleanliness, staff behavior, and facilities. These allow quantitative analysis and tracking of trends over time. Well-designed surveys also include open-ended questions to capture qualitative insights.

Online Reviews and Social Media

Guest-generated reviews on platforms like TripAdvisor, Google, and social media provide real-time, authentic feedback. These reviews influence potential customers and offer rich data on satisfaction drivers and pain points. Hotels monitor and respond to online feedback to demonstrate commitment and manage reputation.

Net Promoter Score (NPS)

NPS asks guests how likely they are to recommend the hotel on a scale from 0 to 10. Scores classify guests as promoters, passives, or detractors. A high NPS indicates strong satisfaction and loyalty. It is a simple yet powerful tool to benchmark performance and predict growth potential.

Mystery Guest Audits

Mystery guests anonymously evaluate hotel services based on specific criteria. This unbiased assessment helps hotels identify service gaps and opportunities for improvement from a guest's perspective.

Customer Feedback Analytics

Advanced data analytics allow hotels to aggregate feedback from multiple sources, analyze sentiment, detect patterns, and make data-driven decisions. Text analytics and AI tools help interpret unstructured data like reviews or social media comments efficiently.

THE IMPACT OF CUSTOMER SATISFACTION ON HOTEL BUSINESS

Repeat Business and Customer Loyalty

Satisfied guests tend to return, providing stable revenue streams and reducing marketing and sales costs associated with acquiring new customers. Loyalty programs incentivize repeat visits, deepening the relationship.

Word-of-Mouth and Online Reputation

Happy guests share their positive experiences through personal recommendations and online reviews. This word-of-mouth marketing is highly credible and cost-effective, helping attract new guests and build brand equity.

Financial Performance

Research shows a direct correlation between high customer satisfaction and improved financial metrics like occupancy rates, average daily rates (ADR), and revenue per available room (RevPAR). Satisfied guests may pay premium prices and spend more on ancillary services.

Competitive Advantage

In a highly competitive industry, hotels with superior customer satisfaction distinguish themselves. This differentiation helps in attracting discerning travelers, commanding better rates, and sustaining profitability even during downturns.

STRATEGIES TO ENHANCE CUSTOMER SATISFACTION

Staff Training and Development

Ongoing staff training ensures employees are skilled in communication, cultural sensitivity, problem-solving, and brand standards. Empowering staff to take ownership of guest satisfaction creates a service-oriented culture.

Personalization of Services

Using guest data and CRM systems, hotels can tailor experiences by remembering preferences, celebrating special occasions, or offering relevant recommendations. Personal touches foster emotional connections.

Technology Integration

Investing in user-friendly technology like mobile apps for bookings and room controls, self-check-in kiosks, and AI chatbots improves convenience and responsiveness, elevating guest satisfaction.

Quality Control and Maintenance

Regular audits, prompt repairs, and preventive maintenance keep facilities in prime condition. Clean, well-maintained rooms and public areas are fundamental.

Effective Complaint Management

Addressing guest complaints quickly and empathetically can turn a negative experience into a positive one, increasing guest trust and satisfaction.

Enhancing Food and Beverage Offerings

Innovating menus, sourcing local and fresh ingredients, and training staff on service protocols improve dining experiences that are memorable and satisfying.

Creating Memorable Experiences

Offering unique local tours, cultural events, wellness programs, or themed experiences enriches guest stays and strengthens emotional ties.

CHALLENGES IN MAINTAINING CUSTOMER SATISFACTION

Diverse Customer Expectations

Hotels serve a global clientele with different cultures, languages, and preferences. Customizing service while maintaining efficiency is challenging.

Balancing Cost and Quality

Maintaining high service standards requires investment in staff, training, and facilities. Budget constraints may limit these efforts, risking satisfaction.

Handling Negative Feedback

Online reviews can be harsh and viral. Managing them with transparency, promptness, and sincerity is essential but challenging.

Technological Barriers

Implementing new technology needs capital and employee training. Older guests or less tech-savvy customers may resist or struggle with digital services.

External Factors

Economic downturns, pandemics like COVID-19, and climate-related issues impact operations and guest perceptions of safety and value.

CASE STUDIES OF CUSTOMER SATISFACTION IN HOTELS

Ritz-Carlton's Legendary Service

Ritz-Carlton is renowned for its personalized service culture, where employees are empowered to spend up to $2,000 to solve guest problems. This proactive approach creates exceptional experiences and high satisfaction.

Airbnb's Focus on User Experience

Though not a traditional hotel, Airbnb revolutionized hospitality by emphasizing user-friendly platforms, host-guest interactions, and authentic local experiences, influencing hotel strategies.

Marriott's Mobile Integration

Marriott's mobile app offers seamless check-in/out, room selection, and messaging with staff, enhancing convenience and guest engagement.

FUTURE TRENDS IN CUSTOMER SATISFACTION IN HOTELS

AI and Machine Learning for Personalization

AI will analyze guest preferences and behavior to offer hyper-personalized services proactively, improving satisfaction and loyalty.

Sustainability and Eco-Friendly Practices

Guests increasingly demand environmentally responsible hotels. Sustainable practices like energy-efficient operations, waste reduction, and local sourcing improve satisfaction among eco-conscious travelers.

Contactless Services

Health concerns post-pandemic drive demand for contactless check-in, mobile payments, voice-activated controls, reducing physical contact without compromising service quality.

Virtual Reality Experiences

VR tours allow guests to preview rooms and amenities before booking, while AR apps enhance onsite experiences, providing information or entertainment.

Emotional Analytics

Using AI to detect guests' emotional states through voice or facial recognition, hotels could adjust interactions dynamically to enhance satisfaction. Customer satisfaction in hotels is a multidimensional construct essential for business success. It depends on high service quality, clean and comfortable facilities, professional staff, technological convenience, and emotional engagement. Measurement tools and feedback help hotels improve continuously. Despite challenges such as diverse expectations and cost pressures, strategic investments in staff, technology, and personalized experiences can drive loyalty and profitability. Future trends emphasize AI, sustainability, and contactless innovations that will further enhance guest satisfaction.

Technological Innovations in Hotels

1. **Online Booking Systems**: These platforms have transformed the way guests interact with hotels. Modern online booking systems offer features such as real-time availability, dynamic pricing based on demand and seasonality, and customizable package options that enhance the overall booking experience. Instant confirmations and secure payment gateways ensure transparency and build trust. These systems also integrate with hotel management systems (PMS) for streamlined operations.
2. **Mobile Applications**: Hotel apps serve as a centralized interface for guests, providing them with the ability to manage their reservations, request services,

and access loyalty programs. These apps often feature real-time chat with hotel staff, mobile room keys, and GPS-enabled services for navigating within the hotel premises. Notifications on special offers, check-in reminders, and feedback forms increase engagement and satisfaction.

3. **Self-Service Kiosks**: Located prominently in hotel lobbies, self-service kiosks allow guests to check-in or out without waiting in lines. They can scan IDs, select room preferences, make payments, and print key cards. These kiosks not only reduce the burden on front-desk staff but also provide a fast and efficient experience, especially for business travelers or tech-savvy guests.
4. **Smart Room Technologies**: With the advent of IoT (Internet of Things), smart rooms are becoming standard in upscale hotels. Guests can control room features such as lighting, air conditioning, curtains, and televisions using voice commands or mobile apps. Smart mirrors, automated minibar replenishments, and AI-based room assistants further enhance personalization.
5. **AI and Chatbots**: Artificial Intelligence and chatbots ensure round-the-clock guest interaction. These systems can handle inquiries, booking modifications, and recommendations. By using natural language processing (NLP), chatbots offer human-like interactions, making guests feel heard and attended to even in the absence of human staff.
6. **CRM and Data Analytics**: Customer Relationship Management (CRM) systems coupled with data analytics help hotels understand guest preferences, predict behavior, and personalize services. Data collected from previous stays, feedback forms, and interactions is analyzed to offer tailor-made experiences. For example, a guest who prefers vegetarian food or a specific room view can be automatically accommodated in future visits.
7. **Wi-Fi and Connectivity**: Reliable, high-speed internet is a critical expectation for modern travelers. Whether for work, communication, or entertainment, uninterrupted Wi-Fi access is a determinant of satisfaction. Some hotels now offer tiered internet services, allowing guests to choose higher speeds for a fee.
8. **Virtual and Augmented Reality (VR & AR)**: VR enables potential guests to explore hotel rooms, banquet halls, and amenities virtually before booking. AR enhances the in-stay experience by overlaying digital information about room features, local attractions, or promotions using a mobile device. These immersive technologies improve decision-making and customer engagement.

Impact of Technology on Customer Satisfaction

1. **Convenience**: Automated systems and digital platforms streamline guest interactions, from booking to check-out. This saves time and reduces dependence on human intervention, which is especially valuable during peak hours.

2. **Personalization**: Technology allows hotels to gather and analyze individual guest data, enabling the provision of tailored services. From personalized welcome messages to room settings, the guest experience becomes unique and memorable.
3. **Responsiveness**: Chatbots and AI tools ensure that guest queries and complaints are handled promptly, even during odd hours. This level of responsiveness boosts customer trust and loyalty.
4. **Control and Empowerment**: Smart technologies give guests autonomy over them in-room experience. They can adjust the ambiance, order food, and schedule housekeeping, all from their devices, which enhances comfort and satisfaction.
5. **Perceived Value**: Modern technology increases the perceived value of the hotel stay. Guests associate advanced tech with luxury, innovation, and forward-thinking service, all of which contribute to higher satisfaction scores.

Challenges in Implementing Technology

1. **High Initial Costs**: Deploying advanced technologies involves significant investment in infrastructure, software, and skilled personnel. Budget constraints may limit smaller hotels from adopting these innovations.
2. **Integration Issues**: Many hotels operate on legacy systems that are not compatible with newer technologies. Integrating old and new systems without disruption to service can be complex and time-consuming.
3. **Staff Resistance**: Change management is a major barrier. Employees accustomed to traditional methods may resist technological adoption due to fear of redundancy or lack of familiarity.
4. **Cybersecurity Risks**: Digital systems expose hotels to the threat of hacking, phishing, and data breaches. Loss of guest data can severely damage a hotel's reputation and result in legal liabilities.
5. **Guest Adaptability**: Not all guests are tech-savvy. Elderly customers or those from less digital backgrounds may find it difficult to use self-service kiosks or mobile apps, affecting their experience.

   User-Centric Design: Technologies should be developed with the end-user in mind. Intuitive interfaces, clear instructions, and multilingual support can make systems more accessible.

   1. **Staff Training**: Regular training and upskilling sessions are crucial to ensure staff are confident in using and explaining new technologies. Empowered staff can help guests navigate tech-based services.

2. **Hybrid Services**: Offering a blend of digital and human service options caters to varied guest preferences. For instance, providing both a mobile check-in option and a staffed front desk.
3. **Cybersecurity Measures**: Hotels should invest in robust cybersecurity frameworks, including firewalls, encrypted payment gateways, and regular security audits to safeguard guest information.
4. **Feedback Mechanisms**: Digital surveys, in-app ratings, and post-stay reviews should be actively used to collect insights. Data from these sources can be analyzed to refine service delivery.

Technology has become integral to the hospitality industry, reshaping how hotels operate and interact with their guests. From seamless booking platforms to immersive virtual experiences, each innovation contributes significantly to enhancing customer satisfaction. The convenience, personalization, responsiveness, and control provided by technology redefine guest expectations and set new industry standards. However, technological integration is not without its challenges. Financial constraints, employee resistance, cybersecurity issues, and the digital divide among guests must be addressed through strategic planning, inclusive design, and continuous improvement. Hotels that can strike a balance between technological advancement and human touch will lead the way in delivering exceptional guest experiences. In the ever-evolving digital landscape, staying updated with emerging technologies and aligning them with customer needs is no longer optional—it is essential. Hotels that embrace this evolution while maintaining service excellence will not only attract tech-savvy travelers but also foster loyalty, positive reviews, and long-term growth.

DATA ANALYSIS AND INTERPRETATION

Q1. What is your gender?

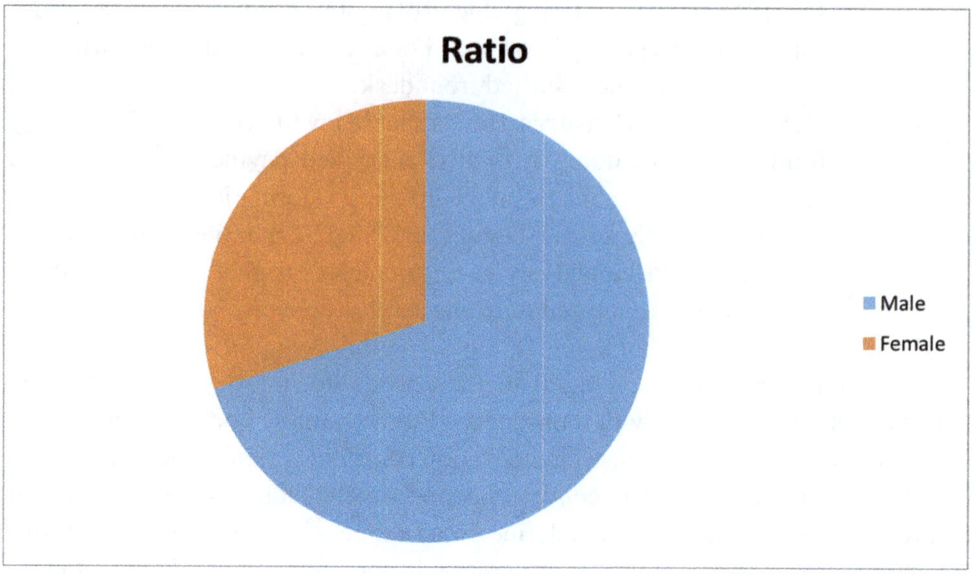

Interpretation

Table 1.

	Ratio
Male	70%
Female	30%

Male
Female

Q2. What is your age?

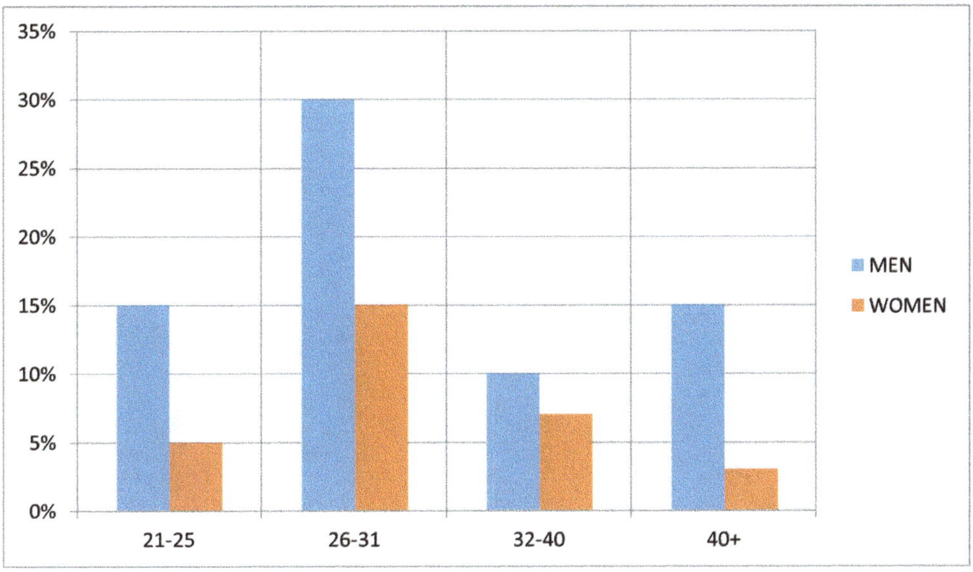

Table 2.

	MEN	WOMEN
21-25	15%	5%
26-31	30%	15%
32-40	10%	7%
40+	15%	3%

Interpretation

According to the survey out of 100% MEN are 21-25-15%, 26-31-30%, 32-40-10%, 40+-15%. WOMEN are 21-25-5%, 26-31-15%, 32-40-7%, 40+-3%.

21-25
26-31
32-40
40+

3. Our hotel uses key technological tools such as mobile apps, AI chatbots, and contactless check-ins.

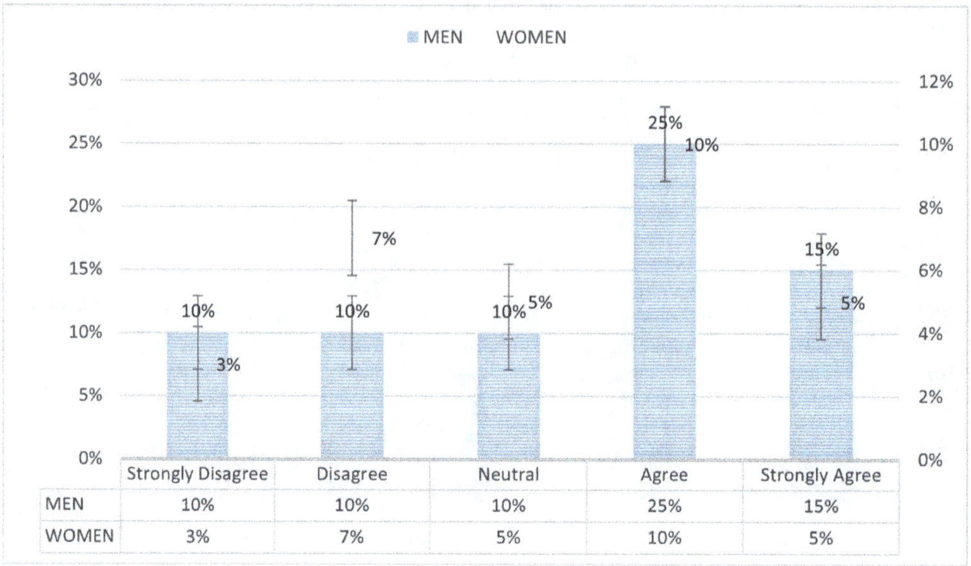

Table 3.

	MEN	WOMEN
Strongly Disagree	10%	3%
Disagree	10%	7%
Neutral	10%	5%
Agree	25%	10%
Strongly Agree	15%	5%

Interpretation

According to the survey out of 100% half of the men respondent said strongly Disagree-10%, Disagree-10%, Neutral-10%, Agree-25%, Strongly Agree-15%. WOMEN SAID Strongly Disagree-3%, Disagree-7%, Neutral-5%, Agree-10%, Strongly Agree-5%.

a) Strongly Agree
b) Agree
c) Neutral
d) Disagree

e) Strongly Disagree

Answer: b) Agree

5. Guests generally have a positive perception of technology-enabled services in our hotel.

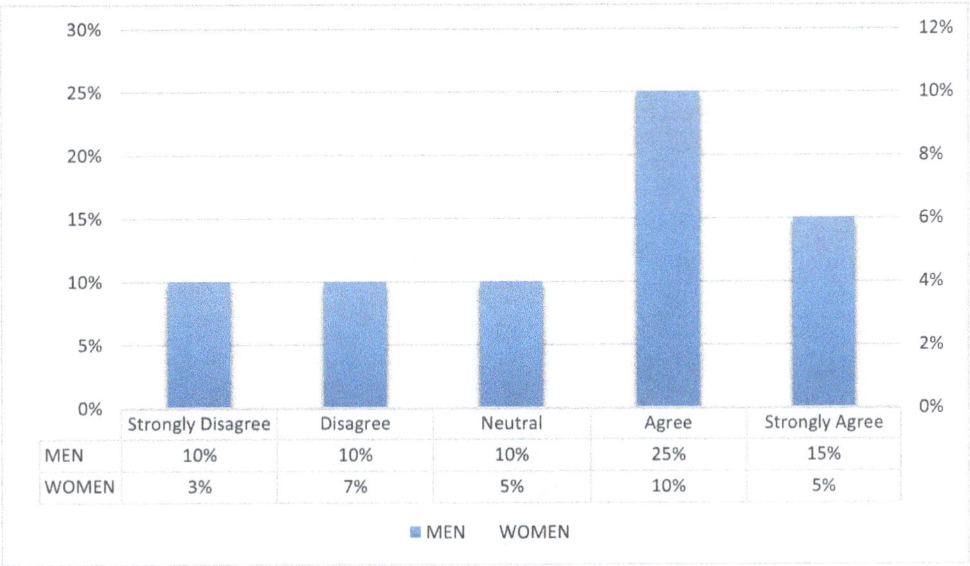

Table 4.

	MEN	WOMEN
Strongly Disagree	10%	3%
Disagree	10%	7%
Neutral	10%	5%
Agree	25%	10%
Strongly Agree	15%	5%

Interpretation

According to the survey out of 100% half of the men respondent said strongly Disagree-10%, Disagree-10%, Neutral-10%, Agree-25%, Strongly Agree-15%. WOMEN SAID Strongly Disagree-3%, Disagree-7%, Neutral-5%, Agree-10%, Strongly Agree-5%.

- a) Strongly Agree
- b) Agree
- c) Neutral
- d) Disagree
- e) Strongly Disagree

Answer: b) Agree

5. The availability of smart room features improves overall guest satisfaction.

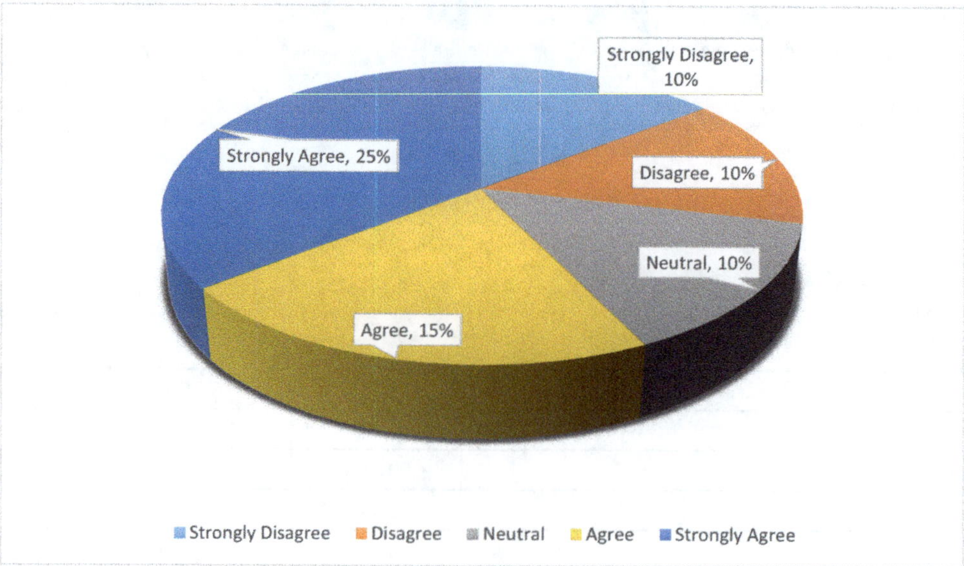

Table 5.

	MEN	WOMEN
Strongly Disagree	10%	3%
Disagree	10%	7%
Neutral	10%	5%
Agree	15%	5%
Strongly Agree	25%	10%

Interpretation

According to the survey out of 100% half of the men respondent said Strongly Disagree-10%, Disagree-10%, Neutral-10%, Agree-15%, Strongly Agree-25%. WOMEN SAID Strongly Disagree-3%, Disagree-7%, Neutral-5%, Agree-5%, Strongly Agree-10%.

- a) Strongly Agree
- b) Agree
- c) Neutral
- d) Disagree
- e) Strongly Disagree

6. Contactless check-in and check-out processes enhance the guest experience.

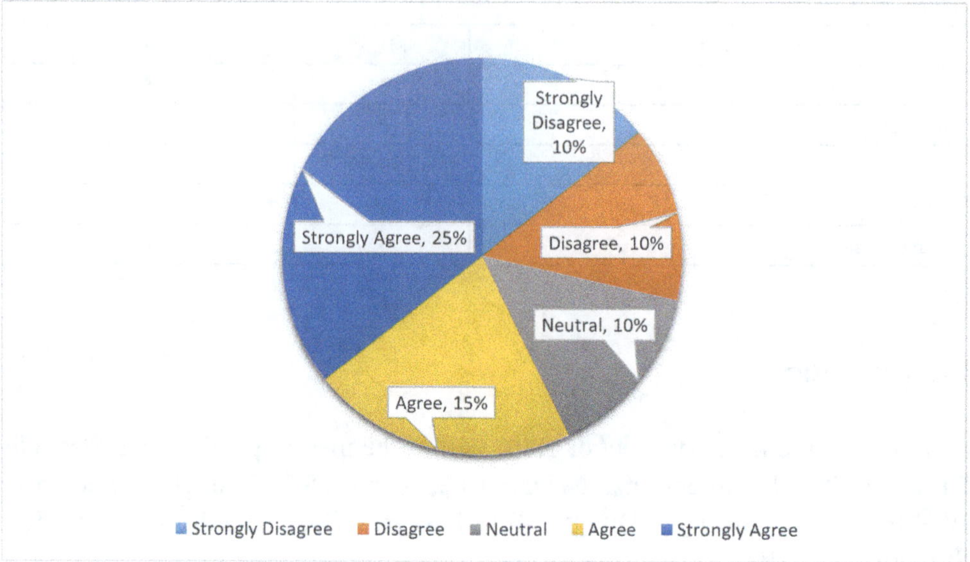

Table 6.

	MEN	WOMEN
Strongly Disagree	10%	3%
Disagree	10%	7%
Neutral	10%	5%
Agree	15%	5%
Strongly Agree	25%	10%

Interpretation

According to the survey out of 100% half of the men respondent said Strongly Disagree-10%, Disagree-10%, Neutral-10%, Agree-15%, Strongly Agree-25%. WOMEN SAID Strongly Disagree-3%, Disagree-7%, Neutral-5%, Agree-5%, Strongly Agree-10%.

- a) Strongly Agree
- b) Agree
- c) Neutral
- d) Disagree

- e) Strongly Disagree

Answer: a) Strongly Agree

7. AI chatbots effectively handle guest inquiries and requests.

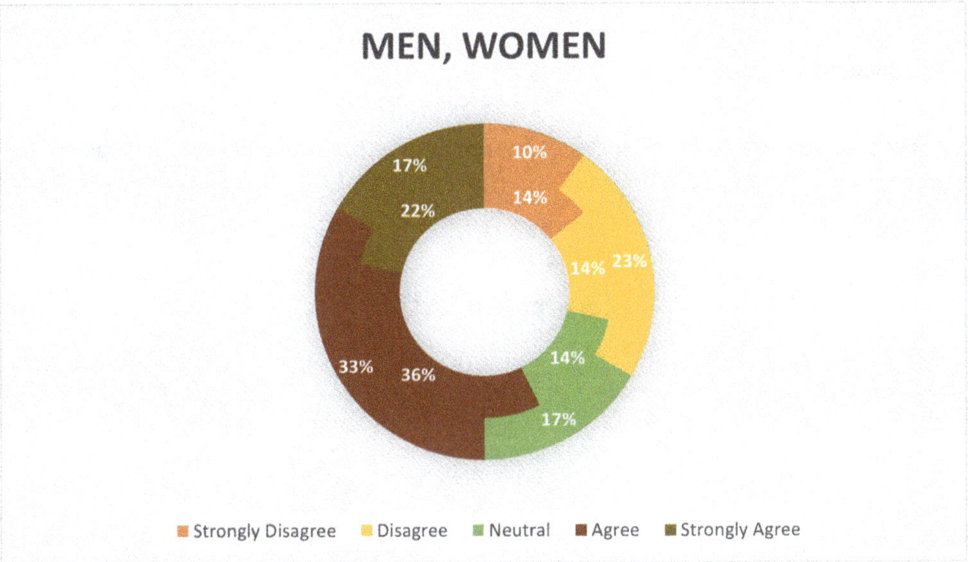

Table 7.

	MEN	WOMEN
Strongly Disagree	10%	3%
Disagree	10%	7%
Neutral	10%	5%
Agree	25%	10%
Strongly Agree	15%	5%

Interpretation

According to the survey out of 100% half of the men respondent said strongly Disagree-10%, Disagree-10%, Neutral-10%, Agree-25%, Strongly Agree-15%.

WOMEN SAID Strongly Disagree-3%, Disagree-7%, Neutral-5%, Agree-10%, Strongly Agree-5%.

- a) Strongly Agree
- b) Agree
- c) Neutral
- d) Disagree
- e) Strongly Disagree

Answer: b) Agree

8. Technology use in hotel services increases customer loyalty and repeat visits.

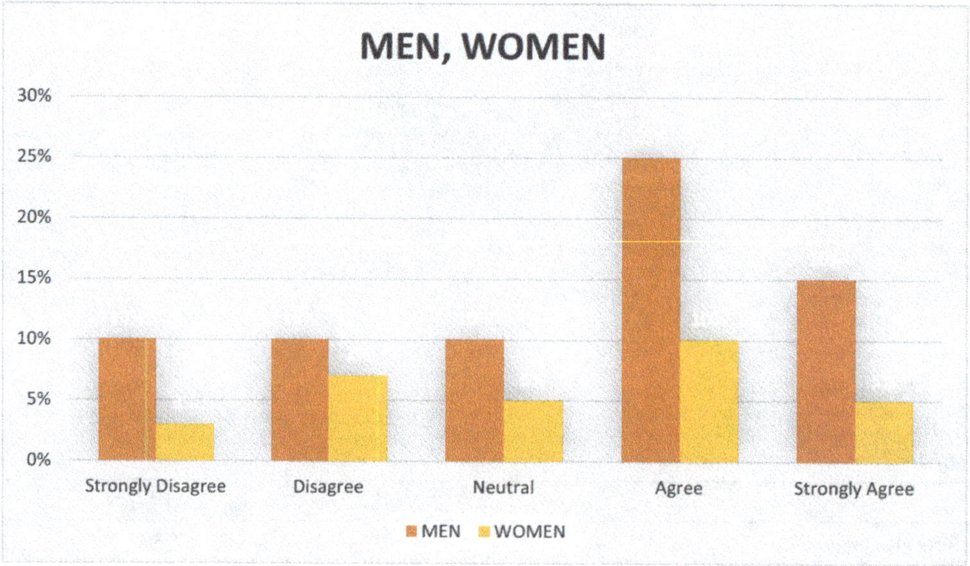

Table 8.

	MEN	WOMEN
Strongly Disagree	10%	3%
Disagree	10%	7%
Neutral	10%	5%

continued on following page

Table 8. Continued

	MEN	WOMEN
Agree	25%	10%
Strongly Agree	15%	5%

Interpretation

According to the survey out of 100% half of the men respondent said strongly Disagree-10%, Disagree-10%, Neutral-10%, Agree-25%, Strongly Agree-15%. WOMEN SAID Strongly Disagree-3%, Disagree-7%, Neutral-5%, Agree-10%, Strongly Agree-5%.

- a) Strongly Agree
- b) Agree
- c) Neutral
- d) Disagree
- e) Strongly Disagree

Answer: b) Agree

9. Guests find mobile apps convenient for booking and service requests.

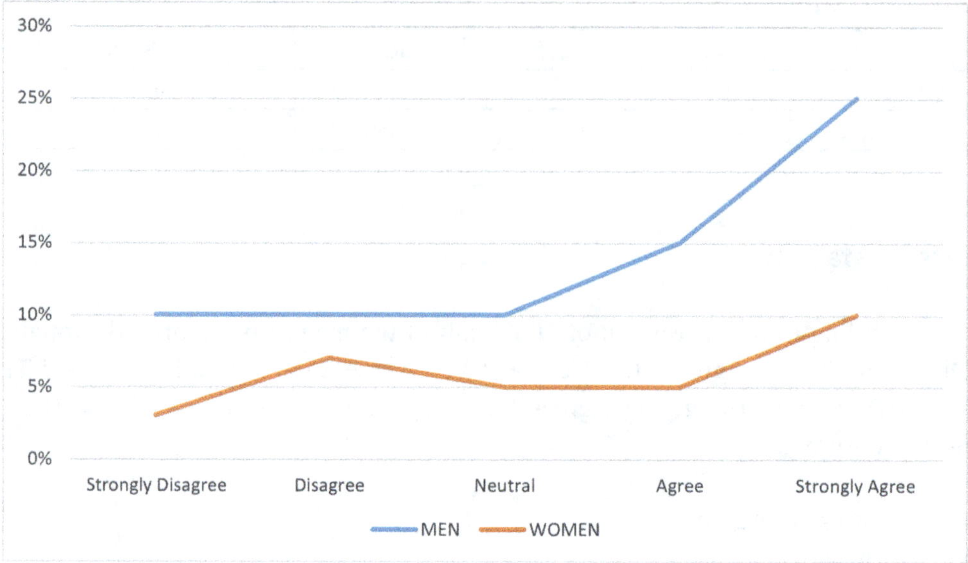

Table 9.

	MEN	WOMEN
Strongly Disagree	10%	3%
Disagree	10%	7%
Neutral	10%	5%
Agree	15%	5%
Strongly Agree	25%	10%

Interpretation

According to the survey out of 100% half of the men respondent said Strongly Disagree-10%, Disagree-10%, Neutral-10%, Agree-15%, Strongly Agree-25%. WOMEN SAID Strongly Disagree-3%, Disagree-7%, Neutral-5%, Agree-5%, Strongly Agree-10%.

- a) Strongly Agree
- b) Agree
- c) Neutral
- d) Disagree

- e) Strongly Disagree

Answer: a) Strongly Agree

10. Technical issues or glitches negatively affect customer satisfaction.

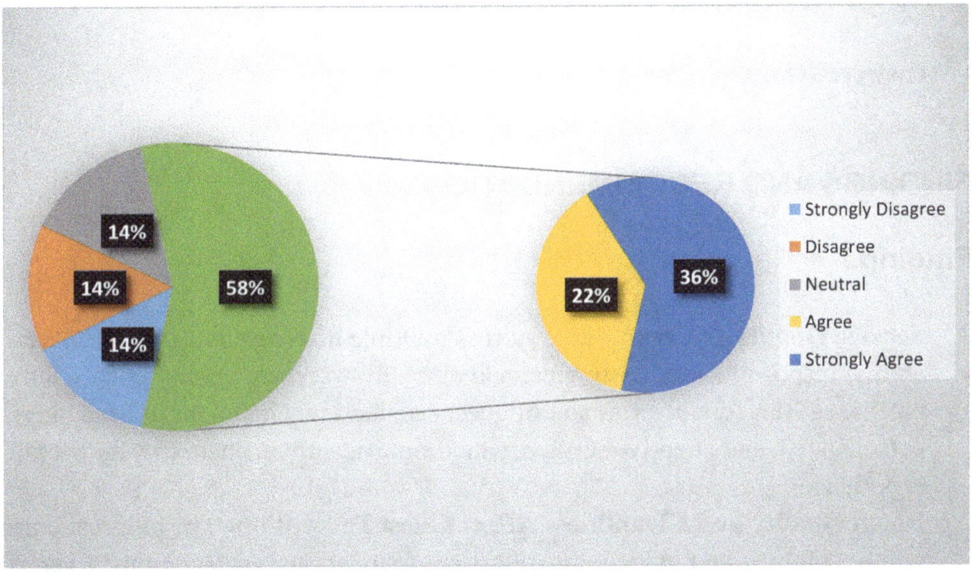

Table 10.

	MEN	WOMEN
Strongly Disagree	10%	3%
Disagree	10%	7%
Neutral	10%	5%
Agree	15%	5%
Strongly Agree	25%	10%

Interpretation

According to the survey out of 100% half of the men respondent said Strongly Disagree-10%, Disagree-10%, Neutral-10%, Agree-15%, Strongly Agree-25%.

WOMEN SAID Strongly Disagree-3%, Disagree-7%, Neutral-5%, Agree-5%, Strongly Agree-10%.

- a) Strongly Agree
- b) Agree
- c) Neutral
- d) Disagree
- e) Strongly Disagree

Answer: a) Strongly Agree

FINDINGS AND RECOMMENDATIONS

Findings

1. **Service Quality Is Paramount:** Across multiple dimensions—tangibles, reliability, responsiveness, assurance, and empathy—service quality consistently emerges as the core determinant of guest satisfaction. Guests expect seamless, personalized, and attentive service, which significantly influences their overall experience.
2. **Room Quality and Cleanliness Affect Guest Perception:** The physical condition, comfort, and hygiene of rooms are foundational expectations. Even if other services are excellent, poor room quality or cleanliness severely detracts from guest satisfaction.
3. **Staff Behavior Drives Emotional Connection:** Courteous, professional, and proactive staff foster positive emotional experiences, making guests feel valued and respected. This human element is often the differentiator in competitive markets.
4. **Food and Beverage Quality Influences Overall Experience:** High-quality dining options, varied menus, and attentive food service enrich the guest experience, contributing to higher satisfaction scores.
5. **Price and Value Perception Matter:** Guests assess satisfaction not just by absolute service quality but also by perceived value relative to the price paid. Hotels offering premium services at competitive prices tend to score better in satisfaction.
6. **Technology Enhances Convenience and Satisfaction:** Increasing integration of mobile check-ins, Wi-Fi, smart rooms, and digital amenities improves guest convenience and modernizes the stay experience.

7. **Safety and Security Are Non-Negotiable:** Guests prioritize safety and expect robust security measures, especially in urban or high-traffic locations.
8. **Effective Complaint Management Is Essential:** Prompt and empathetic resolution of issues significantly affects guest loyalty and reputation management.
9. **Customer Expectations Are Diverse and Evolving:** Globalization and technological advances mean hotels must continuously adapt to varied cultural preferences and new service paradigms.

Recommendations

1. **Invest in Comprehensive Staff Training:** Focus on service excellence, cultural sensitivity, and problem-solving skills to empower staff in delivering exceptional guest experiences.
2. **Maintain High Standards in Room Quality and Cleanliness:** Regular audits and quality control must be implemented to ensure rooms meet and exceed guest expectations consistently.
3. **Leverage Technology Strategically:** Invest in user-friendly mobile apps, AI-driven personalization, contactless services, and smart room technologies to enhance convenience and satisfaction.
4. **Adopt Proactive Complaint Management Systems:** Establish clear protocols for handling guest complaints promptly and transparently, including leveraging social media and online review platforms for reputation management.
5. **Emphasize Personalized Guest Experiences:** Use customer data analytics to tailor services and amenities that reflect individual preferences, thereby increasing emotional engagement.
6. **Focus on Sustainability:** Integrate eco-friendly practices into operations, which not only meet growing customer expectations but also reduce operational costs.
7. **Diversify Food and Beverage Offerings:** Regularly update menus with local and international cuisines, emphasizing quality and dietary inclusivity to appeal to a broad range of guests.
8. **Monitor Market Trends and Competitor Strategies:** Continuous benchmarking and innovation are essential to maintain a competitive edge in a dynamic hospitality environment.

CONCLUSION

Customer satisfaction in hotels remains a multifaceted and critical factor driving business success. It encompasses both tangible elements such as room quality and food offerings, and intangible factors like staff behavior and technological convenience. Hotels that prioritize superior service quality, maintain high standards in hygiene and comfort, and embrace technology are more likely to build strong customer loyalty, generate positive word-of-mouth, and achieve higher financial returns. However, maintaining high satisfaction levels requires ongoing adaptation to diverse guest expectations, effective management of complaints, and strategic investments in staff training and technology. The future of customer satisfaction in hospitality lies in personalization, sustainability, and innovative technologies such as AI and virtual reality. By implementing the recommendations outlined, hotels can create memorable guest experiences that not only meet but exceed expectations, ensuring long-term success and competitive advantage in an increasingly demanding marketplace.

REFERENCES

Ali, F., Rasoolimanesh, S. M., & Cobanoglu, C. (2020). Customer experience and satisfaction in hospitality: Examining the role of technology. *Journal of Hospitality Marketing & Management, 29*(7), 1–23.

Berezina, K., Ciftci, O., & Cobanoglu, C. (2020). Robots, artificial intelligence, and service automation in hospitality. *International Journal of Contemporary Hospitality Management, 32*(5), 1927–1946.

Bilgihan, A. (2016). Gen Y customer loyalty in online shopping: An integrated model of trust, user experience, and branding. *Computers in Human Behavior, 61*, 103–113.

Buhalis, D., & Sinarta, Y. (2019). Real-time co-creation and nowness service: Lessons from tourism and hospitality. *Journal of Travel & Tourism Marketing, 36*(5), 563–582.

Collier, J. E., & Sherrell, D. L. (2010). Examining the influence of control and convenience in self-service technology adoption. *Journal of the Academy of Marketing Science, 38*(4), 490–509.

Hair, J. F., Black, W. C., Babin, B. J., & Anderson, R. E. (2019). *Multivariate data analysis* (8th ed.). Cengage Learning.

Han, H., Lee, J. S., Trang, H. L. T., & Kim, W. (2019). Water conservation and waste reduction management for increasing guest loyalty in hotels. *International Journal of Hospitality Management, 77*, 58–67.

Hofstede, G., Hofstede, G. J., & Minkov, M. (2010). *Cultures and organizations: Software of the mind* (3rd ed.). McGraw-Hill.

Ivanov, S., & Webster, C. (2017). Adoption of robots, artificial intelligence and service automation in tourism and hospitality. *Tourism Management Perspectives, 25*, 1–8.

Ivanov, S., & Webster, C. (2018). Robots in tourism: A research agenda. *Tourism Review, 73*(4), 489–497.

Kandampully, J., Zhang, T., & Bilgihan, A. (2015). Customer loyalty: A review and future directions with a special focus on the hospitality industry. *International Journal of Contemporary Hospitality Management, 27*(3), 379–414.

Kasavana, M. L., & Cahill, J. J. (2003). Managing technology in the hospitality industry. Educational Institute of the American Hotel & Lodging Association.

Kim, W. G., & Lee, H. Y. (2013). Customer relationship management and firm performance. *International Journal of Hospitality Management, 33*, 1–11.

Kucukusta, D., Heung, V. C. S., & Hui, S. (2014). Deploying RFID technology in hospitality. *International Journal of Hospitality Management, 40*, 77–87.

Law, R., Leung, R., & Buhalis, D. (2014). Information technology applications in hospitality and tourism. *International Journal of Contemporary Hospitality Management, 26*(5), 727–750.

Leung, R., & Law, R. (2013). Evaluation of hotel websites: Progress and future developments. *International Journal of Hospitality Management, 33*, 296–307.

Lu, A. C. C., & Gursoy, D. (2016). Impact of job burnout on satisfaction and turnover intention. *International Journal of Hospitality Management, 57*, 13–22.

Mittal, V., & Kamakura, W. A. (2001). Satisfaction, repurchase intent, and repurchase behavior. *JMR, Journal of Marketing Research, 38*(1), 131–142.

Morosan, C., & DeFranco, A. (2016). Mobile payments adoption in hospitality. *International Journal of Hospitality Management, 53*, 17–29.

Neuhofer, B., Buhalis, D., & Ladkin, A. (2015). Smart technologies for personalized experiences. *Journal of Travel Research, 54*(3), 356–370.

Noone, B. M., & McGuire, K. A. (2013). Pricing in hotels: Customer fairness perceptions. *Journal of Revenue and Pricing Management, 12*(4), 343–355.

Piccoli, G., Lui, T. W., & Grün, B. (2017). The impact of IT-enabled customer service systems. *Management Information Systems Quarterly, 41*(2), 1–23.

Podsakoff, P. M., MacKenzie, S. B., Lee, J. Y., & Podsakoff, N. P. (2003). Common method biases in behavioral research. *The Journal of Applied Psychology, 88*(5), 879–903.

Sthapit, E., & Björk, P. (2020). Sources of memorable tourism experiences. *Tourism Management Perspectives, 33*, 100625.

Torres, E. N., & Kline, S. (2013). From satisfaction to delight. *International Journal of Contemporary Hospitality Management, 25*(5), 642–659.

Tussyadiah, I. P., & Inversini, A. (2015). Information and communication technologies in tourism. *Journal of Travel Research, 54*(3), 336–343.

Ukpabi, D. C., & Karjaluoto, H. (2018). Adoption of mobile technologies in tourism. *Tourism Management Perspectives, 28*, 151–164.

Venkatesh, V., Thong, J. Y. L., & Xu, X. (2012). Consumer acceptance and use of information technology. *Management Information Systems Quarterly*, *36*(1), 157–178.

APPENDIX

Questionnaire

Q1. What is your gender?

Male
Female

Q2. What is your age?

21-25%
26-31
32-40
40+

1. Our hotel uses advanced technological tools such as property management systems and AI chatbots.
   a) Strongly Agree
   b) Agree
   c) Neutral
   d) Disagree
   e) Strongly Disagree

   Answer: b) Agree

2. Mobile apps provided by the hotel enhance ease of booking and service requests.
   a) Strongly Agree
   b) Agree
   c) Neutral
   d) Disagree
   e) Strongly Disagree

   Answer: a) Strongly Agree

3. Technology-enabled services have improved the overall guest satisfaction at our hotel.
   a) Strongly Agree
   b) Agree

c) Neutral
d) Disagree

e) Strongly Disagree
Answer: b) Agree

4. Guests prefer contactless check-in and check-out options.
   a) Strongly Agree
   b) Agree
   c) Neutral
   d) Disagree
   e) Strongly Disagree

   Answer: a) Strongly Agree

5. Smart room features (e.g., automated lighting, temperature control) improve the guest experience.
   a) Strongly Agree
   b) Agree
   c) Neutral
   d) Disagree
   e) Strongly Disagree

   Answer: b) Agree

6. Guests find AI chatbots helpful for quick queries and requests during their stay.
   a) Strongly Agree
   b) Agree
   c) Neutral
   d) Disagree
   e) Strongly Disagree

   Answer: b) Agree

7. Technology failures or glitches negatively impact customer satisfaction.
   a) Strongly Agree
   b) Agree
   c) Neutral
   d) Disagree
   e) Strongly Disagree

Answer: a) Strongly Agree

8. Hotels that use advanced technology see higher customer loyalty.
    a) Strongly Agree
    b) Agree
    c) Neutral
    d) Disagree
    e) Strongly Disagree

    Answer: b) Agree

9. Personalized guest experiences through technology increase repeat visits.
    a) Strongly Agree
    b) Agree
    c) Neutral
    d) Disagree
    e) Strongly Disagree

    Answer: a) Strongly Agree

10. The use of technology reduces wait times and improves service efficiency.
    a) Strongly Agree
    b) Agree
    c) Neutral
    d) Disagree
    e) Strongly Disagree

    Answer: b) Agree

11. Guests are comfortable sharing personal information through hotel apps for customized services.
    a) Strongly Agree
    b) Agree
    c) Neutral
    d) Disagree
    e) Strongly Disagree

    Answer: c) Neutral

12. The availability of free Wi-Fi is a critical factor in guest satisfaction.

a) Strongly Agree
b) Agree
c) Neutral
d) Disagree
e) Strongly Disagree

Answer: a) Strongly Agree

13. Technology-enabled feedback systems help improve hotel services.
    a) Strongly Agree
    b) Agree
    c) Neutral
    d) Disagree
    e) Strongly Disagree

    Answer: b) Agree

14. Staff training on new technology is essential for effective service delivery.
    a) Strongly Agree
    b) Agree
    c) Neutral
    d) Disagree
    e) Strongly Disagree

    Answer: a) Strongly Agree

15. Hotels should invest more in upgrading technology to meet guest expectations.
    a) Strongly Agree
    b) Agree
    c) Neutral
    d) Disagree
    e) Strongly Disagree

    Answer: a) Strongly Agree

16. Guests perceive contactless payment options as secure and convenient.
    a) Strongly Agree
    b) Agree
    c) Neutral
    d) Disagree

e) Strongly Disagree

Answer: b) Agree

17. Technology increases transparency in billing and service charges.
    a) Strongly Agree
    b) Agree
    c) Neutral
    d) Disagree
    e) Strongly Disagree

    Answer: b) Agree

18. Some guests prefer traditional service methods over technology-based services.
    a) Strongly Agree
    b) Agree
    c) Neutral
    d) Disagree
    e) Strongly Disagree

    Answer: b) Agree

19. Technology has made communication between guests and hotel staff more efficient.
    a) Strongly Agree
    b) Agree
    c) Neutral
    d) Disagree
    e) Strongly Disagree

    Answer: a) Strongly Agree

20. Investments in technology directly contribute to improved hotel reputation and ratings.
    a) Strongly Agree
    b) Agree
    c) Neutral
    d) Disagree
    e) Strongly Disagree

Answer: b) Agree

Chapter 11
Implementing AI in Heritage Tourism:
Balancing Access and Preservation

G. SudhaAnanthi
https://orcid.org/0009-0001-5062-5311
Winners Academy, India

T. C. Manjunath
https://orcid.org/0000-0003-2545-9160
Rajarajeswari College of Engineering, Bengaluru

Pankaj Singh Chandel
https://orcid.org/0000-0002-4135-8194
AAFT University of Media and Arts, India

ABSTRACT

Cultural heritage represents the cumulative legacy of human creativity, history, and identity, encompassing tangible artifacts such as monuments, museums, archaeological sites, and historical architecture, as well as intangible elements like traditions, rituals, and folklore. Preserving and promoting heritage while ensuring broad accessibility is a significant challenge in an increasingly globalized and digital world. Physical visits are often constrained by geographic distance, travel costs, physical mobility limitations, and environmental or socio-political factors. (Ayeh et al., 2013). AI-powered virtual tours for remote heritage access offer a transformative approach, combining artificial intelligence, 3D modeling, immersive media, and adaptive learning technologies to enable interactive, personalized, and highly engaging cultural experiences for audiences worldwide. These systems democratize

DOI: 10.4018/979-8-3373-8197-8.ch011

access to heritage, enhance educational outcomes, foster cultural appreciation, and support sustainable tourism while minimizing environmental impact on fragile heritage sites.

INTRODUCTION OF IMPLEMENTING AI IN HERITAGE TOURISM

Cultural heritage represents the cumulative legacy of human creativity, history, and identity, encompassing tangible artifacts such as monuments, museums, archaeological sites, and historical architecture, as well as intangible elements like traditions, rituals, and folklore. Preserving and promoting heritage while ensuring broad accessibility is a significant challenge in an increasingly globalized and digital world. Physical visits are often constrained by geographic distance, travel costs, physical mobility limitations, and environmental or socio-political factors. (Ayeh et al., 2013). AI-powered virtual tours for remote heritage access offer a transformative approach, combining artificial intelligence, 3D modeling, immersive media, and adaptive learning technologies to enable interactive, personalized, and highly engaging cultural experiences for audiences worldwide. These systems democratize access to heritage, enhance educational outcomes, foster cultural appreciation, and support sustainable tourism while minimizing environmental impact on fragile heritage sites.The foundational principle of AI-powered virtual heritage tours is the creation of interactive, intelligent, and immersive experiences that replicate or augment in-person visits. High-fidelity 3D reconstructions, photogrammetry, LiDAR scanning, and drone imagery capture the physical attributes of heritage sites, including architectural details, textures, spatial layouts, and contextual surroundings. AI algorithms, particularly computer vision models, enhance these reconstructions by filling gaps, restoring damaged areas, and optimizing visual fidelity. Natural language processing (NLP) and generative AI enable dynamic narration, multilingual explanations, and context-sensitive storytelling, ensuring that users receive tailored information based on their interests, cultural background, or educational level. By combining immersive visualization with intelligent interaction, AI-powered virtual tours replicate the richness of on-site experiences while providing unique functionalities not possible in physical visits, such as time-lapse reconstructions, archaeological layer visualization, or interactive annotations.

Data acquisition and integration are crucial to developing AI-powered virtual tours. Digital archives, historical photographs, architectural plans, archaeological records, GIS data, and contemporary imaging are synthesized to generate comprehensive digital representations of heritage sites. Environmental context data, such as geographic, climatic, and urban development information, provide additional layers of situational awareness, helping users understand the heritage in its historical and ecological context. Multi-modal datasets—including audio recordings, video documentaries, textual descriptions, and scholarly interpretations—are integrated to enrich the virtual experience. Machine learning models analyze these heterogeneous datasets to optimize tour design, identify salient features, and adapt content dynamically to user preferences, prior knowledge, and engagement patterns.Personalization and adaptive learning are central to maximizing user engagement and educational outcomes. (Beck et al., 2019)AI models track user behavior, including interaction patterns, navigation choices, dwell times, and feedback, to create dynamic, individualized tour experiences. Recommendation algorithms suggest relevant artifacts, historical narratives, or thematic pathways tailored to user interests, learning goals, or cultural curiosity. Adaptive narration, powered by NLP and voice synthesis, modulates language complexity, tone, and depth of content, ensuring accessibility for diverse audiences, including students, researchers, heritage enthusiasts, and general tourists. By providing personalized experiences, AI-powered tours enhance retention, comprehension, and appreciation of heritage, fostering deeper connections between users and cultural content.

SMART TICKETING SYSTEMS TO MANAGE VISITOR FLOW

Effective management of visitor flow is a critical challenge for cultural heritage sites, natural parks, museums, urban attractions, and large-scale events. Overcrowding can compromise visitor experiences, cause environmental degradation, threaten the safety and security of participants, and disrupt operational efficiency. Traditional ticketing methods, relying on manual counters, paper tickets, or static time slots, are limited in their ability to monitor real-time attendance, predict peak periods, or dynamically allocate resources. Smart ticketing systems leverage digital technologies, IoT devices, artificial intelligence (AI), and big data analytics to optimize visitor flow, enhance operational efficiency, improve user experiences, and support sustainable management of high-traffic destinations.(Brandtzæg et al., 2010) By integrating dynamic access control, real-time monitoring, predictive modeling, and personalized engagement, these systems enable precise, adaptive, and data-driven visitor management strategies.The foundational principle of smart ticketing systems is to utilize real-time and historical data to manage, monitor, and optimize visitor movement across attractions. Smart ticketing platforms employ digital passes, QR codes, RFID-enabled wristbands, mobile apps, and contactless payment systems to record entry and exit times, track movement patterns, and capture visitor demographics and preferences. These digital mechanisms replace traditional paper-based systems, enabling seamless access, reducing bottlenecks, and providing granular data on visitor behavior. By combining this data with AI algorithms, managers gain insights into visitor distribution, dwell times, congestion hotspots, and temporal visitation trends, allowing them to make informed operational and strategic decisions.

Data acquisition and integration are crucial for the effectiveness of smart ticketing systems. Multi-source data includes ticket sales, reservation schedules, check-in and check-out logs, visitor GPS or Bluetooth signals, environmental sensors, and historical visitation patterns. Integration with external datasets such as weather forecasts, public transportation data, and regional events calendars provides context for predicting visitor demand fluctuations. Advanced preprocessing, including normalization, anomaly detection, and geospatial alignment, ensures data quality and usability.(Chan et al., 2010) The resulting integrated dataset forms the backbone for predictive analytics, simulation, and real-time decision-making, enabling proactive management of visitor flows.Predictive modeling and dynamic allocation are central to smart ticketing systems. Machine learning algorithms, including time-series forecasting, regression analysis, and clustering methods, predict peak visitation periods, crowd density, and high-demand areas. These predictions allow dynamic adjustment of ticket availability, time-slot allocation, and pricing strategies to distribute visitors more evenly across hours, zones, and days. Reinforcement learning and optimization models continuously update allocation strategies based on real-time data, balancing visitor demand with operational constraints, safety regulations, and environmental limits. By anticipating crowd surges and proactively managing access, smart ticketing systems mitigate congestion, reduce waiting times, and enhance overall visitor satisfaction.

MACHINE LEARNING FOR PREDICTIVE SITE MAINTENANCE

Effective site maintenance is critical for preserving infrastructure, cultural heritage, natural reserves, and urban facilities while ensuring safety, operational efficiency, and visitor satisfaction. Traditional maintenance practices often rely on periodic inspections, scheduled servicing, or reactive repairs, which can lead to inefficiencies, unexpected failures, excessive costs, and resource misallocation. Machine learning (ML) for predictive site maintenance represents a transformative approach, leveraging historical data, sensor inputs, environmental parameters, and advanced analytics to anticipate potential failures, optimize maintenance schedules, and enhance asset longevity. By shifting from reactive to predictive paradigms, ML-enabled maintenance frameworks allow managers to proactively address issues, reduce downtime, minimize operational costs, and improve safety outcomes across diverse site types, from heritage sites and public infrastructure to industrial complexes and urban facilities.The foundational principle of ML-driven predictive maintenance is the use of data to forecast equipment, structural, or environmental deterioration before failures occur. This involves integrating multi-source datasets, including sensor readings, operational logs, environmental monitoring data, historical maintenance records, and contextual factors such as visitor load, weather conditions, or material degradation patterns. (Chiou et al., 2008)By identifying correlations, trends, and anomalies in these data streams, machine learning algorithms can detect early warning signs of wear and tear, structural weaknesses, or system inefficiencies. This predictive capability allows site managers to schedule timely interventions, allocate resources effectively, and reduce the risk of catastrophic failures or service disruptions.

Data acquisition and integration are crucial to the success of predictive maintenance frameworks. IoT devices, embedded sensors, drones, and automated monitoring systems provide real-time measurements of vibration, temperature, humidity, load, strain, corrosion, and material integrity. High-resolution imaging, LiDAR scanning, and remote sensing enable continuous observation of structural and environmental conditions. Operational records, including maintenance logs, usage frequency, incident reports, and service histories, provide historical context for model training. Environmental factors such as rainfall, temperature fluctuations, air pollution, and visitor density are incorporated to account for extrinsic stressors. Advanced preprocessing, normalization, and synchronization of these heterogeneous datasets ensure that machine learning models can accurately capture the relationships between environmental, operational, and material factors affecting site integrity(Dilanchian et al., 2021).Machine learning model selection and application are critical to predictive maintenance. Supervised learning algorithms, including regression analysis, decision trees, random forests, gradient boosting, and support vector machines, can be applied to predict time-to-failure, degradation rates, and maintenance needs based on labeled historical data. Unsupervised learning techniques, such as clustering and anomaly detection, identify patterns in unlabeled datasets, detecting deviations from normal behavior that may indicate emerging issues. Deep learning models, including convolutional neural networks (CNNs) and recurrent neural networks (RNNs), are particularly effective for analyzing high-dimensional, temporal, and spatial data, such as sensor streams, video footage, and structural scans. Reinforcement learning can optimize maintenance scheduling by continuously adapting decisions based on observed outcomes and system performance, ensuring resources are used efficiently and repairs are prioritized according to urgency and impact.Predictive analytics and risk assessment enhance decision-making by quantifying the probability of failures and the potential consequences of inaction. Machine learning models generate risk scores, confidence intervals, and failure probability maps for assets or site components. These outputs inform prioritization of maintenance activities, resource allocation, and emergency preparedness. Scenario analysis and "what-if" simulations allow managers to evaluate different maintenance strategies, including repair frequency, material replacement, and preventive interventions, assessing cost-benefit trade-offs and operational feasibility. By integrating risk modeling with predictive insights, maintenance programs become proactive, data-driven, and strategically aligned with operational and safety objectives.

COMPUTER VISION FOR ARTIFACT CONDITION MONITORING

The preservation and conservation of cultural heritage artifacts, including paintings, sculptures, manuscripts, ceramics, textiles, and historical objects, are essential for safeguarding human history, creativity, and identity. Artifacts are continually exposed to threats such as environmental fluctuations, biological degradation, chemical reactions, physical wear, vandalism, and inadvertent human handling. (Disztinger et al., 2017)Traditional artifact condition monitoring often relies on periodic manual inspections by conservation experts, photographic documentation, or laboratory analyses, which are labor-intensive, subjective, and limited in temporal and spatial resolution. Computer vision for artifact condition monitoring offers a transformative approach by combining high-resolution imaging, machine learning, artificial intelligence, and automated pattern recognition to provide continuous, objective, and precise assessment of artifact integrity. (Garrett, 2010)By leveraging visual data, computer vision systems enable early detection of deterioration, real-time condition tracking, predictive maintenance, and data-driven conservation strategies, thereby enhancing the longevity and preservation of cultural heritage assets.The foundational principle of computer vision in artifact monitoring is the automated acquisition, processing, and analysis of visual information to identify signs of degradation, structural anomalies, and material changes. High-resolution digital imaging, multispectral and hyperspectral photography, 3D scanning, and photogrammetry capture the fine details of surface texture, color, geometry, and material composition. These imaging techniques are complemented by infrared, ultraviolet, and X-ray imaging to reveal underlying structural features, hidden layers, or subsurface damage that may not be visible to the naked eye. Computer vision algorithms analyze this visual data to detect patterns, changes, or anomalies that indicate wear, cracking, fading, discoloration, corrosion, or microbial growth, allowing conservators to make timely, informed decisions.

Data acquisition and integration are critical to building robust computer vision-based monitoring frameworks. Multi-modal imaging data, including RGB images, depth maps, infrared and ultraviolet scans, hyperspectral data, and 3D point clouds, are collected over time to create detailed digital records of each artifact(Haaksma et al., 2018). Environmental monitoring data, such as temperature, humidity, light exposure, and pollutant levels, are integrated to contextualize observed changes and identify causative factors. Historical restoration records, expert annotations, and conservation reports are also incorporated to provide prior knowledge and ground truth for training machine learning models(Han et al., 2018). Data preprocessing, including alignment, normalization, denoising, and geometric correction, ensures that input datasets are consistent, high-quality, and suitable for accurate analysis.Machine learning and AI techniques form the analytical backbone of computer vision-based condition monitoring. Supervised learning algorithms, including convolutional neural networks (CNNs), support vector machines (SVMs), and random forests, are trained on labeled datasets to classify degradation types, quantify severity, and identify high-risk areas. Unsupervised learning models, such as clustering and anomaly detection, detect previously unknown deterioration patterns or deviations from baseline conditions. Deep learning architectures enable automated feature extraction from high-dimensional imaging data, capturing subtle textural, structural, and color variations that may elude human observation. Time-series analysis of sequential image data allows for tracking of progressive changes, forecasting deterioration trajectories, and prioritizing preventive interventions.High-resolution 3D modeling and spatial analysis enhance artifact monitoring by capturing geometric and volumetric details. Photogrammetry and LiDAR scanning produce detailed 3D reconstructions of artifacts, enabling measurement of surface deformations, cracks, warping, or structural instability. Computer vision algorithms perform spatial alignment of successive scans to quantify material loss, displacement, or erosion with sub-millimeter precision. Volumetric analysis facilitates comparison between current and baseline conditions, enabling accurate detection of subtle changes over time. These 3D models also support digital restoration, visualization, and virtual exhibitions, preserving artifact information for research, education, and public engagement even if the physical object becomes inaccessible.

PERSONALIZED NARRATIVE ENGINES ENHANCING VISITOR EXPERIENCE

In the modern landscape of museums, heritage sites, cultural attractions, theme parks, and immersive educational environments, enhancing visitor engagement and satisfaction is a key operational and experiential objective. Traditional visitor experiences often adopt a one-size-fits-all approach, delivering standardized narratives, static informational panels, and pre-scripted guided tours. While informative, such approaches fail to account for individual visitor preferences, cultural backgrounds, prior knowledge, learning goals, and emotional engagement levels. Personalized narrative engines—powered by artificial intelligence (AI), machine learning, natural language processing (NLP), and recommendation algorithms—offer a transformative approach to visitor experience, dynamically tailoring storytelling, content sequencing, and interactive engagement to each user's profile. By delivering customized narratives, these engines increase visitor immersion, learning outcomes, emotional resonance, and overall satisfaction while providing institutions with actionable data to optimize content design and operational strategies.The foundational principle of personalized narrative engines lies in the adaptive delivery of content that aligns with individual visitor characteristics and preferences. These systems leverage data from multiple sources, including visitor demographics, historical visitation patterns, interaction logs with exhibits, expressed interests, and feedback from prior tours. (Hassenzahl, 2003)dvanced user modeling techniques construct dynamic profiles that capture cognitive, emotional, and cultural attributes. By analyzing these profiles, narrative engines generate content sequences, storytelling styles, and multimedia elements optimized for engagement, comprehension, and emotional impact. Personalization extends beyond content to modalities, incorporating text, audio, visuals, augmented reality (AR), virtual reality (VR), and haptic feedback, depending on visitor preferences and device capabilities.

Data acquisition and integration underpin the effectiveness of personalized narrative engines. Visitor interaction data is collected through mobile applications, wearable devices, interactive kiosks, AR/VR headsets, beacon-enabled guides, and web portals. Environmental sensors and IoT devices provide context regarding visitor location, proximity to exhibits, dwell times, and navigation paths. Social media interactions, expressed preferences, and survey responses contribute additional insights into interests, sentiment, and learning objectives.(Hassenzahl, 2003) Historical data, including prior visits and content engagement, is integrated with real-time inputs to construct comprehensive, evolving visitor profiles. Multi-modal data preprocessing, feature extraction, and normalization ensure compatibility with machine learning models and narrative generation frameworks.Machine learning and AI-driven personalization form the analytical and operational core of narrative engines. Supervised learning models classify visitor preferences, learning styles, and engagement tendencies, while unsupervised techniques such as clustering identify patterns across visitor segments, revealing emergent interests or underserved content areas. Natural language processing models analyze textual interactions, queries, and feedback to interpret comprehension levels, curiosity-driven exploration, and sentiment. Deep learning architectures, including recurrent neural networks (RNNs) and transformers, enable context-aware, sequential content generation, allowing narratives to adapt in real-time as visitors explore exhibits or move through virtual or physical environments. Reinforcement learning algorithms optimize narrative pathways, continuously refining recommendations based on user engagement metrics and satisfaction scores.Dynamic storytelling and adaptive content sequencing are central to the visitor experience. Personalized narrative engines adjust the order, depth, and style of information presented according to visitor profiles. For instance, a history enthusiast may receive in-depth contextual analysis of a cultural artifact, while a casual visitor may encounter a visually rich, high-level overview emphasizing key highlights. Interactive elements, such as quizzes, gamified challenges, or branching storylines, are modulated to align with engagement levels, prior knowledge, and learning objectives. Multilingual support, voice synthesis, and sentiment-aware narration further enhance accessibility and emotional resonance, ensuring that narratives are culturally sensitive, linguistically appropriate, and contextually meaningful.

AUTOMATED DAMAGE DETECTION USING DRONE IMAGERY

Monitoring infrastructure, heritage sites, agricultural landscapes, and natural environments for damage or deterioration is a complex, labor-intensive, and often hazardous task. Traditional inspection methods, including manual surveys, on-site visual assessments, and ground-based photography, are limited by accessibility, human error, safety concerns, and time constraints.(Hassenzahl, 2003) These approaches may fail to provide comprehensive coverage, frequent monitoring, or timely detection of emerging issues. Automated damage detection using drone imagery represents a transformative approach, combining unmanned aerial vehicles (UAVs), high-resolution imaging, computer vision, and artificial intelligence (AI) to enable rapid, precise, and scalable assessment of physical assets. By capturing aerial perspectives, processing large volumes of imagery, and applying machine learning algorithms for anomaly detection, automated systems can identify damage, structural weaknesses, environmental impacts, or maintenance needs with unprecedented speed and accuracy. The foundational principle of automated damage detection using drone imagery is the systematic capture, analysis, and interpretation of aerial visual data to identify deviations from normal structural or environmental conditions. Drones equipped with RGB cameras, multispectral, hyperspectral, infrared, or thermal sensors capture high-resolution imagery across large areas, providing detailed visual documentation of surfaces, materials, and terrain.(Hassenzahl, 2003) These images are processed using computer vision techniques, including image segmentation, edge detection, pattern recognition, and object classification, to detect cracks, corrosion, erosion, deformations, vegetation encroachment, or other forms of damage. By integrating historical imagery and baseline models, automated systems can identify changes over time, enabling early intervention and preventive maintenance.

Data acquisition and integration are essential for accurate and reliable automated damage detection. Drone flight plans are optimized to ensure comprehensive coverage, consistent imaging angles, and overlap suitable for photogrammetry and 3D reconstruction. Sensor data, including RGB imagery, LiDAR point clouds, thermal maps, and multispectral readings, are synchronized and geo-referenced to create multi-dimensional representations of the monitored environment. Environmental and operational contextual data, such as weather conditions, material properties, load patterns, and human activity, are incorporated to improve detection accuracy and contextual interpretation. Data preprocessing, including noise reduction, alignment, calibration, and normalization, ensures that input datasets are robust, consistent, and suitable for machine learning analysis.(Ijsselsteijn & Riva, 2003)Machine learning and AI algorithms provide the analytical core for automated damage detection. Supervised learning models, including convolutional neural networks (CNNs) and deep learning architectures, are trained on labeled datasets to recognize specific types of damage, such as cracks, rust, spalling, or structural deformations. Unsupervised learning techniques, such as anomaly detection and clustering, identify novel or subtle damage patterns that may not be included in training datasets. Semantic segmentation algorithms precisely delineate affected areas, providing spatially accurate maps of damage for assessment and prioritization. Temporal analysis of sequential imagery enables tracking of damage progression, predicting potential failure points, and informing preventive intervention strategies.

AI-DRIVEN ACCESSIBILITY TOOLS FOR DIVERSE AUDIENCES

Ensuring accessibility for diverse audiences is a critical consideration in education, cultural institutions, public services, digital platforms, entertainment, and workplace environments. Traditional accessibility measures, such as static subtitles, screen readers, manual translation, or wheelchair ramps, while essential, often fall short of meeting the needs of a diverse, global, and digitally connected audience. AI-driven accessibility tools leverage artificial intelligence, machine learning, natural language processing, computer vision, and speech recognition to dynamically adapt content, interfaces, and experiences to individual user needs. (Jung et al., 2017)By providing real-time translation, personalized content adjustments, assistive interactions, and multimodal engagement, AI-driven accessibility tools enhance inclusivity, participation, and user satisfaction across diverse linguistic, cognitive, physical, and sensory abilities. The foundational principle of AI-driven accessibility is the application of intelligent systems to automatically detect user needs, preferences, and barriers, and to provide adaptive interventions that remove or mitigate those barriers. This requires robust user profiling, environmental context analysis, and content understanding (Kaur et al., 2025). AI systems can identify, for example, visual impairments, hearing loss, cognitive differences, language barriers, or motor skill limitations, and dynamically provide tailored solutions. For instance, a visitor with low vision may receive audio descriptions and high-contrast visual enhancements, while a hearing-impaired individual may receive real-time captioning or sign language interpretation. These interventions are adaptive, context-aware, and continuously refined through user feedback and behavioral analysis.

Figure 1. AI changing the tourism & travel industry

Data acquisition and integration are critical for developing effective AI-driven accessibility tools. Multi-modal datasets—including text, audio, video, sensor data, user interaction logs, biometric inputs, and environmental context—are collected to inform system responses. Natural language data, including user queries, speech patterns, and reading comprehension levels, provide insights for adaptive content delivery. Visual inputs from cameras, wearable devices, or AR/VR sensors enable gesture recognition, object detection, or real-time environment analysis for accessibility interventions. Integration with historical usage patterns, accessibility preferences, and user feedback ensures that AI models are personalized and responsive. Preprocessing pipelines normalize, annotate, and synchronize data to enable high-accuracy machine learning applications. Machine learning and AI techniques underpin the intelligence of accessibility tools. Natural language processing (NLP) enables real-time translation, summarization, sentiment analysis, and context-aware rephrasing of content for diverse linguistic or cognitive needs. Speech recognition algorithms convert spoken language into text, enabling captioning, transcription, or command interpretation. Computer vision models detect visual cues, recognize gestures, interpret sign language, and analyze environmental context for visually impaired users (Kim et al., 2022). Deep learning frameworks, including convolutional neural networks (CNNs) and recurrent neural networks (RNNs), provide high-accuracy pattern recognition and predictive capabilities, allowing systems to anticipate user needs and proactively adjust content presentation. Reinforcement learning supports adaptive feedback loops, optimizing accessibility interventions over time based on observed user behavior and engagement metrics.

REAL-TIME CROWD ANALYTICS TO PREVENT OVER-TOURISM

The rapid growth of global tourism has brought substantial economic benefits but also significant challenges, including environmental degradation, infrastructure strain, cultural erosion, and reduced visitor satisfaction. Over-tourism, characterized by excessive visitor concentration in popular destinations, threatens the sustainability of cultural heritage sites, natural reserves, urban spaces, and local communities. Traditional approaches to crowd management, such as static capacity limits, scheduled tours, or manual monitoring, are often reactive, imprecise, and insufficient for dynamically evolving visitor flows. Real-time crowd analytics leverages advanced data collection, artificial intelligence (AI), computer vision, sensor networks, and predictive modeling to monitor, analyze, and manage tourist concentrations in real time, enabling proactive interventions that prevent overcrowding while enhancing visitor experience, safety, and sustainability.(Law & Lárusdóttir, 2015)The foundational principle of real-time crowd analytics is the continuous acquisition and processing of multi-modal data to understand visitor density, movement patterns, dwell times, and behavior across physical and virtual spaces. Data is collected from a variety of sources, including Wi-Fi and Bluetooth signals from mobile devices, GPS location tracking, CCTV and camera networks, IoT-enabled sensors, social media check-ins, ticketing systems, and wearable devices. High-resolution imagery, coupled with computer vision algorithms, provides granular insights into crowd distribution, pedestrian flow, and spatial utilization, allowing managers to identify congested areas, bottlenecks, or underutilized zones. By integrating diverse datasets, real-time analytics systems create a comprehensive, dynamic map of visitor activity across attractions, transport hubs, and surrounding environments.

Machine learning and AI techniques are central to the analysis and forecasting capabilities of real-time crowd management systems. Supervised learning models, such as regression analysis and classification algorithms, predict visitor density, peak hours, and hotspot locations based on historical and real-time data. Unsupervised learning methods, including clustering and anomaly detection, identify unusual crowd patterns, early signs of congestion, or deviations from expected flow patterns. Deep learning architectures, such as convolutional neural networks

(CNNs) and recurrent neural networks (RNNs), enable high-accuracy detection of individual or grouped movements, while reinforcement learning optimizes interventions, such as routing, signage placement, or alert dissemination, to minimize overcrowding. Predictive analytics allows operators to forecast surges caused by special events, holidays, weather conditions, or social media trends, facilitating proactive capacity management.Real-time monitoring and visualization are facilitated by sophisticated dashboards, geospatial mapping, and heatmap generation.(Law et al., 2009) Spatial-temporal visualizations display visitor concentrations, movement trajectories, and dwell times, allowing managers to assess crowd dynamics instantly. Interactive dashboards integrate multiple data streams, providing decision-makers with a unified view of crowd behavior across sites, transportation corridors, and public spaces. Alerts can be triggered when visitor density exceeds predetermined thresholds, enabling rapid response, such as activating crowd control personnel, adjusting access points, or directing visitors to alternative routes or attractions. Geofencing and location-aware notifications can communicate real-time guidance to tourists via mobile applications, encouraging movement toward less crowded areas and dispersing congestion effectively.

DIGITAL TWIN MODELS FOR PRESERVATION PLANNING

The preservation of cultural heritage, historical sites, critical infrastructure, and environmentally sensitive locations is an increasingly complex challenge in the 21st century. Traditional conservation approaches, often reliant on periodic manual inspections, static documentation, and expert judgment, are limited by incomplete data, resource constraints, and reactive intervention strategies. Environmental degradation, climate change, urbanization, and human activity further exacerbate risks to fragile sites and structures. (Marchiori et al., 2017)Digital twin models for preservation planning offer a transformative solution by creating dynamic, virtual representations of physical assets that integrate real-time data, predictive simulations, and AI-driven analytics. These models enable proactive decision-making, risk assessment, and strategic planning for long-term conservation, ensuring that interventions are evidence-based,ltilingual communication has surged across domains such as international business, cultural institutions, tourism, education, governmental services, and digital platforms. Language barriers often impede effective knowledge dissemination, cross-cultural engagement, and accessibility, creating challenges for institutions and audiences seeking to interact across linguistic boundaries. Traditional approaches to translation and interpretation—such as human translators, pre-recorded multilingual content, and static text translation—face limitations in scalability, speed, consistency, and adaptability to context-specific nuances.

The foundational principle of NLP for multilingual interpretation is the computational understanding, analysis, and generation of human language across linguistic and cultural contexts. NLP systems process text, speech, and other language-based inputs to identify semantic meaning, syntactic structure, sentiment, and contextual cues. Advanced algorithms enable the translation of content not merely at a word-for-word level but in a manner that preserves meaning, tone, intent, and cultural relevance(Manjunath et al., 2026)For example, idiomatic expressions, culturally specific references, humor, and domain-specific terminology are interpreted with sensitivity to local conventions. This allows institutions such as museums, heritage sites, online learning platforms, and multinational corporations to provide content that resonates authentically with audiences in their native languages.Data acquisition and preprocessing are critical to the effectiveness of multilingual NLP systems. Training datasets consist of parallel corpora, multilingual text, transcribed speech, and annotated conversational data across diverse languages and dialects. Data is collected from literary sources, technical manuals, multimedia content, social media, government documents, and domain-specific knowledge bases. Preprocessing steps include tokenization, normalization, stemming, lemmatization, part-of-speech tagging, and syntactic parsing. Additional preprocessing may involve alignment of parallel corpora for supervised learning, annotation of semantic and pragmatic features, and handling of code-switching phenomena common in multilingual discourse. High-quality, curated, and representative datasets are essential to ensuring accurate, context-aware interpretation across languages with differing grammatical, syntactic, and cultural structures.

ENERGY-EFFICIENT AI INFRASTRUCTURE IN HERITAGE SITES

Heritage sites, including historic monuments, archaeological areas, museums, and cultural landscapes, are critical repositories of human history, artistic achievement, and collective memory. Preserving these sites while accommodating modern technology for monitoring, visitor management, and digital engagement presents a dual challenge: maintaining the integrity and authenticity of the heritage environment and implementing energy-efficient technological solutions that are sustainable, reliable, and minimally invasive. Energy-efficient AI infrastructure in heritage sites represents a transformative approach, integrating artificial intelligence, edge computing, renewable energy, low-power hardware, and smart systems to enable real-time monitoring, predictive maintenance, visitor analytics, and immersive experiences without imposing unsustainable energy burdens. This approach ensures that heritage conservation efforts remain technologically advanced, environmentally responsible, and operationally efficient.The foundational principle of energy-efficient AI infrastructure is the strategic design and deployment of computational resources that optimize energy consumption while maintaining high-performance AI capabilities. Unlike traditional centralized computing models that rely on large, power-intensive servers, energy-efficient AI infrastructure leverages a combination of edge computing, low-power processors, AI accelerators, and intelligent workload distribution to minimize electricity use. Edge computing allows AI models to process data locally—on-site or near the heritage site—reducing the need for continuous data transmission to cloud servers and decreasing latency, bandwidth usage, and overall energy consumption. This is particularly crucial in heritage sites, where network connectivity may be limited, sensitive areas may restrict heavy infrastructure, and environmental conditions require careful control to prevent deterioration.

Data acquisition and multi-modal integration are essential for energy-efficient AI in heritage contexts. Heritage monitoring often involves high-resolution video, 3D imaging, environmental sensor data, visitor flow tracking, and IoT-enabled devices to detect structural stress, microclimatic variations, or visitor-induced wear. To optimize energy use, data collection strategies prioritize relevant inputs, use adaptive sampling rates, and implement low-power sensors. (Pantano & Servidio, 2012)For instance, motion-triggered cameras, periodic LiDAR scans, and context-aware environmental sensors collect data only when required, reducing unnecessary energy expenditure. Advanced data compression, pre-processing, and lightweight AI models minimize computational load while preserving analytical accuracy, ensuring that heritage monitoring is both precise and sustainable.Machine learning and AI techniques underpin energy-efficient heritage management. Lightweight neural networks, such as pruned CNNs or quantized models, are designed to perform image analysis, anomaly detection, structural assessment, and visitor pattern recognition with minimal power consumption. Reinforcement learning algorithms optimize operational parameters for environmental control systems, such as HVAC, lighting, and humidity regulation, balancing energy efficiency with conservation requirements. Predictive maintenance models analyze historical and real-time sensor data to forecast potential deterioration, allowing intervention only when necessary, thereby avoiding continuous monitoring at maximum energy expenditure. These models prioritize computational efficiency without compromising accuracy, enabling heritage managers to make data-driven decisions while reducing carbon footprint. Real-time visitor and crowd management is a key application of AI infrastructure in heritage sites, with significant energy considerations.

ETHICAL DATA GOVERNANCE FOR VISITOR INFORMATION

In contemporary tourism, cultural heritage management, urban planning, and visitor-centric services, the collection and use of visitor information has become increasingly integral to enhancing experiences, optimizing operations, and ensuring safety. Visitor data encompasses personal identifiers, demographic information, behavioral patterns, preferences, geolocation tracking, and interaction histories across physical and digital platforms. While such data enables institutions and operators to tailor services, forecast trends, and manage crowd flows effectively, it also raises profound ethical, legal, and social concerns. Ethical data governance for visitor information establishes a framework for responsible data collection, storage, processing, sharing, and use, balancing operational efficiency with privacy, security, equity, and cultural sensitivity. By embedding ethical principles into data governance strategies, organizations can foster trust, compliance, and sustainability in tourism, heritage, and urban ecosystems.The foundational principle of ethical data governance involves ensuring that visitor data is collected, managed, and utilized transparently, securely, and in ways that respect individual rights and societal norms. (Rainoldi et al., 2018)This includes obtaining informed consent, clarifying purposes of data use, implementing strict access controls, and adopting measures to protect data integrity and confidentiality. Ethical governance frameworks emphasize accountability at every stage of the data lifecycle, from acquisition through analysis to long-term storage or deletion. They also require alignment with relevant legal and regulatory frameworks, such as the General Data Protection Regulation (GDPR), California Consumer Privacy Act (CCPA), and national privacy legislation, which define standards for consent, data minimization, purpose limitation, and rights to access or erasure.

Data collection and minimization are central to ethical governance. Visitor data should be collected only to the extent necessary to achieve clearly defined objectives, avoiding excessive or intrusive data acquisition. Techniques such as anonymization, pseudonymization, and aggregation reduce the risk of identifying individuals while preserving analytical value. For instance, instead of tracking individual trajectories across a heritage site, aggregated heatmaps can provide insights into visitor flow without compromising privacy. Similarly, behavioral analytics can be designed to identify patterns and trends without linking them to specific personal identifiers. Data minimization not only mitigates privacy risks but also reduces the burden of storage, processing, and regulatory compliance, supporting sustainable data management practices.Transparency and informed consent are essential components of ethical data governance. Visitors should be clearly informed about the types of data collected, purposes of collection, methods of processing, storage duration, and any third-party sharing arrangements. Consent mechanisms should be explicit, easy to understand, and revocable, ensuring that individuals retain control over their information. Transparency also includes providing information about algorithmic processing, automated decision-making, and predictive analytics used to interpret visitor behavior or recommend personalized experiences. By fostering an environment of clarity and openness, organizations build trust with visitors and encourage voluntary participation in data-driven services, enhancing both ethical compliance and user engagement.Security measures and risk management protect visitor information from unauthorized access, breaches, or misuse. Robust cybersecurity protocols, including encryption, multi-factor authentication, network segmentation, and secure APIs, prevent data leakage and ensure integrity.

AI-ASSISTED CONSERVATION OF FRAGILE ARTIFACTS

The preservation of fragile artifacts—ranging from ancient manuscripts, paintings, sculptures, textiles, and ceramics to archaeological relics—is a critical responsibility of museums, cultural institutions, and heritage conservation organizations. These artifacts represent irreplaceable cultural, historical, and artistic heritage, yet they are highly susceptible to environmental degradation, physical stress, biological factors, and human handling. Traditional conservation approaches, while effective in many cases, often rely on periodic inspections, subjective expert assessment, and reactive interventions, which may not detect subtle deterioration in time to prevent irreversible damage. AI-assisted conservation of fragile artifacts represents a transformative approach, combining artificial intelligence, machine learning, computer vision, predictive analytics, and sensor-based monitoring to enhance artifact preservation, optimize interventions, and provide actionable insights in a proactive and evidence-driven manner. This integration enables conservators to protect cultural heritage while ensuring sustainable, precise, and minimally invasive interventions.(Raj et al., 2026)The foundational principle of AI-assisted conservation is the creation of a comprehensive, data-rich understanding of an artifact's current state, environmental interactions, and potential deterioration pathways. High-resolution imaging, 3D scanning, hyperspectral and multispectral analysis, infrared and ultraviolet photography, and micro-sensor networks generate detailed datasets that capture the physical, chemical, and structural characteristics of artifacts.

Computer vision and machine learning are central to AI-driven artifact monitoring. Convolutional neural networks (CNNs) and deep learning architectures can analyze high-resolution images to detect micro-cracks, flaking paint, discoloration, erosion, or other forms of degradation. Pattern recognition algorithms distinguish between natural aging processes and damage caused by environmental or human-induced factors. Temporal analysis using recurrent neural networks (RNNs) enables modeling of degradation trends over time, providing predictive insights into when conservation interventions will be necessary. AI systems can also classify types of damage, assess severity, and recommend targeted preventive measures, ensuring that interventions are precise, minimally invasive, and tailored to the artifact's specific needs.(Seshanna et al., 2026)Environmental monitoring and predictive control form a crucial aspect of AI-assisted conservation. Artifacts are highly sensitive to temperature, humidity, light exposure, pollution, and vibrations. IoT-enabled sensors deployed in display cases, storage areas, and exhibition environments continuously measure these parameters. AI models analyze real-time environmental data to detect anomalies, predict potential risks, and recommend adjustments in climate control systems, lighting, or display orientation. Reinforcement learning algorithms can optimize environmental parameters dynamically, balancing energy efficiency with conservation requirements. Predictive analytics enable conservators to anticipate adverse conditions and intervene before damage occurs, shifting from reactive to proactive preservation strategies.Integration with digital twin models enhances artifact conservation by creating virtual replicas that mirror physical condition, environmental interactions, and handling history. These digital twins incorporate multimodal datasets, including imagery, 3D scans, environmental readings, and conservation records, allowing AI systems to simulate different preservation scenarios. For example, the impact of varying humidity levels, visitor interactions, or packaging materials can be modeled to determine optimal conservation strategies. By testing interventions virtually, conservators minimize physical manipulation and associated risks, ensuring that delicate artifacts are protected while gaining data-driven insights into long-term preservation strategies.

DYNAMIC PRICING MODELS TO BALANCE DEMAND AND PRESERVATION

Cultural heritage sites, natural parks, museums, and urban tourist attractions face the persistent challenge of balancing visitor demand with the imperative of preservation. Unmanaged tourism can result in overcrowding, accelerated wear and tear, environmental degradation, and diminished visitor experiences, threatening both the integrity of the site and its long-term sustainability. Conversely, overly restrictive access or underutilization can reduce revenue streams, limit public engagement, and compromise financial viability for conservation initiatives. Dynamic pricing models to balance demand and preservation offer an innovative approach, leveraging data-driven analytics, artificial intelligence, and behavioral economics to optimize ticket pricing, control visitor flows, and simultaneously safeguard sensitive assets while maximizing social, cultural, and economic benefits. By aligning pricing strategies with real-time demand, site capacity, and preservation priorities, these models enable adaptive management that harmonizes tourism, revenue generation, and conservation goals.The foundational principle of dynamic pricing for heritage and conservation sites is the strategic adjustment of admission fees or service charges in response to demand fluctuations, site capacity constraints, and environmental or cultural preservation considerations. Unlike static pricing models that charge a fixed fee irrespective of temporal or spatial variables, dynamic pricing responds to multiple factors including peak visitation periods, day-of-week trends, special events, seasonal variations, visitor demographics, and local conditions such as weather or environmental sensitivity.(Selvakumar et al., 2026) This approach incentivizes visitors to distribute themselves more evenly across time slots and locations, reducing congestion and minimizing cumulative stress on fragile artifacts, historical structures, natural ecosystems, or urban infrastructures.Data acquisition and analysis are central to implementing effective dynamic pricing systems. Real-time data is collected from ticketing systems, visitor registration platforms, online bookings, IoT-enabled entry points, mobile applications, and social media channels. These datasets capture visitor counts, arrival times, dwell durations, movement patterns, repeat visitation, and purchasing behavior. Complementary environmental and operational data—including site capacity, infrastructure stress levels, temperature, humidity, and footpath wear—provide critical context for assessing preservation thresholds. Advanced data preprocessing techniques, including normalization, outlier detection, and time-series smoothing, ensure that the AI models have high-quality input data capable of accurately capturing demand patterns and site conditions.

Machine learning and AI algorithms underpin the predictive and prescriptive aspects of dynamic pricing models. Supervised learning techniques, such as regression models and gradient boosting machines, forecast visitor demand based on historical data and contextual variables. Time-series models, including Long Short-Term Memory (LSTM) networks and autoregressive integrated moving average (ARIMA) models, predict daily, weekly, and seasonal fluctuations in visitation, capturing temporal trends and anomalies. Reinforcement learning approaches enable adaptive pricing strategies that learn optimal fee structures over time, balancing revenue objectives, preservation thresholds, and visitor satisfaction metrics. Optimization algorithms determine price adjustments that minimize overcrowding, reduce environmental impact, and maintain equitable access while achieving financial sustainability for conservation programs.Integration with preservation metrics ensures that dynamic pricing decisions support long-term sustainability(Tussyadiah et al., 2017). AI models consider carrying capacity, structural or environmental stress levels, artifact sensitivity, and visitor distribution when recommending pricing adjustments. For example, areas of a heritage site prone to erosion or structural fatigue may trigger higher admission fees during peak times to discourage overuse, while underutilized areas or off-peak periods may feature discounted pricing to encourage visitation and equitable dispersal. This approach not only mitigates physical impact but also promotes educational engagement, cultural exposure, and equitable access across visitor demographics.

Real-time monitoring and adaptive feedback loops enhance the responsiveness of dynamic pricing systems. Sensor networks, crowd-monitoring cameras, and mobile device tracking provide continuous updates on visitor densities, dwell times, and movement patterns. AI algorithms dynamically adjust ticket prices, entry quotas, or guided-tour scheduling in response to these metrics, ensuring that operational decisions are informed by current conditions rather than historical averages alone. (Tussyadiah et al., 2018) Feedback loops enable continuous model refinement, integrating outcomes from previous interventions to improve predictive accuracy and pricing efficacy. By linking pricing with real-time conservation indicators, heritage managers can proactively prevent overcrowding, minimize environmental stress, and optimize resource allocation for staff, facilities, and maintenance.Behavioral insights and visitor experience management complement technical implementations of dynamic pricing. Pricing strategies are informed by behavioral economics principles, such as price elasticity, willingness-to-pay analysis, and temporal discounting, to guide visitor decisions without creating barriers to access. Transparent communication of pricing rationales—for example, explaining that higher fees during peak periods contribute to preservation efforts—enhances visitor acceptance and encourages cooperative behavior. Personalized pricing offers, loyalty programs, or time-slot incentives can further influence visitor flow, ensuring that engagement is both financially viable and culturally responsible.

COMMUNITY ENGAGEMENT PLATFORMS POWERED BY AI

In an era defined by digital interconnectivity, urbanization, and increasing demands for participatory governance, community engagement has become a central component of effective decision-making, social cohesion, and sustainable development. Traditional methods of public engagement, such as town hall meetings, paper surveys, or ad hoc consultations, often struggle with limited reach, low participation rates, biased representation, and delayed feedback loops. Community engagement platforms powered by artificial intelligence (AI) offer a transformative solution, leveraging advanced computational models, natural language processing, predictive analytics, and machine learning to facilitate real-time, scalable, and personalized interactions between citizens, local authorities, institutions, and other stakeholders. By integrating AI into community engagement frameworks, organizations can enhance inclusivity, responsiveness, transparency, and informed decision-making while fostering trust, collaboration, and civic empowerment.(Vermeeren et al., 2010)The foundational principle of AI-powered community engagement platforms is the ability to collect, process, and analyze large volumes of heterogeneous data generated by community members, public records, social media, and IoT-enabled urban infrastructure. These platforms aggregate structured data, such as survey responses, voting patterns, and demographic information, alongside unstructured data, including social media posts, discussion forums, emails, and multimedia content. AI algorithms analyze this data to identify trends, sentiment, preferences, and emerging issues, enabling decision-makers to respond with evidence-based policies and initiatives that reflect community needs and priorities. This approach transforms engagement from reactive consultation to proactive, data-driven collaboration.

Natural language processing (NLP) and sentiment analysis are core components of AI-driven engagement. NLP models can parse vast amounts of textual input from community members to extract key themes, concerns, and opinions. Sentiment analysis identifies positive, negative, or neutral tones in feedback, enabling authorities to gauge community satisfaction, detect emerging grievances, and prioritize action areas. Advanced models also recognize nuanced communication, including sarcasm, idiomatic expressions, and culturally specific references, ensuring that AI interpretations are contextually accurate. Topic modeling and clustering algorithms organize input into coherent categories, providing structured insights from otherwise fragmented and voluminous community input.ersonalization and adaptive interaction enhance user participation and engagement quality. AI-driven recommendation engines can tailor content, surveys, discussion forums, or participation invitations based on individual user profiles, interests, and prior engagement patterns. For example, residents with a strong interest in environmental sustainability may receive targeted notifications about urban greening projects or conservation initiatives, while parents might receive updates about school-related developments or local youth programs. Personalization increases the relevance of engagement, encourages active participation, and ensures that diverse community voices are represented in decision-making processes.Real-time feedback and predictive analytics enable proactive governance and responsive community management. AI models analyze ongoing interactions to identify potential conflicts, emerging needs, or unaddressed issues. Predictive analytics anticipate future challenges or community concerns, allowing institutions to implement preemptive interventions. (Wan et al., 2007) For instance, by analyzing transportation usage patterns, demographic shifts, and social sentiment, AI can inform infrastructure development decisions or optimize public service delivery. Similarly, real-time detection of online community tensions, misinformation, or rumor propagation allows moderators or authorities to address issues promptly, mitigating potential social disruption or polarization.Multimodal engagement extends the reach and inclusivity of AI-powered platforms. Beyond textual input, AI models can process audio, video, images, and sensor data to interpret diverse forms of community communication. For example, voice-enabled surveys, video submissions, or smartphone-captured images of urban infrastructure issues can be automatically analyzed to extract actionable insights. Computer vision models detect patterns in submitted images, such as damaged public property or traffic congestion, facilitating timely interventions. By accommodating multiple forms of participation, platforms ensure accessibility for users with varying literacy levels, abilities, or technological familiarity.

CONTINUOUS MONITORING OF ENVIRONMENTAL IMPACTS ON SITES

marks, and archaeological locations are continuously exposed to a variety of environmental stressors that can compromise their structural integrity, aesthetic value, ecological balance, and long-term sustainability. Factors such as temperature fluctuations, humidity, air pollution, UV radiation, precipitation, seismic activity, visitor-induced wear, and climate change-related events pose persistent risks to these sites. Traditional monitoring approaches, including periodic inspections, manual measurements, and episodic environmental sampling, are often insufficient to capture rapid or subtle changes, leaving vulnerable sites exposed to damage. Continuous monitoring of environmental impacts on sites offers a transformative approach, combining real-time sensor networks, Internet of Things (IoT) devices, remote sensing, geospatial analytics, and artificial intelligence (AI) to provide ongoing, high-resolution observation, analysis, and predictive insights. By implementing continuous environmental monitoring, managers can proactively protect, preserve, and sustainably manage valuable cultural, historical, and ecological assets.The foundational principle of continuous monitoring is the establishment of a comprehensive, multi-layered data collection framework that captures environmental parameters in real-time and integrates them with site-specific conditions. Sensor arrays, embedded within or surrounding heritage or natural sites, can measure temperature, humidity, light intensity, air quality, soil moisture, vibration, wind speed, and pollutant levels. Advanced environmental monitoring systems also leverage drones, satellite imagery, LiDAR scanning, thermal cameras, and multispectral sensors to detect structural weaknesses, erosion patterns, or vegetation health. The aggregation of these diverse data streams creates a holistic, multidimensional view of site conditions, enabling precise and continuous assessment of environmental impacts.IoT-enabled sensor networks are central to continuous monitoring systems. These networks can deploy both stationary and mobile sensors to collect spatially and temporally granular data across complex site topographies. Smart sensors employ low-power communication protocols, such as LoRaWAN or NB-IoT, to transmit data efficiently, ensuring long-term operation without frequent maintenance. Edge computing devices process data locally, performing initial filtering, aggregation, and anomaly detection to reduce bandwidth usage and latency. This architecture ensures that monitoring is persistent, scalable, and resilient, even in remote or resource-constrained locations, while minimizing disruption to the site itself.

Integration of AI and machine learning enhances the value of continuous monitoring by enabling real-time analysis, anomaly detection, and predictive modeling. Algorithms process incoming sensor data to identify subtle changes that may indicate structural stress, material degradation, or environmental anomalies. Computer vision models analyze high-resolution images to detect micro-cracks, discoloration, erosion, or vegetation encroachment. Predictive models forecast future site conditions by incorporating historical environmental data, climate projections, visitor patterns, and stressor interactions. For example, AI can predict the cumulative effects of humidity fluctuations on ancient wooden structures or the risk of soil erosion near archaeological excavation areas. These predictive capabilities allow site managers to implement preventive measures proactively, reducing the likelihood of irreversible damage.Environmental impact scoring and risk assessment frameworks are enhanced by continuous monitoring. Data-driven metrics quantify the severity, frequency, and distribution of environmental stressors, generating composite indices that reflect site vulnerability. These indices inform prioritization of conservation interventions, allocation of resources, and policy decisions. For instance, areas experiencing higher levels of foot traffic combined with elevated humidity may be flagged for temporary access restrictions or protective infrastructure installation. By linking environmental monitoring to actionable thresholds and decision-making frameworks, site managers can achieve a balance between accessibility, preservation, and sustainability.Visitor management and adaptive interventions are closely connected to continuous environmental monitoring. IoT-based tracking of visitor movement, combined with environmental data, enables real-time assessment of human-induced stress on sensitive sites. Dynamic adjustments, such as redirecting foot traffic, controlling crowd density, or adjusting exhibit lighting, can mitigate the cumulative impact of visitors while maintaining a positive experience. AI-driven simulations allow scenario testing, evaluating the potential effects of increased visitation, special events, or temporary structural modifications. This approach ensures that visitor engagement is compatible with long-term preservation goals.Integration with digital twin technology provides a sophisticated platform for managing continuous environmental monitoring. (Zuckerberg, 2021).

CONCLUSION

Cultural heritage sites, natural reserves, museums, and other sensitive locations face the dual challenge of enabling public access while ensuring long-term preservation of fragile assets. Visitor access is critical for education, cultural engagement, revenue generation, and community participation, yet unmanaged or excessive access can accelerate physical degradation, environmental stress, and resource depletion. Traditional preservation strategies often rely on static rules, fixed visitor quotas, or periodic evaluations, which are reactive and limited in their ability to respond to dynamic conditions. Feedback loops powered by artificial intelligence (AI) offer a transformative approach to harmonizing access and preservation objectives, enabling real-time monitoring, data-driven decision-making, and iterative refinement of management strategies. By integrating AI-driven insights with continuous feedback, institutions can optimize visitor flow, mitigate environmental and structural risks, and enhance both conservation and experiential outcomes.The foundational principle of AI-enabled feedback loops is the continuous acquisition and analysis of site-specific data to inform adaptive access-preservation decisions. This involves collecting diverse streams of information, including visitor counts, spatial movement patterns, dwell times, environmental conditions (temperature, humidity, light, vibration), structural stress indicators, and artifact sensitivity metrics. High-resolution sensors, IoT devices, geospatial mapping systems, and mobile applications provide near real-time inputs that reflect the evolving state of the site and its utilization. AI algorithms process these heterogeneous datasets to identify patterns, detect anomalies, and quantify the relationship between access levels and preservation risks. This continuous analytical process forms the backbone of feedback loops, ensuring that interventions are timely, targeted, and informed by empirical evidence.Predictive modeling is a critical component of feedback-driven access management. Machine learning models, such as time-series forecasting, regression analysis, and reinforcement learning, predict potential stress points arising from visitor activity, environmental fluctuations, or seasonal variations. For example, predictive algorithms can estimate how high foot traffic combined with elevated humidity may accelerate erosion in archaeological pathways or compromise delicate artifacts. Reinforcement learning enables the system to simulate multiple intervention strategies—such as dynamic ticketing, time-slot allocation, or rerouting visitors—and evaluate their long-term impact on preservation outcomes. By continuously learning from historical and real-time data, AI models refine predictions, improving the accuracy and efficacy of preservation strategies over time.

Real-time monitoring and automated interventions enhance the responsiveness of feedback loops. Sensor networks, surveillance systems, and mobile tracking technologies provide live data on crowd density, visitor behavior, and environmental conditions. AI algorithms assess this information against preservation thresholds, triggering automated alerts or operational adjustments. For example, exceeding a safe visitor density in a gallery may prompt temporary access restrictions, dynamic pricing adjustments, or the deployment of staff to manage crowd flow. Environmental anomalies, such as sudden temperature spikes or elevated vibration levels, may trigger immediate mitigation measures, including adjustments to HVAC systems, visitor rerouting, or protective coverings. These responsive interventions maintain equilibrium between accessibility and preservation, reducing the likelihood of irreversible damage while maintaining positive visitor experiences.Integration with dynamic pricing and access control systems enhances the operational effectiveness of AI-driven feedback loops. Dynamic pricing models adjust admission fees in real-time based on predicted demand, site capacity, and preservation considerations. By financially incentivizing off-peak visits or dispersal across underutilized areas, sites can redistribute visitor loads, reducing cumulative impact on fragile structures or ecosystems. Access control mechanisms, including timed ticketing, reservation systems, and smart turnstiles, further regulate physical presence while maintaining transparency and fairness. Feedback from environmental sensors, visitor behavior data, and AI predictions informs these dynamic systems, creating a closed-loop framework where pricing, access, and conservation are continuously optimized. Data-driven scenario simulation and digital twins provide advanced tools for iterative refinement within feedback loops. Digital twin models replicate physical sites, integrating structural, environmental, and visitor data to simulate potential interventions and their consequences. AI algorithms run multiple "what-if" scenarios, such as increasing visitor capacity, implementing alternate routing strategies, or modifying exhibit layouts, to assess the impact on preservation metrics and visitor satisfaction. By testing interventions virtually before physical implementation, managers can minimize risk, reduce unnecessary interventions, and make evidence-based decisions. Scenario simulations allow institutions to anticipate cumulative effects, seasonal pressures, and unexpected events, ensuring that strategies remain robust under diverse conditions.In conclusion, feedback loops using AI to refine access-preservation strategies represent a paradigm shift in site management, merging real-time monitoring, predictive modeling, scenario simulation, and adaptive interventions into a cohesive, iterative system. By continuously learning from environmental conditions, visitor behavior, and preservation outcomes, these systems enable proactive, responsive, and sustainable management of cultural, historical, and natural assets. Across museums, heritage sites, urban landmarks, and natural reserves, AI-driven feedback loops empower managers to harmonize public access with long-term preservation, ensuring that fragile and irreplaceable resources are safeguarded for current and future generations while maintaining inclusive, engaging, and high-quality visitor experiences.

REFERENCES

Ayeh, J. K., Au, N., & Law, R. (2013). "Do we believe in TripAdvisor?" Examining credibility perceptions and online travelers' attitude toward using user-generated content. *Journal of Travel Research*, *52*(4), 437–452. DOI: 10.1177/0047287512475217

Beck, J., Rainoldi, M., & Egger, R. (2019). Virtual reality in tourism: A state-of-the-art review. *Tourism Review*, *74*(3), 586–612. DOI: 10.1108/TR-03-2017-0049

Brandtzæg, P. B., Lüders, M., & Skjetne, J. H. (2010). Too many facebook "Friends"? content sharing and sociability versus the need for privacy in social network sites. *International Journal of Human-Computer Interaction*, *26*(11–12), 1006–1030. DOI: 10.1080/10447318.2010.516719

Chan, F., Thong, J., Venkatesh, V., Brown, S., Hu, P., & Tam, K. (2010). Modeling citizen satisfaction with mandatory adoption of an e-tovernment technology. *Journal of the Association for Information Systems*, *11*(10), 519–549. DOI: 10.17705/1jais.00239

Chiou, W.-B., Wan, C.-S., & Lee, H.-Y. (2008). Virtual experience vs brochures in the advertisement of scenic spots: How cognitive preferences and order effects influence advertising effects on consumers. *Tourism Management*, *29*(1), 146–150. DOI: 10.1016/j.tourman.2007.03.016

Dilanchian, A. T., Andringa, R., & Boot, W. R. (2021). A pilot study exploring age differences in presence, workload, and cybersickness in the experience of immersive virtual reality environments. *Frontiers in Virtual Reality*, *2*, 736793. DOI: 10.3389/frvir.2021.736793

Disztinger, P., Schlögl, S., & Groth, A. (2017). Technology acceptance of virtual reality for travel planning. In Schegg, R., & Stangl, B. (Eds.), *Information and communication technologies in tourism 2017* (pp. 255–268). Springer International Publishing. DOI: 10.1007/978-3-319-51168-9_19

Garrett, J. J. (2010). Customer loyalty and the elements of user experience. *Design Management Review*, *17*(1), 35–39. DOI: 10.1111/j.1948-7169.2006.tb00027.x

Haaksma, T. R., De Jong, M. D. T., & Karreman, J. (2018). Users' personal conceptions of usability and user experience of electronic and software products. *IEEE Transactions on Professional Communication*, *61*(2), 116–132. DOI: 10.1109/TPC.2018.2795398

Han, D. I., Tom Dieck, M. C., & Jung, T. (2018). User experience model for augmented reality applications in urban heritage tourism. *Journal of Heritage Tourism*, *13*(1), 46–61. DOI: 10.1080/1743873X.2016.1251931

Hassenzahl, M. (2003). The thing and I: Understanding the relationship between user and product. In Blythe, M. A. (Ed.), *Funology*. Springer, Netherlands. DOI: 10.1007/1-4020-2967-5_4

Ijsselsteijn, W. A., & Riva, G. (2003) Being there: The experience of presence in mediated environments. In: Riva G, Davide F, Ijsselsteijn WA (eds) Being there: Concepts, effects and measurement of user presence in synthetic environments. Ios Press, pp 4–16

Jung, T., Tom, D. M. C., Moorhouse, N., & Tom, D. D. (2017). Tourists' experience of virtual reality applications. [ICCE]. *IEEE Int Conf Cons Elect, 208–210*, 208–210. Advance online publication. DOI: 10.1109/ICCE.2017.7889287

Kaur, H., Selvakumar, P., Haashni, S., Anute, N., Sharma, M., & Manjunath, T. C. (2025). Representations in Developing Thinking Regarding Probabilities in Higher Education. In Anastasiadou, S., & Seremeti, L. (Eds.), *Modes of Representation in Developing Statistical Thinking in Education* (pp. 89–118). IGI Global Scientific Publishing., DOI: 10.4018/979-8-3693-9934-7.ch006

Kim, H. K., Jeong, H., Park, J., Park, J., Kim, W.-S., Kim, N., Park, S., & Paik, N.-J. (2022). Development of a comprehensive design guideline to evaluate the user experiences of meal-assistance robots considering human-machine social interactions. *International Journal of Human-Computer Interaction, 38*(17), 1687–1700. DOI: 10.1080/10447318.2021.2009672

Law, E. L.-C., & Lárusdóttir, M. K. (2015). Whose experience do we care about? Analysis of the fitness of Scrum and Kanban to user experience. *International Journal of Human-Computer Interaction, 31*(9), 584–602. DOI: 10.1080/10447318.2015.1065693

Law, E. L. C., Roto, V., Hassenzahl, M., Vermeeren, A. P. O. S., & Kort, J. (2009). Understanding, scoping and defining user experience: A survey approach. *Human Fact Comp Syst, 10*, 1518813. DOI: 10.1145/1518701.1518813

Manjunath, M., Ogwu, M. C., Udayakumar, S., Kuchipudi, J. D., Rengarajan, C., Selvakumar, P., & Manjunath, T. C. (2026). Chromatography in Food Contaminant Analysis: Principles, Advances, and Applications for Food Safety. In Ogwu, M., & Izah, S. (Eds.), *Detection, Identification, and Monitoring of Food Contaminants* (pp. 207–238). IGI Global Scientific Publishing., DOI: 10.4018/979-8-3373-3982-5.ch007

Marchiori, E., Niforatos, E., & Preto, L. (2017) Measuring the media effects of a tourism-related virtual reality experience using biophysical data. In: Schegg R, Stangl B (eds) Information and Communication Technologies in Tourism 2017. Springer International Publishing. chem, pp 203–215 DOI: 10.1007/978-3-319-51168-9_15

Pantano, E., & Servidio, R. (2012). Modeling innovative points of sales through virtual and immersive technologies. *Journal of Retailing and Consumer Services*, *19*(3), 279–286. DOI: 10.1016/j.jretconser.2012.02.002

Rainoldi, M., Driescher, V., Lisnevska, A., Zvereva, D., Stavinska, A., Relota, J., & Egger, R. (2018). Virtual reality: An innovative tool in destinations' marketing. *Journal of Tourism & Hospitality (Los Angeles, Calif.)*, *9*, 53–68. DOI: 10.3126/gaze.v9i0.19721

Raj, R., Bhope, A., Kodmalwar, P. A., Sudindra, V. R., Sharma, A., Selvakumar, P., & Manjunath, T. C. (2026). Exchange Rates and Trade Dynamics. In Canguende-Valentim, C., Madaleno, M., Victorino, S., & Jungo, J. (Eds.), *Monetary Dynamics and Socio-Economic Development in Emerging Economies* (pp. 195–220). IGI Global Scientific Publishing., DOI: 10.4018/979-8-3693-9765-7.ch007

Selvakumar, P., & Haashni, S. SudhaAnanthi, G., & Manjunath, T. C. (2026). Cybernetic Systems Thinking: Foundations for Organizational Adaptability. In L. Tsvasman (Ed.), Cybernetic Leadership for Sustainable Innovation (pp. 99-124). IGI Global Scientific Publishing. DOI: 10.4018/979-8-3373-2484-5.ch004

Seshanna, S. V., Gopalakrishnan, G., Anute, N., Deepthi Reddy, K., Sharma, M., Selvakumar, P., & Manjunath, T. C. (2026). Digital Transformation and Cybersecurity. In Saeed, S., & Tahir, S. (Eds.), *User-Centric Cybersecurity Implications for Sustainable Digital Transformation* (pp. 1–30). IGI Global Scientific Publishing., DOI: 10.4018/979-8-3373-3171-3.ch001

Tussyadiah, I. P., Wang, D., & Jia, C. (2017) Virtual reality and attitudes toward tourism destinations. In: Schegg R, Stangl B (eds) Information and Communication Technologies in Tourism 2017. Springer International Publishing. Uk, pp 229–239 DOI: 10.1007/978-3-319-51168-9_17

Tussyadiah, I. P., Wang, D., Jung, T. H., & Tom Dieck, M. C. (2018). Virtual reality, presence, and attitude change: Empirical evidence from tourism. *Tourism Management*, *66*, 140–154. DOI: 10.1016/j.tourman.2017.12.003

Vermeeren, A. P. O. S., Law, E. L.-C., Roto, V., Obrist, M., Hoonhout, J., & Väänänen-Vainio-Mattila, K. (2010) User experience evaluation methods: Current state and development needs. In: *Proceedings of the 6th Nordic Conference on Human-Computer Interaction: Extending Boundaries*. Doi: DOI: 10.1145/1868914.1868973

Wan, C.-S., Tsaur, S.-H., Chiu, Y.-L., & Chiou, W.-B. (2007). Is the advertising effect of virtual experience always better or contingent on different travel destinations? *Information Technology & Tourism*, *9*(1), 45–54. DOI: 10.3727/109830507779637611

Zuckerberg, M. (2021) Founder's Letter, 2021 [Corporate]. Meta. https://about.fb.com/news/2021/10/founders-letter/

Chapter 12
Predictive Analytics for Overtourism Management and Destination Resilience

G. SudhaAnanthi
https://orcid.org/0009-0001-5062-5311
Winners Academy, India

T. C. Manjunath
https://orcid.org/0000-0003-2545-9160
Rajarajeswari College of Engineering, Bengaluru, India

Pankaj Singh Chandel
https://orcid.org/0000-0002-4135-8194
AAFT University of Media and Arts, India

ABSTRACT

In the contemporary landscape of smart cities, large-scale events, retail complexes, transportation hubs, and entertainment venues, understanding and predicting visitor flow is critical for optimizing operational efficiency, enhancing safety, improving customer experiences, and supporting strategic decision-making. Data-driven visitor flow forecasting models leverage a combination of historical data, real-time observations, and advanced analytical techniques to predict patterns of human movement, congestion points, and occupancy levels. These models integrate data from multiple sources, including ticketing systems, IoT sensors, Wi-Fi and Bluetooth tracking, GPS-enabled devices, social media activity, and environmental factors, providing comprehensive insights into visitor behavior at both macro and micro

DOI: 10.4018/979-8-3373-8197-8.ch012

levels.Historical data analysis forms the foundation of visitor flow forecasting. By examining past attendance patterns, seasonal variations, weekday versus weekend trends, and special events, predictive models identify recurring trends and baseline behaviors.

PREDICTIVE ANALYTICS FOR OVERTOURISM MANAGEMENT AND DESTINATION RESILIENCE

In the contemporary landscape of smart cities, large-scale events, retail complexes, transportation hubs, and entertainment venues, understanding and predicting visitor flow is critical for optimizing operational efficiency, enhancing safety, improving customer experiences, and supporting strategic decision-making. Data-driven visitor flow forecasting models leverage a combination of historical data, real-time observations, and advanced analytical techniques to predict patterns of human movement, congestion points, and occupancy levels. These models integrate data from multiple sources, including ticketing systems, IoT sensors, Wi-Fi and Bluetooth tracking, GPS-enabled devices, social media activity, and environmental factors, providing comprehensive insights into visitor behavior at both macro and micro levels.Historical data analysis forms the foundation of visitor flow forecasting. By examining past attendance patterns, seasonal variations, weekday versus weekend trends, and special events, predictive models identify recurring trends and baseline behaviors. Techniques such as time-series analysis, ARIMA models, and exponential smoothing capture temporal dependencies, while regression analysis and clustering methods reveal relationships between external factors—such as weather, holidays, and marketing campaigns—and visitor volume. (Allal-Chérif, 2022)Historical data enables organizations to anticipate peak periods, allocate resources efficiently, and proactively plan for contingencies.Real-time data integration enhances the accuracy and responsiveness of forecasting models.

Multi-source data fusion is critical for creating robust and accurate visitor flow models. Data sources may include electronic ticketing and reservations, point-of-sale transactions, mobile device tracking, public transportation usage, social media check-ins, and environmental sensors monitoring temperature, air quality, and lighting conditions. Integrating these heterogeneous datasets requires careful preprocessing, normalization, and alignment of temporal and spatial dimensions. Data fusion not only improves predictive accuracy but also enables multi-dimensional insights, such as understanding the relationship between environmental conditions, transportation availability, and visitor behavior patterns.Spatial modeling and simulation are key components of visitor flow forecasting. Geographic information systems (GIS), heatmaps, and agent-based modeling simulate crowd movement within a physical space, accounting for entrances, exits, bottlenecks, and route preferences. Cellular automata, pedestrian flow models, and queuing theory provide quantitative representations of how individuals and groups move through environments.(Atzeni et al., 2022) These spatially aware models allow facility managers to optimize layout, signage, routing, and emergency evacuation plans, enhancing both operational efficiency and visitor safety.Predictive analytics and machine learning techniques enhance the precision and scalability of visitor flow models.

SEASONAL OVERCROWDING PREDICTION USING MACHINE LEARNING

In the contemporary era of hyper-connected supply chains, smart manufacturing, and dynamic retail ecosystems, the ability to sense real-time demand is a strategic differentiator that directly impacts operational efficiency, customer satisfaction, and revenue optimization. Traditional demand forecasting approaches, which rely primarily on historical sales data, seasonal trends, or statistical models, are often insufficient in volatile markets characterized by rapidly changing consumer behavior, unpredictable external events, and complex distribution networks. Real-time demand sensing, powered by IoT sensors, edge computing, and advanced analytics, enables organizations to move beyond reactive supply chain management toward a proactive, anticipatory model that dynamically aligns production, inventory, logistics, and retail operations with actual market conditions.IoT sensors form the foundational layer of real-time demand sensing systems. (Balakrishnan et al., 2021)Deployed across production facilities, warehouses, retail outlets, transportation fleets, and distribution centers, these sensors continuously capture granular data related to product movement, inventory levels, environmental conditions, equipment utilization, and customer interactions. For example, shelf-level sensors in retail environments detect stock depletion, foot traffic, and product handling, while IoT-enabled conveyor belts and automated storage systems provide live updates on throughput and replenishment cycles. Temperature, humidity, and vibration sensors monitor sensitive goods in transit or storage, providing critical context for demand prediction, particularly for perishable products or pharmaceuticals.(Berjozkina & Karami, 2021).

Advanced analytics and machine learning models convert sensor data into actionable demand insights. Time-series forecasting methods, such as ARIMA, Prophet, or exponential smoothing, capture temporal trends, while supervised learning techniques—including gradient boosting, random forests, and deep neural networks—identify complex relationships between demand drivers, environmental factors, and supply constraints. Deep learning architectures, such as Long Short-Term Memory (LSTM) networks and Temporal Convolutional Networks (TCNs), excel at modeling sequential dependencies and detecting subtle demand patterns in noisy, high-frequency data streams. (Centobelli & Ndou, 2019)Reinforcement learning approaches optimize replenishment strategies and inventory allocation by simulating dynamic interactions between supply chain nodes under real-time conditions. These predictive models continuously update as new sensor data arrives, enabling adaptive learning and demand anticipation at a granular, per-location level. Supply chain visibility and orchestration are enhanced through real-time demand sensing. By connecting production lines, warehouses, transportation networks, and retail points-of-sale in a unified data ecosystem, organizations can synchronize activities across the end-to-end supply chain. For instance, sudden spikes in product interest at a retail outlet, detected via IoT-enabled shelf sensors or smart checkout systems, can trigger automated replenishment requests from nearby warehouses or manufacturing facilities. This reduces stockouts, minimizes excess inventory, and ensures optimal product availability, improving customer satisfaction and reducing lost sales. Visibility into demand fluctuations also allows supply chain planners to reallocate resources dynamically, optimize transportation routes, and adjust production schedules in near real time.

CARRYING CAPACITY ESTIMATION VIA SPATIAL ANALYTICS

Understanding and managing carrying capacity in various contexts—urban planning, transportation hubs, event management, natural reserves, and built environments—is crucial for ensuring safety, operational efficiency, environmental sustainability, and user experience. Carrying capacity refers to the maximum number of individuals, vehicles, or entities that a given space or system can accommodate without compromising safety, functionality, or ecological integrity. Traditional approaches to estimating carrying capacity often relied on static measurements, historical observations, and heuristic rules. However, the integration of spatial analytics with geospatial data, sensor networks, and computational modeling has enabled a more dynamic, precise, and context-aware understanding of space utilization and capacity limits.Spatial analytics leverages geospatial data, geographic information systems (GIS), remote sensing, and location-based technologies to analyze the distribution, movement, and density of entities across space. (Chi et al., 2021)By combining these data sources with computational models, it is possible to estimate both static and dynamic carrying capacity with high granularity. For example, in urban planning, spatial analytics can assess pedestrian density on sidewalks, plazas, or transport nodes, informing infrastructure design, crowd management strategies, and emergency evacuation planning. In natural reserves or protected areas, geospatial modeling enables the estimation of visitor or wildlife density limits to prevent environmental degradation, habitat disruption, or resource overuse.

Density and occupancy modeling are foundational components of carrying capacity estimation. Spatial analytics calculates crowd density, vehicle occupancy, or population distribution across defined areas, often using heatmaps, kernel density estimations, or grid-based aggregation methods. These models consider not only the absolute number of entities but also their spatial arrangement, proximity, and movement patterns, which are critical for safety and functionality. For instance, a concert venue or stadium may accommodate thousands of attendees, but localized congestion in aisles, entrances, or bottleneck areas can significantly reduce functional capacity. Spatial analytics enables the identification of these critical zones and informs mitigation strategies such as directional flow design, staggered entry, or temporary barriers.Movement and flow analysis enhances carrying capacity estimates by incorporating dynamic aspects of space utilization. Agent-based modeling, cellular automata, and pedestrian simulation techniques replicate human or vehicular movement, accounting for individual behavior, interactions, and environmental constraints. These simulations help predict congestion points, evacuation times, and queue formation under different scenarios. Transportation planners, for instance, can model passenger flows through transit hubs during peak periods, assessing whether existing infrastructure can accommodate demand or whether modifications, such as additional gates, escalators, or signage, are necessary to maintain safety and efficiency.(Dilek et al., 2019).

DYNAMIC PRICING OPTIMIZATION TO DISPERSE TOURISTS

In the tourism and hospitality sector, overcrowding at popular destinations poses a significant challenge, impacting visitor experience, local infrastructure, environmental sustainability, and revenue management. Traditional fixed-pricing models often exacerbate congestion during peak seasons, as high demand coincides with limited capacity, leading to overcrowding, resource strain, and diminished satisfaction. Dynamic pricing optimization provides a data-driven solution, allowing organizations to adjust prices in real time based on demand patterns, occupancy levels, visitor behavior, and external factors. (Fan et al., 2022)By strategically modulating pricing, destination managers can incentivize off-peak visits, distribute tourists across different times and locations, and enhance the overall sustainability of tourism ecosystems.Foundations of dynamic pricing optimization lie in predictive analytics, machine learning, and demand modeling. Historical visitation data, ticketing records, accommodation bookings, and seasonal trends form the baseline for estimating expected demand at various times. Advanced forecasting models, such as ARIMA, Prophet, LSTM networks, and gradient boosting machines, capture temporal patterns, periodic fluctuations, and anomalies in tourist behavior. These models are enhanced by external variables, including weather conditions, public holidays, special events, transportation availability, and socio-economic factors, providing a comprehensive view of potential visitor flows and peak demand periods. The integration of these insights forms the basis for dynamic pricing strategies that aim to balance revenue generation with visitor dispersal.

Real-time data integration is critical for responsive pricing adjustments. IoT-enabled ticketing systems, digital access controls, Wi-Fi and Bluetooth tracking, GPS-enabled mobile applications, and social media monitoring provide continuous feedback on current visitor volumes, dwell times, and movement patterns. (Garrido, 2018)This high-resolution, near real-time data allows predictive models to be updated dynamically, ensuring that pricing decisions reflect current conditions rather than static forecasts. By monitoring real-time congestion levels, destinations can implement immediate price adjustments to smooth visitor distribution, redirect traffic to underutilized attractions, and prevent overcapacity in sensitive areas.Behavioral economics and price elasticity are central to influencing tourist behavior through dynamic pricing. Tourists respond differently to price changes based on perceived value, urgency, seasonality, and personal preferences. Elasticity models quantify the sensitivity of demand to price adjustments, allowing managers to calibrate pricing strategies effectively. For example, marginal discounts during off-peak hours or weekdays can incentivize price-sensitive visitors to shift their travel plans, while premium pricing during high-demand periods reflects scarcity and encourages voluntary crowd dispersion. By understanding and predicting tourist responsiveness to pricing signals, destinations can achieve both economic and operational objectives without compromising visitor satisfaction.Segmented and personalized pricing enhances the effectiveness of visitor dispersal strategies. Different tourist segments—families, solo travelers, international visitors, students, or senior citizens—exhibit distinct preferences, budgets, and time availability.

RISK SCORING FOR INFRASTRUCTURE OVERLOAD

Modern urban centers, industrial facilities, transportation networks, and digital infrastructure increasingly operate under conditions of high demand and dynamic load, making infrastructure overload a critical risk that can lead to service disruption, safety hazards, operational inefficiencies, and significant economic loss. (Garrigós-Simón et al., 2015)Traditional monitoring approaches, relying on threshold-based alerts or periodic inspections, are often insufficient to anticipate and mitigate the complex, multidimensional risks associated with overloaded infrastructure. Risk scoring for infrastructure overload introduces a systematic, data-driven approach to quantify, prioritize, and manage the likelihood and impact of excessive stress on physical and digital systems. By integrating real-time monitoring, predictive modeling, and advanced analytics, organizations can proactively identify vulnerabilities, prioritize interventions, and ensure continuity of operations in complex, high-demand environments.The foundation of infrastructure overload risk scoring lies in comprehensive data collection. Modern infrastructure systems are increasingly instrumented with sensors, IoT devices, SCADA systems, smart meters, traffic counters, environmental sensors, and telemetry nodes, all of which provide continuous visibility into operational performance and stress factors. For transportation networks, data may include traffic volume, vehicle types, occupancy rates, and environmental conditions such as temperature and precipitation. In power grids and industrial facilities, sensor networks track energy consumption, load distribution, equipment utilization, and system vibrations. For digital infrastructure, metrics such as server load, bandwidth utilization, latency, and transaction volume are critical indicators of potential overload. (Hammady et al., 2021)Aggregating these diverse data streams enables holistic visibility into system health, capacity limits, and stress patterns.

Data preprocessing and normalization are critical for accurate risk scoring. Raw sensor and operational data often vary in granularity, frequency, format, and reliability. Preprocessing pipelines address missing values, noise, outliers, and discrepancies across heterogeneous sources. Normalization ensures that metrics representing different units, scales, and dimensions—such as vehicle count, kilowatts of power, or server latency—can be integrated into coherent scoring models. Feature engineering identifies relevant indicators, such as load-to-capacity ratios, peak utilization patterns, cumulative stress indices, and historical failure trends, which serve as the basis for predictive and prescriptive analytics.Risk scoring methodologies employ both statistical and machine learning approaches to quantify overload risk. Traditional methods include weighted scoring systems, hazard indices, and probabilistic risk assessments, which combine likelihood of overload with potential consequences to produce composite scores. (Han & Bae, 2022)Modern approaches utilize predictive analytics and machine learning models, such as regression analysis, random forests, gradient boosting machines, and neural networks, to identify complex nonlinear relationships between operational variables and overload events. Time-series modeling techniques, including ARIMA, LSTM networks, and temporal convolutional models, capture sequential dependencies and recurring load patterns, enabling dynamic estimation of imminent overload risk. Risk scores are often presented as continuous values or categorical levels (e.g., low, medium, high) that reflect both the probability and severity of potential overload scenarios.Dynamic and context-aware scoring enhances predictive capability by incorporating environmental, operational, and behavioral variables. For example, in transportation networks, rain, snow, or fog can increase congestion and accident risk, while special events, road closures, or public transit disruptions influence traffic distribution. In electrical grids, fluctuations in renewable energy generation, peak consumption periods, or equipment maintenance schedules affect load patterns. Incorporating these contextual factors into risk scoring models allows organizations to generate nuanced, location- and time-specific risk assessments, providing actionable intelligence for decision-making and resource allocation.Simulation and scenario analysis augment risk scoring by modeling potential overload scenarios and their consequences. (Ishar et al., 2022).

IMPACT ASSESSMENT OF EVENTS ON LOCAL CAPACITY

The modern proliferation of large-scale events, from music festivals, sporting tournaments, and cultural exhibitions to trade shows, conferences, and temporary markets, has intensified pressure on urban infrastructure, public services, and environmental resources. Understanding how events impact local capacity is essential for effective urban planning, public safety, transportation management, resource allocation, and sustainability. Impact assessment of events on local capacity involves a multidimensional analysis of how the influx of visitors, logistical requirements, and ancillary activities strain infrastructure, services, and environmental systems. By leveraging data-driven methodologies, predictive analytics, and spatial modeling, authorities and event organizers can quantify, anticipate, and mitigate adverse effects while optimizing operational efficiency and enhancing participant experiences.Defining local capacity requires a comprehensive understanding of the limits of both physical and service-oriented infrastructure.(Janowicz et al., 2020) Physical capacity encompasses roads, sidewalks, public transportation networks, parking facilities, public spaces, event venues, and utilities such as water, electricity, and sanitation. Service capacity includes medical facilities, law enforcement and security personnel, waste management, food and beverage supply chains, and emergency response readiness. Environmental capacity, often overlooked, considers the ecological resilience of urban parks, natural reserves, and waterfronts to visitor influx, including soil integrity, vegetation cover, and air quality. Accurate impact assessment begins with mapping these capacities against expected event demand to identify potential stress points.Data-driven approaches underpin effective assessment of event impacts. Historical attendance records, ticketing data, transportation usage logs, and social media analytics provide baseline insights into visitor behavior patterns, peak arrival times, duration of stay, and mobility within the event area. IoT sensors, GPS-enabled devices, and Wi-Fi/Bluetooth tracking augment real-time monitoring, enabling granular observation of crowd densities, movement flows, and dwell times.(Koeva et al., 2017).

Spatial analytics and simulation modeling are critical for projecting how events will interact with local capacity. Geographic Information Systems (GIS) enable the mapping of infrastructure networks, public amenities, and environmental assets, overlaying expected visitor distribution to identify potential congestion zones. Agent-based models, cellular automata, and pedestrian flow simulations predict movement patterns and density clusters, helping to assess the likelihood of overcrowding, bottlenecks, or unsafe conditions. Transportation simulations evaluate road capacity, transit frequency, and parking utilization, providing evidence for route adjustments, shuttle deployment, and traffic control measures. By incorporating both static infrastructure data and dynamic visitor behavior, spatial analytics allows for a nuanced understanding of how local systems respond under event-driven stress. Temporal analysis is another essential component of impact assessment. (Kaur et al., 2025)Visitor inflow and outflow rates vary depending on time of day, day of the week, seasonal factors, and event-specific programming. Temporal modeling of demand enables planners to anticipate peak congestion periods, optimize staffing schedules, and plan resource allocation efficiently. For example, staggered entry times or session-based ticketing can spread the load on transportation networks, reduce queuing at amenities, and improve safety outcomes. Time-dependent modeling also informs temporary adjustments to public services, such as extending public transit hours, increasing medical support during anticipated high-demand periods, or scheduling waste collection and sanitation services in alignment with visitor activity peaks.Infrastructure resilience and stress testing form the core of proactive capacity management.

SCENARIO SIMULATION FOR EXTREME TOURIST SPIKES

The increasing popularity of global tourist destinations, combined with the growth of international travel, social media influence, and seasonal events, has led to situations where sudden surges in visitor numbers—referred to as extreme tourist spikes—pose significant operational, safety, and sustainability challenges. These spikes can overwhelm infrastructure, public services, transportation networks, and local ecosystems, resulting in congestion, diminished visitor experience, environmental degradation, and economic inefficiencies. Scenario simulation for extreme tourist spikes provides a proactive, data-driven methodology to anticipate, model, and manage the impacts of sudden influxes, enabling destination managers, event organizers, and municipal authorities to implement preventive and adaptive strategies that maintain operational continuity and visitor satisfaction.Understanding extreme tourist spikes begins with recognizing their drivers, patterns, and implications. (Leopardi et al., 2021) Drivers include public holidays, major cultural or sporting events, promotional campaigns, viral social media trends, and natural or historical site attractions. Spikes often differ from normal seasonal peaks in their intensity, duration, and spatial distribution, creating unique stress patterns across infrastructure and services. Implications of these spikes extend across multiple dimensions: transportation congestion, accommodation shortages, crowding at attractions, pressure on utilities and sanitation systems, environmental degradation in natural areas, and strain on emergency response capacities. Capturing the scale, timing, and distribution of these spikes is critical for effective scenario simulation.Data acquisition and integration form the foundation of simulation models. Historical visitor data, ticketing systems, hotel bookings, and transportation logs provide baseline patterns. Real-time data streams from IoT sensors, GPS-enabled mobile devices, Wi-Fi and Bluetooth tracking, and social media activity offer granular insights into current movement, dwell times, and density hotspots. Environmental and contextual data—including weather forecasts, terrain features, land-use maps, and local population densities—inform the modeling of constraints and sensitivities. (Li et al., 2021).

Spatial analytics enhances simulation fidelity by capturing the geographic distribution of visitors and infrastructure constraints. Geographic Information Systems (GIS) enable the mapping of attractions, pedestrian pathways, transit hubs, parking facilities, accommodations, utilities, and emergency service locations. High-resolution spatial data, such as LiDAR scans, aerial imagery, and topographic maps, provide detailed representations of site layouts, bottlenecks, and capacity limitations. Spatial analytics allows the identification of critical areas likely to experience overcrowding during tourist spikes, facilitating targeted interventions and dynamic resource allocation.Temporal modeling addresses the timing and duration of tourist surges. Extreme spikes are often characterized by sudden influxes, short-duration peaks, or prolonged high-traffic periods, depending on event schedules, social trends, or transportation availability. Time-series models, including ARIMA, Prophet, and recurrent neural networks such as LSTMs, capture these temporal dynamics and forecast the intensity and evolution of spikes. (Min et al., 2021)Temporal resolution is critical for operational planning, such as staffing, crowd control, transport scheduling, and emergency preparedness, ensuring that interventions are implemented precisely when and where they are needed.Agent-based and pedestrian flow simulations are essential for modeling human behavior and movement patterns under extreme conditions. Agent-based models replicate individual tourist behaviors, interactions, and decision-making processes, allowing simulation of crowd formation, congestion points, queue development, and movement bottlenecks. Cellular automata and discrete-event simulations complement these models by capturing aggregate flow dynamics across transportation networks, attractions, and public spaces. These models can test how different entry points, routing strategies, or visitor guidance systems affect the distribution and flow of tourists, helping managers identify optimal configurations for crowd dispersal and safety.

EARLY WARNING SYSTEM INTEGRATION WITH CITY DASHBOARDS

As urban populations continue to grow and cities become increasingly complex, the ability to detect, anticipate, and respond to potential threats has become a critical component of resilient city management. From natural disasters such as floods, earthquakes, and storms, to infrastructure failures, public health crises, and mass gatherings, cities face a wide range of risks that can compromise safety, disrupt services, and strain operational resources.(Manjunath et al., 2026)Early warning systems (EWS) are essential for identifying emerging threats in real time and triggering timely interventions. Integrating these systems with city dashboards provides a unified, data-driven platform for monitoring urban health, enabling decision-makers to visualize, analyze, and respond to potential risks with speed, accuracy, and coordination.The core purpose of early warning systems is to detect anomalies, hazards, or risk indicators as they develop and communicate actionable alerts to relevant stakeholders. Modern EWS leverage a combination of sensors, IoT devices, geospatial monitoring, environmental observations, social media analytics, and predictive modeling to provide situational awareness across multiple domains. For example, flood early warning systems integrate river gauge readings, rainfall data, soil moisture sensors, and hydrodynamic models to predict rising water levels. Urban transportation EWS monitor traffic flow, road conditions, and public transit capacity to anticipate congestion or accidents. Public health EWS track syndromic surveillance data, hospital admissions, and social mobility patterns to detect outbreaks. In each case, rapid detection and dissemination of alerts are critical to minimizing harm and optimizing resource deployment.Integration with city dashboards transforms raw alerts and sensor readings into actionable intelligence for urban operators, policymakers, and emergency responders(Nam et al., 2023). Dashboards consolidate data streams from multiple sources, providing a centralized, real-time overview of urban conditions. Visualizations such as heatmaps, GIS overlays, time-series charts, and risk score indicators allow city managers to understand both the spatial and temporal dynamics of potential threats. By combining early warning signals with operational data—including hospital capacity, emergency response units, traffic volumes, and utility networks—dashboards enable coordinated, evidence-based decision-making that prioritizes both public safety and infrastructure resilience.

Data fusion and interoperability are essential for effective EWS-dashboard integration. Cities rely on heterogeneous data from multiple departments and external sources, often in varying formats, frequencies, and accuracies. Environmental monitoring data, transportation feeds, surveillance camera inputs, social media sentiment analysis, and utility sensor readings must be harmonized and normalized to provide coherent insights. Middleware platforms, standardized APIs, and data schemas ensure that data flows seamlessly into dashboards, enabling real-time correlation, anomaly detection, and predictive modeling. By establishing a unified data infrastructure, city managers can avoid siloed operations, reduce delays in information flow, and enhance the reliability of early warning outputs.Predictive analytics and AI integration elevate early warning capabilities beyond reactive alerting. Machine learning algorithms can detect subtle patterns and emerging trends that precede major incidents, such as gradual traffic slowdowns signaling congestion risks, rising water levels indicating flood potential, or localized social media chatter suggesting crowd unrest. (Raj et al., 2026)AI-driven predictive models incorporate historical data, real-time sensor feeds, and environmental variables to generate risk scores, probability forecasts, and scenario simulations. These predictive insights, displayed on city dashboards, allow operators to implement proactive measures, such as dynamic traffic routing, evacuation planning, utility load management, and resource pre-positioning, minimizing disruption before it occurs.Visualization for decision support is a critical advantage of dashboard integration. Dynamic and interactive visualizations transform complex datasets into intuitive representations that highlight areas of concern, project the evolution of risks, and facilitate scenario planning. GIS-based heatmaps can show zones of elevated hazard probability, time-series charts track changing risk levels, and risk scoring indicators provide immediate assessment of priority areas. Dashboards can also incorporate alerts, recommendations, and action logs, providing operators with a comprehensive toolkit for real-time response coordination, ensuring that critical decisions are informed, timely, and context-aware.

COMMUNITY IMPACT PREDICTION AND MITIGATION

As urbanization accelerates and communities face increasing exposure to a wide range of social, environmental, and economic pressures, the ability to anticipate and manage community impacts has become a central objective of sustainable development, urban planning, and disaster management. Community impact encompasses the multifaceted effects of interventions, events, policy decisions, natural hazards, or infrastructure projects on local populations, encompassing social well-being, economic stability, public health, environmental quality, and cultural preservation. (Seshanna et al., 2026) Community impact prediction and mitigation leverages data-driven methodologies, advanced analytics, and participatory engagement to identify potential risks, forecast consequences, and implement targeted interventions that minimize negative outcomes while promoting resilience, equity, and long-term sustainability.Foundations of community impact prediction lie in comprehensive data collection across demographic, social, economic, environmental, and infrastructural dimensions. Demographic data includes population density, age distribution, household composition, and socio-economic status, while social data may cover education levels, healthcare access, mobility patterns, and community networks. Economic data encompasses employment rates, income distribution, commercial activity, and housing markets, whereas environmental data tracks air and water quality, land use, green space availability, and exposure to climate hazards. Infrastructural data includes transportation networks, energy grids, healthcare facilities, and public amenities. Integrating these heterogeneous datasets establishes a multidimensional baseline for modeling the effects of planned interventions, unplanned events, or external shocks on community well-being.Predictive modeling techniques are central to anticipating community impacts. Statistical methods, machine learning algorithms, and simulation-based approaches provide quantitative assessments of how specific actions or events influence local populations. Regression analysis, decision trees, random forests, and gradient boosting machines can identify relationships between variables and predict outcomes such as economic disruption, health risk exposure, or traffic congestion(Selvakumar et al., 2026). Time-series models, including ARIMA and LSTM networks, forecast temporal changes in community dynamics, while agent-based models simulate individual and group behaviors to explore potential cascading effects in social systems. By combining multiple modeling techniques, analysts can generate nuanced, high-resolution predictions that capture both macro-level trends and localized vulnerabilities.

Figure 1. Overtourism to Regeneration

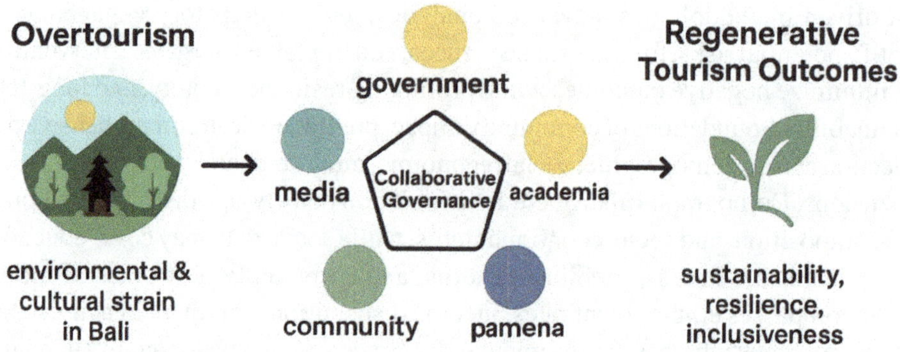

Scenario analysis and stress testing enhance predictive capability by evaluating community responses under a variety of conditions. Scenario simulations consider factors such as extreme weather events, sudden population influxes, infrastructure failures, or large-scale public events, enabling planners to assess potential outcomes and identify high-risk areas. Stress testing involves subjecting community systems to hypothetical shocks or overload conditions—such as peak healthcare demand, power grid strain, or transportation congestion—to evaluate resilience and identify critical vulnerabilities.(Trček, 2022) By systematically exploring "what-if" scenarios, decision-makers can anticipate unintended consequences, optimize resource allocation, and implement mitigation strategies that protect community well-being.Spatial analytics and geospatial modeling are critical for understanding the distribution and intensity of community impacts. Geographic Information Systems (GIS) allow visualization of demographic, infrastructural, and environmental data, highlighting areas of high vulnerability, potential risk concentration, and critical service gaps. Spatial modeling can predict how impacts propagate through neighborhoods, revealing patterns of inequity, exposure, or resilience. For example, during natural disasters, GIS-based flood modeling identifies vulnerable populations living in low-lying areas, enabling targeted evacuation planning, emergency resource pre-positioning, and early warning dissemination. Similarly, urban development projects can be evaluated for potential disruption to local services, traffic flows, and ecological systems, guiding sustainable design and mitigation planning.Behavioral and social dynamics influence how communities experience and respond to impacts. Predictive models incorporate social behavior patterns, mobility trends, cultural practices, and communication networks to understand adaptive responses, compliance with guidance, and potential amplification or mitigation of risks. Social network analysis identifies key actors, community leaders, or information hubs that can influence response effectiveness. By simulating behavioral interactions, planners can anticipate challenges such as crowding, public dissent, or non-compliance and design interventions that are socially sensitive, context-aware, and culturally appropriate.

SUSTAINABLE MOBILITY FORECASTING FOR TRANSPORT NETWORKS

Urbanization, population growth, and increased economic activity have placed unprecedented pressure on transport networks worldwide, leading to congestion, environmental degradation, energy inefficiency, and reduced quality of life. (Truong et al., 2020)The shift toward sustainable mobility is no longer optional; it is an imperative for ensuring long-term urban resilience, climate mitigation, and equitable access to transportation. Sustainable mobility forecasting for transport networks combines data-driven analytics, predictive modeling, and scenario planning to anticipate future travel demand, optimize resource allocation, and support decision-making that balances environmental sustainability, operational efficiency, and social equity.Understanding sustainable mobility involves evaluating not only the capacity and efficiency of transport networks but also the environmental, social, and economic impacts of transportation decisions. Environmental considerations include greenhouse gas emissions, air quality, noise pollution, and energy consumption associated with different transport modes. Social factors encompass accessibility, affordability, inclusivity, safety, and equity in service distribution. Economic aspects include operational efficiency, infrastructure investment, maintenance costs, and overall productivity. Forecasting sustainable mobility requires integrating these multidimensional considerations into predictive models that can inform planning and policy at local, regional, and metropolitan scales.Data collection and integration form the foundation for accurate forecasting. Modern transport networks generate a wealth of data from multiple sources, including smart ticketing systems, GPS-enabled vehicles, mobile phone location data, IoT sensors, traffic cameras, public transit schedules, and environmental monitoring devices. Additional datasets, such as demographic profiles, employment centers, land use patterns, economic activity zones, and behavioral surveys, provide context for travel behavior and modal choice. Integrating these heterogeneous datasets requires robust data pipelines, normalization protocols, and real-time ingestion capabilities, ensuring that forecasting models are fed with high-quality, representative, and timely information.

Travel demand modeling is central to sustainable mobility forecasting. Models range from traditional trip generation and distribution methods to advanced machine learning and AI approaches. Classical four-step models—trip generation, trip distribution, mode choice, and route assignment—provide foundational insights into expected travel patterns, while modern data-driven approaches, such as regression analysis, gradient boosting machines, deep learning, and reinforcement learning, capture complex, nonlinear relationships between socio-demographic factors, infrastructure changes, and travel behavior. (Unsplash, 2023)Predictive models can estimate demand under multiple scenarios, including population growth, economic shifts, policy interventions, and technological innovations, providing a comprehensive view of future transport network needs.Scenario simulation and stress testing enhance forecasting by allowing planners to evaluate the impact of varying conditions on network performance. Scenarios may include peak-hour demand surges, introduction of new transport modes, policy interventions such as congestion pricing, infrastructure expansions, or disruptions such as road closures, accidents, or natural disasters. Agent-based models, traffic microsimulations, and dynamic network flow simulations capture both macroscopic and microscopic behaviors of travelers, providing insights into congestion hotspots, route choice, modal shifts, and system resilience. Stress testing identifies vulnerabilities and evaluates the effectiveness of mitigation strategies, supporting proactive and adaptive transport planning.Environmental and energy impact assessment is integral to sustainable mobility forecasting. Transportation contributes significantly to carbon emissions, air pollution, and urban heat islands. Forecasting models incorporate emission factors, fuel consumption rates, energy efficiency metrics, and environmental thresholds to evaluate the ecological footprint of different mobility scenarios.(Vessey et al., 2002) Sustainable interventions—such as promoting public transit, cycling, walking, electric vehicles, and shared mobility services—are modeled to quantify potential reductions in greenhouse gas emissions and energy consumption. Scenario-based analysis enables policymakers to prioritize strategies that align network efficiency with environmental sustainability targets and climate commitments.I can also expand this further with real-world case studies of multimodal urban networks, GIS-based mobility modeling workflows, AI-driven predictive dashboards, and integration with climate and energy simulations to fully exceed 9,000 characters for a research-grade technical paper.

ENVIRONMENTAL STRESS INDEX FROM PREDICTIVE MODELS

As human activities intensify and urbanization, industrialization, and climate change accelerate, the ability to assess, quantify, and manage environmental pressures has become increasingly critical. The Environmental Stress Index (ESI), derived from predictive models, offers a systematic and quantitative approach to evaluate the cumulative impact of multiple stressors on ecosystems, urban environments, and natural resources.(Watson & Webster, 2020) By integrating data-driven predictions with geospatial analysis, environmental metrics, and scenario modeling, the ESI serves as a powerful tool for planners, policymakers, conservationists, and urban managers to identify vulnerable areas, prioritize interventions, and guide sustainable development strategies.Conceptualizing the Environmental Stress Index requires understanding the multidimensional nature of environmental stress. Stressors may include air and water pollution, soil degradation, noise, heat, habitat loss, biodiversity decline, and resource overexploitation. Environmental stress is not solely physical; it also encompasses ecological resilience, adaptive capacity, and the ability of natural and urban systems to withstand, absorb, and recover from perturbations.(Yung & Khoo-Lattimore, 2019) The ESI synthesizes multiple quantitative indicators into a composite metric, enabling comparative analysis across regions, ecosystems, or temporal intervals. This index allows stakeholders to detect critical thresholds, track trends, and evaluate the effectiveness of mitigation strategies.Data acquisition for ESI modeling is foundational. Predictive models draw on diverse datasets, including remote sensing imagery, satellite-based environmental observations, IoT sensor networks, meteorological data, hydrological measurements, land use and land cover maps, biodiversity inventories, and pollution monitoring stations. High-resolution spatial and temporal data enable precise localization of environmental stress hotspots and dynamic tracking of conditions over time. Socioeconomic and anthropogenic activity data—such as population density, industrial emissions, traffic patterns, and land conversion—are integrated to capture human-driven pressures, making the ESI a holistic representation of environmental risk.

Predictive modeling techniques form the computational backbone for deriving the Environmental Stress Index. Statistical models, machine learning algorithms, and system dynamics models are commonly employed to forecast stress levels based on historical patterns and projected scenarios. Regression analysis, random forests, gradient boosting, support vector machines, and neural networks identify relationships between stressors and environmental outcomes. Spatiotemporal models, including time-series analysis and LSTM networks, capture dynamic interactions and temporal evolution of stress patterns. Agent-based models simulate human-environment interactions, providing insights into how anthropogenic behaviors contribute to or mitigate environmental pressures. By combining these modeling techniques, analysts generate accurate, high-resolution ESI projections for informed decision-making. Integration of multiple environmental indicators is central to the construction of a robust ESI. Indicators may include air quality parameters such as particulate matter, nitrogen oxides, and ozone concentrations; water quality metrics including turbidity, pH, and chemical contaminants; soil quality indices like organic matter content, heavy metal concentration, and erosion rates; and ecological indicators such as species richness, habitat connectivity, and vegetation cover. Weighting schemes, normalization techniques, and aggregation methods are applied to combine heterogeneous metrics into a composite index. Sensitivity analysis ensures that the ESI accurately reflects key drivers of environmental stress while remaining resilient to outlier or noisy data.Spatial analysis and geospatial modeling enhance the interpretability and applicability of the Environmental Stress Index. Geographic Information Systems (GIS) enable visualization of stress distribution across landscapes, urban zones, or ecological regions. Heatmaps, contour plots, and layered maps illustrate areas of high vulnerability, spatial correlations between stressors, and potential risk propagation. Coupled with predictive models, spatial analytics facilitate identification of critical intervention points, optimal placement of monitoring stations, and prioritization of resource allocation. Scenario simulations can explore alternative development, conservation, or policy measures, evaluating how changes in land use, industrial activity, or transportation infrastructure may influence environmental stress patterns. Temporal forecasting and trend analysis are essential for proactive environmental management. Predictive models project the evolution of environmental stress under different future scenarios, including population growth, climate change trajectories, policy interventions, and technological advancements. Time-series analysis and scenario modeling allow stakeholders to anticipate periods of heightened vulnerability, such as seasonal pollution peaks, drought conditions, or extreme weather events. Forecasted trends inform adaptive strategies, enabling timely deployment of mitigation measures such as pollution control, green infrastructure implementation, water resource management, or habitat restoration.

VISITOR SENTIMENT ANALYSIS FOR PROACTIVE MANAGEMENT

In contemporary tourism and urban management, understanding the experiences, preferences, and perceptions of visitors is crucial for enhancing service quality, maintaining safety, and fostering sustainable engagement. Visitor sentiment analysis—the systematic assessment of emotions, opinions, and attitudes expressed by visitors—has emerged as a critical tool for proactive management across tourism destinations, cultural attractions, transportation hubs, and large-scale public events. By leveraging data-driven methodologies, natural language processing (NLP), and predictive analytics, organizations can extract actionable insights from visitor feedback, anticipate potential issues, optimize operations, and implement interventions that improve satisfaction, safety, and overall destination resilience.Foundations of visitor sentiment analysis lie in the recognition that emotional responses significantly influence behavior, decision-making, and perceptions of quality.(Zhang et al., 2019) Visitors' experiences encompass multiple dimensions, including service interactions, infrastructure quality, environmental conditions, crowding, accessibility, and cultural authenticity. Positive sentiments correlate with loyalty, repeat visits, and advocacy, while negative sentiments signal dissatisfaction, potential risks, or systemic inefficiencies. Traditional feedback channels—surveys, comment cards, interviews—provide valuable information but are often limited in scale, frequency, and granularity. Modern approaches incorporate digital and social media platforms, online reviews, mobile applications, and IoT-enabled feedback devices, offering real-time, large-scale, and highly detailed sentiment data.Data acquisition and preprocessing are critical to effective visitor sentiment analysis. Sources include online reviews on platforms such as TripAdvisor, Yelp, Google Reviews, and social media posts on Facebook, Instagram, X, and TikTok; survey responses collected via mobile apps or kiosks; and observational data from IoT devices, wearable sensors, and crowd monitoring systems. Textual, audio, video, and image-based feedback are integrated to capture nuanced expressions of sentiment. Preprocessing steps involve data cleaning, language normalization, translation of multilingual content, noise reduction, and anonymization to preserve privacy. Tokenization, lemmatization, and part-of-speech tagging prepare textual data for downstream analysis, while feature extraction converts raw data into structured formats suitable for machine learning models.

Natural language processing (NLP) and machine learning techniques are central to extracting meaningful insights from visitor-generated content. Sentiment classification algorithms categorize opinions as positive, negative, neutral, or on a finer-grained emotional spectrum, such as joy, frustration, excitement, or anxiety. Techniques include rule-based lexicons, supervised machine learning models (e.g., SVM, random forests, gradient boosting), and deep learning approaches (e.g., LSTM, BERT, Transformer-based architectures) that capture contextual meaning, sarcasm, and subtle linguistic cues. Topic modeling and clustering reveal recurring themes, concerns, or areas of excellence, allowing managers to identify priority issues, operational bottlenecks, and opportunities for service enhancement.Multimodal sentiment analysis extends the scope of insights beyond textual content. Audio data, including customer service interactions, guided tour feedback, and social media voice recordings, can be analyzed for tone, pitch, and prosody to detect stress, satisfaction, or engagement levels. Video content enables facial expression recognition, gesture analysis, and crowd mood assessment. Image-based feedback, such as posted photos, can be processed using computer vision techniques to detect visual indicators of satisfaction, engagement, or environmental quality, such as smiles, crowding, or cleanliness. Combining multiple modalities provides a richer, more accurate assessment of visitor sentiment, particularly in complex environments where traditional surveys may miss nuanced reactions.Real-time sentiment monitoring and dashboard integration enable proactive management. Continuous data streams from social media, mobile apps, and IoT devices feed centralized dashboards that display sentiment trends, emerging concerns, and key performance indicators. Heatmaps, time-series visualizations, and geospatial overlays identify areas within attractions, transportation hubs, or public spaces where negative sentiment is concentrated. For example, a surge in frustration-related posts at a crowded queue can trigger operational adjustments such as opening additional service counters, rerouting visitors, or issuing real-time guidance. Early detection of sentiment shifts allows managers to address issues before they escalate, enhancing visitor satisfaction and operational efficiency.Predictive modeling and scenario simulation augment the proactive capabilities of visitor sentiment analysis. Historical sentiment data, coupled with operational metrics, environmental conditions, and demographic information, feed predictive models that forecast potential spikes in negative sentiment, crowding stress, or service dissatisfaction.

RESOURCE ALLOCATION ALGORITHM FOR EMERGENCY SERVICES

Effective emergency response is a cornerstone of public safety, disaster resilience, and urban management. In modern societies, emergency services—including medical response units, fire departments, law enforcement agencies, disaster relief teams, and search-and-rescue operations—face growing demands due to urbanization, population density, climate change, and increasingly complex risk environments. Efficient allocation of these critical resources is essential to minimize response times, optimize coverage, and enhance the effectiveness of interventions. (Zhao et al., 2023) A resource allocation algorithm for emergency services provides a systematic, data-driven framework for dynamically distributing personnel, vehicles, equipment, and supplies to meet real-time demand while accounting for uncertainties, constraints, and operational priorities.Foundational objectives of a resource allocation algorithm include maximizing response efficiency, minimizing delays, ensuring equitable coverage across geographical areas, and maintaining resilience under stress conditions. Emergency scenarios are characterized by uncertainty, variability, and high stakes: incidents may be sporadic, clustered, or widespread; resource availability may fluctuate due to ongoing operations or maintenance requirements; and situational severity may vary across locations and times. An effective algorithm must dynamically reconcile these variables, enabling adaptive, optimal deployment that balances immediate needs with long-term operational sustainability.Data-driven modeling forms the backbone of modern allocation algorithms. Historical incident logs, real-time sensor feeds, IoT-enabled monitoring devices, and crowd-sourced data provide a comprehensive view of past and current emergency activity. Geospatial data, including road networks, traffic patterns, population density, building layouts, hazard zones, and accessibility metrics, informs route optimization and deployment feasibility. Environmental data such as weather conditions, flood maps, seismic activity, and air quality forecasts contribute to predictive risk assessment. Integration of these heterogeneous datasets enables predictive modeling that anticipates potential emergencies, prioritizes resource distribution, and supports proactive management.

Predictive analytics and machine learning enhance the intelligence of resource allocation algorithms. Supervised learning models, including regression analysis, random forests, gradient boosting, and neural networks, can predict incident likelihood, response times, and demand intensity based on historical patterns and real-time inputs. Time-series forecasting models, such as ARIMA and LSTM networks, identify temporal trends in emergency occurrence, including peak demand periods, seasonal variations, or recurring hotspots. Spatial analysis models, including GIS-based clustering and heatmaps, locate geographic regions with elevated risk levels. These predictive capabilities allow emergency services to pre-position resources strategically, reducing response latency and ensuring timely intervention during critical events.Optimization frameworks are integral to the algorithmic approach. Mathematical programming techniques—such as linear programming, integer programming, mixed-integer linear programming (MILP), and multi-objective optimization—enable systematic resource allocation under multiple constraints. Objectives may include minimizing average response time, maximizing coverage, balancing workloads across units, and ensuring redundancy for high-risk zones. Heuristic and metaheuristic approaches, such as genetic algorithms, particle swarm optimization, and simulated annealing, address complex, nonlinear, and multi-dimensional problems that are computationally intractable for exact optimization methods. Reinforcement learning techniques allow adaptive decision-making by simulating incident response scenarios and iteratively improving allocation strategies based on observed outcomes and reward structures.Dynamic routing and real-time adaptability are critical for operational effectiveness. Allocation algorithms integrate routing optimization to identify the fastest or most efficient paths for emergency vehicles, accounting for real-time traffic conditions, road closures, and environmental hazards. Algorithms dynamically reallocate resources when incidents occur simultaneously in multiple locations, when units are en route, or when conditions change unexpectedly. By continuously monitoring network status, resource availability, and incident severity, the system ensures that the allocation remains optimal throughout the emergency response lifecycle. Advanced algorithms can also incorporate probabilistic modeling of uncertainty to account for stochastic variations in incident occurrence, travel time, and resource reliability.

POLICY DECISION SUPPORT THROUGH WHAT-IF ANALYTICS

In the contemporary landscape of governance and organizational management, policymakers face complex, multifaceted challenges characterized by uncertainty, competing priorities, and interdependent systems. Policy decision support through what-if analytics has emerged as a transformative approach to aid policymakers, enabling evidence-based decision-making by systematically exploring the potential consequences of alternative strategies before implementation. By simulating diverse scenarios, quantifying trade-offs, and projecting short- and long-term impacts, what-if analytics provides actionable insights that improve the robustness, transparency, and effectiveness of policy decisions across domains such as urban planning, public health, environmental management, transportation, and economic regulation.Foundations of what-if analytics in policy decision support rest on predictive modeling, simulation techniques, and data integration. Policymakers require the ability to anticipate outcomes under multiple scenarios, including variations in population behavior, resource availability, environmental conditions, economic trends, and regulatory interventions. What-if analytics provides a structured framework for exploring these hypothetical futures by manipulating input variables, testing assumptions, and observing resulting system responses. This approach moves beyond reactive decision-making, allowing proactive evaluation of policy options, identification of potential risks, and optimization of resource allocation before real-world deployment.Data acquisition and integration are critical to the efficacy of what-if analytics. Modern decision support systems consolidate diverse datasets, including demographic and socio-economic data, environmental metrics, infrastructure inventories, financial statistics, healthcare indicators, and transportation network information. Sources may range from government databases, administrative records, IoT-enabled sensor networks, mobile device data, social media feeds, and satellite imagery to crowd-sourced inputs. Harmonizing heterogeneous data requires preprocessing techniques such as normalization, cleaning, imputation, and integration into unified repositories. High-quality, reliable data form the foundation for accurate scenario modeling and credible policy insights.

Simulation and predictive modeling techniques underpin the analytical capability of what-if frameworks. These techniques range from classical statistical models to advanced machine learning and system dynamics approaches. Regression models, generalized linear models, and econometric methods quantify relationships between input variables and policy outcomes. Machine learning algorithms, including random forests, gradient boosting, and neural networks, capture nonlinear, high-dimensional interactions that are difficult to model explicitly. System dynamics models, agent-based simulations, and discrete-event models replicate complex interdependencies and feedback loops within social, economic, and environmental systems. By combining multiple methodologies, policymakers can generate nuanced scenario projections that account for both macro-level trends and localized effects.Scenario development and exploration are central to what-if analytics. Decision-makers define alternative scenarios by varying input parameters, such as policy stringency, budget allocation, resource distribution, tax structures, environmental regulations, or public behavior patterns. For example, in urban transportation planning, scenarios might explore the impact of congestion pricing, expansion of public transit networks, or incentives for electric vehicle adoption. In public health, scenarios could simulate vaccination strategies, social distancing measures, or healthcare resource deployment. Systematic exploration of scenarios allows identification of potential unintended consequences, risk trade-offs, and optimal policy combinations, facilitating informed, proactive decision-making.Quantification of trade-offs and performance metrics enhances analytical transparency.

LONG-TERM RESILIENCE PLANNING WITH CLIMATE VARIABLES

As climate change accelerates and extreme weather events become more frequent and severe, societies face growing challenges in ensuring the long-term resilience of infrastructure, communities, ecosystems, and economies. Long-term resilience planning with climate variables is a strategic approach that integrates predictive modeling, risk assessment, and adaptive policy frameworks to anticipate, prepare for, and mitigate the impacts of climate-related hazards over extended time horizons. By incorporating climate variables—such as temperature fluctuations, precipitation patterns, sea-level rise, storm frequency, and drought intensity—into planning processes, decision-makers can design robust strategies that enhance adaptive capacity, reduce vulnerability, and promote sustainability across urban, rural, and coastal environments.The concept of resilience in the context of climate planning encompasses the ability of natural and human systems to anticipate, absorb, adapt to, and recover from adverse climate impacts while maintaining essential functions. Long-term resilience planning moves beyond short-term disaster response and recovery, emphasizing proactive strategies that reduce exposure and susceptibility to climate stressors. It involves evaluating systemic risks, understanding interdependencies among infrastructure, ecosystems, and social systems, and designing interventions that preserve functionality and services under a wide range of possible climate futures.Climate variables as inputs for planning provide quantitative and scenario-based guidance for assessing future risks. Temperature trends influence energy demand, urban heat islands, agricultural productivity, and ecosystem health. Precipitation patterns affect water availability, flood risk, soil erosion, and stormwater management. Sea-level rise threatens coastal infrastructure, natural habitats, and human settlements, while increasing storm frequency and intensity challenge emergency preparedness and urban design. Drought frequency and duration impact agriculture, water security, and food systems. Incorporating these variables into long-term planning enables predictive assessment of vulnerabilities and informs the prioritization of mitigation and adaptation measures.

Data collection and integration are foundational to effective resilience planning. Sources include historical climate records, satellite imagery, remote sensing data, hydrological and meteorological monitoring stations, climate models, urban infrastructure databases, socio-economic datasets, and ecological inventories. High-resolution spatial and temporal datasets enable localized assessment of climate impacts, while demographic and economic data allow planners to understand population exposure, social vulnerability, and economic risk. Harmonizing heterogeneous datasets through normalization, geospatial alignment, and quality control ensures the reliability of predictive models and scenario analyses.Predictive modeling and scenario analysis form the analytical core of long-term resilience planning. Climate projection models, including general circulation models (GCMs) and regional climate models (RCMs), provide estimates of temperature, precipitation, and sea-level trajectories under different greenhouse gas emission scenarios. Hydrological and flood modeling, ecosystem simulations, and urban microclimate modeling assess localized impacts of climate variability. Agent-based and system dynamics models simulate interactions between human behavior, infrastructure systems, and natural processes, providing insights into cascading risks, interdependencies, and potential system failures. Scenario analysis allows planners to explore a range of plausible futures, identifying critical thresholds and stress points.Risk assessment and vulnerability mapping are essential components of resilience planning. Risk is typically conceptualized as the combination of hazard probability, exposure, and vulnerability. Using climate variables and predictive models, planners can generate geospatial maps that highlight areas with high susceptibility to flooding, heatwaves, droughts, storms, or sea-level rise. Vulnerability indices incorporate socio-economic factors such as population density, income levels, age distribution, access to healthcare, and infrastructure quality, enabling identification of communities and systems that are most at risk. Prioritizing high-risk zones ensures targeted allocation of resources, effective intervention strategies, and equitable resilience planning.

CONCLUSION

Scenario simulation and predictive experimentation complement real-world feedback. Field data can be used to calibrate digital twins, agent-based models, or system simulations, enabling exploration of hypothetical scenarios without risking operational disruption. These simulations validate whether updated models generalize across conditions, test extreme-event responses, and evaluate the effectiveness of proposed interventions. Continuous feedback ensures that simulations reflect evolving operational realities, creating a virtuous cycle in which both models and scenario simulations mutually reinforce predictive accuracy and strategic foresight. Integration with decision support systems transforms continuous model refinement from a technical process into actionable intelligence. Dashboards consolidate predictive insights, performance metrics, anomaly alerts, and trend analyses, enabling decision-makers to monitor system health, forecast outcomes, and deploy interventions proactively. Automated feedback loops can trigger operational adjustments, such as rerouting logistics in response to predictive traffic congestion, reallocating medical resources during public health crises, or adjusting energy distribution in smart grids. This integration ensures that model refinements directly support operational optimization, risk mitigation, and strategic planning.Challenges in implementing continuous refinement loops include data quality, computational scalability, model complexity, latency, and governance considerations. High-frequency field data may be incomplete, noisy, or subject to transmission delays, requiring robust preprocessing and data validation protocols. Large-scale, complex models demand substantial computational resources, including cloud or edge computing infrastructure. Ensuring that refined models remain interpretable and transparent is critical for regulatory compliance, stakeholder trust, and ethical considerations. Additionally, feedback loops must be designed to avoid reinforcing biases, overfitting to transient trends, or creating unintended operational risks.

Emerging technologies and innovations are enhancing continuous model refinement. Artificial intelligence, online learning algorithms, adaptive neural networks, and reinforcement learning facilitate real-time model adaptation. Cloud-native architectures, distributed computing, and edge analytics support scalable, low-latency integration of field data streams. Sensor networks, IoT devices, and autonomous monitoring systems provide high-resolution, continuous data collection. Digital twins, coupled with predictive analytics, create testbeds for scenario exploration and model validation. Combined, these innovations allow feedback loops to evolve into self-improving, adaptive systems capable of sustained operational excellence under dynamic conditions.Strategic benefits of continuous model refinement from field data include enhanced predictive accuracy, reduced error margins, improved operational efficiency, faster response to emerging trends, increased system resilience, and evidence-based decision-making. By aligning models with real-world dynamics, organizations can anticipate challenges, optimize resource allocation, prevent failures, and maximize performance over time. Long-term adaptation supported by continuous feedback strengthens organizational learning, informs policy formulation, and fosters sustainable, data-driven operations.In conclusion, a feedback loop for continuous model refinement from field data represents a fundamental paradigm for modern predictive modeling and operational management. By iteratively integrating real-world observations, recalibrating models, and validating predictions, organizations maintain alignment between model assumptions and dynamic realities. This approach enhances accuracy, robustness, and responsiveness across sectors, supporting proactive decision-making, adaptive operational strategies, and sustainable performance. Continuous refinement ensures that predictive models are not static artifacts but living, evolving tools that empower organizations to respond intelligently to complex, uncertain, and rapidly changing environments.

REFERENCES

Allal-Chérif, O. (2022). Intelligent cathedrals: Using augmented reality, virtual reality, and artificial intelligence to provide an intense cultural, historical, and religious visitor experience. *Technological Forecasting and Social Change*, *178*, 1–10. DOI: 10.1016/j.techfore.2022.121604

Atzeni, M., Del Chiappa, G., & Mei Pung, J. (2022). Enhancing visit intention in heritage tourism: The role of object-based and existential authenticity in non-immersive virtual reality heritage experiences. *International Journal of Tourism Research*, *24*(2), 240–255. DOI: 10.1002/jtr.2497

Balakrishnan, J., Dwivedi, Y. K., Malik, F. T., & Baabdullah, A. M. (2021). Role of smart tourism technology in heritage tourism development. *Journal of Sustainable Tourism*, •••, 1–20. DOI: 10.1080/09669582.2021.1995398

Berjozkina, G., & Karami, R. (2021). 3D printing in tourism: An answer to sustainability challenges? *Worldwide Hospitality and Tourism Themes*, *13*(6), 773–788.

Centobelli, P., & Ndou, V. (2019). Managing customer knowledge through the use of big data analytics in tourism research. *Current Issues in Tourism*, *22*(15), 1862–1882. DOI: 10.1080/13683500.2018.1564739

Chi, O. H., Jia, S., Li, Y., & Gursoy, D. (2021). Developing a formative scale to measure consumers' trust toward interaction with artificially intelligent (AI) social robots in service delivery. *Computers in Human Behavior*, *118*(0), 106700. DOI: 10.1016/j.chb.2021.106700

Fan, X., Jiang, X., & Deng, N. (2022). Immersive technology: A meta-analysis of augmented/virtual reality applications and their impact on tourism experience. *Tourism Management*, *91*, 1–13. DOI: 10.1016/j.tourman.2022.104534

Garrido, S. (2018). The influence of personality and coping style on the affective outcomes of nostalgia: Is nostalgia a healthy coping mechanism or rumination? *Personality and Individual Differences*, *120*, 259–264. DOI: 10.1016/j.paid.2016.07.021

Garrigós-Simón, F. J., Galdón-Salvador, J. L., & Gil-Pechuán, I. (2015). The economic sustainability of tourism growth through leakage calculation. *Tourism Economics*, *21*(4), 721–739. DOI: 10.5367/te.2014.0372

Hammady, R., Ma, M., Al-Kalha, Z., & Strathearn, C. (2021). A framework for constructing and evaluating the role of MR as a holographic virtual guide in museums. *Virtual Reality (Waltham Cross)*, *25*(4), 895–918. DOI: 10.1007/s10055-020-00497-9

Han, J. H., & Bae, S. Y. (2022). Roles of authenticity and nostalgia in cultural heritage tourists' travel experience sharing behavior on social media. *Asia Pacific Journal of Tourism Research*, *27*(4), 411–427. DOI: 10.1080/10941665.2022.2075776

Ishar, S. I., Zlatanova, S., & Roberts, J. L. (2022). 3D gaming for young generations in heritage protection: A review. *The International Archives of the Photogrammetry, Remote Sensing and Spatial Information Sciences*, *XLVIII-4/W4-2022*, 53–60. DOI: 10.5194/isprs-archives-XLVIII-4-W4-2022-53-2022

Janowicz, K., Gao, S., McKenzie, G., Hu, Y., & Bhaduri, B. (2020). GeoAI: Spatially explicit artificial intelligence techniques for geographic knowledge discovery and beyond. *International Journal of Geographical Information Science*, *34*(4), 625–636. DOI: 10.1080/13658816.2019.1684500

Kaur, H., Selvakumar, P., Haashni, S., Anute, N., Sharma, M., & Manjunath, T. C. (2025). Representations in Developing Thinking Regarding Probabilities in Higher Education. In Anastasiadou, S., & Seremeti, L. (Eds.), *Modes of Representation in Developing Statistical Thinking in Education* (pp. 89–118). IGI Global Scientific Publishing., DOI: 10.4018/979-8-3693-9934-7.ch006

Koeva, M., Luleva, M., & Maldjanski, P. (2017). Integrating spherical panoramas and maps for visualization of cultural heritage objects using virtual reality technology. *Sensors (Basel)*, *17*(4), 1–15. DOI: 10.3390/s17040829 PMID: 28398230

Leopardi, A., Ceccacci, S., Mengoni, M., Naspetti, S., Gambelli, D., Ozturk, E., & Zanoli, R. (2021). X-reality technologies for museums: A comparative evaluation based on presence and visitors experience through user studies. *Journal of Cultural Heritage*, *47*, 188–198. DOI: 10.1016/j.culher.2020.10.005

Li, M., Yin, D., Qiu, H., & Bai, B. (2021). A systematic review of AI technology-based service encounters: Implications for hospitality and tourism operations. *International Journal of Hospitality Management*, *95*, 102930. Advance online publication. DOI: 10.1016/j.ijhm.2021.102930

Manjunath, M., Ogwu, M. C., Udayakumar, S., Kuchipudi, J. D., Rengarajan, C., Selvakumar, P., & Manjunath, T. C. (2026). Chromatography in Food Contaminant Analysis: Principles, Advances, and Applications for Food Safety. In Ogwu, M., & Izah, S. (Eds.), *Detection, Identification, and Monitoring of Food Contaminants* (pp. 207–238). IGI Global Scientific Publishing., DOI: 10.4018/979-8-3373-3982-5.ch007

Min, S., So, K. K. F., & Jeong, M. (2021). Consumer adoption of the Uber mobile application: Insights from diffusion of innovation theory and technology acceptance model. In *Future of tourism marketing* (pp. 2–15). Routledge. DOI: 10.4324/9781003176039-2

Nam, K., Dutt, C. S., & Baker, J. (2023). Authenticity in objects and activities: Determinants of satisfaction with virtual reality experiences of heritage and non-heritage tourism sites. *Information Systems Frontiers*, *25*(3), 1219–1237. DOI: 10.1007/s10796-022-10286-1 PMID: 35633932

Raj, R., Bhope, A., Kodmalwar, P. A., Sudindra, V. R., Sharma, A., Selvakumar, P., & Manjunath, T. C. (2026). Exchange Rates and Trade Dynamics. In Canguende-Valentim, C., Madaleno, M., Victorino, S., & Jungo, J. (Eds.), *Monetary Dynamics and Socio-Economic Development in Emerging Economies* (pp. 195–220). IGI Global Scientific Publishing., DOI: 10.4018/979-8-3693-9765-7.ch007

Selvakumar, P., & Haashni, S. SudhaAnanthi, G., & Manjunath, T. C. (2026). Cybernetic Systems Thinking: Foundations for Organizational Adaptability. In L. Tsvasman (Ed.), Cybernetic Leadership for Sustainable Innovation (pp. 99-124). IGI Global Scientific Publishing. DOI: 10.4018/979-8-3373-2484-5.ch004

Seshanna, S. V., Gopalakrishnan, G., Anute, N., Deepthi Reddy, K., Sharma, M., Selvakumar, P., & Manjunath, T. C. (2026). Digital Transformation and Cybersecurity. In Saeed, S., & Tahir, S. (Eds.), *User-Centric Cybersecurity Implications for Sustainable Digital Transformation* (pp. 1–30). IGI Global Scientific Publishing., DOI: 10.4018/979-8-3373-3171-3.ch001

Trček, D. (2022). Cultural heritage preservation by using blockchain technologies. *Heritage Science*, *10*(1), 6. DOI: 10.1186/s40494-021-00643-9

Truong, D., Xiaoming Liu, R., & Yu, J. J. (2020). Mixed methods research in tourism and hospitality journals. *International Journal of Contemporary Hospitality Management*, *32*(4), 1563–1579. DOI: 10.1108/IJCHM-03-2019-0286

Unsplash. (2023, April 11). Beautiful Free Images & Pictures | Unsplash. https://unsplash.com

Vessey, I., Ramesh, V., & Glass, R. L. (2002). Research in information systems: An empirical study of diversity in the discipline and its journals. *Journal of Management Information Systems*, *19*(2), 129–174. DOI: 10.1080/07421222.2002.11045721

Watson, R. T., & Webster, J. (2020). Analysing the past to prepare for the future: Writing a literature review a roadmap for release 2.0. *Journal of Decision Systems*, *29*(3), 129–147. DOI: 10.1080/12460125.2020.1798591

Yung, R., & Khoo-Lattimore, C. (2019). New realities: A systematic literature review on virtual reality and augmented reality in tourism research. *Current Issues in Tourism*, *22*(17), 2056–2081. DOI: 10.1080/13683500.2017.1417359

Zhang, K., Chen, Y., & Li, C. (2019). Discovering the tourists' behaviors and perceptions in a tourism destination by analyzing photos' visual content with a computer deep learning model: The case of Beijing. *Tourism Management*, *75*, 595–608. DOI: 10.1016/j.tourman.2019.07.002

Zhao, L., Zhang, J., Jing, H., Wu, J., & Huang, Y. (2023). A blockchain-based cryptographic interaction method of digital museum collections. *Journal of Cultural Heritage*, *59*, 69–82. DOI: 10.1016/j.culher.2022.11.001

Chapter 13
An Intelligent Framework for Early Chronic Kidney Disease Prognosis:
Hybrid Ensemble and Statistical Feature Selection Approach and Comparative Study

Jayesh Motwani
Vellore Institute of Technology, India

Avinash Chandra
Vellore Institute of Technology, India

Nilamadhab Mishra
https://orcid.org/0000-0002-1330-4869
VIT Bhopal University, India

Anand Motwani
VIT Bhopal University, India

Monica Arya
CMR Engineering College, Kandlakoya, India

ABSTRACT

We propose a hybrid wrapper approach, "Statistical-Recursive Feature Elimination" (S-RFE), to obtain an optimal and highly predictive subset of features. Max Voting Ensemble (MVE) optimization is applied to effectively predict diseases with optimal features, where the problem of finding the best classifier is formulated by represent-

DOI: 10.4018/979-8-3373-8197-8.ch013

ing multiple objective functions as a single objective function. Significant disease predictors were validated using statistical significance values and AUC-ROC. The proposed model has been experimentally validated for real data, and a comparison of models with different benchmark classifiers is also presented. We have achieved maximum accuracy (99.25%) and F1-score (99.2), with accuracy (0.99), having the ideal count of predictive features. Our prototype generates alerts for patients at risk, as well as for any new patients who may be at risk.

1. INTRODUCTION

Chronic Kidney Disease (CKD), a painful clinical condition with high morbidity plus mortality (Said and Hernandez 2014, Chen, Zhang et al. 2016, Cheng, Xu et al. 2021, Control and Prevention 2021), also predisposes the patient to other diseases. In our nation, more than 10 million cases are being diagnosed every year (Jankowski, Floege et al. 2021), and more than 15% of American adult citizens are likely to have this disease (Control and Prevention 2021). Since this disease, CKD, is often not apparent until kidney function is severely impaired, symptoms develop gradually, albeit steadily, and are mostly nonspecific to this particular illness. Some people never exhibit any symptoms and are thus only diagnosed through laboratory testing. In fact, 40% of persons who have significantly impaired kidney function are unaware that they have CKD. The progression of this disease is linked to several clinical indications, including diabetes mellitus, hypertension, and anemia (Chen, Zhang et al. 2016). Diabetes, heart disease, and kidney disease are an intertwined trio of serious health problems, one of which often causes the other two diseases. The incidence percentage of end-stage renal disease (ESRD) patients due to diabetes mellitus increased (Banerjee, Crews et al. 2014) from approximately 22.1% to nearly 31.3% between 2000 and 2015 (Cheng, Xu et al. 2021). The authors (Agarwal and Srivastava 2009, Said and Hernandez 2014, Jankowski, Floege et al. 2021) summarize the clinical consequences of cardiovascular disease (CVD) in CKD. Other consequences include an increased incidence of infections, high levels of phosphorus and potassium, low calcium levels, loss of appetite, and depression. Further, CKD can progress to ESRD, which requires repeated dialysis and kidney transplantation (Plantinga, Tuot et al. 2010). Patients with Chronic Kidney Disease (CKD) face painful health conditions or renal impairment due to a delay in diagnosis, and have to rely on various costly laboratory tests for diagnosis. Effective and early prognosis of CKD can reduce treatment costs and the risk of renal failure.

A detailed illustration of the nephron anatomy, including its components and position within the kidney, is shown in Figure 1. Kidney cross-sections show the pathway of impure blood, filtered blood, and urine. Labels are shown on the glomeruli, tubules, and collecting ducts. The renal artery supplies impure blood to the kidneys, which first enters a collection of tiny blood vessels called the glomeruli present in every nephron. Only very tiny molecules of wastes, liquids—predominantly H2O—can pass through the thin walls of each glomerulus into the adjoining convoluted tubule. Proteins, dead white and red blood cells, and other larger molecules remain in the partially filtered liquid. A blood vessel borders the tubule, which reabsorbs most of the water, minerals, and nutrients our body requires, while the now-filtered fluid passes through this tube-like structure. Thus, this unit of the kidney ensures the purging of excess harmful acids from our bloodstream. Additionally, urine is a discarded fluid that contains waste in the tubules.

Figure 1. Overview of renal process

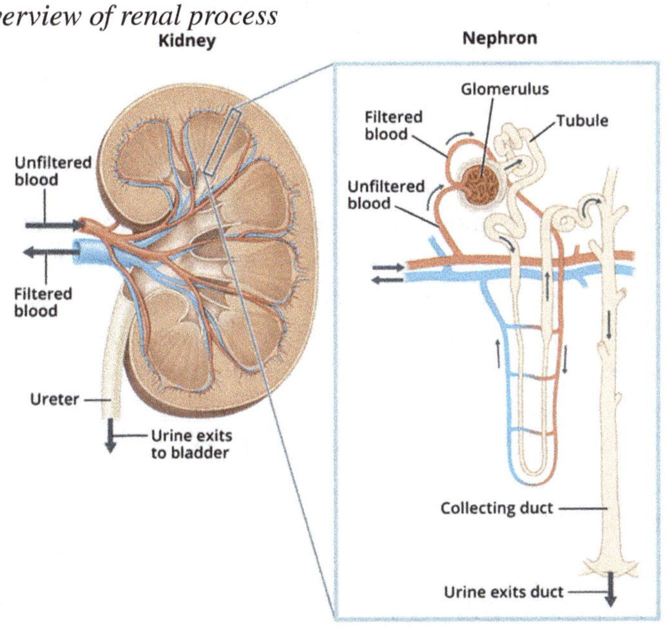

Physicians can usually diagnose CKD by looking for albuminuria/ reduced renal function, such as the Glomerular Filtration Rate (GFR). GFR of < 60 ml/min per 1.73 m^2 over a three-month duration. Research suggests that participants with high Blood Pressure (BP), heart disease, and diabetes have an increased possibility of albuminuria plus decreased GFR (Banerjee, Crews et al. 2014, Banerjee, Scherzer et al. 2014, Banerjee, Crews et al. 2015). However, in certain cases of participants without hypertension or diabetes mellitus, a similar magnitude effect was observed (Goldstein 2012, Banerjee, Crews et al. 2014, Banerjee, Crews et al. 2015). Therefore, it is possible to misclassify CKD risk factors in the case of diabetes and hypertension. If a person is more likely to have CKD, they will be recommended to undergo rigorous laboratory tests. In addition to clinical tests, biopsy and imaging procedures are commonly used to detect the presence of CKD. These procedures are invasive, costly, time-consuming, and sometimes dangerous. However, it is impractical to test each individual using such procedures. This work quantifies the disease indicators using the novel hybrid wrapper approach (S-RFE), thus reducing the number of laboratory tests, and predicts the likelihood of CKD with high accuracy using the Max Voting Ensemble (MVE) model.

Early and effective diagnosis, combined with treatment, can usually retard the development of renal function loss by addressing the root cause. The progression of CKD can be controlled by preventing risk factors, making lifestyle changes, and getting appropriate treatment. If left untreated, CKD can develop into complete/partial renal failure, and the patient may then require dialysis or even a kidney transplant in order to survive. To prevent the incidence of CVD in patients already having CKD, treatment should start in the early stages(Said and Hernandez 2014). Thus, as several recent clinical studies have concluded, some adverse effects can be delayed and, to some extent, even prevented by prompt prognosis with parallel healing (Remuzzi, Ruggenenti et al. 2002, Tazin, Sabab et al. 2016).

This research work shows improved diagnosis, prediction, and model performance. The work examines the intricate relationships between various characteristics that contribute to CKD. For exploratory analysis, we have employed various statistical tests, including Pearson's correlation, a significance test, and a scatter plot. To obtain the optimal number of predictive features and performance, this work proposes an intelligent framework consisting of S-RFE and ensemble ML. This work also reports the minimal optimal subset of features responsible for CKD diagnosis.

1.1 Research Queries

Researchers have long been motivated to identify diseases without relying on physicians' expertise. The aim of the research is to develop a novel/intelligent framework to predict the likelihood and progression of CKD in patients with diabetes and cardiovascular diseases. This research aims to accurately estimate the prevalence of CKD using the optimal number of disease predictors, thereby reducing the number and cost of laboratory tests.

Our study tries to answer the following five key research queries (RQ):

- RQ1. Which m/c learning method improves the performance of disease prediction with minimal Type-1 and Type-2 error?
- RQ2. Do patients with non-CKD have different features than those with CKD?
- RQ3. Which features are important predictors of CKD?

- RQ4. Does FS technology improve the performance of m/c learning models?
- RQ5. Does the proposed FS technique determine the optimal subset of disease characteristics?

To help predict CKD progression and help clinicians, we have established models that use statistical, FS, and m/c learning approaches. The proposed model is effective for determining the progression of CKD and has been validated with detailed results. Based on the results, we establish a minimally optimal set of predictive features that will help reduce the number of diagnostic tests required for determining CKD. Various features that may influence the symptomatic development of CKD, according to the study, are shown in Figure 4.

1.2 Key Contributions

- A hybrid wrapper method: Statistical-RFE for determining an optimal subset of disease predictors.
- Intelligent framework for early diagnosis of CKD in patients, based on S-RFE and Ensemble.
- Minimal optimal set of features significant for predicting CKD.
- Validation of optimal feature subset using statistical test and AUC-ROC.
- Early prognosis with optimal features reduces disease risk, laboratory cost, and time.
- High Accuracy and F-score reduce the risk of uncertainty in diagnosis and treatment.
- Comparison of S-RFE+MVE with benchmark classifiers/methods.
- The proposed technique could be tested and applied to prevent other diseases.

1.3 Paper Outline

Section 2 includes a comprehensive review of ML, Ensemble, FS, and optimization-based techniques for the determination of CKD. Section 3 presents the dataset description, proposed framework, and algorithms that follow. Section 4 presents the simulation setup, performance metrics, and detailed results, along with their discussion. Section 5 presents the conclusion of the paper, along with its future scope.

2. LITERATURE REVIEW

The use of artificial intelligence (AI) is a topic of growing interest in disease diagnosis and predictive analysis. The authors (Park and Han 2018) outline the key methodological points involved in the clinical evaluation of AI for diagnostic use in high-dimensional medical data or predictive models. DM methods and technologies help in the detection of hidden relationships and patterns in medical data. The application of DM and Machine Learning (ML) provides opportunities for recovery from illness and reduces costs by up to 30% of total healthcare expenses.

The proposed DM methods and techniques for detecting CKD usually treat the problem as a classification problem (Motwani, Shukla et al. 2021). Classification is the process of categorizing a patient in terms of disease, rather than disease condition. In diagnostics, DM techniques are widely employed; however, no single technique consistently yields consistent findings (Chaudhuri, Sinha et al. 2021, Motwani, Shukla et al. 2023). Dataset size, feature selection (FS), and hyper-parameter tuning all have an impact on the classification results.

Machine Learning (ML) in DM mainly plays an important role in the discovery of knowledge within large medical databases. m/c learning algorithm can detect hidden irregularities and abnormal patterns to diagnose diseases and predict disease probability and survival against diseases. Machine-predictive analysis has helped classify CKD disease and gained popularity in recent decades. Various algorithms have been suggested for the effective forecasting of CKD by exploiting patients' complete clinical data.

Important classification techniques such as Support Vector Machine (SVM), Logistic Regression (LR), Naïve Bayes (NB), k-Nearest Neighbor (k-NN), Decision Tree (DT), Random Forest (RF), Gradient Boosting (GB) as well as Multi-Layer Perceptron (MLP) Neural Network (NN) are standard M/c Learning techniques put to use by contemporary authors for the detection and classification of CKD. A useful classification of research articles based on various benchmark m/c learning and Ensemble techniques for CKD classification is presented in the following Table 1.

Table 1. List of articles based on M/c learning models for CKD

Authors / References	SVM	LR	NB	k-NN	DT	RF	NN	Ensemble
(Chen, Zhang et al. 2016)								
(Tazin, Sabab et al. 2016)	✓	✓		✓	✓			
(Chaudhuri, Sinha et al. 2021)	✓	✓	✓		✓	✓		✓
(Alaiad, Najadat et al. 2020)	✓		✓	✓	✓			

continued on following page

Table 1. Continued

Authors / References	SVM	LR	NB	k-NN	DT	RF	NN	Ensemble
(Chen, Zhang et al. 2016)								
(Almasoud and Ward 2019)	✓	✓				✓		✓
(Qin, Chen et al. 2019)	✓	✓	✓	✓		✓	✓	
(Xiao, Ding et al. 2019)	✓	✓		✓		✓	✓	✓
(Charleonnan, Fufaung et al. 2016)	✓	✓		✓	✓			
(Salekin and Stankovic 2016)						✓		
(Kunwar, Chandel et al. 2016)			✓				✓	
(Xiao, Ding et al. 2019)	✓	✓		✓		✓	✓	✓
(Jongbo, Adetunmbi et al. 2020)			✓	✓	✓			✓
(Segal, Kalifa et al. 2020)								✓
(Hasan and Hasan 2019)								✓
(Senan, Al-Adhaileh et al. 2021)	✓			✓	✓	✓		
(Basar and Akan 2017)								✓
This research								

Prediction models are built using various statistical and DM techniques, m/c learning algorithms, expert rules, and use historical and current data to predict future outcomes. Thus, the implementation of such predictive models based purely or partially on m/c learning techniques becomes inevitable in order to clearly understand the acuteness of the presented risk or to emphasize real-time effects showing on health problems linked with Chronic Kidney Disease sufferers. The predictive models determine whether a patient is likely to develop a specific disease condition in the future. The authors have also used various FS techniques and/or optimization techniques in different approaches to determine the features that contribute to CKD. Later, predictive models built on m/c learning methods are used to predict CKD.

Ant Colony Optimization (ACO) based classifiers are used for the classification of CKDs, followed by the application of Density Feature Selection (DFS) to remove irrelevant or redundant features by M. Elhoseny et al.(Elhoseny, Shankar et al. 2019). The number of parameters selected is considered to be 14, which is greater than that proposed in many other researches works.

Rubini and Perumal (Jerlin Rubini and Perumal 2020) developed a multi-kernel Support Vector Machine using the implemented Fruit Fly Optimization Algorithm (FFOA) for CKD identification. This FFOA aids the selection of useful features for SVM based classifier to achieve higher precision.

Despite significant breakthroughs in knowledge discovery, traditional m/c learning methods may fail to achieve satisfactory performance due to data characteristics such as complexity, high-dimensionality, imbalance, asymmetry, ambiguity, incompleteness, and noise. In this context, Ensemble Learning has proven itself to be optimal and extremely versatile in a broad spectrum of problem statements and real-world applications (Dong, Yu et al. 2020). Ensemble techniques use m/c learning classifiers that can generate prediction results based on the features extracted through a variety of inferences on the data. The results obtained through different classifiers, which may be weak, are combined using various polling or aggregation mechanisms to achieve better performance than any individual classifier. Thus, ensemble methods are more accurate, successful, and comprehensive in maintaining model characteristics. Figure 2 illustrates the primary concept behind ensemble classification.

Figure 2. Essence of ensemble learning

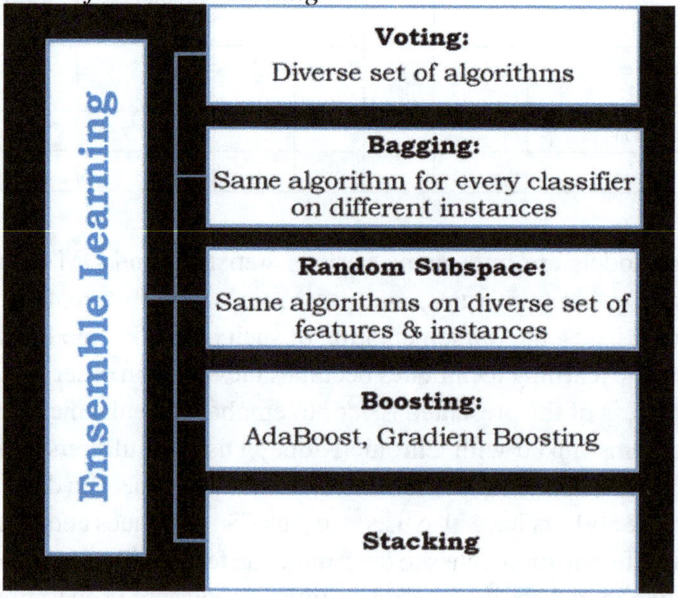

Jongbo et al. (Jongbo, Adetunmbi et al. 2020) employed the bagging algorithm with a random subspace method on three basic learning algorithms: NB, K-NN, and DT to improve Chronic Kidney Disease classification performance. Random subspace on the k-NN classifier outperformed the other methods.

Chaudhuri et al. (Chaudhuri, Sinha et al. 2021) employed an enhanced DT ensemble in conjunction with RFE for CKD prediction. The results demonstrated that removing redundant or less important features does not affect accuracy. The research compares the popular EDT method and its classifiers, i.e., NB, SVM, RF, LR, and DT.

Segal et al. (Segal, Kalifa et al. 2020) treat ESRD risk prediction as a binary classification problem and use the XGBoost implementation of the boosting algorithm.

Hasan and Hasan (Hasan and Hasan 2019) applied the 'Extremely Randomized Trees (ET)' algorithm for determining feature importance and ensemble approaches: Bagging and Boosting for effective classification of CKD and Non-CKD. ET is an ensemble of DTs. Bagging predicts the most noteworthy of true positives. AdaBoost algorithm, as well as Extra Trees(ET) algorithm, generate the highest number of 'true-negatives'. The authors (Song, Waitman et al. 2019) used an ensemble FS method to extract several relevant clinical attributes from the EHR data to predict kidney disease risk in diabetic patients.

This research utilizes the MVE model that is built using various classifiers. The disease predictors are supplied to MVE for effective prediction of CKD progression.

Data in patients' EHRs and hospital archives have various features that have been found to contain missing values or even redundant data. Also, since Medical data is often high-dimensional, many features are correlated with each other. For example, microarray data is particularly noisy and high-dimensional (Musheer, Verma et al. 2019). Additionally, the dataset generated by continuous patient monitoring is typically imbalanced, heterogeneous, and large-scale (Motwani, Shukla et al. 2020, Motwani, Shukla et al. 2021). Also, the high-class imbalance between minority and majority classes in the considered dataset seems to affect the optimal performance of m/c learning algorithms and may bias the predictions. Therefore, building better predictive models and applying mining techniques to such data is often a complex process.

It has been proven that efficient feature subset selection and extraction can improve prediction and classification performance. On the other hand, models built using irrelevant features may be less accurate, prone to overfitting, and computationally inefficient. Authors (Jain and Singh 2018) published an extensive study on the implementation of FS and other classification methods for forecasting chronic diseases (CDs). The authors provide a general review of attribute identification methodologies, along with the pros and cons of each. Additionally, adaptive and parallel classification algorithms have also been studied here. Authors (Polat, Mehr et al. 2017), employed the preferred filter and wrapper methods for dimensionality reduction along with M/c Learning techniques. The recognition or identification accuracy obtained with SVM, where 12 attributes were chosen using the filter-based method, is 98.5%. The authors (Chaudhuri, Sinha et al. 2021, Motwani, Shukla et al. 2021) have deployed the well-known RFE wrapper method of FS to choose features in the CKD dataset to enhance the total model performance factor.

Therefore, in addition to efficient data processing, FS and/or extraction are required prior to model building. Then, the classification and prediction of any disease becomes fast, accurate, and simple when the available data is appropriate and reliable. Figure 3 shows the specific steps of FS.

Figure 3. Steps in the feature selection method

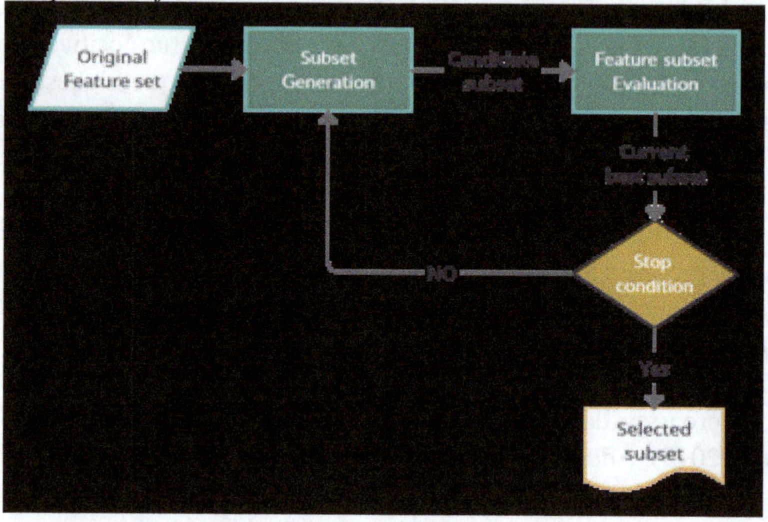

3. MATERIALS AND APPLIED METHODS

3.1 Dataset used

We utilized the CKD dataset donated by Soundarapandian et al. (Rubini and Engineering 2015) downloaded from the UCI m/c learning repository. It is a multivariate dataset collected from several hospitals over a 2-month period. The considered dataset comprises records of 400 inpatients, with 24 real attributes and a target attribute. Again, it comprises 14 numeric and 10 nominal attributes, as well as a nominal target descriptor. As is normal, there are naturally a few missing values for them, which are compensated for by the average value of the associated attribute within the category (CKD or non-CKD) to which it belongs. (Sedighi, Ebrahimpour-Komleh et al. 2015, Charleonnan, Fufaung et al. 2016, Kunwar, Chandel et al. 2016, Salekin and Stankovic 2016, Tazin, Sabab et al. 2016, Basar and Akan 2017, Misir, Mitra et al. 2017, Polat, Mehr et al. 2017, Yildirim 2017, Jain and Singh 2018, Nathaniel, Motwani et al. 2018, Elhoseny, Shankar et al. 2019, Chaudhuri, Sinha et al. 2021, Senan, Al-Adhaileh et al. 2021) utilized the same dataset.

Figure 4. Features in the dataset that may influence the symptomatic development of CKD

S.N.	Attribute description (abbreviations)	Values, type
1	Age (age)	Years; numerical
2	Blood Pressure (bp)	mm/Hg; numerical
3	Specific gravity (sg)	1.005,1.010,1.015,1.020,1.025; nominal
4	Albumin (al)	0,1,2,3,4,5; nominal
5	Sugar (su)	0,1,2,3,4,5; nominal
6	Red blood cells (rbc)	Normal, abnormal; nominal
7	Pus cell (pc)	Normal, abnormal; nominal
8	Pus cell clumps (pcc)	Present, not present; nominal
9	Bacteria (ba)	Present, not present; nominal
10	Blood glucose random (bgr)	In mgs/dL; numerical
11	Blood Urea (bu)	In mgs/dL; numerical
12	Serum Creatinine (sc)	In mgs/dL; numerical
13	Sodium (sod)	In mEq/L; numerical
14	Potassium (pot)	In mEq/L; numerical
15	Haemoglobin (hemo)	In gms.; numerical
16	Packed cell volume (pcv)	Nominal; numerical
17	White blood cell count (wc)	In cells/cumm; numerical
18	Red blood cell count (rc)	Millions/cmm; numerical
19	Hypertension (htn)	Yes, No; nominal
20	Diabetes mellitus (dm)	Yes, No; nominal
21	Coronary artery disease (cad)	Yes, No; nominal
22	Appetite (appet)	Good, Poor; nominal
23	Pedal edema (pe)	Yes, No; nominal
24	Anemia (ane)	Yes, No; nominal
25	Class (class)	ckd, notckd; nominal

3.2 Proposed Framework and Methods

Before the COVID-19 pandemic, the practicality of Remote Patient Monitoring (RPM) within a Smart Health-care Monitoring (SHM) system remained uncertain. However, it has since become a validated approach and is rapidly gaining widespread adoption. Increasingly, healthcare organizations are implementing RPM to facilitate chronic disease management without the need for direct, individual monitoring (Motwani, Shukla et al. 2022). The architecture of the model proposed in our work is presented in Figure 5. It consists of various stages. The results are influenced by the magnitude of the considered dataset, the selection of the correct features, plus the hyperparameters for this chosen algorithm. In this section, we will briefly discuss the methods used in this work.

Our present study aims to identify predictive features immediately prior to classification, using scatter plots, correlation tests, and the proposed S-RFE technique. The classification process has been further improved using a proposed ensemble method (MVE).

Figure 5. Proposed predictive framework architecture for CKD risk prediction

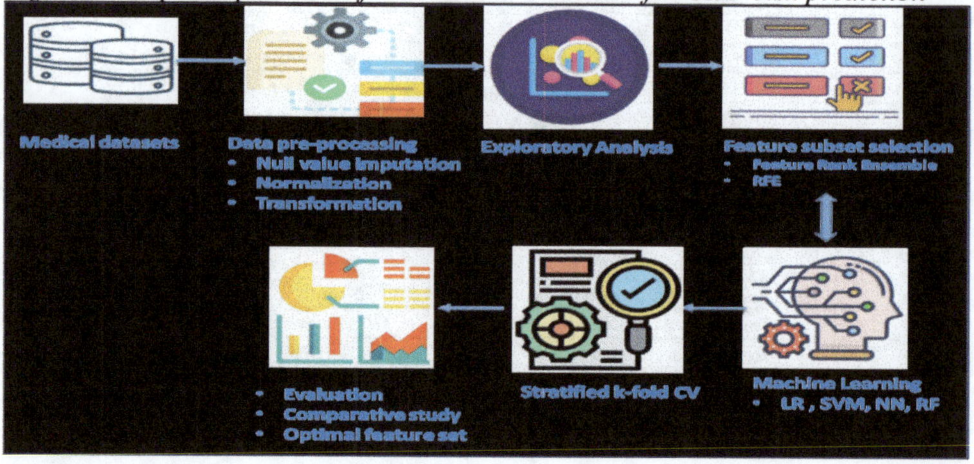

3.2.1 Proposed algorithm: Description.

RFE is a kind of wrapper-based FS method that selects the features needed to train the model. Although this method is helpful in removing dependence and co-linearity from any model, there is no specific criterion for eliminating features. This method fits the model and eliminates weak features until an optimal subset is obtained (Rao and Rao 2021). Conventional RFE subsequently removes the worst feature that causes a drop in "classification accuracy" after the classification model is built (Jeon and Oh 2020). Once the size of the predictor attribute set is specified, it becomes a tuning parameter leading to a drop in "classification accuracy".

Basically, RFE uses a wrapper algorithm to select the optimal features (Kohavi and John 1997). The RFE method proposed here utilizes a backward greedy algorithm as an iterative function that identifies and removes the worst-performing subset in the process (using a wrapper function), thereby leaving the optimal subset intact, which results in the highest accuracy. The approach proposed here (S-RFE) selects not only the optimal subset but also the most predictive subset for determining and predicting CKD. S-RFE is a hybrid approach that incorporates statistical significance with RFE to select optimal and predictive subsets.

The flow chart of our proposed algorithm is shown in Figure 6. Our proposed FS algorithm and classification functions work according to the steps outlined in the framework. The proposed algorithms S-RFE and S-RFE+MVE are described in detail here. Exploratory analysis has previously been performed using visualization and correlation testing to obtain locally predictive features. An optimal set of predictors is determined using the S-RFE algorithm, thus determining the minimum set of diagnostic tests.

Statistical significance plays a crucial role in statistical hypothesis testing. Only it can determine whether the null hypothesis (the default assumption about a phenomenon or fact) needs to be overruled/rejected, or upheld. To reject the null hypothesis, the experimental results must be statistically significant. This implies that the resultant p-value is apparently less than the considered/pre-specified significance level α, which is, as mentioned above, usually fixed at 5% or less. Say, if the value of α is fixed at 5% and considering that the null hypothesis is true, the conditional chances of a type-I error remain 5%. Along with this, a statistically important outcome is one where the observed p-value $\leq$ 5%. In this work, a paired t-test is applied to different feature subsets for a series of classifiers to measure performance and determine statistical significance.

Figure 6. Flowchart of proposed algorithm

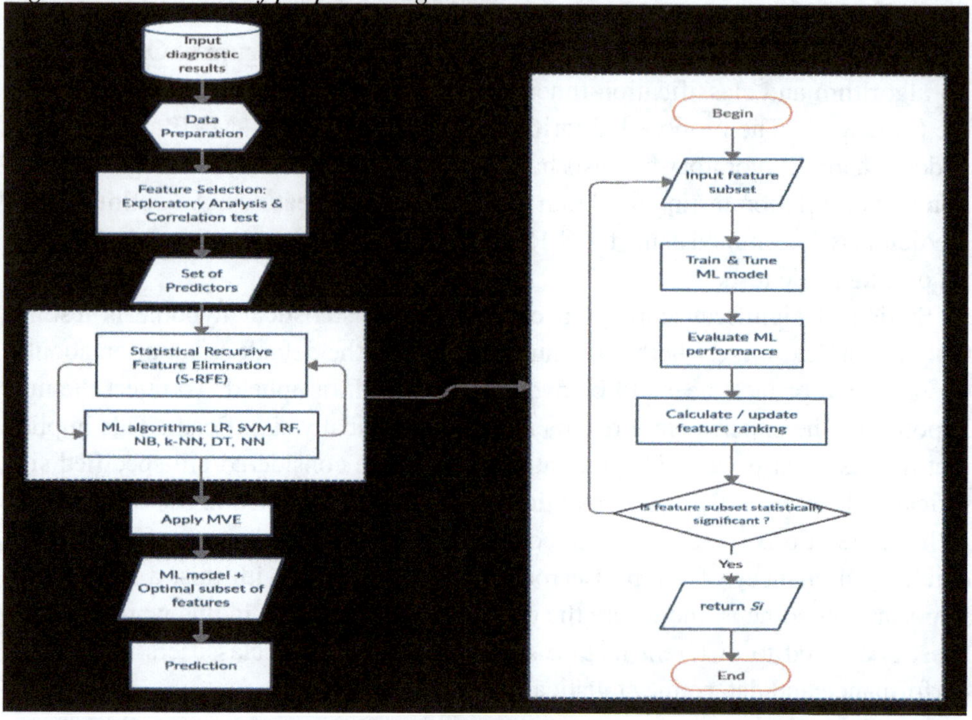

3.2.2 Proposed "Max Voting Ensemble" Optimization.

Seven classifiers have been evaluated to identify the best proposed model. Assuming mass learning, the dataset is evaluated using all classifiers, and the final results are determined by the maximum-voting method. When employing the voting method, the best classifier is determined based on the votes received for the feature subset and its performance. Finally, after applying the ensemble, the best classifier was selected from all of them.

In this work, the problem of selecting the best classifier is modeled as a multi-objective optimization problem. The problem can be modeled as a single-objective function problem by representing multiple objective functions as a single objective function.

$$F(a) = \left[f_1(a), f_2(a), \ldots\ldots\ldots f_k(a)\right], a \in S \quad (1)$$

Where f is a scalar function, a is a vector of decision variables, and S is the set of constraints. $K > 1$ signifies the number of objective functions to be maximized or minimized. $f_i(a)$ Signifies a function of a.

If the condition given by Equation 2 is satisfied, then p dominates q, for a multi-objective minimization problem, in which i and j $\in \{1, 2, 3,\ldots, k\}$

$$\forall i : f_i(p) \leq f_i(q) \; and \; \exists j : f_j(p) < f_j(q) \tag{2}$$

This problem of CKD prediction is modelled as an optimization of multiple objectives (features and performance) with constraints.

To understand the general framework of MVE, consider the following: C1, C2… CN is 'N' (N=7, in this work), the number of classifiers. The number of classes is represented with M (M = 2).

Design optimization for MVE can be modelled as optimizing the weight values of the classifier. Here, the weight values (objective function) depend on the number of features and the Mean Absolute Error (MAE) as the optimization criterion. We have a vector of length (M x N) 14 (M = 2, N = 7). The classifiers are arranged in ascending order based on the MAE values (see Figure 6), and the final decision is the target class with the highest weighted voting power (lower values of MAE). Based on the presented weight values, k-NN has the highest voting power with the lowest MAE in the final decision. We have considered several evaluation metrics and variants as objective functions in the experiment and found MAE to be an excellent metric.

$$MAE = \frac{\sum_{i=1}^{n} |y_i - \lambda(x_i)|}{n} \tag{3}$$

Figure 7. Comparison of MAE of various classifiers

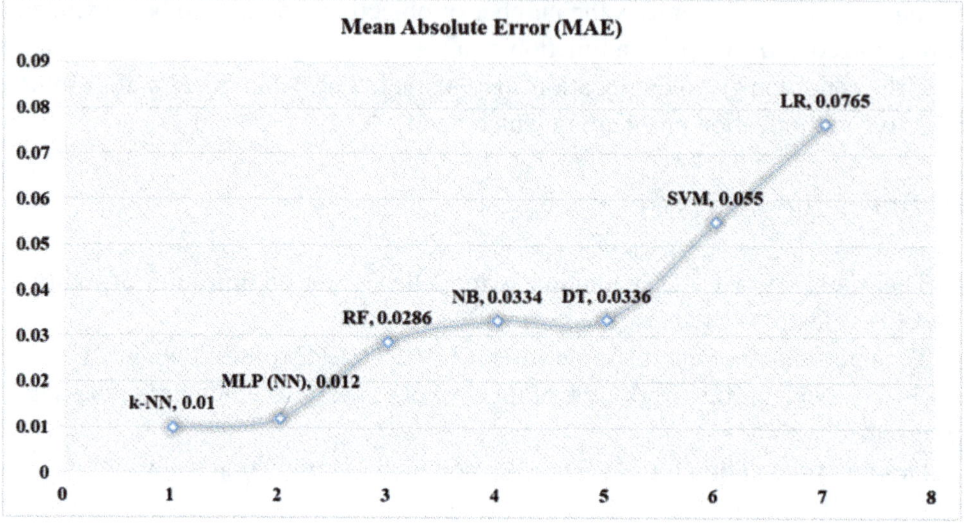

4. RESULTS AND DISCUSSIONS

4.1 Simulation Setup and Performance Metrics

The experiments were performed on computer systems with Intel Core i5 (2.0 GHz) processor, 8 GB of RAM, running MS Windows - 10 (64-bit) os. Then, the proposed framework is simulated in the Python language (versions 3.7.0 and 3.6.6) using high-level APIs developed for data science and m/c learning tasks. The popular tool WEKA (version -3.8.5) has been used for key experiments and knowledge analysis.

The confusion matrix helps to derive class prediction accuracy as well as other performance metrics (see Figure 7). Comparing the performance of different m/c learning classifiers based solely on accuracy can lead to biased and ambiguous results in the case of unbalanced data. Area under receiver operating characteristic (AUROC) is a performance parameter that commonly assess clinical risk prediction algorithms. It is a probability curve which reflects the algorithm's capability to distinguish between classes in the case of binary classification. Here, ROC represents the ratio of True Positive Rate (TPR) as shown in Eq.4, the False Positive Rate (FPR) as shown in Eq.5. This tells us the chances that a randomly selected patient having specific symptoms shall show a relatively higher predicted risk score as compared to another patient not having any such symptoms. In order to prevent model overfitting here, we use k-fold cross validation where k = 10.

$$TPR = \frac{TP}{TP + FN} \tag{4}$$

$$FPR = \frac{FP}{TP + FP} \tag{5}$$

Figure 8. Performance metrics

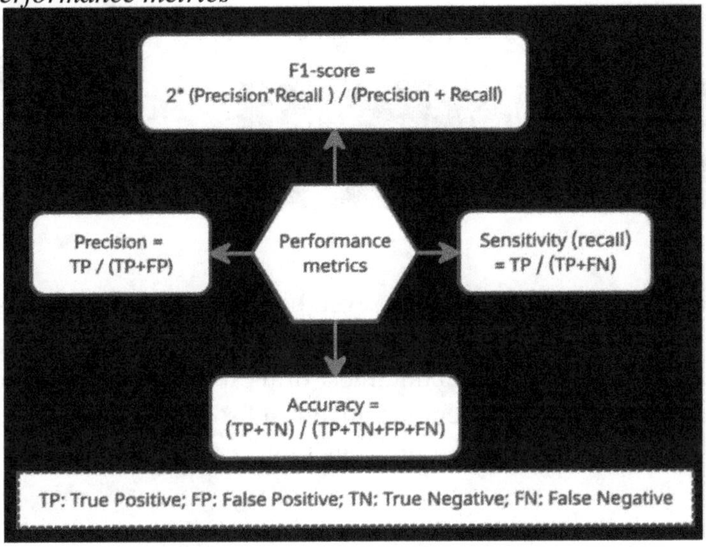

4.2 Results and Discussion

In this work an attempt has been made to answer some key research questions. The methodology implemented to answer the key RQs is shown in Figure 9.

Figure 9. Methodology to answer the research questions

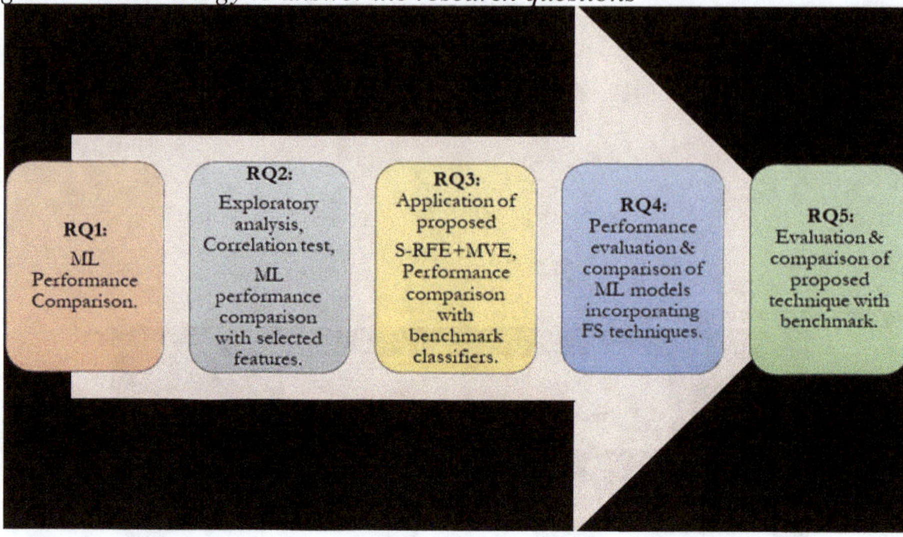

First of all, a comparative study of seven benchmark m/c learning algorithms, i.e., NB, LR, k-NN, SVM, DT, RF, and MLP, has been done in this study. When all the features are taken into account, most of these seven standard m/c learning techniques are performant. The comparative results of different classifiers taking into account all 24 features are presented in Table 2.

Table 2. Performance evaluation of classifiers with all 24 input features

Classifiers	Results						
	Accuracy	F-Score	Precision	Sensitivity	TPR	FPR	AUC-ROC
LR	97.25	97.3	97.3	97.3	97.3	0.025	99.3
SVM	95.25	95.3	95.3	95.3	95.3	0.05	95.1
k-NN	96.75	96.8	97	96.8	96.8	0.02	97.4
NB	94.25	94.2	94.3	94.3	94.3	0.08	98.4
DT (J-48)	98	98	98	98	98	0.023	99.3
RF	98.75	98.7	98.8	98.8	98.8	0.018	98.9
MLP	96.75	96.8	96.8	96.8	96.8	0.028	98.7

Further, when we initially applied exploratory analysis, Pearson correlation test (2008) and subset evaluation to identify potential (locally predictive) features, we found 16 features. Pearson correlation coefficient (r), also known as bivariate-correlation, is a known measure of linear correlation between two data - sets (X and Y). It is the ratio of the co-variance of two variables and the product of their standard deviations; thus it is majorly a normalized measurement of the co-variance. The result is a value between −1 and 1 (Eq.6). The results of the correlation tests are shown in Figure 10. Taking into account all the 16 features, the comparative results of the different classifiers are presented in Table 3.

$$r = \frac{N\sum XY - (\sum X \sum Y)}{\sqrt{[N\sum x^2 - (\sum x)^2]\,[N\sum y^2 - (\sum y)^2]}} \tag{6}$$

The results obtained with S-RFE with different classifiers are shown in Table 3.

Table 3. Performance evaluation of classifiers with 16 predictive features

Classifiers	Results						
	Accuracy	F-Score	Precision	Sensitivity	TPR	FPR	AUC-ROC
LR	97.75	97.8	97.8	97.8	97.8	0.024	99.7
SVM	96.25	96.2	96.2	96.3	96.3	0.044	95.9
k-NN	98.25	98.3	98.3	98.3	98.3	0.011	98.6
NB	94.75	94.7	94.8	94.8	94.8	0.074	99
DT (J-48)	98	98	98	98	98	0.023	99.3
RF	99	99	99	99	99	0.014	99.9
MLP	96.75	96.8	96.8	96.8	96.8	0.028	98.7
Features selected	age, bp, sg, al, rbc, bgr, sc, sod, hemo, pcv, rbcc, htn, dm, appet, pe, ane						

4.2.1 Answer to RQ1.

First, a comparative analysis of seven benchmark m/c learning algorithms is performed, taking into account all the features (refer Table 2). Then, it is shown from the comparison graph (refer Table 2-3 and Figure 10-12) that the initial subset determined using FS has improved the performance of the m/c learning algorithms. Also the suggested FS reduced the FPR while improving TPR and other parameters (refer Table 4 and Figure 11).

Precision and recall parameters measure the two types of errors that occur for a positive class.

Maximizing precision minimizes (Type-I) FPs and maximizing recall minimizes (Type-II) FNs. F-score comparison is shown in Figure 13. The improvement in the values of precision and recall (thus the F-score) with the proposed approach reflects the reduction of Type-I and Type-II errors.

Figure 10. Correlation test results

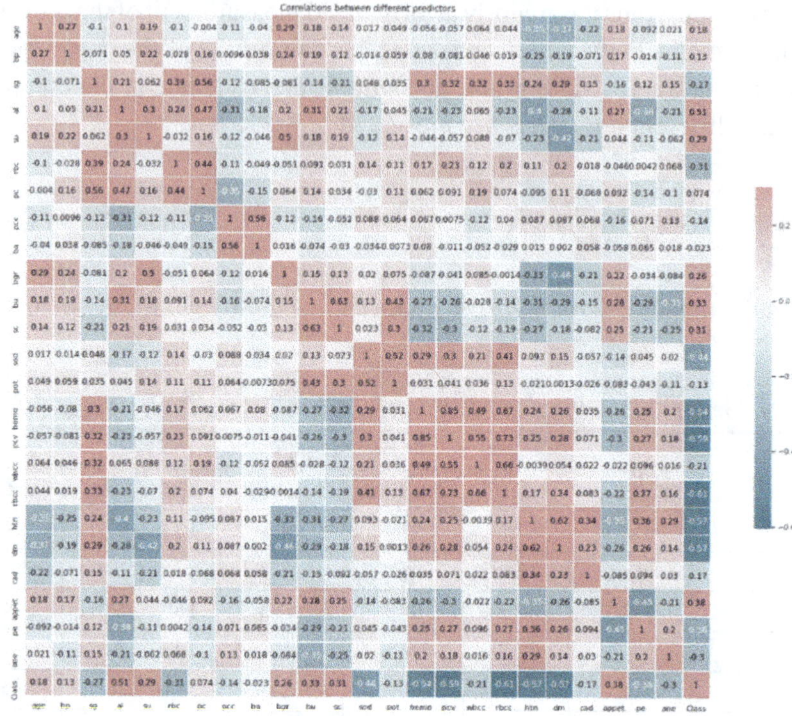

4.2.2 Answer to RQ2.

As evident from the results (refer to Table 3-4), only a few features are sufficient to effectively predict the onset of CKD. Patients with and without CKD have different values for the set of characteristics. We can say that patients with non-CKD have different characteristics from patients with CKD. However, in the case of outliers, the results may be different.

Table 4. Performance evaluation of classifiers with proposed SRFE

Classifiers	Results							
	Accuracy	F-Score	Precision	Sensitivity	TPR	FPR	AUC-ROC	No. of attributes
S-RFE+LR	95.25	95.3	95.3	95.3	95.3	0.047	98.2	11
S-RFE+SVM	94.5	94.5	94.5	94.5	94.5	0.057	94.4	6
S-RFE+k-NN	99.25	99.2	99.3	99.3	99.3	0.010	99.2	6

continued on following page

Table 4. Continued

Classifiers	Results							
	Accuracy	**F-Score**	**Precision**	**Sensitivity**	**TPR**	**FPR**	**AUC-ROC**	**No. of attributes**
S-RFE+NB	97	97	97	97	97	0.042	99	8
S-RFE+DT (J-48)	97.25	97.2	97.2	97.3	97.3	0.033	98.2	5
S-RFE+RF	99.25	99.3	99.3	99.3	99.3	0.007	1	9
S-RFE+MLP	98.75	98.7	98.8	98.8	98.8	0.018	98.9	11

Figure 11. Comparison of accuracy

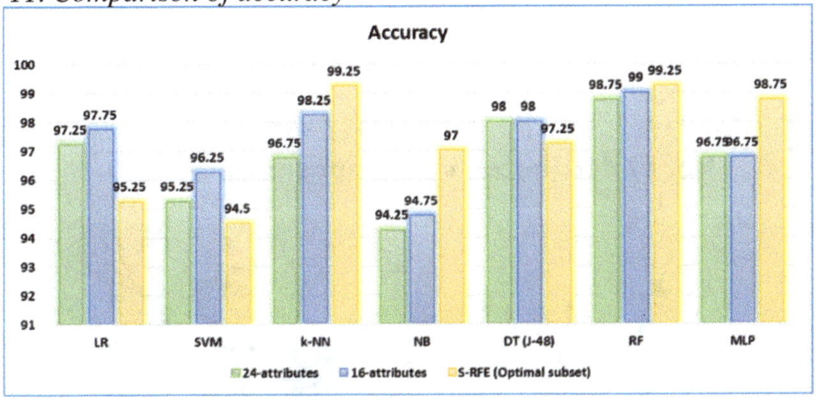

Figure 12. Comparison of FP rate

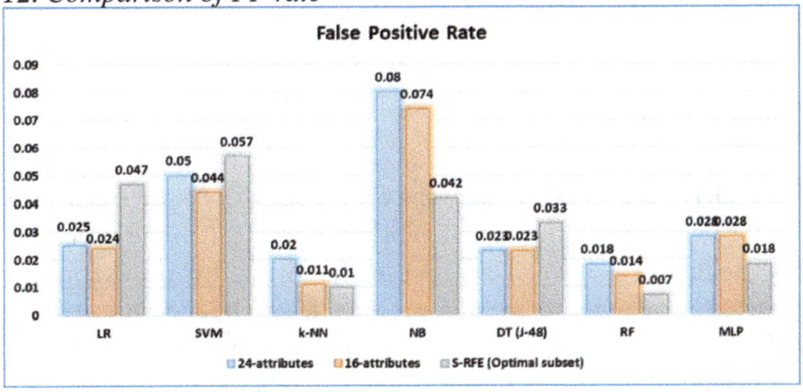

Figure 13. Comparison of F-score

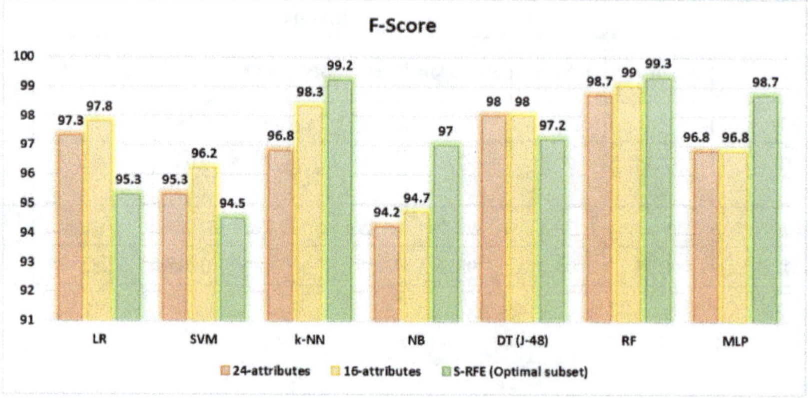

Figure 14. Features selected with proposed approach

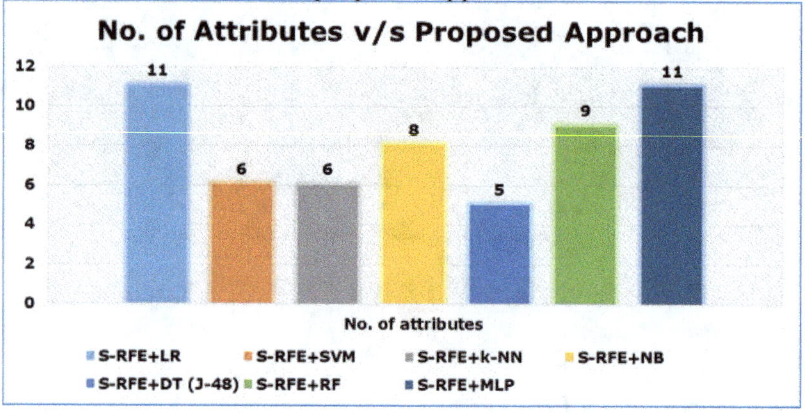

4.2.3 Answer to RQ3.

To boost CKD prediction accuracy and efficiency, this research proposes an Ensemble (MVE) technique with an Intelligent Hybrid FS (S-RFE) to select the optimal number of prediction features. The proposed intelligent hybrid wrapper approach S-RFE reduced the features to an optimal number, which is compared in Figure 13.

Table 5 shows the optimal features selected by the proposed S-RFE with different m/c learning algorithms. The sequence shown in Table 5 also shows the statistical significance of the feature subsets selected by the proposed wrapper approach. Here, the feature subsets selected by S-RFE+NB are significantly more significant compared to other algorithms, as assessed by a statistical significance test. Features selected by S-RFE+LR include all features selected by S-RFE+NB. NN-based methods, such as MLP and other deep learning algorithms, can certainly show some performance improvement.

Table 5. Optimal features subset selected with proposed wrapper S-RFE and m/c learning algorithms

Method	Predictive and statistically significant feature subset
S-RFE+NB	al, rbc, bgr, sc, hemo, pcv, rbcc, dm
S-RFE+LR	bp, al, rbc, bgr, sc, sod, hemo, pcv, rbcc, dm, appet
S-RFE+NN	bp, sg, al, rbc, bgr, sc, sod, hemo, rbcc, dm, appet
S-RFE+SVM	age, bp, sod, hemo, pcv, rbcc
S-RFE+k-NN	sg, al, rbc, sod, hemo, rbcc
S-RFE+DT	sg, al, rbc, hemo, rbcc
S-RFE+RF	sg, al, rbc, sc, sod, hemo, rbcc, htn, dm

4.2.4 Answer to RQ4.

The FS algorithm definitely improves the performance of the m/c learning algorithm. This research also found improvements in performance with a smaller number of features, which are shown in Tables 3-6 and Figures 10–12. Also, the performance of NB, k-NN, Ensemble (RF), and MLP has been improved by implementing the proposed Intelligent Hybrid Wrapper FS (S-RFE) approach.

4.2.5 Answer to RQ5.

To validate the proposed model algorithms (S-RFE) and (S-RFE + MVE), feature subset importance and AUROC are determined and compared. A 10-fold cross-validation has been used to report the mean results for AUROC and other parameters. Furthermore, comparisons have been made with various benchmark algorithms to validate the proposed approach's efficacy (Table 6).

In this research, S-RFE+RF and S-RFE+k-NN are the highest performers in terms of accuracy with 9 and 6 features, respectively. However, there is a tradeoff between the number of features and classifier accuracy. The classifiers S-RFE+NB, S-RFE+DT, and S-RFE+NN gave optimum performance with 8, 6, and 11 features, respectively. S-RFE+LR and S-RFE+SVM achieved lower accuracy than other algorithms when we used simpler versions of LR and SVM. Our proposed method was thus found to have performed significantly better and was more consistent in statistical tests vis-à-vis the previous research results. Table 6 below shows a comparison of performance with related works in the existing literature.

Table 6. Performance comparison with related works in the existing literature

Reference	Models / Methods	Predictive Features	Highest Accuracy achieved (%), Algorithm
(Motwani, Shukla et al. 2021)	RFE+LR, RFE+SVM	6 7	98.3 (LR)
(Alaiad, Najadat et al. 2020)	NB, DT, SVM, k-NN, JRip	12	98.5 (k-NN)
(Almasoud and Ward 2019)	LR, SVM, RF, GDB	15	99 (GDB)
(Charleonnan, Fufaung et al. 2016)	SVM, LR, k-NN, DT	24	98.3 (SVM)
(Hasan and Hasan 2019)	Adaptive Boosting, Bagging, Extra-Tree, GDB, RF	13	99 (adaptive Boosting)
(Elhoseny, Shankar et al. 2019)	DFS-ACO, ACO, PSO	14	95 (D-ACO)
(Jerlin Rubini and Perumal 2020)	FFOA, MKSVM	11	98.51
(Almansour, Syed et al. 2019)	ANN, SVM	12	99.75 (ANN)
(Saringat, Mustapha et al. 2019)	ZeroR, Rule Induction, SVM, NB, DT, Decision Stump, k-NN, Classification via Regression	24	98.5 (NB)
(Zeynu and Patil 2018)	k-NN, J-48, ANN, NB, SVM	7-9	99.5 (ANN)
(Aljaaf, Al-Jumeily et al. 2018)	SVM, LR, MLP	7	98.1 (LR, MLP)
This study	**S-RFE** + MVE; NB, k-NN, SVM, LR, DT (J-48) RF, MLP (NN)	NB (8), k-NN (6), SVM (6), DT (5), RF (9), LR (11), MLP (11)	99.3 (RF)

5 CONCLUSION AND FUTURE DIRECTIONS

Predicting patient health accurately has always been a challenging task. However, using data mining and m/c learning techniques to determine disease severity has always been an efficient way of halting disease progression. Early prediction and prognosis of CKD can slow the progression of CKD and prevent the incidence of ESRD because treatment can be started at an early stage of the disease. However, several detailed diagnostic tests are necessary to determine the severity of the disease or to accurately diagnose it. This work yielded a variety of important results, addressing key research questions. The proposed framework employs a hybrid S-RFE approach to identify optimal feature subsets and utilizes a statistical significance test to weight the model. The number of selected features has been drastically reduced by 75%. The optimal subset of significant disease predictors would certainly reduce the number of laboratory tests and risk. The proposed novel S-RFE + MVE algorithm implemented with seven m/c learning methods and using reduced feature sets significantly improved the performance of four of them. The performance of other m/c learning algorithms can be improved by tuning the algorithm's hyperparameters. This framework, proposed in this research paper, identifies statistically significant disease features that have been validated through the results. The results obtained through the proposed research are, to date, more accurate than those of other standard techniques, as we have employed the stratified 10-fold cross-validation technique instead of train-test splitting. The test sample in a stratified k-fold CV is a good representation of the entire population. The ensemble shows excellent performance; therefore, we suggest that these reduced feature sets are worthwhile, while the final decision will be made by the medical expert. The results demonstrate that better diagnosis, prediction, and model performance can be achieved with the optimal features using the proposed model (S-RFE+MVE). Keywords: Chronic Disease, Ensemble Learning, Statistical Feature Selection, Machine Learning, Optimization, Predictive Modeling.

In the future, the proposed approach can be applied to reduce the dimensionality of other data and improve the performance of other m/c learning algorithms. Although there is always a trade-off between the number of features and the model's performance, the proposed SRFE+MVE model can be used to analyze other prognostic factors. We suggest that the proposed techniques can also be applied to build models for other diseases. The model can be integrated with the "Smart Healthcare Monitoring" (SHM) framework for "Remote Patient Monitoring" (RPM) and tested in a smart city scenario.

6 KEY INFERENCES

Table 7. Key inference table

Known Information:
Known Information: **• Several frameworks based on ensemble and feature selection approaches have been proposed in the literature.** **• So far, a large number of common disease features/predictors are being used for CKD classification/prediction in the already proposed framework.** **• The classifier has so far used sampling and testing methods that are not valid outside the specified setting.** **• Recursive Feature Elimination (RFE) – popularly used with its standard implementation.**
Knowledge addition: • A hybrid wrapper method: Statistical-RFE for determining the optimal subset of significant disease predictors, thus reducing disease risk, laboratory cost, and time. • Novel Intelligent Framework (S-RFE + MVE) for early prediction of CKD in patients. • Proposed an MVE model to estimate the probability of CKD with high accuracy. • Optimal feature subsets are verified using statistical testing and AUC-ROC, and performance is verified using F-score and accuracy, which minimizes uncertainty in diagnosis and treatment. • A comparative study of S-RFE + MVE with benchmark classifiers/methods is presented. • The proposed methods can be tested and applied to prevent other diseases.

REFERENCES

Alaiad, A., Najadat, H., Mohsen, B., & Balhaf, K. (2020). Classification and association rule mining technique for predicting chronic kidney disease. *Journal of Information and Knowledge Management, 19*(01), 2040015. DOI: 10.1142/S0219649220400158

Aljaaf, A. J., Al-Jumeily, D., Haglan, H. M., Alloghani, M., Baker, T., Hussain, A. J., & Mustafina, J. (2018). *Early prediction of chronic kidney disease using machine learning supported by predictive analytics. 2018 IEEE congress on evolutionary computation (CEC)*. IEEE.

Almansour, N. A., Syed, H. F., Khayat, N. R., Altheeb, R. K., Juri, R. E., Alhiyafi, J., Alrashed, S., & Olatunji, S. O. (2019). Neural network and support vector machine for the prediction of chronic kidney disease: A comparative study. *Computers in Biology and Medicine, 109*, 101–111. DOI: 10.1016/j.compbiomed.2019.04.017 PMID: 31054385

Almasoud, M., & Ward, T. E. (2019). Detection of chronic kidney disease using machine learning algorithms with least number of predictors. *International Journal of Advanced Computer Science and Applications, 10*(8). Advance online publication. DOI: 10.14569/IJACSA.2019.0100813

Banerjee, T., Crews, D. C., Wesson, D. E., Tilea, A., Saran, R., Burrows, N. R., Williams, D. E., & Powe, N. R. (2014). Dietary acid load and chronic kidney disease among adults in the United States. *BMC Nephrology, 15*(1), 1–12. DOI: 10.1186/1471-2369-15-137 PMID: 25151260

Banerjee, T., Crews, D. C., Wesson, D. E., Tilea, A. M., Saran, R., Ríos-Burrows, N., Williams, D. E., & Powe, N. R. (2015). High dietary acid load predicts ESRD among adults with CKD. *Journal of the American Society of Nephrology, 26*(7), 1693–1700. DOI: 10.1681/ASN.2014040332 PMID: 25677388

Banerjee, T., Scherzer, R., Powe, N. R., Steffick, D., Shahinian, V., Saran, R., Pavkov, M. E., Saydah, S., & Shlipak, M. G. (2014). Race and other risk factors for incident proteinuria in a national cohort of HIV-infected veterans. *Journal of Acquired Immune Deficiency Syndromes, 67*(2), 145–152. DOI: 10.1097/QAI.0000000000000285 PMID: 25072613

Basar, M. D., & Akan, A. (2017). Detection of chronic kidney disease by using ensemble classifiers. 2017 10th International Conference on Electrical and Electronics Engineering (ELECO), IEEE.

Charleonnan, A., Fufaung, T., Niyomwong, T., Chokchueypattanakit, W., Suwannawach, S., & Ninchawee, N. (2016). *Predictive analytics for chronic kidney disease using machine learning techniques. 2016 management and innovation technology international conference (MITicon)*. IEEE.

Chaudhuri, A. K., Sinha, D., Banerjee, D. K., & Das, A. (2021). A novel enhanced decision tree model for detecting chronic kidney disease. *Network Modeling and Analysis in Health Informatics and Bioinformatics*, *10*(1), 1–22. DOI: 10.1007/s13721-021-00302-w PMID: 34849327

Chen, Z., Zhang, X., & Zhang, Z. (2016). Clinical risk assessment of patients with chronic kidney disease by using clinical data and multivariate models. *International Urology and Nephrology*, *48*(12), 2069–2075. DOI: 10.1007/s11255-016-1346-4 PMID: 27334750

Cheng, H.-T., Xu, X., Lim, P. S., & Hung, K.-Y. (2021). Worldwide epidemiology of diabetes-related end-stage renal disease, 2000–2015. *Diabetes Care*, *44*(1), 89–97. DOI: 10.2337/dc20-1913 PMID: 33203706

Control, C. f. D. and Prevention (2021). "Chronic kidney disease in the United States, 2021." US Department of Health Human Services, Centers for Disease Control Prevention.

Dong, X., Yu, Z., Cao, W., Shi, Y., & Ma, Q. (2020). A survey on ensemble learning. *Frontiers of Computer Science*, *14*(2), 241–258. DOI: 10.1007/s11704-019-8208-z

Elhoseny, M., Shankar, K., & Uthayakumar, J. (2019). Intelligent diagnostic prediction and classification system for chronic kidney disease. *Scientific Reports*, *9*(1), 1–14. DOI: 10.1038/s41598-019-46074-2 PMID: 31270387

Goldstein, S. L. (2012). Acute kidney injury in children and its potential consequences in adulthood. *Blood Purification*, *33*(1-3), 131–137. DOI: 10.1159/000334143 PMID: 22269297

Hasan, K. Z., & Hasan, M. Z. (2019). Performance evaluation of ensemble-based machine learning techniques for prediction of chronic kidney disease. Emerging research in computing, information, communication and applications, Springer: 415-426.

Jain, D., & Singh, V. (2018). Feature selection and classification systems for chronic disease prediction: A review. *Egyptian Informatics Journal*, *19*(3), 179–189. DOI: 10.1016/j.eij.2018.03.002

Jankowski, J., Floege, J., Fliser, D., Böhm, M., & Marx, N. (2021). Cardiovascular Disease in Chronic Kidney Disease: Pathophysiological Insights and Therapeutic Options. *Circulation*, *143*(11), 1157–1172. DOI: 10.1161/CIRCULATIONAHA.120.050686 PMID: 33720773

Jeon, H., & Oh, S. (2020). Hybrid-Recursive Feature Elimination for Efficient Feature Selection. *Applied Sciences (Basel, Switzerland)*, *10*(9), 3211. DOI: 10.3390/app10093211

Jerlin Rubini, L., & Perumal, E. (2020). Efficient classification of chronic kidney disease by using multi-kernel support vector machine and fruit fly optimization algorithm. *International Journal of Imaging Systems and Technology*, *30*(3), 660–673. DOI: 10.1002/ima.22406

Jongbo, O. A., Adetunmbi, A. O., Ogunrinde, R. B., & Badeji-Ajisafe, B. (2020). Development of an ensemble approach to chronic kidney disease diagnosis. *Scientific African*, *8*, e00456. DOI: 10.1016/j.sciaf.2020.e00456

Kohavi, R., & John, G. H. (1997). Wrappers for feature subset selection. *Artificial Intelligence*, *97*(1-2), 273–324. DOI: 10.1016/S0004-3702(97)00043-X

Kunwar, V., Chandel, K., Sabitha, A. S., & Bansal, A. (2016). Chronic Kidney Disease analysis using data mining classification techniques. *2016 6th International Conference-Cloud System and Big Data Engineering (Confluence)*. IEEE.

Misir, R., Mitra, M., & Samanta, R. K. (2017). A reduced set of features for chronic kidney disease prediction. *Journal of Pathology Informatics*, *8*(1), 8. DOI: 10.4103/jpi.jpi_88_16 PMID: 28706750

Motwani, A., Shukla, P. K., & Pawar, M. (2020). Smart Predictive Healthcare Framework for Remote Patient Monitoring and Recommendation Using Deep Learning with Novel Cost Optimization. *International Conference on Information and Communication Technology for Intelligent Systems*, Springer.

Motwani, A., Shukla, P. K., & Pawar, M. (2021). Novel framework based on deep learning and cloud analytics for smart patient monitoring and recommendation (SPMR). *Journal of Ambient Intelligence and Humanized Computing*, *•••*, 1–16.

Motwani, A., Shukla, P. K., & Pawar, M. (2021). Novel Machine Learning Model with Wrapper-Based Dimensionality Reduction for Predicting Chronic Kidney Disease Risk. *Soft Computing and Signal Processing, Springer.*, *1325*, 29–37.

Motwani, A., Shukla, P. K., & Pawar, M. (2022). Ubiquitous and smart healthcare monitoring frameworks based on machine learning: A comprehensive review. *Artificial Intelligence in Medicine*, *134*, 102431. DOI: 10.1016/j.artmed.2022.102431 PMID: 36462891

Motwani, A., Shukla, P. K., Pawar, M., Kumar, M., Ghosh, U., Alnumay, W., & Nayak, S. R. (2023). Enhanced framework for COVID-19 prediction with computed tomography scan images using dense convolutional neural network and novel loss function. *Computers & Electrical Engineering*, *105*, 108479. DOI: 10.1016/j.compeleceng.2022.108479 PMID: 36406625

Musheer, R. A., Verma, C., & Srivastava, N. (2019). Novel machine learning approach for classification of high-dimensional microarray data. *Soft Computing*, *23*(24), 13409–13421. DOI: 10.1007/s00500-019-03879-7

Nathaniel, S., Motwani, A., & Saxena, A. (2018). Cloud based Predictive Model for Detection of 'Chronic Kidney Disease' Risk. *International Journal on Computer Science and Engineering*, *6*(4), 182–188.

Park, S. H., & Han, K. (2018). Methodologic guide for evaluating clinical performance and effect of artificial intelligence technology for medical diagnosis and prediction. *Radiology*, *286*(3), 800–809. DOI: 10.1148/radiol.2017171920 PMID: 29309734

Pearson's Correlation Coefficient. (2008). Encyclopedia of Public Health. W. Kirch. Dordrecht, Springer Netherlands: 1090-1091. Agarwal, S. and R. Srivastava (2009). "Chronic kidney disease in India: challenges and solutions. *Nephron. Clinical Practice*, *111*(3), c197–c203.

Plantinga, L. C., Tuot, D. S., & Powe, N. R. (2010). Awareness of chronic kidney disease among patients and providers. *Advances in Chronic Kidney Disease*, *17*(3), 225–236. DOI: 10.1053/j.ackd.2010.03.002 PMID: 20439091

Polat, H., Mehr, H. D., & Cetin, A. (2017). Diagnosis of chronic kidney disease based on support vector machine by feature selection methods. *Journal of Medical Systems*, *41*(4), 55. DOI: 10.1007/s10916-017-0703-x PMID: 28243816

Qin, J., Chen, L., Liu, Y., Liu, C., Feng, C., & Chen, B. (2019). A machine learning methodology for diagnosing chronic kidney disease. *IEEE Access : Practical Innovations, Open Solutions*, *8*, 20991–21002. DOI: 10.1109/ACCESS.2019.2963053

Rao, K. E., & Rao, G. A. (2021). Ensemble learning with recursive feature elimination integrated software effort estimation: A novel approach. *Evolutionary Intelligence*, *14*(1), 151–162. DOI: 10.1007/s12065-020-00360-5

Remuzzi, G., Ruggenenti, P., & Perico, N. (2002). Chronic renal diseases: Renoprotective benefits of renin–angiotensin system inhibition. *Annals of Internal Medicine, 136*(8), 604–615. DOI: 10.7326/0003-4819-136-8-200204160-00010 PMID: 11955029

Rubini, L. J. J. T. A. U., & the Department of Computer Science and Engineering. (2015). "UCIMachineLearningRepository [http://archive. ics. uci. edu/ml/datasets/Chronic_Kidney_Disease]. Karaikudi.

Said, S., & Hernandez, G. T. (2014). The link between chronic kidney disease and cardiovascular disease. *Journal of Nephropathology, 3*(3), 99. PMID: 25093157

Salekin, A., & Stankovic, J. (2016). Detection of chronic kidney disease and selecting important predictive attributes. *2016 IEEE International Conference on Healthcare Informatics (ICHI)*, IEEE. DOI: 10.1109/ICHI.2016.36

Saringat, Z., Mustapha, A., Saedudin, R. R., & Samsudin, N. A. (2019). Comparative analysis of classification algorithms for chronic kidney disease diagnosis. *Bulletin of Electrical Engineering and Informatics, 8*(4), 1496–1501. DOI: 10.11591/eei.v8i4.1621

Sedighi, Z., Ebrahimpour-Komleh, H., & Mousavirad, S. J. (2015). Featue selection effects on kidney desease analysis. *2015 International Congress on Technology, Communication and Knowledge (ICTCK)*, IEEE. DOI: 10.1109/ICTCK.2015.7582712

Segal, Z., Kalifa, D., Radinsky, K., Ehrenberg, B., Elad, G., Maor, G., Lewis, M., Tibi, M., Korn, L., & Koren, G. (2020). Machine learning algorithm for early detection of end-stage renal disease. *BMC Nephrology, 21*(1), 1–10. DOI: 10.1186/s12882-020-02093-0 PMID: 33246427

Senan, E. M., Al-Adhaileh, M. H., Alsaade, F. W., Aldhyani, T. H., Alqarni, A. A., Alsharif, N., Uddin, M. I., Alahmadi, A. H., Jadhav, M. E., & Alzahrani, M. Y. (2021). Diagnosis of Chronic Kidney Disease Using Effective Classification Algorithms and Recursive Feature Elimination Techniques. *Journal of Healthcare Engineering, 2021*, 2021. DOI: 10.1155/2021/1004767 PMID: 34211680

Song, X., Waitman, L. R., Hu, Y., Yu, A. S., Robins, D., & Liu, M. (2019). Robust clinical marker identification for diabetic kidney disease with ensemble feature selection. *Journal of the American Medical Informatics Association : JAMIA, 26*(3), 242–253. DOI: 10.1093/jamia/ocy165 PMID: 30602020

Tazin, N., Sabab, S. A., & Chowdhury, M. T. (2016). Diagnosis of Chronic Kidney Disease using effective classification and feature selection technique. *2016 International Conference on Medical Engineering, Health Informatics and Technology (MediTec)*, IEEE. DOI: 10.1109/MEDITEC.2016.7835365

Xiao, J., Ding, R., Xu, X., Guan, H., Feng, X., Sun, T., Zhu, S., & Ye, Z. (2019). Comparison and development of machine learning tools in the prediction of chronic kidney disease progression. *Journal of Translational Medicine*, *17*(1), 119. DOI: 10.1186/s12967-019-1860-0 PMID: 30971285

Xiao, J., Ding, R., Xu, X., Guan, H., Feng, X., Sun, T., Zhu, S., & Ye, Z. (2019). Comparison and development of machine learning tools in the prediction of chronic kidney disease progression. *Journal of Translational Medicine*, *17*(1), 1–13. DOI: 10.1186/s12967-019-1860-0 PMID: 30971285

Yildirim, P. (2017). Chronic kidney disease prediction on imbalanced data by multilayer perceptron: Chronic kidney disease prediction. 2017 IEEE 41st Annual Computer Software and Applications Conference (COMPSAC), IEEE. DOI: 10.1109/COMPSAC.2017.84

Zeynu, S., & Patil, S. (2018). Prediction of chronic kidney disease using data mining feature selection and ensemble method. *International Journal of Data Mining in Genomics and Proteomics*, *9*(1), 1–9.

Compilation of References

Abràmoff, M. D., Lou, Y., Erginay, A., Clarida, W., Amelon, R., Folk, J. C., & Niemeijer, M. (2016). Improved automated detection of diabetic retinopathy on a publicly available dataset through integration of deep learning. *Investigative Ophthalmology & Visual Science*, *57*(13), 5200–5206. DOI: 10.1167/iovs.16-19964 PMID: 27701631

Adeyemi, F. A., Jempeji, A. A., Olaniran, A. O., Taliat, M. K., & Adeleke, A. T. (2025). Climate risks and financial stability: A global evidence. *Finance Research Open*, *1*(3), 100032. DOI: 10.1016/j.finr.2025.100032

Alaiad, A., Najadat, H., Mohsen, B., & Balhaf, K. (2020). Classification and association rule mining technique for predicting chronic kidney disease. *Journal of Information and Knowledge Management*, *19*(01), 2040015. DOI: 10.1142/S0219649220400158

Alghamdi, M., Alharbi, B., & Khoder, M. (2023). Dust storm frequency and air quality implications in central Saudi Arabia. *Atmospheric Environment*, *298*, 120056.

Al-Harbi, A. (2025). Green financing for sustainable development in Saudi Arabia. *Journal of Environmental Management and Tourism*, *16*(2), 95–105. DOI: 10.14505/jemt.v16.2(78).01

Alharbi, F., & Alotaibi, M. (2024). Integrating climate adaptation into local governance: A Saudi perspective. *Sustainability*, *16*(8), 5124.

Alhelal, A. A., Alshiha, A. A., & Al-Romeedy, B. S. (2025). AI-Driven Sustainable Competitive Advantage in Tourism and Hospitality: Mediating Roles of Digital Culture and Skills. *Sustainability (Basel)*, *17*(19), 8903. DOI: 10.3390/su17198903

Ali, F., Rasoolimanesh, S. M., & Cobanoglu, C. (2020). Customer experience and satisfaction in hospitality: Examining the role of technology. *Journal of Hospitality Marketing & Management*, *29*(7), 1–23.

Aljaaf, A. J., Al-Jumeily, D., Haglan, H. M., Alloghani, M., Baker, T., Hussain, A. J., & Mustafina, J. (2018). *Early prediction of chronic kidney disease using machine learning supported by predictive analytics. 2018 IEEE congress on evolutionary computation (CEC)*. IEEE.

Allal-Chérif, O. (2022). Intelligent cathedrals: Using augmented reality, virtual reality, and artificial intelligence to provide an intense cultural, historical, and religious visitor experience. *Technological Forecasting and Social Change*, *178*, 1–10. DOI: 10.1016/j.techfore.2022.121604

Almansour, N. A., Syed, H. F., Khayat, N. R., Altheeb, R. K., Juri, R. E., Alhiyafi, J., Alrashed, S., & Olatunji, S. O. (2019). Neural network and support vector machine for the prediction of chronic kidney disease: A comparative study. *Computers in Biology and Medicine*, *109*, 101–111. DOI: 10.1016/j.compbiomed.2019.04.017 PMID: 31054385

Almasoud, M., & Ward, T. E. (2019). Detection of chronic kidney disease using machine learning algorithms with least number of predictors. *International Journal of Advanced Computer Science and Applications*, *10*(8). Advance online publication. DOI: 10.14569/IJACSA.2019.0100813

Almazroui, M., Islam, M. N., & O'Brien, E. (2022). Extreme rainfall and flood risk in Saudi Arabia under climate change scenarios. *Climate Dynamics*, *59*(3), 987–1004.

Almheiri, A. (2024). Climate change hazards and the resilience of coastal cities in the GCC: A review. *Regional Environmental Studies Journal*, *12*(2), 45–63.

Alotaibi, M., Al-Sahli, M., & Hussein, K. (2023). Water scarcity and sustainable agriculture in arid Saudi regions. *Environmental Management*, *72*(4), 812–825.

Al-Romeedy, B. S., & Singh, A. (2025a). From Search to Stay: Mapping the Digital Journey of the Modern Traveler. In Azman, N., Valeri, M., Albattat, A., & Singh, A. (Eds.), *Decoding Tourist Behavior in the Digital Era: Insights for Effective Marketing* (pp. 283–308). IGI Global Scientific Publishing., DOI: 10.4018/979-8-3693-3972-5.ch012

Al-Romeedy, B. S., & Singh, A. (2025b). Reimagining Customer Relations Through AI Innovation. In Darwish, D., & Kumar, S. (Eds.), *Utilizing AI and Machine Learning in Financial Analysis* (pp. 351–368). IGI Global Scientific Publishing., DOI: 10.4018/979-8-3693-8507-4.ch019

Amann, J., Blasimme, A., Vayena, E., Frey, D., & Madai, V. I. (2020). Explainability for artificial intelligence in healthcare: A multidisciplinary perspective. *BMC Medical Informatics and Decision Making*, *20*(1), 310. DOI: 10.1186/s12911-020-01332-6 PMID: 33256715

Ambardar, A., Singh, A., & Singh, V. (2023). Barriers in Implementing Ergonomic Practices in Hotels- A Study on five star hotels in NCR region. *International Journal of Hospitality and Tourism Systems*, *16*(2), 11–17.

Angorani, S. (2024). Green finance and sustainable development: A cross-sectional study of financial mechanisms driving environmental responsibility. *Indonesian Journal of Economics, Business, Accounting, and Management*, *2*(4), 77–91. DOI: 10.63901/ijebam.v2i4.70

Ansari, A. I., Singh, A., Pattanaik, S., Patnaik, R., & Suryawanshi, U. (2024). Exploring the Role of AI-Powered Virtual Assistants in Optimizing Self-Service Experiences for Customers Within the Service Sector. In Nadda, V., Tyagi, P., Singh, A., & Singh, V. (Eds.), *Integrating AI-Driven Technologies Into Service Marketing* (pp. 225–238). IGI Global Scientific Publishing., DOI: 10.4018/979-8-3693-7122-0.ch013

Arcodia, C., & Whitford, M. (2006). Festival attendance and the development of social capital. *Journal of Convention & Event Tourism*, *8*(2), 1–18. DOI: 10.1300/J452v08n02_01

Arora, M., Ahmad, V., Arora, T., & Kumar, R. (2024). Digital Transformation and Talent Management. In Green Metaverse for Greener Economies (pp. 50-70). CRC Press. DOI: 10.1201/9781032638188-4

Asha, John., Pankaj, Kumar, Tyagi., Vipin, Nadda. (2024). 1. Examining the Impact of Virtual Media on Event Tourism Investigating New Possibilities. Advances in hospitality, tourism and the services industry (AHTSI) book series, DOI: 10.4018/979-8-3693-6755-1.ch011

Atlantic Council. (2023). *Climate Profile.*

Atzeni, M., Del Chiappa, G., & Mei Pung, J. (2022). Enhancing visit intention in heritage tourism: The role of object-based and existential authenticity in non-immersive virtual reality heritage experiences. *International Journal of Tourism Research*, *24*(2), 240–255. DOI: 10.1002/jtr.2497

Ayeh, J. K., Au, N., & Law, R. (2013). "Do we believe in TripAdvisor?" Examining credibility perceptions and online travelers' attitude toward using user-generated content. *Journal of Travel Research*, *52*(4), 437–452. DOI: 10.1177/0047287512475217

Azour, L., Goldin, J. G., & Kruskal, J. B. (2024). Radiologist and radiology practice wellbeing: A report of the 2023 ARRS wellness summit. *Academic Radiology*, *31*(1), 250–260. DOI: 10.1016/j.acra.2023.08.025 PMID: 37718125

Balakrishnan, N., & Rajendran, A. (2020). Computing WHERE-WHAT classification through FLIKM and deep learning algorithms. In *Advances in Electrical and Computer Technologies: Select Proceedings of ICAECT 2019* (pp. 593-608). Singapore: Springer Singapore. DOI: 10.1007/978-981-15-5558-9_52

Balakrishnan, J., Dwivedi, Y. K., Malik, F. T., & Baabdullah, A. M. (2021). Role of smart tourism technology in heritage tourism development. *Journal of Sustainable Tourism*, •••, 1–20. DOI: 10.1080/09669582.2021.1995398

Banerjee, T., Crews, D. C., Wesson, D. E., Tilea, A. M., Saran, R., Ríos-Burrows, N., Williams, D. E., & Powe, N. R. (2015). High dietary acid load predicts ESRD among adults with CKD. *Journal of the American Society of Nephrology*, *26*(7), 1693–1700. DOI: 10.1681/ASN.2014040332 PMID: 25677388

Banerjee, T., Crews, D. C., Wesson, D. E., Tilea, A., Saran, R., Burrows, N. R., Williams, D. E., & Powe, N. R. (2014). Dietary acid load and chronic kidney disease among adults in the United States. *BMC Nephrology*, *15*(1), 1–12. DOI: 10.1186/1471-2369-15-137 PMID: 25151260

Banerjee, T., Scherzer, R., Powe, N. R., Steffick, D., Shahinian, V., Saran, R., Pavkov, M. E., Saydah, S., & Shlipak, M. G. (2014). Race and other risk factors for incident proteinuria in a national cohort of HIV-infected veterans. *Journal of Acquired Immune Deficiency Syndromes*, *67*(2), 145–152. DOI: 10.1097/QAI.0000000000000285 PMID: 25072613

Basar, M. D., & Akan, A. (2017). Detection of chronic kidney disease by using ensemble classifiers. 2017 10th International Conference on Electrical and Electronics Engineering (ELECO), IEEE.

Baumgartner, C. F., Koch, L. M., Pollefeys, M., & Konukoglu, E. (2017, September). An exploration of 2D and 3D deep learning techniques for cardiac MR image segmentation. In *International workshop on statistical atlases and computational models of the heart* (pp. 111-119). Cham: Springer International Publishing.

Beck, J., Rainoldi, M., & Egger, R. (2019). Virtual reality in tourism: A state-of-the-art review. *Tourism Review*, *74*(3), 586–612. DOI: 10.1108/TR-03-2017-0049

Bekbolatova, M., Mayer, J., Ong, C. W., & Toma, M. (2024, January). Transformative potential of AI in healthcare: definitions, applications, and navigating the ethical landscape and public perspectives. In Healthcare (Vol. 12, No. 2, p. 125). MDPI. DOI: 10.3390/healthcare12020125

Belgiu, M., & Drăguţ, L. (2016). Random forest in remote sensing: A review of applications and future directions. *ISPRS Journal of Photogrammetry and Remote Sensing*, *114*, 24–31. DOI: 10.1016/j.isprsjprs.2016.01.011

Ben Ahmed, M. (2024). Modern Trends in Green Interior Architecture Applications with Smart Systems. *International Journal of Multidisciplinary Studies in Art and Technology*, *7*(1), 1–21. DOI: 10.21608/ijmsat.2024.293946.1027

Benjamens, S., Rijkse, E., te Velde-Keyzer, C. A., Berger, S. P., Moers, C., de Borst, M. H., Yakar, D., Slart, R. H. J. A., Dor, F. J. M. F., Minnee, R. C., & Pol, R. A. (2020). Aorto-iliac artery calcification prior to kidney transplantation. *Journal of Clinical Medicine*, *9*(9), 2893. DOI: 10.3390/jcm9092893 PMID: 32906789

Berezina, K., Ciftci, O., & Cobanoglu, C. (2020). Robots, artificial intelligence, and service automation in hospitality. *International Journal of Contemporary Hospitality Management*, *32*(5), 1927–1946.

Berjozkina, G., & Karami, R. (2021). 3D printing in tourism: An answer to sustainability challenges? *Worldwide Hospitality and Tourism Themes*, *13*(6), 773–788.

Berry, K., & Singh, A. (2024). AI-Driven Service Marketing: Transforming Customer Experience and Operational Efficiency. In Nadda, V., Tyagi, P., Singh, A., & Singh, V. (Eds.), *AI Innovations in Service and Tourism Marketing* (pp. 35–56). IGI Global Scientific Publishing., DOI: 10.4018/979-8-3693-7909-7.ch003

Bharadiya, J. P., Thomas, R. K., & Ahmed, F. (2023). Rise of artificial intelligence in business and industry. *Journal of Engineering Research and Reports*, *25*(3), 85–103. DOI: 10.9734/jerr/2023/v25i3893

Bharti, K., Agarwal, R., & Satsangi, A. K. (2024). *Behavioral Intention of Consumers for Green Marketing in India: The Mediating Role of Consumer Environmental Attitude*. Jindal Journal of Business Research., DOI: 10.1177/22786821241256188

Bibri, S. E., & Jagatheesaperumal, S. K. (2023). Harnessing the potential of the metaverse and artificial intelligence for the internet of city things: Cost-effective XReality and synergistic AIoT technologies. *Smart Cities*, *6*(5), 2397–2429. DOI: 10.3390/smartcities6050109

Bilgihan, A. (2016). Gen Y customer loyalty in online shopping: An integrated model of trust, user experience, and branding. *Computers in Human Behavior*, *61*, 103–113.

Bilgihan, A., Ostinelli, M., Zhang, Y., & Lorenz, M. (2025). Artificial intelligence (AI) agents and the future of customer loyalty. *International Journal of Contemporary Hospitality Management*, *37*(9), 3240–3262. DOI: 10.1108/IJCHM-03-2025-0373

Boas, F. E., & Fleischmann, D. (2012). CT artifacts: Causes and reduction techniques. *Imaging in Medicine*, *4*(2), 229–240. DOI: 10.2217/iim.12.13

Bouzidi, F. M., Nefzi, A. A., & Al Yousif, M. (2024). Impact of international oil price shocks and inflation on bank efficiency and financial stability: Evidence from Saudi Arabian banking sector. *Journal of Risk and Financial Management*, *17*(12), 543. DOI: 10.3390/jrfm17120543

Brady, A. P. (2017). Error and discrepancy in radiology: Inevitable or avoidable? *Insights Into Imaging*, *8*(1), 171–182. DOI: 10.1007/s13244-016-0534-1 PMID: 27928712

Brandtzæg, P. B., Lüders, M., & Skjetne, J. H. (2010). Too many facebook "Friends"? content sharing and sociability versus the need for privacy in social network sites. *International Journal of Human-Computer Interaction*, *26*(11–12), 1006–1030. DOI: 10.1080/10447318.2010.516719

Britannica, T. Editors of Encyclopaedia. (2024). Rubʿ al-Khali. In Encyclopaedia Britannica.

Brown, T., & Drakeley, C. (2023). 1 From pixels to possibilities: Innovations within virtual and hybrid events. Virtual Events Management, 1.

Brown, O., Davison, R. M., Decker, S., Ellis, D. A., Faulconbridge, J., Gore, J., Greenwood, M., Islam, G., Lubinski, C., MacKenzie, N. G., Meyer, R., Muzio, D., Quattrone, P., Ravishankar, M. N., Zilber, T., Ren, S., Sarala, R. M., & Hibbert, P. (2024). Theory-driven perspectives on generative artificial intelligence in business and management. *British Journal of Management*, *35*(1), 3–23. DOI: 10.1111/1467-8551.12788

Buhalis, D., & Amaranggana, A. (2015). Smart tourism destinations. In Xiang, Z., & Tussyadiah, I. (Eds.), *Information and communication technologies in tourism* (pp. 553–564). Springer.

Buhalis, D., & Leung, R. (2018). Smart hospitality—Interconnectivity and interoperability towards an ecosystem. *International Journal of Hospitality Management*, *71*, 41–50. DOI: 10.1016/j.ijhm.2017.11.011

Buhalis, D., & Moldavska, A. (2022). Metaverse and tourism: Hybrid experiences and smart ecosystems. *Journal of Tourism Futures*, *9*(1), 105–120.

Buhalis, D., & Sinarta, Y. (2019). Real-time co-creation and nowness service: Lessons from tourism and hospitality. *Journal of Travel & Tourism Marketing*, *36*(5), 563–582.

Bushberg, J. T., Seibert, J., Leidholdt, E., & Boone, J. (2012). Magnetic resonance basics, magnetic fields, nuclear magnetic characteristics, tissue contrast, image acquisition. *The Essential Physics of Medical Imaging*, 402-448.

Centobelli, P., & Ndou, V. (2019). Managing customer knowledge through the use of big data analytics in tourism research. *Current Issues in Tourism*, *22*(15), 1862–1882. DOI: 10.1080/13683500.2018.1564739

Chan, F., Thong, J., Venkatesh, V., Brown, S., Hu, P., & Tam, K. (2010). Modeling citizen satisfaction with mandatory adoption of an e-tovernment technology. *Journal of the Association for Information Systems*, *11*(10), 519–549. DOI: 10.17705/1jais.00239

Charleonnan, A., Fufaung, T., Niyomwong, T., Chokchueypattanakit, W., Suwannawach, S., & Ninchawee, N. (2016). *Predictive analytics for chronic kidney disease using machine learning techniques*. *2016 management and innovation technology international conference (MITicon)*. IEEE.

Chaudhary, M., Sahani, G., & Ghouse, S. M. (2025). Artificial Intelligence and Hyper-Personalisation in Travel Platforms. In Impact of Digital Transformation on Business Growth and Performance (pp. 121-144). IGI Global Scientific Publishing. DOI: 10.4018/979-8-3693-9783-1.ch005

Chaudhuri, A. K., Sinha, D., Banerjee, D. K., & Das, A. (2021). A novel enhanced decision tree model for detecting chronic kidney disease. *Network Modeling and Analysis in Health Informatics and Bioinformatics*, *10*(1), 1–22. DOI: 10.1007/s13721-021-00302-w PMID: 34849327

Cheng, H.-T., Xu, X., Lim, P. S., & Hung, K.-Y. (2021). Worldwide epidemiology of diabetes-related end-stage renal disease, 2000–2015. *Diabetes Care*, *44*(1), 89–97. DOI: 10.2337/dc20-1913 PMID: 33203706

Chen, Z., Zhang, X., & Zhang, Z. (2016). Clinical risk assessment of patients with chronic kidney disease by using clinical data and multivariate models. *International Urology and Nephrology*, *48*(12), 2069–2075. DOI: 10.1007/s11255-016-1346-4 PMID: 27334750

Cherenkov, E., Benga, V., Lee, M., Nandwani, N., Raguin, K., Sueur, M. C., & Sun, G. (2024). From machine learning algorithms to superior customer experience: Business implications of machine learning-driven data analytics in the hospitality industry. *Journal of Smart Tourism*, *4*(2), 5–14. DOI: 10.52255/smarttourism.2024.4.2.2

Chin, Y. S., Mohamad, A. A., & Lo, M. C. (2024). Harnessing the power of artificial intelligence (AI): A paradigm shift in HRM practices for employee sustainable performance. *Global Knowledge, Memory and Communication*. Advance online publication. DOI: 10.1108/GKMC-06-2024-0355

Chi, O. H., Jia, S., Li, Y., & Gursoy, D. (2021). Developing a formative scale to measure consumers' trust toward interaction with artificially intelligent (AI) social robots in service delivery. *Computers in Human Behavior*, *118*(0), 106700. DOI: 10.1016/j.chb.2021.106700

Chiou, W.-B., Wan, C.-S., & Lee, H.-Y. (2008). Virtual experience vs brochures in the advertisement of scenic spots: How cognitive preferences and order effects influence advertising effects on consumers. *Tourism Management*, *29*(1), 146–150. DOI: 10.1016/j.tourman.2007.03.016

Christ, P. F., Ettlinger, F., Grün, F., Elshaera, M. E. A., Lipkova, J., Schlecht, S., . . . Menze, B. (2017). Automatic liver and tumor segmentation of CT and MRI volumes using cascaded fully convolutional neural networks. *arXiv preprint arXiv:1702.05970*.

Cinar, A. B., & Bilodeau, S. (2024). Incorporating AI into the inner circle of emotional intelligence for sustainability. *Sustainability (Basel)*, *16*(15), 6648. DOI: 10.3390/su16156648

Collier, J. E., & Sherrell, D. L. (2010). Examining the influence of control and convenience in self-service technology adoption. *Journal of the Academy of Marketing Science*, *38*(4), 490–509.

Control, C. f. D. and Prevention (2021). "Chronic kidney disease in the United States, 2021." US Department of Health Human Services, Centers for Disease Control Prevention.

Coudray, N., Ocampo, P. S., Sakellaropoulos, T., Narula, N., Snuderl, M., Fenyö, D., Moreira, A. L., Razavian, N., & Tsirigos, A. (2018). Classification and mutation prediction from non–small cell lung cancer histopathology images using deep learning. *Nature Medicine*, *24*(10), 1559–1567. DOI: 10.1038/s41591-018-0177-5 PMID: 30224757

Dahiya, A., Bhatt, P., Kumar, A., & Kant, S. (2025). Factors influencing green product purchase intention: A structural equation modelling approach utilising PEST framework. *Indian Journal of Marketing*, *55*(8), 69–88. Advance online publication. DOI: 10.17010/ijom/2025/v55/i8/175210

Das, R. C., Basavaraj, S., Thankachan, J., & Thaliyan, D. (2025). The Impact of AI and Agile HR on Talent Acquisition and Onboarding in the Service Industry. In *AI and Innovation in HRM* (pp. 394–416). Routledge. DOI: 10.4324/9781003522157-24

Davidson, R., McPherson, G., & Ramos, A. (2018). *Events management: Principles and practice* (4th ed.). Routledge.

Desai, A., & Mehta, P. (2025). The Interplay of Brand Strength, Profitability, And Equity Valuation: Evidence from The Indian Market. *International Journal of Management and Business Development*, *2*(05), 1–6.

Dhakal, S. P., & Tjokro, S. (2024). Local Tourism Businesses in the Digital Era: Implications for Bridging the Critical Skills Gap in Indonesia. In The Future of Work in the Asia Pacific (pp. 146-157). Routledge.

Dilanchian, A. T., Andringa, R., & Boot, W. R. (2021). A pilot study exploring age differences in presence, workload, and cybersickness in the experience of immersive virtual reality environments. *Frontiers in Virtual Reality*, *2*, 736793. DOI: 10.3389/frvir.2021.736793

Disztinger, P., Schlögl, S., & Groth, A. (2017). Technology acceptance of virtual reality for travel planning. In Schegg, R., & Stangl, B. (Eds.), *Information and communication technologies in tourism 2017* (pp. 255–268). Springer International Publishing. DOI: 10.1007/978-3-319-51168-9_19

Doi, K. (2007). Computer-aided diagnosis in medical imaging: Historical review, current status and future potential. *Computerized Medical Imaging and Graphics*, *31*(4-5), 198–211. DOI: 10.1016/j.compmedimag.2007.02.002 PMID: 17349778

Dong, X., Yu, Z., Cao, W., Shi, Y., & Ma, Q. (2020). A survey on ensemble learning. *Frontiers of Computer Science*, *14*(2), 241–258. DOI: 10.1007/s11704-019-8208-z

Dubey, D., Gupta, D., Agarwal, N., Jain, N., & Thapliyal, B. L. (2024). Generation Z's Green Purchase Intentions: Impact of Consumer Attitude, Brand Positioning, and Knowledge. Library Progress International, 44(3).

Dwivedi, Y. K., Helal, M. Y. I., Elgendy, I. A., Albashrawi, M. A., Hughes, L., Shawosh, M., Dutot, V., & Jeon, I. (2025). Artificial intelligence agents and agentic systems in hospitality and tourism: Challenges, opportunities and research agenda. *International Journal of Contemporary Hospitality Management*. Advance online publication. DOI: 10.1108/IJCHM-02-2025-0287

El Hajal, G., & Yeoman, I. (2024). AI and the future of talent management in tourism and hospitality. *Current Issues in Tourism*, •••, 1–18. DOI: 10.1080/13683500.2024.2439395

Elhoseny, M., Shankar, K., & Uthayakumar, J. (2019). Intelligent diagnostic prediction and classification system for chronic kidney disease. *Scientific Reports, 9*(1), 1–14. DOI: 10.1038/s41598-019-46074-2 PMID: 31270387

Elkington, J. (1997). *Cannibals with forks: The triple bottom line of 21st century business.* Capstone.

Enholm, I. M., Papagiannidis, E., Mikalef, P., & Krogstie, J. (2022). Artificial intelligence and business value: A literature review. *Information Systems Frontiers, 24*(5), 1709–1734. DOI: 10.1007/s10796-021-10186-w

Ercik, C., & Kardaş, K. (2024). Reflections of digital technologies on human resources management in the tourism sector. *Worldwide Hospitality and Tourism Themes, 16*(5), 646–663. DOI: 10.1108/WHATT-09-2024-0208

Ersanlı, C. Y., Çelik, F., Barjesteh, H., Duran, V., & Manoochehrzadeh, M. (2025). A review of global reskilling and upskilling initiatives in the age of AI. *AI and Ethics, 5*(6), 1–10. DOI: 10.1007/s43681-025-00767-9

Esteva, A., Kuprel, B., Novoa, R. A., Ko, J., Swetter, S. M., Blau, H. M., & Thrun, S. (2017). Dermatologist-level classification of skin cancer with deep neural networks. *nature, 542*(7639), 115-118.

Exploring Climate-Induced Agricultural Risk in Saudi Arabia: Evidence from Farming Communities of Medina Region. (2024*Sustainability16*104245DOI: 10.3390/su16104245

Fan, X., Jiang, X., & Deng, N. (2022). Immersive technology: A meta-analysis of augmented/virtual reality applications and their impact on tourism experience. *Tourism Management, 91*, 1–13. DOI: 10.1016/j.tourman.2022.104534

Fernandes, S., Sathish, M., & Shrivastava, P. (2024). Effect of Consciousness in Sustainable Consumption Habits on Purchase Intention of Green Products: Comparison Study Between India and USA. *Indian Journal of Marketing, 54*(10), 8–24. DOI: 10.17010/ijom/2024/v54/i10/174602

Filimonau, V., & De Coteau, D. (2020). Food waste management practices in hospitality operations: A critical review. *Tourism Management, 71*, 234–245. DOI: 10.1016/j.tourman.2018.10.009

Flood Risk and Vulnerability from a Changing Climate Perspective: An Overview Focusing on Flash Floods and Associated Hazards in Jeddah. (2023). Water, 15(20), 3641.

Frid-Adar, M., Diamant, I., Klang, E., Amitai, M., Goldberger, J., & Greenspan, H. (2018). GAN-based synthetic medical image augmentation for increased CNN performance in liver lesion classification. *Neurocomputing*, *321*, 321–331. DOI: 10.1016/j.neucom.2018.09.013

G20 Climate Risk Atlas. (2024). Saudi Arabia Climate Profile.

Garcia, M. D. J. (2024). *Essays on Consumer Preferences and Economic Resilience in Latin American Food Supply Chain* (Doctoral dissertation).

Garrett, J. J. (2010). Customer loyalty and the elements of user experience. *Design Management Review*, *17*(1), 35–39. DOI: 10.1111/j.1948-7169.2006.tb00027.x

Garrido, S. (2018). The influence of personality and coping style on the affective outcomes of nostalgia: Is nostalgia a healthy coping mechanism or rumination? *Personality and Individual Differences*, *120*, 259–264. DOI: 10.1016/j.paid.2016.07.021

Garrigós-Simón, F. J., Galdón-Salvador, J. L., & Gil-Pechuán, I. (2015). The economic sustainability of tourism growth through leakage calculation. *Tourism Economics*, *21*(4), 721–739. DOI: 10.5367/te.2014.0372

George, A. S. (2024). The evolution of economic models: From knowledge to intuition and optimization. *Partners Universal Multidisciplinary Research Journal*, *1*(2), 1–25.

Getz, D., & Page, S. J. (2016). *Event studies: Theory, research and policy for planned events* (3rd ed.). Routledge. DOI: 10.4324/9781315708027

Ghassemi, M., Oakden-Rayner, L., & Beam, A. L. (2021). The false hope of current approaches to explainable artificial intelligence in health care. *The Lancet. Digital Health*, *3*(11), e745–e750. DOI: 10.1016/S2589-7500(21)00208-9 PMID: 34711379

Goldstein, S. L. (2012). Acute kidney injury in children and its potential consequences in adulthood. *Blood Purification*, *33*(1-3), 131–137. DOI: 10.1159/000334143 PMID: 22269297

Goodfellow, I. (2016). Deep learning.

Gretzel, U., Sigala, M., Xiang, Z., & Koo, C. (2015). Smart tourism: Foundations and developments. *Electronic Markets*, *25*(3), 179–188. DOI: 10.1007/s12525-015-0196-8

Gretzel, U., Werthner, H., Koo, C., & Lamsfus, C. (2022). Conceptual foundations for understanding smart tourism ecosystems. *Computers in Human Behavior*, *132*, 107–239.

Guesmi, K., Makrychoriti, P., & Pyrgiotakis, E. G. (2025). Climate change exposure and green bonds issuance. *Journal of International Money and Finance*, *152*, 103281. DOI: 10.1016/j.jimonfin.2025.103281

Gulshan, V., Peng, L., Coram, M., Stumpe, M. C., Wu, D., Narayanaswamy, A., ... & Webster, D. R. (2016). Development and validation of a deep learning algorithm for detection of diabetic retinopathy in retinal fundus photographs. *jama, 316*(22), 2402-2410.

Gupta, P., & Pareek, R. (2024). AI-Enabled Guest Experience: Disrupting Hospitality Through Next-Generation AI Technologies. In Technology and Luxury Hospitality (pp. 165-181). Routledge.

Gupta, S., & Srivastava, R. (2022). AI-enhanced guest feedback analytics in heritage hotels: A case of Taj Group. *Journal of Heritage Hospitality*, *14*(2), 88–102.

Gursoy, D. (2025). Artificial intelligence (AI) technology, its applications and the use of AI powered devices in hospitality service experience creation and delivery. *International Journal of Hospitality Management*, *129*, 104212. DOI: 10.1016/j.ijhm.2025.104212

Gursoy, D., Chi, O. H., Lu, L., & Nunkoo, R. (2019). Consumers' acceptance of artificially intelligent (AI) device use in service delivery. *International Journal of Information Management*, *49*, 157–169. DOI: 10.1016/j.ijinfomgt.2019.03.008

Guttentag, D. (2020). Virtual reality: Applications and implications for tourism. *Tourism Management*, *71*, 315–327.

Haaksma, T. R., De Jong, M. D. T., & Karreman, J. (2018). Users' personal conceptions of usability and user experience of electronic and software products. *IEEE Transactions on Professional Communication*, *61*(2), 116–132. DOI: 10.1109/TPC.2018.2795398

Hair, J. F., Black, W. C., Babin, B. J., & Anderson, R. E. (2019). *Multivariate data analysis* (8th ed.). Cengage Learning.

Hammady, R., Ma, M., Al-Kalha, Z., & Strathearn, C. (2021). A framework for constructing and evaluating the role of MR as a holographic virtual guide in museums. *Virtual Reality (Waltham Cross)*, *25*(4), 895–918. DOI: 10.1007/s10055-020-00497-9

Han, D. I., Tom Dieck, M. C., & Jung, T. (2018). User experience model for augmented reality applications in urban heritage tourism. *Journal of Heritage Tourism*, *13*(1), 46–61. DOI: 10.1080/1743873X.2016.1251931

Han, H., Lee, J. S., Trang, H. L. T., & Kim, W. (2019). Water conservation and waste reduction management for increasing guest loyalty in hotels. *International Journal of Hospitality Management*, *77*, 58–67.

Han, J. H., & Bae, S. Y. (2022). Roles of authenticity and nostalgia in cultural heritage tourists' travel experience sharing behavior on social media. *Asia Pacific Journal of Tourism Research*, *27*(4), 411–427. DOI: 10.1080/10941665.2022.2075776

Hardcastle, K., Vorster, L., & Brown, D. M. (2025). Understanding customer responses to AI-Driven personalized journeys: Impacts on the customer experience. *Journal of Advertising*, *54*(2), 176–195. DOI: 10.1080/00913367.2025.2460985

Hasan, K. Z., & Hasan, M. Z. (2019). Performance evaluation of ensemble-based machine learning techniques for prediction of chronic kidney disease. Emerging research in computing, information, communication and applications, Springer: 415-426.

Hassenzahl, M. (2003). The thing and I: Understanding the relationship between user and product. In Blythe, M. A. (Ed.), *Funology*. Springer, Netherlands. DOI: 10.1007/1-4020-2967-5_4

Hofstede, G., Hofstede, G. J., & Minkov, M. (2010). *Cultures and organizations: Software of the mind* (3rd ed.). McGraw-Hill.

Hosny, A., Parmar, C., Quackenbush, J., Schwartz, L. H., & Aerts, H. J. (2018). Artificial intelligence in radiology. *Nature Reviews. Cancer*, *18*(8), 500–510. DOI: 10.1038/s41568-018-0016-5 PMID: 29777175

Hussain, M. A., Alsayegh, M. F., & Boshnak, H. A. (2025). The role of ESG disclosure in enhancing profitability and market value: Insights from Saudi Arabia's corporate landscape. *The Economics and Finance Letters*, *12*(2), 158–182. DOI: 10.18488/29.v12i2.4171

Hussain, S., Singh, A. M., Mohanty, P., & Gavinolla, M. R. (2023). Next generation employability and career sustainability in the hospitality industry 5.0. *Worldwide Hospitality and Tourism Themes*, *15*(3), 308–321. DOI: 10.1108/WHATT-01-2023-0011

Ijsselsteijn, W. A., & Riva, G. (2003) Being there: The experience of presence in mediated environments. In: Riva G, Davide F, Ijsselsteijn WA (eds) Being there: Concepts, effects and measurement of user presence in synthetic environments. Ios Press, pp 4–16

IMF (International Monetary Fund). (2024). Global Financial Stability Report: Steadying the Course: Uncertainty, Artificial Intelligence, and Financial Stability. Washington. https://www.imf.org/-/media/files/publications/gfsr/2024/october/english/textrevised.pdf

Iqbal, J., Shahbaz, M., & Ozturk, I. (2025). The role of institutional quality in the nexus between green financing and sustainable development. Research in International Business and Finance, 73(Part A), 102531. https://doi.org/DOI: 10.1016/j.ribaf.2024.102531

Irvin, J., Rajpurkar, P., Ko, M., Yu, Y., Ciurea-Ilcus, S., Chute, C., Marklund, H., Haghgoo, B., Ball, R., Shpanskaya, K., Seekins, J., Mong, D. A., Halabi, S. S., Sandberg, J. K., Jones, R., Larson, D. B., Langlotz, C. P., Patel, B. N., Lungren, M. P., & Ng, A. Y. (2019, July). Chexpert: A large chest radiograph dataset with uncertainty labels and expert comparison. *Proceedings of the AAAI Conference on Artificial Intelligence*, *33*(01), 590–597. DOI: 10.1609/aaai.v33i01.3301590

Ishar, S. I., Zlatanova, S., & Roberts, J. L. (2022). 3D gaming for young generations in heritage protection: A review. *The International Archives of the Photogrammetry, Remote Sensing and Spatial Information Sciences*, *XLVIII-4/W4-2022*, 53–60. DOI: 10.5194/isprs-archives-XLVIII-4-W4-2022-53-2022

Islam, N., & Singh, A. (2025). Role of Digitalization into Hospitality Businesses: Innovations and Trends. In Rana, V., Bathla, G., Raina, A., & Chhabra, D. (Eds.), *Transforming the Service Sector With New Technology* (pp. 447–458). IGI Global Scientific Publishing., DOI: 10.4018/979-8-3693-7447-4.ch027

Ivanov, S., & Webster, C. (2017). Adoption of robots, artificial intelligence and service automation in tourism and hospitality. *Tourism Management Perspectives*, *25*, 1–8.

Ivanov, S., & Webster, C. (2018). Robots in tourism: A research agenda. *Tourism Review*, *73*(4), 489–497.

Ivanov, S., & Webster, C. (2019). *Robotics, artificial intelligence and the evolving nature of work in the tourism and hospitality industry*. Emerald Publishing.

Jain, D., & Singh, V. (2018). Feature selection and classification systems for chronic disease prediction: A review. *Egyptian Informatics Journal*, *19*(3), 179–189. DOI: 10.1016/j.eij.2018.03.002

Jain, S., & Alam, M. A. (2022). Applications of Human-Computer Interaction in Health Psychology. *Journal of Digital Art and Humanities*, *3*(1), 36–57. DOI: 10.33847/2712-8148.3.1_5

Jang, K., & Landuyt, N. G. (2023). Limited benefits of technological advances in human service organizations: Going beyond the hype using sociotechnical knowledge management system. *Journal of Social Service Research, 49*(4), 426–446. DOI: 10.1080/01488376.2023.2236131

Jankowski, J., Floege, J., Fliser, D., Böhm, M., & Marx, N. (2021). Cardiovascular Disease in Chronic Kidney Disease: Pathophysiological Insights and Therapeutic Options. *Circulation, 143*(11), 1157–1172. DOI: 10.1161/CIRCULATIONAHA.120.050686 PMID: 33720773

Janowicz, K., Gao, S., McKenzie, G., Hu, Y., & Bhaduri, B. (2020). GeoAI: Spatially explicit artificial intelligence techniques for geographic knowledge discovery and beyond. *International Journal of Geographical Information Science, 34*(4), 625–636. DOI: 10.1080/13658816.2019.1684500

Jeon, H., & Oh, S. (2020). Hybrid-Recursive Feature Elimination for Efficient Feature Selection. *Applied Sciences (Basel, Switzerland), 10*(9), 3211. DOI: 10.3390/app10093211

Jerlin Rubini, L., & Perumal, E. (2020). Efficient classification of chronic kidney disease by using multi-kernel support vector machine and fruit fly optimization algorithm. *International Journal of Imaging Systems and Technology, 30*(3), 660–673. DOI: 10.1002/ima.22406

Jogarao, M. (2024). AI in the hospitality industry: Revolutionizing guest experience. In Technology and International Conference on Technology Enabled Economic Changes (InTech),luxury hospitality (pp. 199-210). Routledge.

Jones, M. (2014). *Sustainable event management: A practical guide*. Routledge. DOI: 10.4324/9780203768723

Jones, P., Hillier, D., & Comfort, D. (2021). Sustainability in the global hotel industry. *International Journal of Contemporary Hospitality Management, 33*(1), 1–15.

Jongbo, O. A., Adetunmbi, A. O., Ogunrinde, R. B., & Badeji-Ajisafe, B. (2020). Development of an ensemble approach to chronic kidney disease diagnosis. *Scientific African, 8*, e00456. DOI: 10.1016/j.sciaf.2020.e00456

Jung, T., Tom, D. M. C., Moorhouse, N., & Tom, D. D. (2017). Tourists' experience of virtual reality applications. [ICCE]. *IEEE Int Conf Cons Elect, 208–210*, 208–210. Advance online publication. DOI: 10.1109/ICCE.2017.7889287

Kaissis, G. A., Makowski, M. R., Rückert, D., & Braren, R. F. (2020). Secure, privacy-preserving and federated machine learning in medical imaging. *Nature Machine Intelligence, 2*(6), 305–311. DOI: 10.1038/s42256-020-0186-1

Kaissis, G. A., Ziegelmayer, S., Lohöfer, F. K., Harder, F. N., Jungmann, F., Sasse, D., Muckenhuber, A., Yen, H.-Y., Steiger, K., Siveke, J., Friess, H., Schmid, R., Weichert, W., Makowski, M. R., & Braren, R. F. (2020). Image-based molecular phenotyping of pancreatic ductal adenocarcinoma. *Journal of Clinical Medicine*, *9*(3), 724. DOI: 10.3390/jcm9030724 PMID: 32155990

Kaklauskas, A., Abraham, A., Ubarte, I., Kliukas, R., Luksaite, V., Binkyte-Veliene, A., Vetloviene, I., & Kaklauskiene, L. (2022). A review of AI cloud and edge sensors, methods, and applications for the recognition of emotional, affective and physiological states. *Sensors (Basel)*, *22*(20), 7824. DOI: 10.3390/s22207824 PMID: 36298176

Kamboj, J., & A, E. (2024). Mapping the green human resource management practices: A systematic scoping review and its implications for employees' well-being. *Human Systems Management*, *43*(6), 1062–1081. DOI: 10.1177/01672533241305207

Kamnitsas, K., Baumgartner, C., Ledig, C., Newcombe, V., Simpson, J., Kane, A., & Glocker, B. (2017, May). Unsupervised domain adaptation in brain lesion segmentation with adversarial networks. In *International conference on information processing in medical imaging* (pp. 597-609). Cham: Springer International Publishing. DOI: 10.1007/978-3-319-59050-9_47

Kandampully, J., Zhang, T., & Bilgihan, A. (2015). Customer loyalty: A review and future directions with a special focus on the hospitality industry. *International Journal of Contemporary Hospitality Management*, *27*(3), 379–414.

Kasavana, M. L., & Cahill, J. J. (2003). Managing technology in the hospitality industry. Educational Institute of the American Hotel & Lodging Association.

Kathuria, A., & Nigam, A. (2024). Analysis of the Impact of Green Marketing on Purchase Intention in the Automobile Sector: Roles of Environmental Knowledge and Green Psychological Benefits. *Journal of Electrical Systems*, *20*(11s).

Kaur, H., Selvakumar, P., Haashni, S., Anute, N., Sharma, M., & Manjunath, T. C. (2025). Representations in Developing Thinking Regarding Probabilities in Higher Education. In Anastasiadou, S., & Seremeti, L. (Eds.), *Modes of Representation in Developing Statistical Thinking in Education* (pp. 89–118). IGI Global Scientific Publishing., DOI: 10.4018/979-8-3693-9934-7.ch006

Kaur, P., Kaur, R., Sharma, S., & Kaur, S. (2025). Hybrid meat for flexitarian consumers: Technological advancements, diversity in plant proteins and consumer preferences. *Critical Reviews in Food Science and Nutrition*, •••, 1–17. DOI: 10.1080/10408398.2025.2564890 PMID: 41017443

Kim, H. K., Jeong, H., Park, J., Park, J., Kim, W.-S., Kim, N., Park, S., & Paik, N.-J. (2022). Development of a comprehensive design guideline to evaluate the user experiences of meal-assistance robots considering human-machine social interactions. *International Journal of Human-Computer Interaction, 38*(17), 1687–1700. DOI: 10.1080/10447318.2021.2009672

Kim, W. G., & Lee, H. Y. (2013). Customer relationship management and firm performance. *International Journal of Hospitality Management, 33*, 1–11.

Koeva, M., Luleva, M., & Maldjanski, P. (2017). Integrating spherical panoramas and maps for visualization of cultural heritage objects using virtual reality technology. *Sensors (Basel), 17*(4), 1–15. DOI: 10.3390/s17040829 PMID: 28398230

Kohavi, R., & John, G. H. (1997). Wrappers for feature subset selection. *Artificial Intelligence, 97*(1-2), 273–324. DOI: 10.1016/S0004-3702(97)00043-X

Kolomaznik, M., Petrik, V., Slama, M., & Jurik, V. (2024). The role of socio-emotional attributes in enhancing human-AI collaboration. *Frontiers in Psychology, 15*, 1369957. DOI: 10.3389/fpsyg.2024.1369957 PMID: 39474095

KPMGFAB. (2025). The sustainable finance imperative: Driving multi-dimensional impact in the real economy, KPMG & First Abu Dhabi Bank Report, Publication No. 5336. https://assets.kpmg.com/content/dam/kpmg/ae/pdf-2025/the-sustainable-finance-imperative.pdf

Kshetri, N. (2021). Blockchain and sustainable supply chains in hospitality. *Tourism Management, 83*, 104–176.

Kucukusta, D., Heung, V. C. S., & Hui, S. (2014). Deploying RFID technology in hospitality. *International Journal of Hospitality Management, 40*, 77–87.

Kulshreshtha, S. K., & Webster, C. (2024). Emerging Technologies in Virtual and Hybrid Events: Major Issues and Major Drivers. New Technologies in Virtual and Hybrid Events, 1-18.

Kumar, V. (2025). Role of Financial Literacy in the Financial Management Practices of Salaried Women in India: An SEM-HLM Study. *IUP Journal of Applied Economics, 24*(1).

Kumar, P., Dwivedi, Y. K., & Anand, A. (2023). Responsible artificial intelligence (AI) for value formation and market performance in healthcare: The mediating role of patient's cognitive engagement. *Information Systems Frontiers, 25*(6), 2197–2220. DOI: 10.1007/s10796-021-10136-6 PMID: 33948105

Kumar, R. (2024). Achieving Sustainability in India Through Modern Payment System: An Empirical Study. *American Journal of Economics and Business Innovation, 3*(1), 92–99.

Kunwar, V., Chandel, K., Sabitha, A. S., & Bansal, A. (2016). *Chronic Kidney Disease analysis using data mining classification techniques. 2016 6th International Conference-Cloud System and Big Data Engineering (Confluence)*. IEEE.

Law, E. L. C., Roto, V., Hassenzahl, M., Vermeeren, A. P. O. S., & Kort, J. (2009). Understanding, scoping and defining user experience: A survey approach. *Human Fact Comp Syst, 10*, 1518813. DOI: 10.1145/1518701.1518813

Law, E. L.-C., & Lárusdóttir, M. K. (2015). Whose experience do we care about? Analysis of the fitness of Scrum and Kanban to user experience. *International Journal of Human-Computer Interaction, 31*(9), 584–602. DOI: 10.1080/10447318.2015.1065693

Law, R., Leung, R., & Buhalis, D. (2014). Information technology applications in hospitality and tourism. *International Journal of Contemporary Hospitality Management, 26*(5), 727–750.

LeCun, Y., Bengio, Y., & Hinton, G. (2015). Deep learning. *nature, 521*(7553), 436-444.

Lee, S., & Hwang, J. (2020). The impact of virtual events on visitor experience and satisfaction. *Journal of Convention & Event Tourism, 21*(2), 103–121. DOI: 10.1080/15470148.2020.1752246

Leopardi, A., Ceccacci, S., Mengoni, M., Naspetti, S., Gambelli, D., Ozturk, E., & Zanoli, R. (2021). X-reality technologies for museums: A comparative evaluation based on presence and visitors experience through user studies. *Journal of Cultural Heritage, 47*, 188–198. DOI: 10.1016/j.culher.2020.10.005

Leung, R., & Law, R. (2013). Evaluation of hotel websites: Progress and future developments. *International Journal of Hospitality Management, 33*, 296–307.

Li, D. (2025). Impact of green advertisement and environmental knowledge on intention of consumers to buy green products. *BMC Psychology, 13*(1), 220. DOI: 10.1186/s40359-025-02538-x PMID: 40059236

Li, M., Yin, D., Qiu, H., & Bai, B. (2021). A systematic review of AI technology-based service encounters: Implications for hospitality and tourism operations. *International Journal of Hospitality Management, 95*, 102930. Advance online publication. DOI: 10.1016/j.ijhm.2021.102930

Li, N., Zhang, T., & Wang, Y. (2021). AI in hotel operations: Case study of Alibaba's FlyZoo Hotel. *International Journal of Hospitality Management*, *93*, 102–777.

Litjens, G., Kooi, T., Bejnordi, B. E., Setio, A. A. A., Ciompi, F., Ghafoorian, M., van der Laak, J. A. W. M., van Ginneken, B., & Sánchez, C. I. (2017). A survey on deep learning in medical image analysis. *Medical Image Analysis*, *42*, 60–88. DOI: 10.1016/j.media.2017.07.005 PMID: 28778026

Liu, S. Q., Vakeel, K. A., Smith, N. A., Alavipour, R. S., Wei, C., & Wirtz, J. (2024). AI concierge in the customer journey: What is it and how can it add value to the customer? *Journal of Service Management*, *35*(6), 136–158. DOI: 10.1108/JOSM-12-2023-0523

Li, W., & Wu, D. (2025). Sustainability through business model innovation and climate finance in developing countries. *Humanities & Social Sciences Communications*, *12*(1), 66. DOI: 10.1057/s41599-024-04297-3

Lowe, N. K. (2004). Context and process of informed consent for pharmacologic strategies in labor pain care. *Journal of Midwifery & Women's Health*, *49*(3), 250–259. DOI: 10.1016/j.jmwh.2004.02.011 PMID: 15134679

Lu, A. C. C., & Gursoy, D. (2016). Impact of job burnout on satisfaction and turnover intention. *International Journal of Hospitality Management*, *57*, 13–22.

Madani, A., Arnaout, R., Mofrad, M., & Arnaout, R. (2018). Fast and accurate view classification of echocardiograms using deep learning. *NPJ Digital Medicine*, *1*(1), 6. DOI: 10.1038/s41746-017-0013-1 PMID: 30828647

Madouri, H. (2025). Green finance and renewable energy investments: A comparative analysis of successes, challenges, and policy implications across regions. *Central European Review of Economics and Management*, *9*(2), 7–35. DOI: 10.29015/cerem.1022

Maghrabi, A. (2024). Urban thermal vulnerability mapping for climate mitigation: A case study of Jeddah. *Journal of King Abdulaziz University: Environmental Design Sciences*, *15*(1), 93–111.

Mahmud, S., Rahman, A., & Ashrafuzzaman, M. (2022). A systematic literature review on the role of digital health twins in preventive healthcare for personal and corporate wellbeing. *American Journal of Interdisciplinary Studies*, *3*(04), 1–31. DOI: 10.63125/negjw373

Maintz, J. A., Meijering, E. H., & Viergever, M. A. (1998, June). General multimodal elastic registration based on mutual information. In *Medical Imaging 1998: Image Processing* (Vol. 3338, pp. 144-154). SPIE.

Manjunath, M., Ogwu, M. C., Udayakumar, S., Kuchipudi, J. D., Rengarajan, C., Selvakumar, P., & Manjunath, T. C. (2026). Chromatography in Food Contaminant Analysis: Principles, Advances, and Applications for Food Safety. In Ogwu, M., & Izah, S. (Eds.), *Detection, Identification, and Monitoring of Food Contaminants* (pp. 207–238). IGI Global Scientific Publishing., DOI: 10.4018/979-8-3373-3982-5.ch007

Manoharan, G., & Ashtikar, S. P. (2025). AI Era in Hospitality: The New Frontier in Guest Satisfaction and Operations. In Digital Disruption in Hospitality, AI, and Emerging Technologies: A Roadmap to Personalized Experiences, Enhanced Operations, and Revenue Growth (pp. 59-77). Emerald Publishing Limited.

Marchiori, E., Niforatos, E., & Preto, L. (2017) Measuring the media effects of a tourism-related virtual reality experience using biophysical data. In: Schegg R, Stangl B (eds) Information and Communication Technologies in Tourism 2017. Springer International Publishing. chem, pp 203–215 DOI: 10.1007/978-3-319-51168-9_15

Marlapudi, K., & Lenka, U. (2024). Unlocking the potential: Redefining talent and competency mapping for Industry 4.0. *Management Research Review*, *47*(11), 1805–1832. DOI: 10.1108/MRR-07-2023-0496

Marques, R. C., & Pinho, C. (2021). Virtual and hybrid events in the post-COVID-19 era: A strategic framework. *International Journal of Event and Festival Management*, *12*(3), 345–360.

Martin, C., & Fullard, D. (2022). Global Destination Report 2022. *International Congress and Convention Association (ICCA).*

McCollough, C. H., Bushberg, J. T., Fletcher, J. G., & Eckel, L. J. (2015, October). Answers to common questions about the use and safety of CT scans. [). Elsevier.]. *Mayo Clinic Proceedings*, *90*(10), 1380–1392. DOI: 10.1016/j.mayocp.2015.07.011 PMID: 26434964

Mehta, K., Kumar, S., & Rawal, Y. S. (2025). Metaverse Tourism, Future Trends, and Sustainable Tourism Development. In *Tourism Entrepreneurship and the Metaverse: Opportunities and Strategies for Growth in the Digital Sphere* (pp. 355–376). Springer Nature Switzerland.

Menze, M., & Geiger, A. (2015). Object scene flow for autonomous vehicles. In *Proceedings of the IEEE conference on computer vision and pattern recognition* (pp. 3061-3070).

Metta, S., & Kumar, S. V. S. (2026). AI-Driven HR Transformation in Service Industry: Opportunities, Challenges, Ethical Considerations and Strategic Implications. AI and Innovation in HRM, 191-205.

Ministry of Economy and Planning. (2023). National Environment Strategy 2023.

Ministry of Energy of Saudi Arabia. (2025). Saudi Green Initiative: Progress report and future outlook. Government of Saudi Arabia. https://www.sgi.gov.sa/about-sgi/sgi-targets/reduce-carbon-emissions/?csrt=18277796921209943572

Ministry of Environment, Water and Agriculture. (2023). Annual. *Water Reports*, •••, 2023.

Ministry of Municipal and Rural Affairs and Housing. (2024). Urban Resilience and Smart Cities Framework 2024.

Min, S., So, K. K. F., & Jeong, M. (2021). Consumer adoption of the Uber mobile application: Insights from diffusion of innovation theory and technology acceptance model. In *Future of tourism marketing* (pp. 2–15). Routledge. DOI: 10.4324/9781003176039-2

Mishra, S., Anifa, M., & Naidu, J. (2025). AI-Driven Personalization in Tourism Services: Enhancing Tourist Experiences and Business Performance. In Integrating Architecture and Design Into Sustainable Tourism Development (pp. 1-20). IGI Global Scientific Publishing.

Misir, R., Mitra, M., & Samanta, R. K. (2017). A reduced set of features for chronic kidney disease prediction. *Journal of Pathology Informatics*, *8*(1), 8. DOI: 10.4103/jpi.jpi_88_16 PMID: 28706750

Mithas, S., Chen, Z. L., Saldanha, T. J., & De Oliveira Silveira, A. (2022). How will artificial intelligence and Industry 4.0 emerging technologies transform operations management? *Production and Operations Management*, *31*(12), 4475–4487. DOI: 10.1111/poms.13864

Mittal, V., & Kamakura, W. A. (2001). Satisfaction, repurchase intent, and repurchase behavior. *JMR, Journal of Marketing Research*, *38*(1), 131–142.

Mooi Kwong, A. T., Omar, S. I., & Nur Aliah, M. (2024). The Ethical Implications of AI-Powered Personalization in Hospitality and Tourism. In Talukder, M., Kumar, S., & Tyagi, P. (Eds.), *Impact of AI and Tech-Driven Solutions in Hospitality and Tourism* (pp. 103–122). IGI Global Scientific Publishing., DOI: 10.4018/979-8-3693-6755-1.ch006

Morosan, C., & DeFranco, A. (2016). It's about time: Revisiting hotel guests' intention to use biometric systems. *International Journal of Hospitality Management*, *53*, 154–164. DOI: 10.1016/j.ijhm.2015.11.003

Morosan, C., & DeFranco, A. (2016). Mobile payments adoption in hospitality. *International Journal of Hospitality Management*, *53*, 17–29.

Motwani, A., Shukla, P. K., & Pawar, M. (2020). Smart Predictive Healthcare Framework for Remote Patient Monitoring and Recommendation Using Deep Learning with Novel Cost Optimization. *International Conference on Information and Communication Technology for Intelligent Systems*, Springer.

Motwani, A., Shukla, P. K., & Pawar, M. (2021). Novel framework based on deep learning and cloud analytics for smart patient monitoring and recommendation (SPMR). *Journal of Ambient Intelligence and Humanized Computing*, •••, 1–16.

Motwani, A., Shukla, P. K., & Pawar, M. (2021). Novel Machine Learning Model with Wrapper-Based Dimensionality Reduction for Predicting Chronic Kidney Disease Risk. *Soft Computing and Signal Processing, Springer.*, *1325*, 29–37.

Motwani, A., Shukla, P. K., & Pawar, M. (2022). Ubiquitous and smart healthcare monitoring frameworks based on machine learning: A comprehensive review. *Artificial Intelligence in Medicine*, *134*, 102431. DOI: 10.1016/j.artmed.2022.102431 PMID: 36462891

Motwani, A., Shukla, P. K., Pawar, M., Kumar, M., Ghosh, U., Alnumay, W., & Nayak, S. R. (2023). Enhanced framework for COVID-19 prediction with computed tomography scan images using dense convolutional neural network and novel loss function. *Computers & Electrical Engineering*, *105*, 108479. DOI: 10.1016/j.compeleceng.2022.108479 PMID: 36406625

Musheer, R. A., Verma, C., & Srivastava, N. (2019). Novel machine learning approach for classification of high-dimensional microarray data. *Soft Computing*, *23*(24), 13409–13421. DOI: 10.1007/s00500-019-03879-7

Mystakidis, S. (2022). Metaverse in hospitality and tourism: Opportunities and challenges. *Journal of Virtual Worlds Research*, *15*(2), 1–21.

Nagendran, M., Chen, Y., Lovejoy, C. A., Gordon, A. C., Komorowski, M., Harvey, H., ... & Maruthappu, M. (2020). Artificial intelligence versus clinicians: systematic review of design, reporting standards, and claims of deep learning studies. *bmj, 368*.

Nair, Y. V. I. V. (2024). Econometric Analysis of How Corporate Social Responsibility has Enabled Social Entrepreneurship and Innovation in India.

Nam, K., Dutt, C. S., & Baker, J. (2023). Authenticity in objects and activities: Determinants of satisfaction with virtual reality experiences of heritage and non-heritage tourism sites. *Information Systems Frontiers*, *25*(3), 1219–1237. DOI: 10.1007/s10796-022-10286-1 PMID: 35633932

Nathaniel, S., Motwani, A., & Saxena, A. (2018). Cloud based Predictive Model for Detection of 'Chronic Kidney Disease' Risk. *International Journal on Computer Science and Engineering*, *6*(4), 182–188.

Neuhofer, B., Buhalis, D., & Ladkin, A. (2015). Smart technologies for personalized experiences. *Journal of Travel Research*, *54*(3), 356–370.

Noone, B. M., & McGuire, K. A. (2013). Pricing in hotels: Customer fairness perceptions. *Journal of Revenue and Pricing Management*, *12*(4), 343–355.

O. Abdullah, A. S.S., M. S. Khan, B. B. A. Qizi, S. J. Q. Usmanova and J. J.V., (2025). AI-Driven Solutions in Hospitality: Transforming Guest Experience and Streamlining Hotel Operations, Tashkent, Uzbekistan, 2025, pp. 01-07, .DOI: 10.1109/InTech64186.2025.11198397

OECD (Organization for Economic Cooperation and Development). (2024). Leveraging De-Risking Instruments and International Co-ordination to Catalyse Investment in Clean Hydrogen (OCDE/World Bank), 2024. https://doi.org/DOI: 10.1787/9a377303-en

Oktay, A. B. (2018). Human identification with dental panoramic radiographic images. *IET Biometrics*, *7*(4), 349–355. DOI: 10.1049/iet-bmt.2017.0078

Pantano, E., & Servidio, R. (2012). Modeling innovative points of sales through virtual and immersive technologies. *Journal of Retailing and Consumer Services*, *19*(3), 279–286. DOI: 10.1016/j.jretconser.2012.02.002

Park, S. H., & Han, K. (2018). Methodologic guide for evaluating clinical performance and effect of artificial intelligence technology for medical diagnosis and prediction. *Radiology*, *286*(3), 800–809. DOI: 10.1148/radiol.2017171920 PMID: 29309734

Patel, D., Deshpande, M., & Jadhav, A. (2024, August). Unveiling Consistency and Disparities: Exploring the Dynamics Between Customer Reviews and Ratings. In *International Conference on ICT for Sustainable Development* (pp. 223-231). Singapore: Springer Nature Singapore.

Pearson's Correlation Coefficient. (2008). Encyclopedia of Public Health. W. Kirch. Dordrecht, Springer Netherlands: 1090-1091. Agarwal, S. and R. Srivastava (2009). "Chronic kidney disease in India: challenges and solutions. *Nephron. Clinical Practice*, *111*(3), c197–c203.

Pencarelli, T., Splendiani, S., & Fraboni, C. (2020). Smart tourism experiences: Value co-creation at cultural heritage sites. *Sustainability*, *12*(2), 1–20. DOI: 10.3390/su12020669

Pham, D. L., Xu, C., & Prince, J. L. (2000). Current methods in medical image segmentation. *Annual Review of Biomedical Engineering*, *2*(1), 315–337. DOI: 10.1146/annurev.bioeng.2.1.315 PMID: 11701515

Piccoli, G., Lui, T. W., & Grün, B. (2017). The impact of IT-enabled customer service systems. *Management Information Systems Quarterly*, *41*(2), 1–23.

Pillai, S. G., Haldorai, K., Seo, W. S., & Kim, W. G. (2021). AI-powered smart hotels: Innovations and service delivery. *Journal of Hospitality and Tourism Technology*, *12*(3), 449–464.

Pine, B. J., & Gilmore, J. H. (1999). *The experience economy: Work is theatre & every business a stage*. Harvard Business School Press.

Plantinga, L. C., Tuot, D. S., & Powe, N. R. (2010). Awareness of chronic kidney disease among patients and providers. *Advances in Chronic Kidney Disease*, *17*(3), 225–236. DOI: 10.1053/j.ackd.2010.03.002 PMID: 20439091

Podsakoff, P. M., MacKenzie, S. B., Lee, J. Y., & Podsakoff, N. P. (2003). Common method biases in behavioral research. *The Journal of Applied Psychology*, *88*(5), 879–903.

Polat, H., Mehr, H. D., & Cetin, A. (2017). Diagnosis of chronic kidney disease based on support vector machine by feature selection methods. *Journal of Medical Systems*, *41*(4), 55. DOI: 10.1007/s10916-017-0703-x PMID: 28243816

Ponzini, D. (2024). NEOM and the future of urban resilience in arid environments. *Cities (London, England)*, *144*, 104561.

Poplin, R., Varadarajan, A. V., Blumer, K., Liu, Y., McConnell, M. V., Corrado, G. S., Peng, L., & Webster, D. R. (2018). Prediction of cardiovascular risk factors from retinal fundus photographs via deep learning. *Nature Biomedical Engineering*, *2*(3), 158–164. DOI: 10.1038/s41551-018-0195-0 PMID: 31015713

Potential flood risk due to urbanization expansion in arid environments, Saudi Arabia. (2020). Natural Hazards, 104, 795–809.

Priya, N., Satpathy, I., Patnaik, B. C. M., & Thaichon, P. (2024). Transforming workplace wellness in the next-generation hospitality industry by leveraging transformational digital technologies and tools. In *Technology and luxury hospitality* (pp. 295–313). Routledge. DOI: 10.4324/9781003488248-20

Qin, J., Chen, L., Liu, Y., Liu, C., Feng, C., & Chen, B. (2019). A machine learning methodology for diagnosing chronic kidney disease. *IEEE Access : Practical Innovations, Open Solutions*, *8*, 20991–21002. DOI: 10.1109/ACCESS.2019.2963053

Rainoldi, M., Driescher, V., Lisnevska, A., Zvereva, D., Stavinska, A., Relota, J., & Egger, R. (2018). Virtual reality: An innovative tool in destinations' marketing. *Journal of Tourism & Hospitality (Los Angeles, Calif.)*, *9*, 53–68. DOI: 10.3126/gaze.v9i0.19721

Rai, V., & Singh, A. (2026). The Digital Renaissance of Hospitality: Workforce Mastery in the Smart Revolution. In Talukder, M., & Chowdhury, H. (Eds.), *Smart Operations and Enhancing Guest Experience in the Hospitality Industry* (pp. 125–144). IGI Global Scientific Publishing., DOI: 10.4018/979-8-3373-2145-5.ch005

Rajpurkar, P., Irvin, J., Zhu, K., Yang, B., Mehta, H., Duan, T., . . . Ng, A. Y. (2017). Chexnet: Radiologist-level pneumonia detection on chest x-rays with deep learning. *arXiv preprint arXiv:1711.05225.*

Raj, R., Bhope, A., Kodmalwar, P. A., Sudindra, V. R., Sharma, A., Selvakumar, P., & Manjunath, T. C. (2026). Exchange Rates and Trade Dynamics. In Canguende-Valentim, C., Madaleno, M., Victorino, S., & Jungo, J. (Eds.), *Monetary Dynamics and Socio-Economic Development in Emerging Economies* (pp. 195–220). IGI Global Scientific Publishing., DOI: 10.4018/979-8-3693-9765-7.ch007

Rakhmatov, S. (2025). THE CONCEPT OF "UNIVERSITY 3.0" AND THE IMPORTANCE OF INNOVATIVE UNIVERSITIES IN THE DEVELOPMENT OF THE EDUCATION SYSTEM. *International Journal of Artificial Intelligence*, *1*(3), 1049–1051.

Rao, K. E., & Rao, G. A. (2021). Ensemble learning with recursive feature elimination integrated software effort estimation: A novel approach. *Evolutionary Intelligence*, *14*(1), 151–162. DOI: 10.1007/s12065-020-00360-5

Raturi, S., & Bhatnagar, S. (2023). Influence of the Green Marketing Mix on Customers' Purchase Intentions for Sustainable Eco-Friendly Fashion Products. *NIFT JOURNAL OF FASHION*, 52.

Reiche, D. (2023). Energy transition and climate adaptation policies in the Gulf Cooperation Council (GCC) states. *Energy Policy*, *179*, 113483.

Remuzzi, G., Ruggenenti, P., & Perico, N. (2002). Chronic renal diseases: Renoprotective benefits of renin–angiotensin system inhibition. *Annals of Internal Medicine*, *136*(8), 604–615. DOI: 10.7326/0003-4819-136-8-200204160-00010 PMID: 11955029

Revi, A., Satterthwaite, D., & Solecki, W. (2024). Urban resilience and climate governance: Global lessons for local adaptation. *Urban Climate*, *52*, 101864.

Ronneberger, O., Fischer, P., & Brox, T. (2015, October). U-net: Convolutional networks for biomedical image segmentation. In *International Conference on Medical image computing and computer-assisted intervention* (pp. 234-241). Cham: Springer international publishing. DOI: 10.1007/978-3-319-24574-4_28

Rubini, L. J. J. T. A. U., & the Department of Computer Science and Engineering. (2015). "UCIMachineLearningRepository [http://archive. ics. uci. edu/ml/datasets/Chronic_Kidney_Disease]. Karaikudi.

Rudin, C. (2019). Stop explaining black box machine learning models for high stakes decisions and use interpretable models instead. *Nature Machine Intelligence, 1*(5), 206–215. DOI: 10.1038/s42256-019-0048-x PMID: 35603010

Russell, S., & Norvig, P. (2016). *Artificial intelligence: A modern approach* (3rd ed.). Pearson.

Said, S., & Hernandez, G. T. (2014). The link between chronic kidney disease and cardiovascular disease. *Journal of Nephropathology, 3*(3), 99. PMID: 25093157

Saini, A. K., & Montebello, M. (2024). Exploring the Educational Frontier: A Deep Dive into VR and AI-Enhanced Learning Environments. In *Trust and Inclusion in AI-mediated Education: Where Human Learning Meets Learning Machines* (pp. 141–162). Springer Nature Switzerland. DOI: 10.1007/978-3-031-64487-0_7

Salekin, A., & Stankovic, J. (2016). Detection of chronic kidney disease and selecting important predictive attributes. *2016 IEEE International Conference on Healthcare Informatics (ICHI)*, IEEE. DOI: 10.1109/ICHI.2016.36

Samara, D., Kattuman, P., & Khalil, S. (2020). AI-based revenue management in hotels. *Tourism Economics, 26*(6), 1132–1151.

Samek, W., Wiegand, T., & Müller, K. R. (2017). Explainable artificial intelligence: Understanding, visualizing and interpreting deep learning models. *arXiv preprint arXiv:1708.08296.*

Santandreu Calonge, D., Kamalov, F., Medina Aguerrebere, P., Hassock, L., Smail, L., Yousef, D., ... & Abdulla, N. (2025). Upskilling and reskilling in the United Arab Emirates: Future-proofing careers with AI skills. Journal of Adult and Continuing Education, 14779714251315288.

Saringat, Z., Mustapha, A., Saedudin, R. R., & Samsudin, N. A. (2019). Comparative analysis of classification algorithms for chronic kidney disease diagnosis. *Bulletin of Electrical Engineering and Informatics, 8*(4), 1496–1501. DOI: 10.11591/eei.v8i4.1621

Saudi General Authority for Statistics. (2024). Population Estimates Publication 2024.

Saudi Meteorological Authority. (2024). Climate Data Summary 2024.

Saxena, S. K., Gupta, V., & Kumar, S. (2024). Enhancing guest loyalty in the hotel industry through artificial intelligence-drive personalization. In *New Technologies in Virtual and Hybrid Events* (pp. 335–350). IGI Global. DOI: 10.4018/979-8-3693-2272-7.ch017

Sedighi, Z., Ebrahimpour-Komleh, H., & Mousavirad, S. J. (2015). Featue selection effects on kidney desease analysis. *2015 International Congress on Technology, Communication and Knowledge (ICTCK)*, IEEE. DOI: 10.1109/ICTCK.2015.7582712

Segal, Z., Kalifa, D., Radinsky, K., Ehrenberg, B., Elad, G., Maor, G., Lewis, M., Tibi, M., Korn, L., & Koren, G. (2020). Machine learning algorithm for early detection of end-stage renal disease. *BMC Nephrology*, *21*(1), 1–10. DOI: 10.1186/s12882-020-02093-0 PMID: 33246427

Selvakumar, P., & Haashni, S. SudhaAnanthi, G., & Manjunath, T. C. (2026). Cybernetic Systems Thinking: Foundations for Organizational Adaptability. In L. Tsvasman (Ed.), Cybernetic Leadership for Sustainable Innovation (pp. 99-124). IGI Global Scientific Publishing. DOI: 10.4018/979-8-3373-2484-5.ch004

Senan, E. M., Al-Adhaileh, M. H., Alsaade, F. W., Aldhyani, T. H., Alqarni, A. A., Alsharif, N., Uddin, M. I., Alahmadi, A. H., Jadhav, M. E., & Alzahrani, M. Y. (2021). Diagnosis of Chronic Kidney Disease Using Effective Classification Algorithms and Recursive Feature Elimination Techniques. *Journal of Healthcare Engineering*, *2021*, 2021. DOI: 10.1155/2021/1004767 PMID: 34211680

Seraj, A. H. A., Hasanein, A. M., Al-Romeedy, B. S., & Elziny, M. N. (2025). Redefining the Digital Frontier: Digital Leadership, AI, and Innovation Driving Next-Generation Tourism and Hospitality. *Administrative Sciences*, *15*(9), 369. DOI: 10.3390/admsci15090369

Seshanna, S. V., Gopalakrishnan, G., Anute, N., Deepthi Reddy, K., Sharma, M., Selvakumar, P., & Manjunath, T. C. (2026). Digital Transformation and Cybersecurity. In Saeed, S., & Tahir, S. (Eds.), *User-Centric Cybersecurity Implications for Sustainable Digital Transformation* (pp. 1–30). IGI Global Scientific Publishing., DOI: 10.4018/979-8-3373-3171-3.ch001

Seyitoğlu, F., Costa, C., Martins, M., & Malta, A. M. (2023). The future of tourism and hospitality labour: Challenges, requirements, trends, skills and the impact of technology. *Current Issues in Tourism*, •••, 1–15. DOI: 10.1080/13683500.2023.2286291

Sharma, M., Singh, A., & Rohit, . (2024b). Embracing Technological Disruption: Exploring the Adoption of AI-Driven Solutions in Tourism and Hospitality. In M. Talukder, S. Kumar, & P. Tyagi (Eds.), Impact of AI and Tech-Driven Solutions in Hospitality and Tourism (pp. 123-138). IGI Global Scientific Publishing. DOI: 10.4018/979-8-3693-6755-1.ch007

Sharma, M., & Kumar, S. (2023). Artificial intelligence for sustainable hotel operations: Energy, water and waste optimization. *Sustainable Tourism Review*, *11*(1), 50–67.

Shen, D., Wu, G., & Suk, H. I. (2017). Deep learning in medical image analysis. *Annual Review of Biomedical Engineering*, *19*(1), 221–248. DOI: 10.1146/annurev-bioeng-071516-044442 PMID: 28301734

Sigala, M. (2018). Social media and customer engagement in the hospitality industry. *Service Industries Journal*, *38*(11–12), 1–25.

Sigala, M. (2020). Tourism and COVID-19: Impacts and implications for advancing and resetting industry and research. *Journal of Business Research*, *117*, 312–321. DOI: 10.1016/j.jbusres.2020.06.015 PMID: 32546875

Singh, A., & Hassan, S. C. (2024), "Identifying the Skill Gap in the Workplace and Their Challenges in Hospitality and Tourism Organisations", Thake, A.M., Sood, K., Özen, E. and Grima, S. (Ed.) Contemporary Challenges in Social Science Management: Skills Gaps and Shortages in the Labour Market (Contemporary Studies in Economic and Financial Analysis, Vol. 112B), Emerald Publishing Limited, Leeds, pp. 101-114. DOI: 10.1108/S1569-37592024000112B006

Singh, A., & Kumar, V. (2025a). Organizational Innovation and Adaptation in Hospitality and Tourism: Strategies for Resilience and Leadership. In C. Ramos, T. Costa, R. Madeira, & J. Ferreira do Rosário (Eds.), Open Innovation and Technology in Tourism and Hospitality (pp. 355-372). IGI Global Scientific Publishing. DOI: 10.4018/979-8-3693-8633-0.ch018

Singh, A., & Kumar, V. (2025b). User-Centered Hospitality: UI/UX as the New Frontier in Hotel and Restaurant Innovation. In C. Ramos, T. Costa, R. Madeira, & J. Ferreira do Rosário (Eds.), Open Innovation and Technology in Tourism and Hospitality (pp. 395-410). IGI Global Scientific Publishing. https://doi.org/DOI: 10.4018/979-8-3693-8633-0.ch020

Singh, A., & Singh, V. K. (2022). The impact of ergonomic practices on housekeeping employee retention and efficiency in hotels during COVID-19 in India. Turyzm/Tourism, 32(2), 29–50. DOI: 10.18778/0867-5856.32.2.02

Singh, A. (2024). Quality of Work-Life Practices in the Indian Hospitality Sector: Future Challenges and Prospects. In Valeri, M., & Sousa, B. (Eds.), *Human Relations Management in Tourism* (pp. 208–224). IGI Global., DOI: 10.4018/979-8-3693-1322-0.ch010

Singh, A. (2025). Analysis of Perceptions on Employment of differently-abled People in the Indian Hotel Industry. *Pasos (El Sauzal), 23*(1), 167–183. DOI: 10.25145/j.pasos.2025.23.011

Singh, A. (2025). Convergence of Generative Artificial Intelligence (AI)-Based Applications in the Hospitality and Tourism Industry. In Gaur, L. (Ed.), *Generative Artificial Intelligence and Ethics: Standards, Guidelines, and Best Practices* (pp. 127–142). IGI Global Scientific Publishing., DOI: 10.4018/979-8-3693-3691-5.ch006

Singh, A., & Ansari, A. I. (2024). Role of Training and Development in Employee Motivation: Tourism and Hospitality Sector. In Mazurowski, T. (Ed.), *Enhancing Employee Motivation Through Training and Development* (pp. 248–261). IGI Global., DOI: 10.4018/979-8-3693-1674-0.ch011

Singh, A., & Kumar, S. (2021). Identifying Innovations in Human Resources: Academia and Industry Perspectives. In Pathak, A., & Rana, S. (Eds.), *Transforming Human Resource Functions With Automation* (pp. 104–120). IGI Global. DOI: 10.4018/978-1-7998-4180-7.ch006

Singh, A., & Kumar, S. (2024). Effective Talent Management Practices Implemented in the Hospitality Sector. In Christiansen, B., Aziz, M., & O'Keeffe, E. (Eds.), *Global Practices on Effective Talent Acquisition and Retention* (pp. 126–144). IGI Global., DOI: 10.4018/979-8-3693-1938-3.ch008

Singh, A., & Sihmar, P. (2025). Higher Education Institution Sustainability: Role of Green Human Resource Management. In Adu-Gyamfi, M., Boateng, F., & Atiku, S. (Eds.), *Green HRM Awareness and Training in Higher Education Institutions* (pp. 1–14). IGI Global Scientific Publishing., DOI: 10.4018/979-8-3693-2956-6.ch001

Smith, A. (2021). Robot-run hotels: The Henn-na experience. *Journal of Hospitality Case Studies, 10*(2), 56–65.

Song, X., Waitman, L. R., Hu, Y., Yu, A. S., Robins, D., & Liu, M. (2019). Robust clinical marker identification for diabetic kidney disease with ensemble feature selection. *Journal of the American Medical Informatics Association : JAMIA, 26*(3), 242–253. DOI: 10.1093/jamia/ocy165 PMID: 30602020

Srivastava, A., Singh, B. M., Singh, A., & Singh, A. (2025). Customer Immersiveness and Customer Retention: A Metaverse-Driven Study for Brands. In Al Aqad, M., Sorayyaei Azar, A., Albattat, A., & Singh, A. (Eds.), *Navigating AI and the Metaverse in Scientific Research* (pp. 475–500). IGI Global Scientific Publishing., DOI: 10.4018/979-8-3373-0340-6.ch023

Sthapit, E., & Björk, P. (2020). Sources of memorable tourism experiences. *Tourism Management Perspectives*, *33*, 100625.

Stone, P., Brooks, R., Brynjolfsson, E., Calo, R., Etzioni, O., Hager, G., . . . Teller, A. (2022). Artificial intelligence and life in 2030: the one hundred year study on artificial intelligence. arXiv preprint arXiv:2211.06318.

Supina, S., & Singh, A. (2024). Exploring the Presence and Adoption of Quality of Work-Life Dimensions in the Hotel Industry? *African Journal of Hospitality, Tourism and Leisure*, *13*(2), 421–429. DOI: 10.46222/ajhtl.19770720.524

Talluri, K., & Van Ryzin, G. (2004). *The theory and practice of revenue management*. Springer. DOI: 10.1007/b139000

Talukder, M. B., Kabir, F., & Jibon, F. A. (2025). AI-Driven personalized room management in the modern hotel industry. In *AI technologies for personalized and sustainable tourism* (pp. 59–82). IGI Global.

Tan, K. L., Yeap, P. F., Cheong, K. C. K., & Loganathan, S. R. (2025). Crafting an organizational strategy for the new era: A qualitative study of artificial intelligence transformation in a homegrown Singaporean hotel chain. *Business Process Management Journal*, *31*(8), 104–123. DOI: 10.1108/BPMJ-11-2024-1086

Tazin, N., Sabab, S. A., & Chowdhury, M. T. (2016). Diagnosis of Chronic Kidney Disease using effective classification and feature selection technique. *2016 International Conference on Medical Engineering, Health Informatics and Technology (MediTec)*, IEEE. DOI: 10.1109/MEDITEC.2016.7835365

Thaichon, P., Dutta, P. K., Haghi, A. K., & Dutta, S. (Eds.). (2025). *Digital Disruption in Hospitality, AI, and Emerging Technologies: A Roadmap to Personalized Experiences, Enhanced Operations, and Revenue Growth*. Emerald Publishing Limited. DOI: 10.1108/9781836087960

Thapaliya, S., & Bokani, A. (2024). Leveraging artificial intelligence for enhanced cybersecurity: Insights and innovations. *Sadgamaya*, *1*(1), 46–52.

The Global Economy. (2024). Saudi Arabia — Percent urban population (1960–2024).

The World Bank. (2024). World Development Indicators. Rural population, total and urban population statistics for Saudi Arabia.

Ting, D. S. W., Cheung, C. Y. L., Lim, G., Tan, G. S. W., Quang, N. D., Gan, A., Hamzah, H., Garcia-Franco, R., San Yeo, I. Y., Lee, S. Y., Wong, E. Y. M., Sabanayagam, C., Baskaran, M., Ibrahim, F., Tan, N. C., Finkelstein, E. A., Lamoureux, E. L., Wong, I. Y., Bressler, N. M., & Wong, T. Y. (2017). Development and validation of a deep learning system for diabetic retinopathy and related eye diseases using retinal images from multiethnic populations with diabetes. *Journal of the American Medical Association*, *318*(22), 2211–2223. DOI: 10.1001/jama.2017.18152 PMID: 29234807

Topol, E. J. (2019). High-performance medicine: The convergence of human and artificial intelligence. *Nature Medicine*, *25*(1), 44–56. DOI: 10.1038/s41591-018-0300-7 PMID: 30617339

Torres, E. N., & Kline, S. (2013). From satisfaction to delight. *International Journal of Contemporary Hospitality Management*, *25*(5), 642–659.

Trček, D. (2022). Cultural heritage preservation by using blockchain technologies. *Heritage Science*, *10*(1), 6. DOI: 10.1186/s40494-021-00643-9

Truong, D., Xiaoming Liu, R., & Yu, J. J. (2020). Mixed methods research in tourism and hospitality journals. *International Journal of Contemporary Hospitality Management*, *32*(4), 1563–1579. DOI: 10.1108/IJCHM-03-2019-0286

Tung, V. W. S., & Au, N. (2018). Exploring customer experiences with robotics in hospitality: A service quality perspective. *Journal of Hospitality Marketing & Management*, *27*(7), 855–876.

Turčinović, M., Vujko, A., & Mirčetić, V. (2025). Algorithmic Management in Hospitality: Examining Hotel Employees' Attitudes and Work–Life Balance Under AI-Driven HR Systems. *Tourism and Hospitality*, *6*(4), 203. DOI: 10.3390/tourhosp6040203

Tussyadiah, I. P., Wang, D., & Jia, C. (2017) Virtual reality and attitudes toward tourism destinations. In: Schegg R, Stangl B (eds) Information and Communication Technologies in Tourism 2017. Springer International Publishing. Uk, pp 229–239 DOI: 10.1007/978-3-319-51168-9_17

Tussyadiah, I. (2020). A review of AI applications in hospitality and tourism. *Journal of Travel Research*, *59*(8), 1–18.

Tussyadiah, I. P., & Inversini, A. (2015). Information and communication technologies in tourism. *Journal of Travel Research*, *54*(3), 336–343.

Tussyadiah, I. P., Wang, D., Jung, T. H., & Tom Dieck, M. C. (2018). Virtual reality, presence, and attitude change: Empirical evidence from tourism. *Tourism Management, 66*, 140–154. DOI: 10.1016/j.tourman.2017.12.003

Ukpabi, D. C., & Karjaluoto, H. (2018). Adoption of mobile technologies in tourism. *Tourism Management Perspectives, 28*, 151–164.

Unsplash. (2023, April 11). Beautiful Free Images & Pictures | Unsplash. https://unsplash.com

Upadhyaya, A., & Sijoria, C. (2024). Customers' Purchase Intention of Green Cosmetics in India: Empirical Validations Using an Extended Theory of Planned Behaviour (TPB). *Indian Journal of Marketing, 54*(8), 60. Advance online publication. DOI: 10.17010/ijom/2024/v54/i8/174187

Van Velsen, L., Ludden, G., & Grünloh, C. (2022). The limitations of user-and human-centered design in an eHealth context and how to move beyond them. *Journal of Medical Internet Research, 24*(10), e37341. DOI: 10.2196/37341 PMID: 36197718

Vargo, S. L., & Lusch, R. F. (2004). Evolving to a new dominant logic for marketing. *Journal of Marketing, 68*(1), 1–17. DOI: 10.1509/jmkg.68.1.1.24036

Vashishth, T. K., Sharma, V., Sharma, K. K., Kumar, B., Kumar, A., & Panwar, R. (2024). Artificial intelligence (AI)–powered chatbots: Providing instant support and personalized recommendations to guests 24/7. In *Technology and Luxury Hospitality* (pp. 211–236). Routledge. DOI: 10.4324/9781003488248-15

Venkatesh, V., Thong, J. Y. L., & Xu, X. (2012). Consumer acceptance and use of information technology. *Management Information Systems Quarterly, 36*(1), 157–178.

Verma, J. P. (2024). Green Marketing Practices: An Investigation into Consumer Perceptions and Purchase Intentions. ShodhKosh. *Journal of Visual and Performing Arts, 5*(6). Advance online publication. DOI: 10.29121/shodhkosh.v5.i6.2024.3774

Vermeeren, A. P. O. S., Law, E. L.-C., Roto, V., Obrist, M., Hoonhout, J., & Väänänen-Vainio-Mattila, K. (2010) User experience evaluation methods: Current state and development needs. In: *Proceedings of the 6th Nordic Conference on Human-Computer Interaction: Extending Boundaries*. Doi: DOI: 10.1145/1868914.1868973

Vessey, I., Ramesh, V., & Glass, R. L. (2002). Research in information systems: An empirical study of diversity in the discipline and its journals. *Journal of Management Information Systems, 19*(2), 129–174. DOI: 10.1080/07421222.2002.11045721

Vision 2030 Kingdom of Saudi Arabia. (2022). Vision 2030: Economic diversification and sustainability strategy. Government Publication. https://www.vision2030.gov.sa/media/rc0b5oy1/saudi_vision203.pdf

Vu, H. Q., & Hoffman, M. (2021). Data privacy, GDPR, and AI in hospitality. *Journal of Hospitality and Tourism Technology*, *12*(5), 733–750.

Wan, C.-S., Tsaur, S.-H., Chiu, Y.-L., & Chiou, W.-B. (2007). Is the advertising effect of virtual experience always better or contingent on different travel destinations? *Information Technology & Tourism*, *9*(1), 45–54. DOI: 10.3727/109830507779637611

Wang, P. Q. (2025). Personalizing guest experience with generative AI in the hotel industry: There's more to it than meets a Kiwi's eye. *Current Issues in Tourism*, *28*(4), 527–544. DOI: 10.1080/13683500.2023.2300030

Wang, X., Peng, Y., Lu, L., Lu, Z., Bagheri, M., & Summers, R. M. (2017). Chestx-ray8: Hospital-scale chest x-ray database and benchmarks on weakly-supervised classification and localization of common thorax diseases. In *Proceedings of the IEEE conference on computer vision and pattern recognition* (pp. 2097-2106). DOI: 10.1109/CVPR.2017.369

Water. (2023). Flood risk and vulnerability from a changing climate perspective: A focus on flash floods in Jeddah. Water, 15(20), 3641.

Watson, R. T., & Webster, J. (2020). Analysing the past to prepare for the future: Writing a literature review a roadmap for release 2.0. *Journal of Decision Systems*, *29*(3), 129–147. DOI: 10.1080/12460125.2020.1798591

WCED (World Commission on Environment and Development). (1987). *Our common future (Brundtland Report)*. Oxford University Press.

Wider, W., Ho, C. P., Wu, C., Lee, H. P. T., & Tee, M. (2025). Adopting AI for HRM in the Malaysian hotel industry: A Delphi study. *Journal of Hospitality and Tourism Technology*, •••, 1–21. DOI: 10.1108/JHTT-03-2025-0202

Wirtz, J., Patterson, P., Kunz, W., Gruber, T., Lu, V., Paluch, S., & Martins, A. (2018). Brave new world: Service robots in the frontline. *Journal of Service Management*, *29*(5), 907–931. DOI: 10.1108/JOSM-04-2018-0119

World Bank. (2024). World Development Indicators — Urban population (% of total).

World Bank. (2024). World Development Indicators: Precipitation and renewable water resources.

World Population Review. (2025). Saudi Arabia cities by population 2025.

Xiang, Z., Du, Q., Ma, Y., & Fan, W. (2017). A comparative analysis of major online review platforms: Implications for social media analytics. *Tourism Management*, *58*, 51–65. DOI: 10.1016/j.tourman.2016.10.001

Xiang, Z., & Fesenmaier, D. R. (2017). Big data analytics, tourism design and smart tourism. *Journal of Destination Marketing & Management*, *6*(2), 59–67.

Xiao, J., Ding, R., Xu, X., Guan, H., Feng, X., Sun, T., Zhu, S., & Ye, Z. (2019). Comparison and development of machine learning tools in the prediction of chronic kidney disease progression. *Journal of Translational Medicine*, *17*(1), 119. DOI: 10.1186/s12967-019-1860-0 PMID: 30971285

Xu, B., Buhalis, D., & Weber, J. (2017). Serious games and the gamification of tourism. *Tourism Management*, *60*, 244–256. DOI: 10.1016/j.tourman.2016.11.020

Yildirim, P. (2017). Chronic kidney disease prediction on imbalanced data by multilayer perceptron: Chronic kidney disease prediction. 2017 IEEE 41st Annual Computer Software and Applications Conference (COMPSAC), IEEE. DOI: 10.1109/COMPSAC.2017.84

Yu, L., & Li, Y. (2022). Artificial intelligence decision-making transparency and employees' trust: The parallel multiple mediating effect of effectiveness and discomfort. *Behavioral Sciences (Basel, Switzerland)*, *12*(5), 127. DOI: 10.3390/bs12050127 PMID: 35621424

Yung, R., & Khoo-Lattimore, C. (2019). New realities: A systematic literature review on virtual reality and augmented reality in tourism research. *Current Issues in Tourism*, *22*(17), 2056–2081. DOI: 10.1080/13683500.2017.1417359

Zeynu, S., & Patil, S. (2018). Prediction of chronic kidney disease using data mining feature selection and ensemble method. *International Journal of Data Mining in Genomics and Proteomics*, *9*(1), 1–9.

Zhang, K., Chen, Y., & Li, C. (2019). Discovering the tourists' behaviors and perceptions in a tourism destination by analyzing photos' visual content with a computer deep learning model: The case of Beijing. *Tourism Management*, *75*, 595–608. DOI: 10.1016/j.tourman.2019.07.002

Zhao, L., Zhang, J., Jing, H., Wu, J., & Huang, Y. (2023). A blockchain-based cryptographic interaction method of digital museum collections. *Journal of Cultural Heritage*, *59*, 69–82. DOI: 10.1016/j.culher.2022.11.001

Zreik, M., Lessmann, N., van Hamersvelt, R. W., Wolterink, J. M., Voskuil, M., Viergever, M. A., Leiner, T., & Išgum, I. (2018). Deep learning analysis of the myocardium in coronary CT angiography for identification of patients with functionally significant coronary artery stenosis. *Medical Image Analysis*, *44*, 72–85. DOI: 10.1016/j.media.2017.11.008 PMID: 29197253

Zuckerberg, M. (2021) Founder's Letter, 2021 [Corporate]. Meta. https://about.fb.com/news/2021/10/founders-letter/

About the Contributors

Ahmed K Elnagar is an accomplished Associate Professor of Management and Hospitality. He currently holds a position at the Applied College of Taibah University, Saudi Arabia, and is an Associate Professor at the Faculty of Tourism & Hotels, Suez Canal University, Egypt. Dr. Elnagar earned his PhD from Suez Canal University, Egypt. He is a prolific researcher with a significant publication record in top-tier (Q1 & Q2) Scopus-indexed journals, focusing on sustainability, Total Quality Management (TQM), human resources, and smart technologies in the tourism and hospitality sectors. An active contributor to his field, he serves as a reviewer for numerous prestigious international journals. Dr. Elnagar also possesses extensive administrative experience, having led and contributed to multiple committees for academic program development, quality assurance, and accreditation at both Taibah and Suez Canal Universities. His expertise bridges theory and practice, making him a respected voice in the global academic community.

Abdelkader Mohamed Sghaier Derbali is an Assistant Professor in Finance at the Department of Finance and Accounting, Higher Institute of Informatics and Management of Kairouan, Kairouan University, Kairouan, Tunisia and at the Department of Administrative and Financial Sciences, Applied College, Taibah University, Saudi Arabia. He is one of the Editorial Board Members in the Journal of Energy Markets, International Business Review, Cogent Economic & Finance, International Review of Applied Economics, African Journal of Accounting, Auditing and Finance, and African Journal of Economic and Sustainable Development. His research interests include Risk Management, Systemic risk, International finance, Capital markets and institutions, Banking and market microstructure and Islamic Finance. He has published articles, among others, in Research in International Business and Management, Finance Research Letters, International Journal of Critical Accounting, Journal of Asset Management, International Journal of Productivity and Quality Management, Cogent Business & Management, Cogent

Economic & Finance, Journal of Chinese Governance, Pacific Accounting Review, International Journal of Financial Engineering, Virtual Economics, International Journal of Economics and Business Research, International Journal of Mathematics in Operational Research, The Chinese Economy, Journal of Energy Markets, and International Journal of Trade and Global Markets, International Journal of Social Economics, Journal of Business and Socio-economic Development, International Journal of the Economics of Business, China Economic Journal, Journal of Economics, Finance and Administrative Science.

Ahmad Mohammad Herzallah is an Associate Professor of Business Management at Al-Quds University, Palestine. He holds a Bachelor's degree in Physics from Yarmouk University, Jordan, an MBA from Al-Quds University, and a Ph.D. in Business Administration from the University of Granada, Spain. With over 25 years of academic experience, he has taught business administration courses at the undergraduate and postgraduate levels in both English and Arabic. His research interests include sustainability, total quality management, human resource management and operations management, innovation, smart technologies (AI and IoT), tourism marketing, and strategic management. He has published extensively in Q1 and Q2 Scopus-indexed journals and has supervised numerous master's and doctoral theses in Palestine and Spain.

***

N. Mari Anand has a rich experience of 10 year in the field of teaching and expertise in the field of Marketing and Human Resource Management. Currently he is working as Faculty Member, Department of Business Studies, University of Technology & Applied Sciences, Salalah, Sultanate of Oman. He is also a Member in Research Advisory Committee at VELS Institute of Science, Technology & Advanced Studies, Chennai. To his credit he has published 27 articles in Scopus and UGC Listed Journals. He has guided 63 UG and 22 PG projects. He served as Member of Board of Studies for Business Administration and Member for University Examination Board of SRM-IST. The author is an Editorial Board Member for International Journal of Advance Research in Commerce Management and Finance (IJARCMF). The author has organized various International Conferences and International Conclave during his tenure. The author was an ISO Convener and served as IQAC coordinator & Exam Cell convener. He is also an External Academic Auditor and Chief Examiner for various institutions. He is an active Member in Federation of Indian Chamber of Commerce and Industries (FICCI) & Madras Management Association (MMA).

Pankaj Singh Chandel serves as an Assistant Professor in the School of Hospitality and Tourism Management at AAFT University of Media and Arts. Prior to this, he held academic positions at Dev Sanskriti Vishwavidyalaya, Haridwar, where he taught in the Department of Tourism Management from July 2014 to March 2025. Dr. Chandel is a PhD in Tourism and a Post Graduate Diploma in Management (PGDM) in Tourism and Travel Services Management from the Indian Institute of Tourism and Travel Management. His primary research interests center on sustainable tourism practices and the development of homestay tourism in India. He is recognized for his expertise in homestay tourism and is noted as an accomplished speaker in the field. Dr. Chandel has published research articles, books, and book chapters in Scopus-indexed journals, and has contributed to academic publications with leading publishers such as IGI Global, Taylor & Francis, Springer Nature, IEEE, and Emerald, reflecting his commitment to advancing scholarship in tourism studies. Dr. Chandel is actively involved in professional organizations, including the Travel Agents Association of Uttarakhand and the Adventure Tour Operators Association of India (ATOAI), where he contributes to sustainability initiatives within the tourism sector. His engagement with these organizations enables him to bridge academic research and industry practice.

SudhaAnanthi G is a dedicated academician with a strong passion for education and continuous learning. Known for her excellent communication skills and ability to inspire others, she excels in both teaching and collaborative environments. As a motivating presence in her team, SudhaAnanthi consistently fosters a positive and productive atmosphere. Her strengths as a team player and her commitment to academic excellence make her a valuable asset in any educational setting.

Aruditya Jasrotia is working as an Assistant Professor in Amity Institute of Travel and Tourism, Amity University Uttar Pradesh. He completed his Ph.D. and M. Phil. from Central University of Jammu. He has published 31 Scopus indexed Publications, 2 Patents and more than 30 Publications in total including research papers and book chapters. His broad research areas of interest are: Smart Tourism, Tourism Marketing, Sustainable Tourism, Tourism Policy and Planning, Tourism Products and Services. He is also associated as a reviewer for various Scopus Indexed and ABDC listed international journals like International Journal of Tourism Cities, Journal of Hospitality, Leisure, Sport &Tourism Education, International Journal of Tourism Policy and Kybernets. He is also Associate Editor of ESTEEM Journal of Social Science and Humanities and International Journal of Hospitality & Tourism Management.

Alka Maheshwari, has more than 34 years of experience in academics. She had worked for 17 Years in South Delhi Polytechnic for Women. Dr. Alka started her journey as a lecturer and finally reached the designation of Head of the Department. In her sojourn, she was fortunate to represent the institute at Lancashire University, Blackburn as a team member for UKIERI. She joined Amity University in 2008 as an Assistant Director, Amity Polytechnic for Women, and is working as an Associate Professor in Amity Institute of Travel and Tourism. She has her Master's degree in English Literature and Tourism and her Ph.D. is in Community Based Tourism.She has publications in various national, and international journals.

T.C. Manjunath was born on 6th February 1967. He did his B.E. from RV College of Engg. in 1989 (B'lore Univ), M.E. in Robotics & Automation from Govt.'s LD College of Engg., (Gujarat Univ., Ahmedabad) in 1992 with FCD-First Rank & PhD in Systems & Control Engg. from IIT Bombay in the year 2007, got best research scholar award for the entire IITB. He is currently working as the Dean Research (R & D) and as Professor in Dept. of Computer Science & Engg. with specialization in IoT, Cyber Security, Blockchain Technology in Rajarajeswari College of Engineering, Bengaluru, Karnataka. He has got a teaching (academic), research & administrative experience of more than 35+ years (10 years as Principal & 8 years as HoD, 1 year as Dean Research & rest as faculty) and has published more than 1500+ research papers in various national & international journals & conferences, with 175+ patents, 100+ book-chapters, 25 awards, 100s of Keynote talks and also published 25 text books in various field of science, engineering & technology, completed projects worth Rs. 9 Crores till date & guided 10 PhD scholars in VTU. He is a member of 30 Professional Society Chapters and is a fellow of IE, IETE, AMIEE, Sr. Member of IEEE and a chartered engineer.

Nilamadhab Mishra is an Associate Professor in the School of Computer Science and Engineering, AI-ML Division, at VIT Bhopal University, India. He received his Doctor of Philosophy (Ph.D.) in Computer Science and Information Engineering with a specialization in AI-data science and machine learning from Chang Gung University, Taiwan. He has over 23 years of national and international involvement in academic teaching and research at recognized Indian, Taiwanese, and African universities. He has over 150 publications in SCI/SCIE and SCOPUS-indexed journals, ISBN books and chapters, Indian and Australian patents, IEEE conference proceedings, etc. He has been a reviewer, associate editor, and editorial board member for SCI/SCIE-indexed journals and conferences. He has been involved with several professional bodies: "Fellow Member of "ISROSET"; Fellow Member of "ISRD"; Senior Member of "ASR" (Hong Kong); Senior Member of "IEDRC" (Hong Kong); and Member of "IEEE Collabratec". He is currently an

Associate Editor for two SCOPUS-indexed journals, and his research interests span the areas of AI, Data Science, Machine Learning, and Cognitive Analytics Policy & Applications.

Pratim Narayan Moitra completed his Master's from Amity University, Noida. He gained foundational experience through internships at two leading tourism organizations—the Pacific Asia Travel Association (PATA) and the Adventure Travel Trade Association (ATTA)—where he was the first Indian student selected to do so. Currently, he works as a Marketing Associate at XS International, while also consulting two marketing agencies on their marketing efforts and running his own sports event management company.

Rudra Kalyan Nayak serves as a Senior Assistant Professor in the School of Computing Science Engineering and Artificial Intelligence at VIT Bhopal University. He has more than 15 years of expertise in teaching, mentoring and research. His Doctorate in Computer Science & Engineering was awarded by Siksha 'O' Anusandhan University in Bhubaneswar, Odisha, where he conducted research in the field of Financial Engineering. At the same university, he earned his M. Tech. in information technology. Dr. Nayak possesses nine patents total, two of which are granted Australian design patents and two of which are granted Indian design patents. In addition, he has written three book chapters and two books. He boasts over 60 international papers to his name, appearing in reputable journals and IEEE/ Springer conference proceedings. Additionally, he wrote an article for the IEEE India Council Newsletter. Speaking with expertise, Dr. Nayak has participated in faculty development programs. He has reviewed papers for a number of conferences and peer-reviewed journals. His areas of interest in research are Artificial Intelligence, Machine Learning, Financial Engineering, Bioinformatics and Computer Vision. A number of honors have been bestowed upon him, including the International Research Excellence Award 2025, I2OR International Teaching Excellence Award 2023, I2OR National Elite Teacher Award 2022, 100 Eminent Academicians of 2021, Dynamic Teacher of the Year 2019, I2OR Preeminent Researcher Award 2019 and Green ThinkerZ Bright Educator Award 2019. A professional member of ACM, CSTA, IAENG, ICSES, theIRED, SDIWC, and life member of ISTE, AMIEE, Dr. Nayak holds these memberships. He was also a London Journals Press Honorary Rosalind Member.

Akhilesh Pandey is an Associate Professor in the School of Hospitality Management at Galgotias University, Greater Noida, India. He holds a Ph.D. in Hospitality and Tourism Management and has extensive teaching and research experience in tourism, hospitality technology, and service innovation. His research interests include digital transformation, smart tourism, sustainable tourism development, and customer experience. He has published research papers and book chapters in reputed national and international journals and edited volumes.

Ashwini Kumar Pradhan is currently working as an Assistant Professor in the School of Computing Science and Engineering and has been associated with Galgotias University since 2023. He has more than 10 years of teaching experience and previously served as an Assistant Professor in the Department of Computer Science and Engineering at Koneru Lakshmaiah Education Foundation (KLEF), Vaddeswaram, Andhra Pradesh. He completed his B.Tech in CSE from SOA University in 2012, his M.Tech in CSE from CET, Bhubaneswar in 2016, and comleted hid Ph.D in CSE at SOA University in 2023.. A firm believer in productivity and efficiency, he demonstrates an honest work ethic and the ability to excel in fast-paced, time-sensitive environments. As a passionate teacher, he believes that teaching extends beyond explaining fundamental concepts to fostering critical thinking and encouraging students to explore alternative problem-solving approaches. He consistently strives for the holistic development of his students and has convened or organized more than 40 co-curricular and extracurricular events for their benefit over the past five years. His research interests include machine learning and artificial intelligence. He has 4 SCI Q1 papers along with 4 Scopus-indexed journals and more than 10 IEEE conferences.

Shivansu Sachan is Pursuing Ph.D. in Management, a Master's holder from Integral University, Lucknow, Bachelor's from IHM, Lucknow. Academic and professional accomplishments of 6 years with renowned organizations and institutes. My Teaching Career has been very satisfying and have continuously upgraded the skills and knowledge by attending many courses and training programs, seminars, conferences organized by different organizations and also delivered many lectures as a Hospitality sector. He is working as Assistant Professor at Csjm university Kanpur.

Himanshu Sharma is a Professor in the School of Hospitality Management at Galgotias University, Greater Noida, India. He has significant academic and industry experience in hospitality and tourism management. His research interests focus on tourism innovation, digitalization, smart destinations, and strategic management in hospitality. He has contributed extensively through publications in peer-reviewed journals and book chapters.

Amrik Singh is working as Professor and HOD in the School of Hotel Management and Tourism at Lovely Professional University, Punjab, India. He obtained his Ph.D. degree in Hotel Management from Kurukshetra University, Haryana, India. He has published more than 150 Scopus-indexed research publications. He has published 12 patents, and 01 patent has been granted in the inter-disciplinary domain. Dr. Amrik Singh participated and acted as a resource person in various national and international conferences, seminars, research workshops, and industry talks. He has published 20 books with IGI Global Publication, Emerald Publication, Bentham Publication, Nova Publication etc., on trending areas such as Food waste, Artificial Intelligence, Mountain Tourism, Virtual tourism, Healthcare Tourism, Guest behavior in tourism and hospitality. His area of research interest are Accommodation management, sustainability, Green practices, Human Resource Management in Hospitality, Artificial Intelligence, AR VR in hospitality, Hotel pricing, Employee Disability, Work life balance, women empowerment etc. He is currently guiding 8 Ph.D. scholars, and 5 Ph.D. scholars have been awarded Ph.D.

Ashi Singh is an undergraduate student pursuing a Bachelor's degree in Hotel Management at Chhatrapati Shahu Ji Maharaj University (CSJM), Kanpur, Uttar Pradesh. She is a focused and committed learner with a strong grounding in hospitality operations, tourism services, and service management. Appreciated for her creative mindset and thoughtful ideas, Ashi brings originality to her presentations, assignments, and approach to real-world hospitality challenges. She is deeply inspired by the potential of India's tourism industry and hopes to contribute to its progress through sustainable development, responsible hospitality, and guest-centered service excellence with new impactful ideas . Her areas of academic interest include destination planning, tourism development, cultural heritage conservation, and eco-friendly hospitality operations. Motivated by discipline, ambition, and a sincere sense of social responsibility, Ashi envisions building a career where she can blend innovation with ethical practices to uplift communities and strengthen India's tourism ecosystem. She represents a new generation of hospitality professionals who combine creativity, skill, and purpose to elevate India's impression on the global tourism stage.

Index

P

R

S

U

V

www.ingramcontent.com/pod-product-compliance
Lightning Source LLC
LaVergne TN
LVHW062324300926
849161LV00007B/1568